CAMBRIDGE STUDIES IN
ANGLO-SAXON ENGLAND

6

THE IRISH TRADITION IN OLD ENGLISH LITERATURE

CAMBRIDGE STUDIES IN ANGLO-SAXON ENGLAND

Editors' preface

Cambridge Studies in Anglo-Saxon England is a series of scholarly texts and monographs intended to advance our knowledge of all aspects of the field of Anglo-Saxon studies. The scope of the series, like that of *Anglo-Saxon England*, its periodical counterpart, embraces original scholarship in various disciplines: literary, historical, archaeological, philological, art-historical, palaeographical, architectural, liturgical and numismatic. It is the intention of the editors to encourage the publication of original scholarship which advances our understanding of the field through interdisciplinary approaches.

Volumes published:

1 *Anglo-Saxon Crucifixion Iconography and the Art of the Monastic Revival* by BARBARA C. RAW

2 *The Cult of the Virgin Mary in Anglo-Saxon England* by MARY CLAYTON

3 *Religion and Literature in Western England, 600–800*, by PATRICK SIMS-WILLIAMS

4 *Visible Song: Transitional Literacy in Old English Verse* by KATHERINE O'BRIEN O'KEEFFE

5 *The Metrical Grammar of* Beowulf by CALVIN B. KENDALL

6 *The Irish Tradition in Old English Literature* by CHARLES D. WRIGHT

7 *Anglo-Saxon Medicine* by M. L. CAMERON

THE IRISH TRADITION IN OLD ENGLISH LITERATURE

CHARLES D. WRIGHT

Associate Professor of English

University of Illinois at Urbana-Champaign

CAMBRIDGE UNIVERSITY PRESS

Published by the Press Syndicate of the University of Cambridge
The Pitt Building, Trumpington Street, Cambridge CB2 1RP
40 West 20th Street, New York, NY 10011-4211, USA
10 Stamford Road, Oakleigh, Melbourne 3166, Australia

First published 1993

Printed in Great Britain at the University Press, Cambridge

A catalogue record for this book is available from the British Library

Library of Congress cataloguing in publication data

Wright, Charles Darwin, 1954–
The Irish tradition in Old English literature / Charles D. Wright.
p. cm. (Cambridge Studies in Anglo-Saxon England)
Includes bibliographical references and index.
ISBN 0-521-41909-3
1. English literature – Old English, *c.* 450–1100 – Irish influences. 2. Christian literature, English (Old) – History and criticism. 3. Sermons, English (Old) – History and criticism. 4. England – Civilization – Irish influences. 5. Cosmology, Medieval, in literature. 6. Mythology, Celtic, in literature. 7. Devil in literature. 8. Hell in literature. 9. Vercelli book. I. Title. II. Series.
PR182.W75 1992
829.09–dc20 92–7319 CIP

ISBN 0521 41909 3 hardback

UP

Slóged lebar nÉrenn,
asa trebar tóiden,
ro túrsem a ndírman ...

Félire Oengusso

Contents

Contents

Acknowledgements

Portions of this book have previously appeared in various journals. Ch. 2 was published in an earlier form in *Cambridge Medieval Celtic Studies* 18 (Winter 1989), 27–74. Brief sections in other chapters have been excerpted from articles in *Anglia*, *Anglo-Saxon England*, *Ériu*, *Manuscripta*, *Neuphilologische Mitteilungen* and *Notes and Queries*. I am grateful to the editors of these journals for permission to reprint this material in revised form here. The following libraries provided microfilms of manuscripts in their collections: the Parker Library, Corpus Christi College, Cambridge; the Hill Monastic Microfilm Library, Collegeville, Minnesota; the Royal Irish Academy, Dublin; the Badische Landesbibliothek, Karlsruhe; the British Library, London; the Bayerische Staatsbibliothek, Munich; the Bodleian Library, Oxford; the Bibliothèque Nationale, Paris; the Stiftsbibliothek, St Gallen; the Österreichische Nationalbibliothek, Vienna; and the Zentralbibliothek, Zurich.

Completion of the book was aided by an appointment to the Center for Advanced Study at the University of Illinois and by an Arnold O. Beckman Research Award. I am grateful to my Department Head, Richard Wheeler, who supported my applications for funding and released time.

This book is based on a doctoral dissertation directed by Thomas D. Hill, whom I thank for his unfailing guidance and friendship. I was fortunate also to have as teacher and adviser the late R. E. Kaske, whose learning and generosity were equally inspiring. I am grateful to many others who have helped me along the way: Camille Bennett, Frederick M. Biggs, Margot Fassler, John B. Friedman, Joseph Harris, Jay Jasanoff, Joseph F. Kelly, James Marchand, James J. O'Donnell, Joel

Relihan, Paul E. Szarmach and Mary F. Wack. Durrell Dew provided valuable assistance in checking references and quotations. Special thanks are due to John Carey, J. E. Cross, Thomas N. Hall and J. P. Hermann, each of whom read the entire manuscript and made many suggestions for its improvement, and also to Donald G. Scragg, who has kindly allowed me to cite the text of Vercelli Homily IX from his forthcoming edition of the Vercelli Homilies for the Early English Text Society. The generosity of these teachers, friends and colleagues is responsible in large measure for whatever merits the book may have; but that responsibility does not extend to its failings.

I owe the most to my family: to my father, who loved books and who would have been pleased that I became a scholar; to my mother and my sisters Cathy, Rebecca and Lisa, who have always been supportive; and to my wife Shwu-Hua, daughter Millie and son Benjamin, who have patiently tolerated my long preoccupation with this book. It is for them.

Abbreviations

AB	*Analecta Bollandiana*
Archiv	*Archiv für das Studium der neueren Sprachen und Literaturen*
ASE	*Anglo-Saxon England*
ASPR	The Anglo-Saxon Poetic Records, ed. Krapp and Dobbie
BBCS	*Bulletin of the Board of Celtic Studies*
BCLL	*A Bibliography of Celtic-Latin Literature 400–1200*, ed. Lapidge and Sharpe [cited by no.]
BL	British Library (London)
BM	Bibliothèque Municipale
BN	Bibliothèque Nationale (Paris)
CCCM	Corpus Christianorum, Continuatio Mediaevalis
CCSL	Corpus Christianorum, Series Latina
CLA	*Codices Latini Antiquiores*, ed. Lowe [cited by volume and no.]
CMCS	*Cambridge Medieval Celtic Studies*
CSEL	Corpus Scriptorum Ecclesiasticorum Latinorum
DIL	*Dictionary of the Irish Language*, gen. ed. Quin
EEMF	Early English Manuscripts in Facsimile
EETS	Early English Text Society
os	Original Series
ss	Supplementary Series
ES	*English Studies*
ESt	*Englische Studien*
FFC	Folklore Fellows Communications
HBS	Henry Bradshaw Society

HE	Bede, *Historia ecclesiastica*, ed. and trans. Colgrave and Mynors
Hib.	*Collectio Canonum Hibernensis*, ed. Wasserschleben
ITS	Irish Texts Society
JCS	*Journal of Celtic Studies*
JEGP	*Journal of English and Germanic Philology*
JTS	*Journal of Theological Studies*
MÆ	*Medium Ævum*
MGH	Monumenta Germaniae Historica
Auct. antiq.	Auctores antiquissimi
SS rer. Merov.	Scriptores rerum Merovingicarum
MMIS	Medieval and Modern Irish Series
MLN	*Modern Language Notes*
MLR	*Modern Language Review*
MP	*Modern Philology*
MS	*Mediaeval Studies*
NM	*Neuphilologische Mitteilungen*
NQ	*Notes and Queries*
PBA	*Proceedings of the British Academy*
PHCC	*Proceedings of the Harvard Celtic Colloquium*
PL	Patrologiae cursus completus, Series Latina, ed. Migne
PLS	Patrologiae cursus completus, Series Latina: Supplementum, ed. Hamman
PMLA	*Publications of the Modern Language Association*
PQ	*Philological Quarterly*
PRIA	*Proceedings of the Royal Irish Academy*
RB	*Revue bénédictine*
RC	*Revue celtique*
RES	*Review of English Studies*
SC	*Studia Celtica*
SLH	Scriptores Latini Hiberniae
SM	*Studi Medievali*
SP	*Studies in Philology*
TLS	Todd Lecture Series
TU	Texte und Untersuchungen zur Geschichte der altchristlichen Literatur
ZCP	*Zeitschrift für celtische Philologie*

List of abbreviations

Biblical quotations are from *Biblia Sacra iuxta Vulgatam versionem*, ed. R. Weber, 3rd ed. (Stuttgart, 1983); translations are from the Douai-Rheims version. I have not attempted to standardize the presentation of Old and Middle Irish in quotations from printed editions. Unless otherwise noted, translations are my own.

1
Introduction

A pivotal fact in the ecclesiastical history of the English nation, according to Bede, was that the Irish monks and missionaries who came to England during the first century of the conversion had certain distinctive customs that attracted the attention, and disapproval, of their counterparts who had been dispatched from Rome. Irish irregularities (from the point of view of the Romanists) in the calculation of Easter, the form of tonsure and the ordination of bishops were the focus of dissension, but the Irish were distinctive in other ways, notably in their rigorously ascetic devotional practices.[1] Inevitably, Irish forms of devotional expression were adopted by English ecclesiastics educated in the Irish tradition. Cuthbert, for example, was an Anglo-Saxon bishop whose way of life bore a distinctively Celtic impress.[2] It is natural to suppose that Irish Christian literature of the early Middle Ages would have reflected characteristic emphases of Irish learning and spirituality, and that Irish literary traditions would also have been assimilated by English authors trained in Irish schools or exposed to Irish books.[3]

[1] On Irish devotional practices, see L. Gougaud, *Devotional and Ascetic Practices in the Middle Ages* (London, 1927).

[2] See C. Stancliffe, 'Cuthbert and the Polarity between Pastor and Solitary', in *St Cuthbert*, ed. G. Bonner *et al.*, pp. 21–44, at 39–42. Later legend actually made Cuthbert an Irishman. See the references given by D. Ó Cróinín, 'Is the Augsburg Gospel Codex a Northumbrian Manuscript?', *ibid.*, pp. 189–201, at 190, n. 4.

[3] Bede (*HE* III.3) states that during the rule of King Oswald, 'inbuebantur praeceptoribus Scottis paruuli Anglorum una cum maioribus studiis et obseruatione disciplinae regularis'. Aldhelm and Bede both testify to the frequency with which English monks were schooled in Ireland (see below, pp. 42–3). Prominent Anglo-Saxons who spent periods of study in Ireland include Aldfrith, Ecgberht, Willibrord and Æthelwine, to name only a few (for a fuller list from Bede and other sources,

Certainly, the potential for such influence existed, for the Irish played a formative role in the Christianization of the pagan Anglo-Saxons – as Bede often warmly acknowledges – and scholars no longer assume that Irish cultural influence in England evaporated after the Synod of Whitby.[4] David Dumville has spoken of

> Anglo-Celtic contacts ... which might at any point in Anglo-Saxon history have made possible the borrowing or imitation of Celtic literary forms, themes, or motifs by English literary artists (or vice versa, indeed); given a history of constant (if varying) contacts between England and the Celtic-speaking countries in this period, we can never hope fully to understand the culture of the one without reference to those of the others.[5]

see Ó Cróinín, 'Rath Melsigi', p. 23, n. 2). On Rath Melsigi, which Bede (*HE* III.27) identifies as a destination for many Englishmen, see Ó Cróinín, 'Rath Melsigi'. The Irish monastery at Mayo, called 'Mayo of the Saxons', founded by Colmán after the Synod of Whitby, was also occupied by English monks up to Bede's time (*HE* IV.4) and beyond. See N. K. Chadwick, 'Bede, St Colmán and the Irish Abbey of Mayo', in *Celt and Saxon*, ed. Chadwick, pp. 186–205 (Ó Cróinín, 'Rath Melsigi', p. 26, n. 1, doubts that Ecgberht was connected with Mayo). Hughes, 'Evidence for Contacts', pp. 51–3, discusses the case of Mayo and other apparent English foundations in Ireland. The island monasteries of Iona and Lindisfarne were, of course, the major centres for the transmission of Irish learning to England. On Iona and its *paruchia*, to which Mayo belonged, see H. Moisl, 'Das Kloster Iona und seine Verbindungen mit dem Kontinent im siebenten und achten Jahrhundert', in *Virgil von Salzburg*, ed. Dopsch and Juffinger, pp. 27–37.

4 See especially Hughes, 'Evidence for Contacts', and Kelly, 'Irish Influence in England'. For contacts in the tenth and eleventh centuries, see also Bethell, 'English Monks and Irish Reform'.

5 '"Beowulf" and the Celtic World', p. 110. Since I do not think there can be any *a priori* objection on historical grounds to the possibility of Irish influence on Old English Christian literature, and because the historical evidence is generally well known and has frequently been surveyed in previous scholarship, I do not intend to offer a general survey of my own here; I do discuss, however, the evidence for Mercia and for an Irish-influenced Mercian literary milieu in ch. 5 (below, pp. 267–70). For convenient surveys of the Irish mission and Irish cultural influence in Anglo-Saxon England, see C. H. Slover, 'Early Literary Channels between Britain and Ireland', *University of Texas Studies in English* 6 (1926), 5–52, and 7 (1927), 5–111; N. K. Chadwick, 'The Celtic Background of Early Anglo-Saxon England', in *Celt and Saxon*, ed. Chadwick, pp. 323–52; C. L. Wrenn, 'Saxons and Celts in South-West Britain', in *Transactions of the Honourable Society of Cymmrodorion* 1959, pp. 38–75; Dunleavy, *Colum's Other Island*; R. W. D. Fenn, 'Irish Sea Influence on the English Church', in *The Irish Sea Province in Archaeology and History*, ed. D. Moore (Cardiff, 1970), pp. 78–85; Bieler, 'Ireland's Contribution'; M. McNamara, 'Ireland

Historical circumstances, then, were clearly favourable for literary relations between Ireland and England; but it has proved difficult to define precisely how Irish Christianity and literature did influence Anglo-Saxon writers.

Scholars who have tried to isolate Irish and 'Roman' strands in the English cultural weave have often resorted to impressionistic characterizations of 'Celtic' temperament. Typically, Roman and English 'gravity' and 'sobriety' are contrasted with Irish 'imagination' and 'exuberance' – a colourful Celtic fringe around a sturdy Saxon warp and Roman weft. The great palaeographer E. A. Lowe argued that one can attribute an Insular manuscript of uncertain origins to an Irish or an Anglo-Saxon scribe 'by paying heed to the temperamental differences of the two nations, which existed even then'.[6] Lowe suggested that 'The variability in the treatment of d, n, r, s ... may spring from the exuberance of the Irish imagination',[7] and hazarded a rough typology of the palaeographical manifestations of the 'temperamental differences' between the Irish and English:

> With the departure of the Irish from Northumbria their influence wanes; the English pupils begin to find their feet and English genius for sobriety and orderliness asserts itself. It now becomes possible to distinguish an English from an Irish manuscript. Broadly speaking, the Irish type of Insular differs from the English in that it is freer, more incalculable, in short, less bound by rules and regulations than the English type modelled upon it. The Irish scribe often behaves as if the written line were something elastic, not a fixed and determined space which has to be filled in a particular way. He seems often guided by whim and fancy. The English scribe, by comparison, is balanced and disciplined.[8]

Applying these criteria to the Book of Durrow, Lowe argued that 'perhaps English workmanship accounted for the orderliness of its script and the balance and sobriety of its ornamentation'.[9]

and Northumbria as Illustrated by a Vatican Manuscript', *Thought* 54 (1979), 274–90; Campbell, 'The Debt of the Early English Church to Ireland'. On Bede's generally sympathetic attitude towards the Irish, see now the analysis of W. Goffart, *The Narrators of Barbarian History (A. D. 550–800)* (Princeton, NJ, 1989), pp. 306, 309–13 and 326–7.

[6] *CLA* II, 2nd ed., p. xvi.

[7] *Ibid.* But Lowe cautiously added, 'On the other hand it may go back to the unknown models from which the first Irish scribes learned the art of writing.'

[8] *Ibid.*

[9] *Ibid.*, p. xviii.

A. B. Kuypers distinguished between confessional prayers of Irish or Roman inspiration by appealing to similar temperamental differences. Contrasting the 'sobriety and restraint' of certain prayers in the Book of Cerne (Cambridge, University Library, Ll. 1. 10) with the 'pious *abandon*' and 'emotional effusiveness' of others,[10] Kuypers concluded that 'we are in the presence of two currents of influence, issuing in two types of prayer: – the Roman type which, while keeping in check devotional feeling, manifests a high quality of thought, art, and liturgical culture; and the Irish, which is predominantly an outpouring of feeling and devotion'.[11] These polarities were elaborated by Edmund Bishop:

In the devotional products of the first period [the end of the seventh century and the eighth], ... the Celt (that is, the Irishman) and the Roman are pouring their respective pieties into this devoted isle, and we absorb both kinds; but the English mind and religious sense assert themselves in the process of fusion and contribute to the resultant a quality and measure possessed by neither Celt nor Roman alone; the Celt brings 'all heart' and much fluency with little mind; the Roman brings all mind and – I was going to say 'no', but had better perhaps prefer 'small' – heart. The one commonly by excess of words and sometimes by extravagance of form brings us easily and soon within the verge of unreality; the other has the right sense, the right mind, but leaves us cold as marble.[12]

It is no longer fashionable to attribute stylistic distinctions such as these to supposed differences of racial character or national temperament.[13] The Irish palaeographer Leonard Boyle, for example, points out that Lowe 'simply applied to the past some commonly accepted versions of "typical" Irish and English "national characteristics"'.[14] Moreover, historians such as H. R. Loyn and James Campbell have lately cautioned that the contrast between the Roman

[10] *The Book of Cerne*, ed. Kuypers, p. xix (emphasis in the original).

[11] *Ibid.*, p. xxix.

[12] *Liturgica Historica*, p. 385. On Bishop's attitude towards the Irish, see N. Abercrombie, *The Life and Work of Edmund Bishop* (London, 1959), pp. 287 and 363.

[13] The stereotypical contrasts between Celt and Saxon have a complex history tainted by racism and nationalism on the one hand, and Romanticism on the other. See H. A. MacDougall, *Racial Myth in English History: Trojans, Teutons, and Anglo-Saxons* (Hanover, NH, 1982), pp. 97–101, and Sims-Williams, 'The Visionary Celt'.

[14] 'Saints, Scholars and Others, 500–800 A. D.', in *Myth and Reality in Irish Literature*, ed. J. Ronsley (Waterloo, Ontario, 1977), pp. 17–28, at 18.

and Irish missions has been too sharply drawn, and that Roman and Irish strands of influence are often inextricably intertwined.[15] No one denies, however, that significant differences did exist, and many scholars still find that the qualities contrasted by Lowe and Kuypers do, after all, correspond to real differences in literary style and devotional expression manifested in Anglo-Saxon culture. 'Racially the theories are so much nonsense', Loyn concedes, referring to the stereotypical contrast between 'simple German and tortuous Celt'; but he goes on to suggest that, 'From the point of view of educational theory ... the contrast does acquire some significance in any attempt to analyse the two main elements of the Northumbrian Renaissance, the Celtic and the Roman.'[16] Another historian, Henry Mayr-Harting, follows Kuypers and Bishop in contrasting Irish and Roman elements in Anglo-Saxon prayer and worship, although he would now qualify the contrast in other areas.[17] Thomas D. Hill discriminates between the three Old English *Christ* poems by drawing attention to various parallels with Irish eschatological writings for *Christ III*, in contrast with the mainstream patristic sources of *Christ I* and *Christ II*. Hill concludes:

> To turn from Bede to the vernacular or Latin Irish saints' lives or to the *Evernew Tongue* is to move from 'Roman' caution, sobriety, and intellectual restraint to an exotic, Insular, imaginative thought-world which is fervently Christian but clearly reflects the imaginative exuberance of the deeply traditional barbarian world in which it existed ... *Christ I* and *Christ II* are themselves quite different from the *Christ III* poem in that these poems are based upon Latin sources of a specific kind, texts firmly situated in the great tradition of orthodox Christian Latin literature from Augustine to Bede and Alcuin. By contrast, the *Christ III* poet derives much of his lore from apocryphal Insular sources, a very different literary tradition indeed.[18]

[15] Loyn, 'The Conversion of the English', pp. 5–6; J. Campbell, 'The First Century of Christianity in England', *The Ampleforth Journal* 76 (1971), 12–29, at 26–7. See also Sims-Williams, *Religion and Literature*, p. 114.

[16] *Anglo-Saxon England and the Norman Conquest* (London, 1962), p. 272. The comment is unchanged in the 2nd ed. (Harlow, Essex, 1991), p. 282. Compare his remarks in 'The Conversion of the English', p. 6. See also Campbell, 'The Debt of the Early English Church to Ireland'.

[17] *The Coming of Christianity*, pp. 182–90. In the Preface to the third edition Mayr-Harting states that 'My emphasis has been too much on the Roman/Irish antithesis, even though at various points I have tried to make it not so' (p. 6).

[18] 'Literary History and Old English Poetry', pp. 18–19.

Hill places the word 'Roman' in quotation marks, marking it as a term of convenience rather than an absolute historical essence, and employs the broader term 'Insular' to avoid suggesting that the contrary qualities are wholly the result of Irish influence on a passive and non-creative Anglo-Saxon culture. Although Hill supports these characterizations by detailed comparative source analysis, his distinctions between 'Roman' and 'Insular' traditions in Old English poetry echo those of Lowe and Kuypers.

Allen J. Frantzen makes a similar but more explicitly qualified use of the traditional distinctions between Roman and Irish piety and stylistic expression as applied to penitential and confessional texts:

> Amid the lucidity of England's Roman heritage, and the simplicity of its Germanic culture, the enigmatic and the recherché, we are invited to assume, is Irish. The racial assumptions behind such categorization may be 'nonsense', an oversimplified division of English piety into 'Roman' and 'Celtic' strains. But the implied tensions are useful in illuminating the process of adaptation through which Irish customs were assimilated by the English church.[19]

Frantzen alludes to Kuypers's characterization of the differences between prayers of Roman and Irish inspiration, with a cautious appraisal of their value:

> 'Sobriety and restraint' might well be said to characterize English adaptations of both disciplinary and devotional materials from the Irish tradition. Because the Irish penitentials and prayers have been seen as more exotic than they really are, their differences from English disciplinary and devotional materials are easily exaggerated. But it would be difficult to deny that these differences exist.[20]

Finally, after offering some impressionistic judgements of his own, Frantzen concludes:

> Inviting though such contrasts are, they are also admittedly superficial. Nonetheless, they offer a useful if limited way to gain a perspective on 'English' as opposed to 'Irish' qualities in both prayers and penitentials. English texts are less varied and colorful than the Irish for several reasons. It may be that the English were, after all, soberer and more restrained. But it is also obvious that they were working with materials foreign to their own culture and seeking to adapt them to administrative purposes and pastoral conditions which, if not entirely new, were at least substantially different from those of the early Irish mission.[21]

[19] *The Literature of Penance*, pp. 61–2. [20] *Ibid.*, p. 90. [21] *Ibid.*, p. 91.

Like these scholars, I believe that the traditional contrast between 'Roman' and 'Irish' piety and stylistic expression can still be useful, so long as it is not exaggerated or hypostatized. We may fairly question whether the English temperament was inherently more congenial to either 'Irish' or 'Roman' influences, since the Anglo-Saxons were receptive to both, and we should probably abandon such impressionistic criteria as 'sobriety' and 'imagination' as tests of national origin; but we need not abandon all distinctions between Irish and Roman influences in Anglo-Saxon culture and literature. Our understanding of these differences should, however, be tested and exemplified by careful source and stylistic analysis – as Kathleen Hughes and Allen J. Frantzen have done for English private prayer and penitential literature,[22] and as Thomas D. Hill and Frederick Biggs have done for the Old English *Christ III*.[23] One aim of such analysis should be to establish, as far as possible, a reliable thematic and stylistic inventory of Irish influences in Anglo-Saxon literary texts. The present book attempts a preliminary and limited stock-taking by focusing on Irish influences on Old English homiletic literature, especially in Vercelli Homily IX and its remarkable exemplum, 'The Devil's Account of the Next World'.[24] Vercelli IX and other Old English homilies that draw on Irish sources differ, I shall argue, in definable ways from those that depend exclusively on patristic and continental sources, including the homilies of Ælfric and Wulfstan.

Studies of Irish influence on Old English literature have traditionally concentrated on the poetry, especially on possible connections between Celtic folklore and *Beowulf*, or between Celtic lyric and gnomic poetry and the Old English elegies. The papers in a recent collection entitled *Connections between Old English and Medieval Celtic Literature*,[25] including one on *Beowulf* and two on the elegies, reflect the focus of most modern research.[26] Studies of specifically Christian influences have generally

[22] Hughes, 'Some Aspects of Irish Influence'; Frantzen, *The Literature of Penance*.

[23] See Hill, 'Literary History and Old English Poetry'; Biggs, *The Sources of Christ III*; *idem*, 'The Fourfold Division of Souls: the Old English "Christ III" and the Insular Homiletic Tradition', *Traditio* 45 (1989–90), 35–51.

[24] See the Appendix, below, pp. 273–91, for the text and translation of the entire homily and exemplum.

[25] Ed. Ford and Borst.

[26] The few monographs devoted to the subject share the same focus. Puhvel's *Beowulf and Celtic Tradition* seeks to identify Irish folk motifs behind many of the 'marvelous elements' in *Beowulf*. Henry's *The Early English and Celtic Lyric* mounts a detailed

dealt with the same group of poems. Charles Donahue and James Carney, for example, have detected an Irish background to the *Beowulf*-poet's account of the descent of monsters from Cain and apparent confusion of Cain and Cham.[27] Donahue's bold and speculative approach to the poem finds Irish Christianity a subtle and pervasive influence, especially on the poet's depiction of virtuous pagan heroes who lived according to natural law.[28] Dorothy Whitelock's interpretation of *The Seafarer* as an expression of the ideal of spiritual pilgrimage cultivated by Irish monks has been particularly influential.[29] R. F. Leslie has suggested that certain themes and stylistic features in *The Wanderer* reflect the influence of Irish and Hiberno-Latin writings.[30] There have also been scattered attempts, with varying degrees of success, to relate other Old English religious poems to Irish models or sources.[31]

argument for the indebtedness of the Old English elegies to Celtic models, both Irish and Welsh. Dunleavy's *Colum's Other Island*, a study of the Irish cultural presence at Lindisfarne, detects Irish influence in poems as diverse as *The Wife's Lament* and *The Ruin*.

27 Donahue, 'Grendel and the *Clanna Cain*', *JCS* 1 (1950), 167–75; Carney, 'The Irish Elements in *Beowulf*', in his *Studies in Irish Literature and History*, pp. 77–128, at 102–14. Cross, 'Identification', pp. 82–3, has drawn attention to a lengthy exposition of the origin of monsters in the Hiberno-Latin 'Reference Bible' (*BCLL*, no. 762; Wright, 'Hiberno-Latin', no. 1).

28 'Beowulf, Ireland and the Natural Good'; see also Donahue's later article, '*Beowulf* and Christian Tradition: a Reconsideration from a Celtic Stance', *Traditio* 21 (1965), 55–116. J. R. R. Tolkien had already suggested that this aspect of the poem might be influenced by the 'inquisitive and less severe Celtic learning' ('*Beowulf*: the Monsters and the Critics', *PBA* 22 (1936), 245–95, at 266). See also M. Pepperdene, 'Irish Christianity and *Beowulf*: Basis for a New Interpretation of the Christian Elements' (unpubl. PhD dissertation, Vanderbilt Univ., 1953); J. Travis, 'Hiberno-Saxon Christianity and the Survival of *Beowulf*', *Lochlann: a Review of Celtic Studies* 4 (1969), 226–34; Dumville, '"Beowulf" and the Celtic World'.

29 'The Interpretation of *The Seafarer*', in *The Early Cultures of North-West Europe*, ed. C. Fox and B. Dickins (Cambridge, 1950), pp. 259–72. See also the recent study by C. Ireland, 'Some Analogues of the OE *Seafarer* from Hiberno-Latin Sources', *NM* 92 (1991), 1–14.

30 *The Wanderer*, ed. R. F. Leslie (Manchester, 1966), pp. 27–30 and 34–7.

31 J. Hennig, 'The Irish Counterparts of the Anglo-Saxon *Menologium*', *MS* 14 (1952), 98–106; E. McLoughlin, 'OE *Exodus* and the *Antiphonary of Bangor*', *NM* 70 (1969), 658–67; T. D. Hill, 'An Irish-Latin Analogue for the Blessing of the Sods in the Old English *Æcer-bot* Charm', *NQ* 213 (1968), 362–3; A. R. Duckert, '*Erce* and Other Possibly Keltic Elements in the Old English Charm for Unfruitful Land', *Names* 20

Arguments for Irish influence on Old English poems have not always found wide acceptance. A recent survey by Karl Reichl of the question of Irish influence on Old English secular literature, for example, arrives at mainly negative conclusions.[32] As for the religious poetry, arguments for Irish Christian influence, though often suggestive and tantalizing, have tended to rely on broad characterizations of Irish spirituality rather than specific textual correspondences. Recent work focusing on the anonymous homilies and other prose texts has achieved more concrete results, especially since Anglo-Saxonists have begun to examine Hiberno-Latin writings from the early Middle Ages.[33] While the Alfredian translations and the homilies of Ælfric and Wulfstan are based firmly upon patristic and continental sources, recent studies have shown that Hiberno-Latin literature exercised significant influence elsewhere, especially on the anonymous homilies,[34] but also on texts as diverse as the *Old English Martyrology*,[35] the prose introductions to the psalms in

(1972), 83–90; J. Earl, 'Hisperic Style in the Old English "Rhyming Poem"', *PMLA* 102 (1987), 187–96. Earlier studies include C. F. Brown, 'Irish-Latin Influence in Cynewulfian Texts', *ESt* 40 (1909), 1–29, whose arguments are discounted by P. Gradon, ed., *Cynewulf's 'Elene'*, rev. ed. (Exeter, 1977), p. 20 (although Dumville, '"Beowulf" and the Celtic World', p. 120, n. 63, endorses Brown's findings regarding Hiberno-Latin name-forms in the poem); and H. Meroney, 'Irish in the Old English Charms', *Speculum* 20 (1945), 172–82.

32 'Zur Frage des irischen Einflusses auf die altenglische weltliche Dichtung', in *Die Iren und Europa*, ed. Löwe I, 138–68.

33 See Cross, 'Identification', pp. 77–83, who stresses Hiberno-Latin literature as a promising area of research on the sources and analogues of Old English prose. Previous research on the influence of Hiberno-Latin writings in Anglo-Saxon England is summarized by Wright, 'Hiberno-Latin', to which the reader is referred for more detailed information on the Hiberno-Latin texts cited in this book (titles generally follow Lapidge and Sharpe, *BCLL*; references to *BCLL* and Wright, 'Hiberno-Latin' will be given in the notes by entry numbers).

34 See especially the following by J. E. Cross: 'Portents and Events at Christ's Birth'; '*De ordine creaturarum liber* in Old English Prose'; *Cambridge Pembroke College MS 25*, pp. 64–87. See also Bazire and Cross, *Rogationtide Homilies*, pp. 8–9. I have drawn attention to further Irish sources and analogues for passages in Old English homilies in several articles: '*Docet Deus, Docet Diabolus*'; 'Blickling Homily III'; 'The Irish "Enumerative Style"' (reprinted in revised form below as ch. 2); and 'The Pledge of the Soul'. See also Lees, 'The "Sunday Letter" and the "Sunday Lists"'; *idem*, 'Theme and Echo'.

35 Cross, 'The Influence of Irish Texts and Traditions'.

the Paris Psalter,[36] the *Prose Solomon and Saturn* and *Adrian and Ritheus*[37] and the *Prose Solomon and Saturn Pater Noster Dialogue*.[38] These studies of the Hiberno-Latin sources of Old English prose have brought certain characteristic features of Irish literary influence into sharper focus, and the results may enable us to describe with greater precision the Irish element in Old English religious verse.[39]

In the present book I hope to contribute to our understanding of the literary impact of the Irish mission, and of the continuing cultural relationship it established, not through a comprehensive survey – which would be premature in view of our present knowledge – but by way of a detailed analysis of the Irish background of Vercelli IX and 'The Devil's Account of the Next World'. Because Vercelli IX is so thoroughly indebted to Irish models, it makes an ideal case study of the assimilation of Irish literary forms and learned traditions by an Anglo-Saxon author. The scope of the book, however, is not so narrow as its focus on a single anonymous homily may suggest. I have chosen this homily because it exemplifies literary motifs, stylistic features and theological preoccupations characteristic of much Irish Christian literature and of certain other Old English texts formed under Irish influence. Vercelli IX itself was evidently quite popular, and some of its distinctive themes enjoyed a wide circulation in the vernacular. The book reconstructs the Irish background of the peculiar contents of Vercelli IX and traces the dissemination of related stylistic and thematic elements elsewhere in Old English literature. In this way, Vercelli IX serves as a convenient frame for a broader study of Irish literary influence in Anglo-Saxon England.

An attempt to identify Irish elements in Old English literature raises certain problems of definition and methodology. It may be necessary,

36 O'Neill, 'The Old English Introductions'.

37 See Cross and Hill, *The Prose Solomon and Saturn*, pp. 9–11.

38 See Wright, 'The Three "Victories" of the Wind', and below, pp. 248–55.

39 For example, Hildegard Tristram's suggestion that 'The elegiac tone and the ascetic aspect of Cynewulf's poetry recall the early Celtic concern with penitence and eschatology' ('Early Modes of Insular Expression', in *Sages, Saints and Storytellers*, ed. Ó Corráin *et al.*, pp. 427–48, at 444) finds concrete support in the discovery of a Latin source in the *Apocrypha Priscillianistica* (*BCLL*, no. 1252) for the motif of the 'pledge' of the soul in an Old English Rogationtide homily, since Cynewulf alludes to this theme in the eschatological passage concluding *Elene* (see Wright, 'The Pledge of the Soul', and below, pp. 225–6).

first of all, to specify that by 'Irish influence' I refer to the direct or indirect transmission of specific themes and rhetorical formulations from Irish or Hiberno-Latin writings, not to an infusion of a transcendental Celtic spirit or *mentalité*. The simplest manifestations of such influence are Old English texts that translate or adapt passages from identifiable Irish sources, but many other Old English texts include material which can be identified as characteristically Irish in formulation and dissemination, even if the source cannot be traced to a specific Irish or Hiberno-Latin text.[40]

Although certain characteristic features of the Irish tradition in the early Middle Ages can be defined on the basis of the surviving literary sources, the relative paucity and general inaccessibility to Anglo-Saxonists of these sources have presented serious obstacles to the study of Irish influence on Old English literature. Much of the literary heritage of the early Irish church was lost during the Viking period. As Kathleen Hughes has remarked, 'The shortage of pre-ninth-century evidence affects almost all branches of Irish history, and makes it necessary to use later sources when discussing the earlier period.'[41] Most of what has survived, from the earliest period up to the Anglo-Norman invasion, has been meticulously catalogued by James F. Kenney in his magnificent but aging *The Sources for the Early History of Ireland: Ecclesiastical*, which appeared in 1926. Kenney's massive inventory is still the indispensable starting-point for research on the Irish church in the early Middle Ages, but many of the texts catalogued by Kenney are unedited, untranslated or otherwise difficult of access.[42] Our understanding of early Christian Ireland and its literary traditions is therefore inevitably fragmentary and imperfect; certainly nothing approaching a definitive and comprehensive study of the intellectual history, theology and spirituality of the early Irish church could be made at present, even if there were a scholar equipped to write one.[43]

[40] See Wright, 'Hiberno-Latin', p. 89.

[41] 'The Cult of St Finnian of Clonard from the Eighth to the Eleventh Century', *Irish Historical Studies* 9 (1954–5), 13–27, at 27, n. 74.

[42] Kenney himself omitted 'many short devotional pieces, in prose and verse, of unknown authorship and uncertain date, the majority untranslated' (*The Sources*, p. 732).

[43] The most serviceable general guides are still Gougaud, *Christianity in Celtic Lands*, and Hughes, *Early Christian Ireland.* See also the recently published volumes of selected essays by Kathleen Hughes, Ludwig Bieler and Mario Esposito, three of the

There have been, of course, many significant advances in the years since Kenney's work first appeared.[44] Among the most important was Bernhard Bischoff's publication in 1954 of a catalogue of over thirty Hiberno-Latin and Irish-influenced biblical commentaries that were written up to the beginning of the ninth century, many of which had previously been unknown, neglected or misattributed.[45] Bischoff's research has made available to scholars an extensive body of Hiberno-Latin exegesis, and his identification of distinctive Irish literary 'symptoms' has made possible a more precise understanding of the characteristic features of Irish Christian learning and literature in the early Middle Ages. Many of the commentaries in Bischoff's catalogue remain unedited, however, and Anglo-Saxonists have only begun to explore this rich resource.

Since the corpus of biblical commentaries established by Bischoff is of such fundamental importance for the study of the Irish tradition in the early Middle Ages, the methods by which it was established require close attention. Beginning with biblical commentaries and other Latin theological or grammatical works whose Irish authorship is firmly established, Bischoff classified certain recurrent methods and idiosyncrasies as 'Irish symptoms',[46] whose presence in an anonymous

most important modern scholars of early Christian Ireland: Hughes, *Church and Society in Ireland, A.D. 400–1200*, ed. D. Dumville (London, 1987); Bieler, *Ireland and the Culture of Early Medieval Europe*, ed. R. Sharpe (London, 1987); Esposito, *Latin Learning in Mediaeval Ireland* and *Irish Books and Learning in Mediaeval Europe*, ed. M. Lapidge (London, 1988 and 1990, respectively).

[44] The 1966 reprint of Kenney's work includes addenda by Ludwig Bieler. The material compiled by Kenney can also be supplemented with Hayes, *Manuscript Sources*; Lapidge and Sharpe, *BCLL*; and R. Baumgarten, *Bibliography of Irish Linguistics and Literature 1942–71* (Dublin, 1986), updating R. Best, *Bibliography of Irish Philology and of Printed Irish Literature* (Dublin, 1913) and *idem*, *Bibliography of Irish Philology and Manuscript Literature: Publications 1913–1941* (Dublin, 1942). Important recent scholarship has been published in the proceedings of three conferences held in Tübingen and Dublin: *Die Iren und Europa*, ed. Löwe; *Irland und Europa*, ed. Ní Chatháin and Richter; and *Irland und die Christenheit*, ed. Ní Chatháin and Richter.

[45] Bischoff, 'Turning-Points' (I cite from this English translation; see the Bibliography for the German version). See also now Kelly, 'A Catalogue of Early Medieval Hiberno-Latin Biblical Commentaries'.

[46] The metaphor echoes the 'Spanish symptoms' described earlier by Ludwig Traube and Edmund Bishop.

commentary of unknown origin therefore suggests Irish authorship or influence. Bischoff argued that Irish and Irish-influenced commentaries betray a striking 'family resemblance', sharing characteristic organizational schemes, peculiar phraseology or favoured expressions, distinctive motifs and recurrent stylistic features.[47] 'Irish' methods of format and organization, for example, include beginning a commentary with a series of questions regarding the place, time and authorship (*locus*, *tempus*, *persona*) of the book being commented upon (and in general a marked preference for the question-and-answer form); referring chapters in gospel commentaries to the appropriate canon;[48] and grouping non-literal interpretations under the headings *moraliter* and *spiritualiter*. Peculiar phraseology and favoured expressions are encountered in certain title-forms (*pauca* and *ecloga* are common) and suprascriptions (*in nomine Dei summi*); in ways of introducing and citing authorities (listing alternative interpretations with *aliter* or *alii dicunt*, or referring to Augustine's *De ciuitate Dei* as *Augustinus de urbe*) and of signalling transitions and connections with phrases such as *hic est ordo*, *nunc* (or *hucusque*) *accedens*, *haeret*, *coniungitur ad locum*; and finally in the habit of prefacing the response to a question with *non difficile* or a like phrase, corresponding to Irish *ní anse*.[49] Other stylistic features include frequent comparisons using *more* or *mos est*[50] and – perhaps the most ingrained and persistent habit – a penchant for enumeration. Among

[47] Several Irish symptoms had earlier been identified in the *Catechesis Celtica* by Grosjean, 'A propos du manuscrit 49'. For general surveys of the Irish symptoms identified by Grosjean, Bischoff and R. E. McNally, see McNally, 'The Imagination and Early Irish Biblical Exegesis'; McNamara, 'A Plea for Hiberno-Latin Biblical Studies'; *idem*, 'Early Irish Exegesis: Some Facts and Tendencies', *Proceedings of the Irish Biblical Association* 8 (1984), 57–96; Kelly, 'Hiberno-Latin Exegesis and Exegetes'; Ó Laoghaire, 'Irish Elements in the *Catechesis Celtica*'. The following list includes merely a few representative examples, most of which are discussed by Bischoff, 'Turning-Points', pp. 83–8.

[48] See below, pp. 268–9, for an elaborate board game based on the Eusebian canons and called 'gospel dice' (*Alea euangelii*), depicted in an Irish gospel book with a note stating that it was brought away from the court of King Athelstan by Dub Innse, bishop of Bangor (d. 953).

[49] The corresponding Welsh phrase *nit abruid* occurs in the Old Welsh Computus fragment. See T. M. Charles-Edwards, 'The *Corpus Iuris Hibernici*', *Studia Hibernica* 20 (1980), 141–62, at 147 and 151.

[50] See Ó Laoghaire, 'Irish Elements in the *Catechesis Celtica*', p. 154, for parallels in vernacular Irish texts.

the recurrent motifs in these commentaries are references to the active and contemplative lives as *uita actualis* and *uita theorica* and to the Mosaic law as *lex litterae*,[51] and lists of the names of things and persons in the 'three sacred languages' (Hebrew, Greek and Latin).[52] Distinctive explanations of specific biblical verses and topics include the identification of the 'one place' in which God commanded the waters to congregate (Gen. I.7) as the seventh part of the earth;[53] the correlation of the seven Catholic Epistles with the seven trumpets before the walls of Jericho; and the description of the pinnacle of the temple in the narrative of Christ's temptation (Matth. IV.5) as the *sedes doctorum*.[54]

Apart from such specific symptoms, Irish exegesis is characterized more broadly, according to Bischoff, by its heightened interest in the literal level.[55] Irish exegetes drew on the Latin version of Theodore of Mopsuestia's psalm commentary, for example, in constructing a scheme of psalm exegesis that included not one but two distinct historical levels – a scheme that passed to Anglo-Saxon England and survives in the prose introductions to the psalms in the Paris Psalter.[56] Again, Irish commentaries on Genesis tend to place the major emphasis on historical and scientific questions, often devoting considerable space to these

[51] On the term *lex litterae* (Irish *recht litre*), see McNamara, 'Plan and Source Analysis of *Das Bibelwerk*, Old Testament', in *Irland und die Christenheit*, ed. Ní Chatháin and Richter, pp. 84–112, at 94–5, who traces the expression to Eucherius. Donahue, 'Beowulf, Ireland and the Natural Good', p. 275, n. 74, suggests that the term *wordriht* in the Old English *Exodus* (in *The Junius Manuscript*, ed. Krapp, p. 91, line 3) 'is apparently an English equivalent of Irish *recht litre*'.

[52] See R. E. McNally, 'The "Tres Linguae Sacrae" in Early Irish Bible Exegesis', *Theological Studies* 19 (1958), 395–403; for an example in Old English, see Cross, 'The Influence of Irish Texts and Traditions', p. 191. For Bede's criticism of misguided questions concerning which of the three languages God spoke, see below, n. 177.

[53] For an echo of this interpretation in 'The Devil's Account', see below, pp. 185–8.

[54] For the equivalent expression in a late Old English homily (Belfour X), see below, p. 227.

[55] 'Turning-Points', p. 87; see also McNally, 'The Imagination and Early Irish Biblical Exegesis', p. 12.

[56] See O'Neill, 'The Old English Introductions'. That the Irish used the commentaries of Theodore of Mopsuestia on the psalms and of Pelagius on the Pauline Epistles as sources of literal expositions does not have the 'heretical implications' some scholars have suggested (see Bradshaw, 'The Wild and Woolly West', pp. 9–10, and below, pp. 37–8).

questions for a series of verses before rounding off the discussion with a rather perfunctory list of significations *spiritualiter* and *moraliter*.[57] Of course, Irish exegetes inevitably adopted the allegorical methods of the Fathers, so that their interest in explicating the literal level of Scripture should not be exaggerated or oversimplified as a deliberate shift away from 'Alexandrian' in favour of 'Antiochene' exegesis.[58] But the scholastic and encyclopaedic cast of Irish learning focused considerable attention on historical, linguistic and scientific questions whose answers were most likely to be found in glossarial compilations and in scientific or historical treatises such as Orosius's *Historiarum aduersum paganos libri VII*, Jerome's *Liber interpretationis Hebraicorum nominum* and above all Isidore's *Etymologiae* and *De natura rerum*.[59] At the same time, the analytical and schematic tendencies of Irish exegetes all too often degenerated into a pedantic and literal-minded approach, manifested in hairsplitting distinctions and trivial obsessions with noting biblical 'firsts' (a virtual 'mania' in the Irish 'Reference Bible')[60] and parading the names of things in the 'three sacred languages'.

Bischoff's identification of anonymous commentaries as Irish or Irish-influenced by means of Irish 'symptoms' raises another methodological question: how can a given literary feature be defined as 'Irish' within the larger context of the Christian-Latin literary heritage common to Western Europe as a whole? Although Bischoff's conclusions have in the main been corroborated by subsequent research, his methods have been criticized by Clare Stancliffe[61] and Edmondo Coccia.[62] Stancliffe's

57 This is the technique of the 'Reference Bible' (*BCLL*, no. 762; Wright, 'Hiberno-Latin', no. 1) and the *Commemoratio Geneseos* (*BCLL*, no. 1259; Wright, 'Hiberno-Latin', no. *7). The exegesis of the St Gallen Commentary on the Creation and Fall (*BCLL*, no. 1260; Wright, 'Hiberno-Latin', no. *8) is predominantly literal, although allegorical interpretations are offered as well.

58 Aldhelm's letter to Heahfrith specifically extols the study in Ireland of 'the fourfold honeyed oracles of allegorical or rather tropological disputation of opaque problems in aetherial mysteries', which clearly implies an emphasis on 'Alexandrian' methods (*Aldhelm: the Prose Works*, trans. Lapidge and Herren, pp. 161–2; see their note on the passage, p. 201, n. 31).

59 On the transmission of the works of Isidore to Ireland, see M. W. Herren, 'On the Earliest Irish Acquaintance with Isidore of Seville', in *Visigothic Spain: New Approaches*, ed. E. James (Oxford, 1980), pp. 243–50.

60 See Bischoff, 'Turning-Points', pp. 88 and 102.

61 'Early "Irish" Biblical Exegesis'.

62 'La cultura irlandese precarolina'.

article, despite its sceptical title (with the word 'Irish' in quotation marks), makes limited objections to certain of Bischoff's arguments. Stancliffe prefers to stress the fundamental unity of Irish and continental exegesis, which derives from a common patristic background, rather than the idiosyncratic elements of the commentaries Bischoff considered Irish or Irish-influenced. But Stancliffe agrees that 'we can allow the main picture to stand',[63] and in another article she accepts without argument the Irish character of several of the anonymous commentaries in Bischoff's catalogue, in several cases offering further corroborative evidence of her own.[64] Coccia's critique is part of a broader and concerted effort to devalue the intellectual quality of Hiberno-Latin literature and to minimize its significance for the culture of early medieval Europe. He quarrels with Bischoff and R. E. McNally over the attribution of a few commentaries, finding their arguments circular when the Irish character of one commentary is supported by reference to others which have themselves been established as Irish by the presence of some of the same 'symptoms'.[65] But the hypothesis of Irish authorship or influence for anonymous commentaries is based, in the first place, upon parallels with works of known Irish authorship; moreover, the evidence of Irish literary symptoms is often corroborated by external evidence such as Irish palaeographical or orthographical features, or the presence in the manuscript of Irish glosses or of other Hiberno-Latin works. For some anonymous works, such as the Reference Bible,[66] the Karlsruhe Commentary on the Catholic Epistles,[67] and the *Liber de numeris*,[68] the evidence for Irish authorship – bearing in mind that 'authorship' embraces compilation as well as composition – is both extensive and compelling. The peculiar features shared by these works can thus be added to the inventory of Irish

[63] 'Early "Irish" Biblical Exegesis', p. 366.

[64] 'Red, White and Blue Martyrdom'. Bischoff's attribution of the pseudo-Hieronymian commentary on Mark to Cummian, disputed by Stancliffe, has recently received support from M. Walsh and D. Ó Cróinín (see Wright, 'Hiberno-Latin', no. 29).

[65] 'La cultura irlandese precarolina', p. 346.

[66] *BCLL*, no. 762; Wright, 'Hiberno-Latin', no. 1.

[67] *BCLL*, no. 340; Wright, 'Hiberno-Latin', no. 34. The author of this seventh-century commentary names five Irish teachers as authorities.

[68] On this text, see below, p. 55.

'symptoms' upon which a hypothesis of Irish authorship or influence for other commentaries can be based.

Most scholars have accepted Bischoff's inventory of Irish symptoms as well as his more general characterizations of Irish exegesis. What remains controversial is the degree to which these symptoms are sufficient to establish Irish authorship as opposed to Irish influence. Stancliffe emphasizes that it is 'extremely difficult when we meet an "Irish symptom" to know whether this betokens Irish authorship in our sense of the word, or an Irishman's way of expressing an idea found in his source, or even some one else's adaptation of an Irishman's sentence',[69] and Michael Herren cautions that 'there was nothing to prevent the spread of literary fads outside Irish circles'.[70] It seems generally agreed that an isolated Irish symptom does not suffice to establish Irish authorship of a work, but that when a series of such symptoms occurs in the same work Irish authorship is a strong if still not a certainty. Most scholars are more comfortable asserting Irish authorship when multiple Irish symptoms are corroborated by linguistic or palaeographical evidence. Herren, for example, would expect to see distinctive Hibernicisms in a text written by an Irish author.[71] Vivien Law, on the other hand, who focuses on the attribution of anonymous grammatical treatises, is sceptical about linguistic and palaeographical evidence for Irish authorship because in her view such features, although valuable as corroborative evidence of an Insular origin, cannot normally distinguish an Irish from an Anglo-Saxon work. Law would place greater reliance on the presence of Bischoff's

69 'Early "Irish" Biblical Exegesis', p. 362.

70 'Hiberno-Latin Philology: the State of the Question', in *Insular Latin Studies: Papers on Latin Texts and Manuscripts of the British Isles: 550–1066*, ed. M. W. Herren (Toronto, 1981), pp. 1–22, at 10.

71 *Ibid.* On the linguistic features of Hiberno-Latin, see especially B. Löfstedt, *Der hiberno-lateinischer Grammatiker Malsachanus* (Uppsala, 1965); M. W. Herren, 'Sprachliche Eigentümlichkeiten in den hibernolateinischen Texten des 7. und 8. Jahrhunderts', in *Die Iren und Europa*, ed. Löwe I, 425–33; J. Picard, 'The Schaffhausen Adomnán – a Unique Witness to Hiberno-Latin', *Peritia* 1 (1982), 216–49; P. Breatnach, 'The Pronunciation of Latin in Medieval Ireland', in *Scire litteras: Forschungen zum mittelalterlichen Geistesleben*, ed. S. Krämer and M. Bernhard, Abhandlungen der Bayerischen Akademie der Wissenschaften, phil.-hist. Klasse, nf 99 (Munich, 1988), 59–72. Other references are given by Lapidge and Sharpe, *BCLL*, p. 77.

Irish symptoms, some of which also occur in grammatical works, as evidence of Irish as opposed to Anglo-Saxon authorship;[72] but she cautions that because of the dissemination of Irish methods in England and the Continent, 'only when there are other clear indications of Irish provenance can a work displaying some or all of these symptoms be declared to be from the pen of an Irish author'.[73]

It may not be possible to resolve the question of Irish authorship versus Irish influence for many of the commentaries in Bischoff's catalogue.[74] But for my purpose it is not crucial to do so, since I do not propose any specific commentary as a direct source for Vercelli IX, or for any other Old English text; my concern is with the reception and assimilation of characteristically Irish thematic and stylistic elements in Old English literature. As Bischoff realized, the Irish symptoms he identified are seldom wholly original, but generally have an ultimate source or antecedent, whether in the Fathers, the apocrypha or the grammarians. What makes them 'Irish' is not merely their persistent occurrence in Irish sources, but also in many cases their reformulation in distinctive ways. If the matter is frequently borrowed, the form and expression may be unique or unusual, reflecting typically Irish intellectual concerns and literary forms. In R. E. McNally's words, 'the Irish *point de départ* is invariably the conventional, the traditional and the common-place'; yet 'the trend is towards the ultimate – the fantastic, the unexpected, the odd, the quaint, the fanciful, the eccentric and even, at times, the grotesque'.[75] The Irish 'imagination', in other words,

[72] 'Notes on the Dating and Attribution of Anonymous Latin Grammars of the Early Middle Ages', *Peritia* 1 (1982), 250–67, at 264–6.

[73] V. Law, *The Insular Latin Grammarians*, Studies in Celtic History 3 (Woodbridge, 1982), 85; see also *idem*, 'Irish Symptoms and the Provenance of Sixth- and Seventh-Century Latin Grammars', in *Matériaux pour une histoire des théories linguistiques*, ed. S. Auroux, M. Glatigny, A. Joly, A. Nicolas and I. Rosier (Lille, 1984), pp. 77–85.

[74] In Stancliffe's words, 'there is a hard core of commentaries which are definitely Irish, but outside this we have a gradual shading off through probabilities to possibilities; through compilations in which an Irishman had a hand to ones in which some Irish influence is discernible' ('Early "Irish" Biblical Exegesis', p. 366). Lapidge and Sharpe, *BCLL*, list some of the anonymous commentaries in Bischoff's catalogue under the headings 'Ireland' and 'Celtic *Peregrini* on the Continent', others under 'Works of Possible or Arguable Irish Authorship', but without explicit justification of their classifications for individual cases.

[75] 'The Imagination and Early Irish Biblical Exegesis', p. 26.

generates inventive combinations and reformulations of inherited materials rather than novel doctrines. From a theological point of view such transformations may appear superficial, but their literary interest as stylistic techniques, thematic elements and structural devices does not depend upon their theological significance or profundity.

Detailed studies by McNally and others of specific themes characteristic of Irish writings have brought into sharper focus an Irish learned tradition at once derivative and idiosyncratic.[76] An instructive example, carefully investigated by Clare Stancliffe, of 'a theme whose germ can be found in Continental writings, but which was later developed by the Irish in their own idiosyncratic way',[77] is 'the three martyrdoms'. Irish authors distinguished each 'martyrdom' by colour: red for literal martyrdom, white for the 'martyrdom' of ascetic mortification and blue for the 'martyrdom' of penance. Although the notion of non-literal 'martyrdoms', and to some extent the correlation with colours, derived from continental sources, it was the Irish – whose country had few if any 'red' martyrs prior to the Viking invasions – who distilled the idea into a triad which suited their own emphasis on ascetic and penitential discipline.

As the example of the three martyrdoms suggests, motifs regarded as Irish symptoms because they occur frequently in known Irish works and in the relatively small group of anonymous works regarded as Hiberno-Latin or Irish-influenced are not disqualified simply because they have patristic or continental models. Of course, since Irish missionaries and scholars were active in England and the Continent during the early Middle Ages, one is likely to encounter these symptoms in some non-Irish texts.[78] But if the formulation of a motif in Irish sources distinguishes it from the standard patristic and continental formulation, or if a motif appears persistently in Irish sources and only rarely elsewhere, it can be regarded as an indication of Irish influence when it does occur in a text of non-Irish or unknown origin, especially when accompanied by further symptoms or other corroborative

[76] In addition to the articles by McNally listed in the Bibliography, the materials he collected in his source-analysis of the *Liber de numeris* are especially valuable for identifying characteristically Irish motifs and determining their degree of originality.

[77] 'Red, White and Blue Martyrdom', p. 21.

[78] On the absorption of Irish exegetical methods on the Continent, see Contreni, 'Carolingian Biblical Studies', pp. 94–6.

evidence in the same text or manuscript. Only when it can be shown to be commonplace in demonstrably non-Irish texts must its diagnostic value as an indication of Irish influence be dismissed.

The question of Irish influence can be more problematic when Irish symptoms occur in Anglo-Saxon texts, precisely because the close interaction between the Irish and the Anglo-Saxons led to the formation of certain common 'Insular' traditions. Hence the difficulty that expert palaeographers and art historians have in distinguishing between Irish and Anglo-Saxon hands and styles of illumination. In the same way, a scholar may be able to classify a distinctive literary motif common to Irish and Anglo-Saxon sources as 'Insular', but not be able to determine whether the Anglo-Saxons borrowed it from the Irish or vice versa.[79] A careful weighing of the evidence, however, may tip the balance of probabilities in one direction or another. When, for example, as Patrick Sims-Williams has shown, the Whitby *Vita S. Gregorii* and Werferth's translation of Gregory's *Dialogi* both state that Gregory was called 'golden mouth' (*os aureum*, *gyldenmuþ*), an epithet normally reserved for St John Chrysostom,

> the writer is probably drawing, directly or indirectly, on an Irish source. In Ireland, as early as *c.* 632, Gregory was commonly styled *os aureum*; in vernacular texts this is *bél óir* or *gin óir* which suggests that the epithet had its origin in an etymological interpretation of the termination of *Grigoir*, the Irish form of *Gregorius*, which might be associated both with Latin *os*, *oris* 'mouth' and with Irish *óir* 'of gold, golden'.[80]

In focusing on Irish influences in Old English literature, I do not wish to discount English influence on the Irish. Literary influences must have been reciprocal during the entire period, and the Anglo-Saxons were not always the students of the Irish. Indeed, by the eleventh century we find that Irishmen were being trained in England.[81] Yet even at the end of the Anglo-Saxon period, as Denis Bethell has demonstrated, 'English and Irish monks shared a common cultural world in

[79] I refer to motifs that are unusual or unknown in continental (non-Celtic) sources, or motifs that are formulated unusually in Insular sources. Naturally, many motifs found in both Irish and Anglo-Saxon sources derive independently from continental sources, as Hildegard Tristram has stressed (*Sex aetates mundi*, pp. 90, n. 128 and 190–2).

[80] *Religion and Literature*, p. 187.

[81] Patrick, bishop of Dublin (d. 1084), was trained at Worcester (see Gwynn, *The Writings of Bishop Patrick*, p. 6).

which the Irish could still be teachers'.[82] As for Vercelli IX and other texts which I would associate with its milieu, the evidence presented in the following chapters, taken as a whole, points to the reception and assimilation of Irish traditions by Anglo-Saxon authors in the period preceding the tenth-century Benedictine reform.

A sequence of numerical motifs in Vercelli IX, for example, illustrates what has been called the Irish 'enumerative style'. Both patristic and native Irish traditions contributed to the Irish habit of couching fact, lore and wisdom in enumerative form. In comparison to most continental sources, Irish biblical commentaries, florilegia and homily collections are remarkable for their persistent use of numerical motifs, often grouped in sequence or employed as a structural principle, as in the influential tract *De duodecim abusiuis saeculi*. One Hiberno-Latin text, the *Liber de numeris*, is made up entirely of enumerations, arranged in numerical order. Ch. 2 describes these and other Irish compilations and traces the influence of the enumerative style in Vercelli IX and elsewhere in Old English homiletic literature. Although not every enumeration in Old English is a symptom of Irish influence, certain enumerations and sequences of enumerations in Old English are based on distinctively Irish enumerative themes. The first part of Vercelli IX incorporates several enumerations from Irish tradition, arranged in an ascending sequence, as well as a list of the joys of heaven based on a widespread Hiberno-Latin numerical motif. But by making enumeration a structural principle of his text, the Vercelli homilist has not merely borrowed a few motifs; he has also adopted the Irish 'enumerative style'.

In addition to numerical motifs, Vercelli IX and several other Old English anonymous homilies draw on apocryphal lore transmitted through Irish sources. Irish writers made surprisingly free use of apocrypha and of certain otherwise rare, and occasionally heretical, authors. As Bischoff noted, 'in the early period of Irish Christianity, in many respects still dark, a refuge was offered for some of the heretical and apocryphal literature which on the Continent was destined to disappear'.[83] The question of heretical sources and the orthodoxy of the Irish theological tradition is a controversial one which I will defer for now. On the other hand, there is no question that apocryphal sources contributed heavily to the Irish learned tradition. It has long been

[82] 'English Monks and Irish Reform', p. 125.

[83] 'Turning-Points', p. 78.

realized that the Irish had access to a wide range of apocryphal texts, including rarities otherwise preserved only in Syriac.[84] In Irish exegesis, as Bischoff remarked, 'unrestrained entrance was allowed to apocryphal narratives'.[85] The historical data available in Scripture often failed to satisfy Irish *curiositas* and was freely supplemented by apocryphal sources for minor literal details, particularly for numbers and names – the age of Adam,[86] the number of the Holy Innocents[87] or the names of the seven archangels and of the wives of Noah and his sons[88] – and also for narratives of episodes in salvation history passed over in Scripture, such as the creation and fall of the angels[89] and the childhood of Jesus.[90] If the information gleaned from an apocryphal source was contradicted by, or inconsistent with, another authority, Irish scholars were usually content to pass over the discrepancy with an *alii dicunt* or like phrase. The St Gallen Commentary on the Creation and Fall, for example,

[84] The fundamental study is McNamara, *The Apocrypha in the Irish Church*; see the important reviews by D. Dumville, *JTS* ns 27 (1976), 491–4, and D. Ó Cróinín, *Éigse* 16 (1976), 348–56. See also Herbert and McNamara, *Irish Biblical Apocrypha*. A *Corpus Apocryphorum Hiberniae* is now planned, under McNamara's direction. Among earlier studies should be mentioned M. R. James, 'Notes on Apocrypha, II: Syriac Apocrypha in Ireland', *JTS* 11 (1909–10), 290–1; *idem*, 'Irish Apocrypha'; Seymour, 'Notes on Apocrypha in Ireland'; and Dumville, 'Biblical Apocrypha and the Early Irish'. See also Wright, 'Apocryphal Lore'. Determining the routes of transmission of Eastern apocrypha to Ireland is a fundamental problem. See M. Schlauch, 'On Conall Corc and the Relations of Old Ireland with the Orient', *JCS* 1 (1950), 152–66, and Hall, 'Apocryphal Lore and the Life of Christ', pp. 217–19. Dumville, 'Biblical Apocrypha and the Early Irish', pp. 322–8, citing several studies by J. N. Hillgarth, favours the theory of Spanish influence. But concrete evidence for Spanish transmission of apocrypha to Ireland is slender, depending largely on De Bruyne's theory of Priscillianist origins for the so-called *Apocrypha Priscillianistica* (see below, pp. 64–5).

[85] 'Turning-Points', p. 88.

[86] On this detail in Irish exegesis and in Old English, see Cross, 'Identification', p. 79; Wright, 'Apocryphal Lore', p. 128.

[87] See Cross, *Cambridge Pembroke College MS 25*, pp. 68–9; Wright, 'Some Evidence for an Irish Origin of Redaction XI', p. 36.

[88] On the names of the archangels in Irish and Anglo-Saxon texts, see McNally, *Der irische Liber de numeris*, pp. 126–7; J. Carey, 'Angelology in *Saltair na Rann*', *Celtica* 19 (1987), 1–8, at 6–7; James, 'Names of Angels'. On the names Rumiel and Satiel–Sathiel, see below, pp. 255–6, n. 147. On the names of the wives of Noah and his sons (which are listed in the Old English *Genesis A*), see the references in Wright, 'Hiberno-Latin', p. 114.

[89] See Wright, 'Apocryphal Lore', pp. 130–3.

[90] See McNamara, *The Apocrypha in the Irish Church*, pp. 37–57.

juxtaposes the standard patristic account of the rebellion of Satan, based on Isaiah XIV, with an alternative version based on the apocryphal *Vita Adae et Euae* and vaguely authenticated with the phrases *dicunt quidam* and *ut aiunt sapientes.*[91]

Irish authors also mined apocryphal texts for information on two subjects which the Bible treats sketchily or obscurely: eschatology and cosmology. One of the most richly and imaginatively developed genres in Irish secular literature was the journey to the Otherworld.[92] In Irish Christian literature one finds a corresponding emphasis on the eschatological vision, including tours of heaven and hell and revelations of the fates of good and bad souls after death.[93] Early Irish visions of the next world such as those attributed to Fursa, Adomnán and Laisrén are part of a long tradition that culminated in the elaborate and influential *Visio Tnugdali.*[94] Other Irish texts plot the exit and transit of souls before their consignment to heaven or hell. The Hiberno-Latin Three Utterances sermon describes the struggle of demons and angels for souls as they leave the body and the exclamations of the souls as they are led to heaven or to hell. Several Irish vernacular texts enumerate 'seven journeys of the soul', while the Irish versions of the Seven Heavens apocryphon, including a section of *Fís Adamnán*, describe the punishment or purgation of souls through each of the heavens.[95]

[91] For this passage, see Wright, 'Apocryphal Lore', p. 130; on the St Gallen commentary, see above, n. 57. In the Irish annals *sapiens* is a formal term for a scholar (Irish *suí*); see Hughes, 'The Distribution of Irish Scriptoria', p. 247.

[92] See K. Meyer and A. Nutt, *The Voyage of Bran*, I: *The Happy Otherworld* (London, 1895); Patch, *The Other World*, pp. 27–59; C. M. Löffler, *The Voyage to the Otherworld Island in Early Irish Literature*, 2 vols., Salzburg Studies in English Literature 103 (Salzburg, 1983).

[93] See Seymour, *Irish Visions*; *idem*, 'The Bringing Forth of the Soul in Irish Literature'; Boswell, *An Irish Precursor of Dante.*

[94] *Fís Adamnán* is ed. Best and Bergin, *Lebor na Huidre*, pp. 67–76 (see p. xxx for other editions). Boswell's *An Irish Precursor of Dante* is a study of this vision, with an English translation. For a more recent translation, see Herbert and McNamara, *Irish Biblical Apocrypha*, pp. 137–48. See also Dumville, 'Towards an Interpretation of *Fís Adamnán*'. The fragmentary Vision of Laisrén is ed. Meyer, 'Stories and Songs from Irish MSS'. On Fursa's vision, see further below. For the *Visio Tnugdali* (*BCLL*, no. 730) and its connections with Irish traditions, see Seymour, 'Studies in the Vision of Tundal'; *idem*, *Irish Visions*, pp. 161–7; Spilling, *Die Visio Tnugdali.*

[95] For the Three Utterances and Seven Heavens texts, see below, pp. 215–21. 'The Seven Journeys of the Soul' texts are ed. M. Herbert, *Éigse* 27 (1977), 1–11; an

To suggest that medieval Irish authors were concerned with eschatological and visionary themes one need not subscribe to the Romantic stereotype of the 'Visionary Celt' which Patrick Sims-Williams has so effectively discredited.[96] The Irish had no monopoly on revelations of heaven and hell, nor did they corner the Anglo-Saxon market. But the vision of the Irish hermit Fursa, for example, was obviously influential (Bede, Ælfric and the author of the *Old English Martyrology* all recount Fursa's vision),[97] while the Three Utterances exemplum survives in no fewer than three Old English versions.[98] Eschatological themes adapted by the Irish from apocryphal sources also contributed to a common stock shared with the Anglo-Saxons. For descriptions of hell, one apocryphal source was particularly influential: the *Visio S. Pauli*. Ch. 3 surveys the transmission of this apocryphal vision in both Ireland and Anglo-Saxon England, and discusses

analogue in Redaction *Br* of the *Visio S. Pauli* (ed. Silverstein, 'New Links and Patterns', p. 238) has not been pointed out. 96 'The Visionary Celt'.

97 I am aware that the *Vita prima* of Fursa (*BCLL*, no. 384 (ii)) is a continental work, but its background is certainly Irish; see P. Ó Riain, 'Les vies de saint Fursy: les sources irlandaises', *Revue du Nord* 68 (1986), 405–13. For an edition of the visions from the *Vita prima*, see M. P. Ciccarese, 'Le visioni di S. Fursa', *Romanobarbarica* 8 (1984–5), 231–303, at 279–303. A *Fís Fursa* is listed in the Irish tale-lists (see P. Mac Cana, *The Learned Tales of Medieval Ireland* (Dublin, 1980), pp. 48, 58 and 107). Bede (*HE* III.19) used a *libellus* based on an early redaction of the *Vita prima*. On Ælfric's use of the vision, see P. Szarmach, 'Ælfric, the Prose Vision, and the *Dream of the Rood*', in *Studies in Honour of René Derolez*, ed. A. M. Simon-Vandenbergen (Ghent, 1987), pp. 592–602. On the *Martyrology*, see Cross, 'The Influence of Irish Texts and Traditions', pp. 178–80. The vision of the Englishman Dryhthelm (*HE* V.12) occurs in a context that suggests the influence of Irish spirituality (see Hughes, 'Evidence for Contacts', p. 58). Dryhthelm follows the Irish penitential practice of extended immersion in a cold river, and his confidants included the monk Hæmgisl, who later retired to Ireland to live a solitary life, and King Aldfrith, who had spent many years in Ireland. Bede's story of the vision of the thegn of Cenred in the following chapter (*HE* V.13) includes a possible reminiscence of a phrase in the Three Utterances sermon (see the note by Colgrave and Mynors, *Bede's Ecclesiastical History*, p. 500, n. 1, citing Willard, *Two Apocrypha*, pp. 95–7). Bede also alludes to the devils' book containing the sinner's thoughts, words and deeds, a triad made popular by the Irish (see Sims-Williams, 'Thought, Word and Deed', pp. 109–10, and below, pp. 79–80; on the devils' book, see also Willard, *Two Apocrypha*, pp. 62–3, and L. Jordan, 'Demonic Elements in Anglo-Saxon Iconography', in *Sources of Anglo-Saxon Culture*, ed. Szarmach, pp. 283–317, at 284).

98 See below, pp. 215–16.

eschatological motifs in Vercelli IX and other Old English homilies which derive ultimately from interpolations in the redactions of the vision: the Hanging Sinner, the Men with Tongues of Iron and the Monster of Hell. In Irish and Anglo-Saxon sources these motifs were developed and reformulated in a distinctive, and distinctively Insular, vision of hell. The description of the hanging punishment in Vercelli IX has striking parallels with the descriptions of hell in Blickling XVI and of Grendel's mere in *Beowulf*, which combine features from two interpolated scenes in redactions of the *Visio*, the Hanging Sinners and the Bridge of Hell. This same combination of elements occurs in a recently discovered ninth-century text of the *Visio*, which both internal and external evidence suggests is an Irish redaction. A vernacular Irish legend concerning an apparition of Mael Sechnaill mac Maele Ruanaig, king of Tara, to Cairpre Crom, bishop of Clonmacnois, provides another analogue, not only for the infernal setting of the hanging punishment in Old English, but also for its specific rhetorical function in Vercelli IX as a hypothetical torment within an inexpressibility topos. The other two motifs, the Men with Tongues of Iron and the Monster of Hell, occur in numerous Irish and Anglo-Saxon vernacular sources in a rhetorical formulation common in Irish literature, the numerical *gradatio*.

Caesar testifies that cosmology and the fate of souls in the afterlife were among the chief concerns of the druids.[99] The writings of medieval Irish scholars reveal a similar preoccupation with cosmological lore, particularly concerning measurements of this world and of the next: the distances between the seven heavens and between earth, heaven and hell, and similar computations were meticulously recorded by Irish scholars, and even versified by Irish poets.[100] In the Christian period

[99] 'They are chiefly anxious to have men believe the following: that souls do not suffer death, but after death pass from one body to another... They have also much knowledge of the stars and their motion, of the size of the world and of the earth' (*De bello Gallico* XIV.6, trans. J. J. Tierney, 'The Celtic Ethnography of Posidonius', *PRIA* 60C (1959–60), 189–275, at 272). Tierney (p. 215) cautions that the beliefs ascribed to the druids by Caesar have a 'Pythagorean and Stoic quality'.

[100] See O. Bergin, 'A Mystical Interpretation of the Beati', *Ériu* 9 (1932), 103–6, and D. Ó Cróinín, *The Irish Sex Aetates Mundi* (Dublin, 1983), pp. 129–30 (on the number of journeys, paces and stadia between heaven and hell); McNamara, *The Apocrypha in the Irish Church*, p. 24 (no. 8, on the distance between the Garden of

such lore derived mainly from foreign sources,[101] including classical and Christian authors such as Pliny the Elder[102] and Isidore of Seville,[103] and from apocryphal texts such as the *Visio S. Pauli*. The Middle Irish *Saltair na Rann* ('The Psalter of the Quatrains') is a particularly rich depository of cosmological lore.[104] *Saltair na Rann* and the Hiberno-Latin treatise *Liber de ordine creaturarum*, for example, transmit a Neo-Platonic cosmological image comparing the earth surrounded by the heavens to an egg surrounded by its shell.[105] By the ninth and tenth

Eden and the House of the Trinity); *Irish Texts*, ed. J. Fraser, P. Grosjean and J. G. O'Keeffe, fasc. I–V (London, 1931–4) I, 24 (on the distance to the Trinity, trans. D. Ó Laoghaire, 'Old Ireland and Her Spirituality', in *Old Ireland*, ed. McNally, pp. 29–59, at 35). On the distances between the heavens in *Saltair na Rann*, see Carey, 'Cosmology in *Saltair na Rann*', pp. 40–5.

101 For cosmological learning in seventh-century Ireland, see Smyth, 'The Physical World'; *idem*, 'Isidore of Seville and Early Irish Cosmography'. Smyth stresses that at this early period Irish cosmology was based largely on patristic sources rather than classical scientific tradition. For cosmological traditions in Irish narrative, see Sayers, 'Ringing Changes on a Cosmic Motif'.

102 Carey, 'Cosmology in *Saltair na Rann*', p. 45, points out that a collection of excerpts from Pliny the Elder, including a calculation of celestial distances attributed to Pythagoras, was used by the Irish monk Dicuil in his *Liber de astronomia* (*BCLL*, no. 660).

103 Isidore was apparently not, however, an important source prior to the end of the seventh century, according to Smyth, 'Isidore of Seville and Early Irish Cosmography'.

104 See especially Carey, 'Cosmology in *Saltair na Rann*'; *idem*, 'The Heavenly City in *Saltair na Rann*'. The *Cosmographia* of Aethicus Ister, if it is indeed the work of the Irish bishop of Salzburg, Virgilius, as Heinz Löwe has argued, provides another indication of the fantastic nature of Irish learning in this area. See Löwe, 'Ein literarischer Widersacher des Bonifatius: Virgil von Salzburg und die Kosmographie des Aethicus Ister', *Abhandlungen der Akademie der Wissenschaften und der Litteratur in Mainz, 1951* (Mainz, 1952). The attribution, however, has been disputed, most recently by M. W. Herren, 'Wozu diente die Fälschung der Kosmographie des Aethicus?', in *Lateinische Kultur im VIII. Jahrhundert*, ed. Lehner and Berschin, pp. 145–59, at 146–7. For further references, see *BCLL*, no. 647. Four manuscripts of the *Cosmographia* of Aethicus Ister which were written or owned in Anglo-Saxon England have survived (Gneuss, 'A Preliminary List', nos. 386, 439, 718 and 839); see also K. O'B. O'Keeffe, 'The Geographic List'.

105 See P. Dronke, *Fabula: Explorations into the Uses of Myth in Medieval Platonism* (Leiden, 1974), pp. 80–1 and 154–66. For other references, see Smyth, 'The Physical World', p. 219, n. 57. As J. E. Cross has shown, the *Liber de ordine creaturarum* (*BCLL*, no. 342) was the source for the image in the *Old English Martyrology* ('*De*

centuries, however, there is some evidence that Irish scholars were attempting to synthesize native traditions concerning the Otherworld with Christian cosmological and apocryphal traditions.[106] John Carey has suggested that Virgil of Salzburg's speculations regarding the Antipodes, paralleled in Irish texts such as *Saltair na Rann* ('The Psalter of the Quatrains') and *Tenga Bithnua* ('The Evernew Tongue'), reflect Irish scholars' 'desire to accommodate as many as possible of their inherited beliefs to the prestigious and exciting world view afforded by Christian revelation and Graeco-Roman science'.[107] Perhaps the most striking is the notion of a sinless race living in the Otherworld, which has been traced in Irish literature by James Carney and John Carey.[108] The same conception appears even in Hiberno-Latin exegesis. The Reference Bible, in answer to the question 'upon whom does the sun shine when it is not visible to us', states, 'Id est, ebrei tradunt quod sol aliis gentibus lucet quas genuit Adam ante peccatum.'[109]

In medieval Ireland native mythology and literary forms were freely combined with foreign influences. The learned classes of the *filid* (poets) and *brithemin* (legal specialists) existed side by side with the ecclesiastical scholars (*fir léginn*, 'men of reading'), and frequently overlapped, so that harmonization and syncresis of native and Christian learning were

ordine creaturarum liber in Old English Prose', p. 134). It occurs elsewhere in Old English in the *Metres of Boethius* (in *The Paris Psalter and the Meters of Boethius*, ed. Krapp, p. 182, lines 169–71a). Krapp notes (p. xlviii) that this image is 'the one important addition' in the *Metres* to the prose source.

106 According to Smyth, 'The Physical World', p. 212, the earliest Irish treatises on cosmology and natural science, the seventh-century *De mirabilibus sacrae scripturae* of the Irish Augustine (*BCLL*, no. 291) and the *Liber de ordine creaturarum*, do not show any influence of native Irish traditions.

107 'Ireland and the Antipodes', p. 5.

108 See Carney, 'The Deeper Level of Irish Literature', *Capuchin Annual* 36 (1969), 160–71, at 165; Carey, 'The Irish Vision of the Chinese', pp. 76–7; *idem*, 'Ireland and the Antipodes', pp. 5–6; Mac Cana, 'The Sinless Otherworld'.

109 Paris, BN, lat. 11561, 66ra: 'That is, the Hebrews relate that the sun shines over other races which Adam begot before his sin.' The Old English *Adrian and Ritheus* takes up the same question about the course of the sun, listing three places it shines at night, including an island called 'Glið', where the souls of holy men rest until Doomsday. See Cross and Hill, *The Prose Solomon and Saturn*, pp. 131–4. The question and answer are also generally paralleled in 'The Evernew Tongue', ed. Stokes, pp. 124–6, which suggests that the problem preoccupied both Irish and Anglo-Saxon scholars.

inevitable.[110] According to Donnchadh Ó Corráin, during the sixth century 'there came into being a mandarin class of literati who ranged over the whole of learning from scriptural exegesis, canon law and computistics to inherited native law, legend and genealogy'.[111] Hermann Moisl argues that by the mid-eighth century 'the canonical stratum of the extant corpus of law tracts ... comprehensively integrates the Church into the native legal framework', while 'principles and terminology taken from secular law had by the early eighth century been incorporated into Irish Church law'.[112] In much the same way, native historical traditions, the province of the *filid*, were carefully synchronized and conflated with classical, biblical and Christian historical sources, resulting in the curious hybrid history narrated in such texts as the *Lebor Gabála Érenn* ('Book of the Invasions of Ireland')[113] and *Auraicept na n-Éces* ('The Scholar's Primer').[114] The same process of assimilation took place in imaginative literature, where we find strikingly original syntheses of Celtic, Christian and Oriental legends such as the Irish voyage tales (*immrama*), a genre which includes the immensely popular *Nauigatio S. Brendani*.[115] Recent scholarship has shown that even the saga literature has been influenced by Old Testament narratives and other Latin models.[116] Irish Christian

110 Cf. the story of Cenn Faelad mac Ailella, who was said to have memorized and committed to writing the accumulated traditions of ecclesiastical learning, native law and native poetry. See P. Mac Cana, 'The Three Languages and the Three Laws', *SC* 5 (1970), 62–78, and for an anti-nativist perspective McCone, *Pagan Past and Christian Present*, pp. 23–4.

111 'Irish Origin Legends and Genealogy: Recurrent Aetiologies', in *History and Heroic Tale*, ed. Nyberg, pp. 51–96, at 52.

112 'The Church and the Native Tradition of Learning in Early Medieval Ireland', in *Irland und die Christenheit*, ed. Ní Chatháin and Richter, pp. 258–71, at 262.

113 *Lebor Gabála Érenn*, ed. Macalister.

114 *Auraicept na n-Éces: the Scholar's Primer*, ed. G. Calder (Edinburgh, 1912). See also A. Ahlqvist, *The Early Irish Linguist: an Edition of the Canonical Part of the Auraicept na nÉces*, Commentationes Litterarum Humanarum 73 (Helsinki, 1983).

115 *Navigatio Sancti Brendani*, ed. Selmer. On the *immrama*, see H. P. A. Oskamp, *The Voyage of Máel Dúin* (Groningen, 1970), and for a collection of texts, see van Hamel, *Immrama*. On the genre, see Dumville, '*Echtrae* and *Immram*'.

116 See K. McCone, 'A Tale of Two Ditties: Poet and Satirist in *Cath Maige Tuired*', in *Sages, Saints and Storytellers*, ed. Ó Corráin *et al.*, pp. 125–43; McCone, *Pagan Past and Christian Present*; J. Carey, 'Vernacular Irish Learning: Three Notes', *Éigse* 24 (1990), 37–44.

literature was in turn influenced by native traditions,[117] for Irish secular literature was transmitted and cultivated in ecclesiastical centres at an early date.[118] As a rule, however, secular literary themes are found not in Hiberno-Latin biblical commentaries or theological treatises,[119] but in genres such as saints' lives and visions of the Otherworld which allow greater imaginative freedom, and especially in texts which have Irish subjects (such as lives or visions of Irish saints) and which were intended (in the first place at least) for Irish readers. One finds the greatest freedom in Irish vernacular literature, but the *Nauigatio S. Brendani* and *Visio Tnugdali* also incorporate specifically Irish themes and Irish subjects, and both profoundly influenced the popular religious legends of the later Middle Ages.

Ch. 4 focuses on a remarkable synthesis of apocryphal cosmology and Celtic myth in 'The Devil's Account of the Next World'. The cosmological setting of this tale combines two visionary topoi, the journey to the world-river Oceanus and the vision of the tiny 'point' of earth, with an apocryphal tradition concerning the ratio of dry land to water, an Irish symptom transmitted by Hiberno-Latin commentaries on the book of Genesis. Yet the cosmological setting leads not to the expected vision of hell and heaven, but to descriptions of hypothetical torments and joys formulated as elaborate inexpressibility topoi in place of the vision *manqué*. These descriptions conflate Christian and Celtic Otherworlds: the devil's account of a fiery torment in an iron-walled Ocean combines motifs from Christian apocrypha and exempla with a 'demonized version' of a narrative paradigm of the malevolent Otherworld, known to Celticists as the Iron House, while his account of a regal pleasure-dome combines imagery of Paradise with a catalogue of

117 For some secular themes in Irish hagiography, see *Vitae Sanctorum Hiberniae*, ed. Plummer I, cxxxii-cxxxiii; F. Ó Briain, 'Saga Themes in Irish Hagiography', in *Essays and Studies presented to Professor Tadhg Ua Donnchadha* (*Féilscríbhinn Torna*), ed. S. Pender (Cork, 1947), pp. 33–42; L. Bieler, 'Hagiography and Romance in Medieval Ireland', *Medievalia et Humanistica* ns 6 (1975), 13–24; W. W. Heist, 'Irish Saints' Lives, Romance, and Cultural History', *ibid.*, pp. 25–40.

118 See Dumville, '"Beowulf" and the Celtic World', pp. 157–8.

119 This should hardly be surprising, and must be viewed, as Stancliffe ('Early "Irish" Biblical Exegesis', pp. 369–70) suggests, as a generic constraint and not taken as an argument against Irish authorship. Apocryphal works, however, could more easily be influenced by native Celtic traditions; cf. Dumville, 'Biblical Apocrypha and the Early Irish', p. 337.

sensual delights reminiscent of those in the sinless Otherworld of Irish legend. Both descriptions employ a rhetorical formula found in Irish narrative tradition, according to which the hyperbolic pains and pleasures associated with the pagan Otherworld appear inconsequential to the soul who has experienced the inexpressible realities of heaven or hell for a single night.

Any attempt to trace the influence of what Josef Szövérffy has termed *irisches Erzählgut*[120] in medieval literature involves its own methodological problems. One immediate difficulty which scholars face when dealing with Irish literary folklore is that motifs listed in T. P. Cross's *Motif-Index of Early Irish Literature* have a way of showing up in motif indices of many other world literatures. Given the international character of most folklore motifs and tale-types, how can a narrative motif be considered specifically Irish? The problem is further complicated by the existence of common Celtic narrative traditions.[121] Arguments for the influence of Irish mythological or secular narrative traditions in Old English literature often fail to convince precisely because the motifs or narrative structures compared, even when sufficiently similar to suggest a common background, have rarely been shown to be distinctively Irish or Celtic.[122] On the other hand, it is easy to forget that folklore motifs and tale-types registered in scholarly indices are reduced and abstracted to their lowest common denominators or narrative functions, with little consideration of differences in formulation and stylistic expression which often characterize a particular national or linguistic narrative tradition. Upon closer examination, the implementation and realization of an international motif or tale-type in

[120] *Irisches Erzählgut im Abendland* (Berlin, 1957).

[121] See the cautionary remarks of P. Sims-Williams, 'The Significance of the Irish Personal Names', p. 600: 'In the absence of internal or external evidence of borrowing from Ireland one has to suspend judgement as to whether a motif or tale came from Ireland to Wales or passed the other way, or whether it was inherited from a remote Common Celtic period, or was common to many early literatures through polygenesis or oral dissemination.'

[122] See P. Sims-Williams, '"Is it Fog or Smoke or Warriors Fighting?": Irish and Welsh Parallels to the *Finnsburg* Fragment', *BBCS* 27 (1978), 505–14. Dumville, '"Beowulf" and the Celtic World', p. 120, doubts any links between *Beowulf* and Irish secular literature, remarking that 'the common ethos and the inevitably common folk-tale elements of this kind of literature ensure that any investigations must be pursued at the fruitless level of comparative folklore studies'.

Irish narrative tradition may indeed reveal unique features and stylistic formulations which may be regarded as distinctively Celtic, or more specifically Irish. In the case of the Iron House motif, Kenneth Jackson has noted an analogue in the Grimms' tale 'Six Go Through the Whole World', but the motif can be traced in Irish narrative tradition at least back to the tenth century, and occurs there in a highly specific and stable form which consistently characterizes its Celtic implementation. Moreover, although one of the Celtic tales that incorporates the Iron House motif is Welsh rather than Irish, it is set within a context that strongly suggests it was borrowed from an Irish source.[123]

In its indebtedness to Irish traditions Vercelli IX is neither unique nor isolated. Ch. 5 discusses other Old English texts that draw on Irish sources, including three sermons whose apocryphal contents can be traced to Ireland: the Three Utterances exemplum, the Seven Heavens apocryphon and the 'Niall' redaction of the Sunday Letter. One Old English homily, entitled *Be heofonwarum ⁊ be helwarum*, incorporates the Three Utterances and material from the Seven Heavens apocryphon together with variations of two of the eschatological motifs found in Vercelli IX, the Men with Tongues of Iron and the Monster of Hell. Other Old English homilies draw selectively on Irish sources, sometimes for exegesis of a pericope, but more commonly for eschatological and cosmological motifs.

Ch. 5 also discusses the influence of Irish rhetorical style in Old English homilies. As Irish ascetics were given to extravagant mortifications, Irish scholars were inclined to extravagant displays of learning and rhetoric.[124] The most notorious examples, the perversely obscure compositions known as the *Hisperica Famina*,[125] are an extreme case, but

[123] For details, see below, pp. 194–201.

[124] On Irish Latinity and style, see the comments of Gougaud, *Christianity in Celtic Lands*, pp. 52–3, and for medieval testimonies to Irish extravagance in private devotion and liturgy, *ibid.*, pp. 337–8. It is well to bear in mind, however, Kathleen Hughes's qualification that 'simplicity and directness ... [are] as much a part of the Irish monastic tradition as the pedantic obscurities of hisperic Latin' ('Irish Monks and Learning', p. 65).

[125] Ed. Herren, *Hisperica Famina*. I accept the view of Michael Herren that the *Hisperica Famina* (*BCLL*, nos. 325–30) are Irish compositions. For a Hibernicism in the vocabulary of the A-text, see my article 'The Three "Victories" of the Wind', and below, pp. 253–5. Also disputed is the nationality of Virgilius Maro Grammaticus, although Herren ('Some New Light on the Life of Virgilius Maro Grammaticus')

hardly an isolated phenomenon. Other poems in Irish and in Latin were composed in a dense rhetorical style (*Amra Coluim Cille* is a notable early example of *bérla na filed* or *iarmbérla*).[126] Vernacular prose texts are sometimes embellished with obscure metrical passages called *roscada* or *retoiric*,[127] while Hiberno-Latin prose texts, especially in didactic and paranetic genres and in eschatological contexts, often contain lengthy runs of short parallel or antithetical clauses, a technique derived from antique Christian-Latin *Kunstprosa* but characteristically extended by the Irish.[128] Irish liturgical and paraliturgical texts in particular are frequently effusive, and typically litanic and enumerative in structure. The influence of the Irish litanic style can be traced in several Old English texts, including Vercelli Homily IV and a Lenten homily in Oxford, Bodleian Library, Junius 85/86 that contains an extended series of antitheses closely paralleled in a Hiberno-Latin sermon. But for its concentrated rhetorical extravagance and fantastic hyperbole, Vercelli IX is exceptional. Its closest affinities in Old English are with the Old English *Solomon and Saturn* texts, especially the *Prose Solomon and Saturn Pater Noster Dialogue*.[129] Solomon and Saturn in fact make a cameo

has brought forward additional evidence that Virgilius was Irish. Lapidge and Sharpe assign Virgilius to Ireland (*BCLL*, nos. 295–7).

126 For *bérla na filed* or 'poets' jargon', see the references in *DIL*, s.v. *bélrae* II b; for *iarmbérla*, falsely analysed as 'iron speech', see O'Rahilly, *Early Irish History and Mythology*, pp. 85–91. The *Amra* is ed. Best and Bergin, *Lebor na Huidre*, pp. 11–41, and V. Hull, 'Amra Choluim Chille', *ZCP* 28 (1960–1), 242–51 (partial). For earlier editions, see Kenney, *The Sources*, pp. 426–7 (no. 212).

127 See P. Mac Cana, 'On the Use of the Term *Retoiric*', *Celtica* 7 (1966), 65–90; D. Binchy, 'Varia Hibernica, 1. The So-called "Rhetorics" of Irish Saga', in *Indo-Celtica: Gedächtnisschrift für Alf Sommerfelt*, ed. H. Pilch and J. Thurow (Munich, 1972), pp. 29–41; S. Tranter, 'Marginal Problems', in *Early Irish Literature*, ed. Tranter and Tristram, pp. 221–40; McCone, *Pagan Past and Christian Present*, pp. 44–5.

128 See E. Norden, *Die antike Kunstprosa*, 2 vols. (Leipzig, 1909) II, 619–23. On the use of the technique in Hiberno-Latin, see McNally, '"Christus" in the Pseudo-Isidorian "Liber de ortu et obitu patriarcharum"', pp. 172–3; *idem*, *Der irische Liber de numeris*, pp. 145–7. Tristram, *Sex aetates mundi*, pp. 335–6, discusses the rhythmic prose style found in Irish texts such as *Fís Adamnán*. She also suggests tentatively (p. 152) the influence of Hiberno-Latin models such as the *Catechesis Celtica* on the rhythmic prose of Old English anonymous homilies, but without concrete illustration.

129 *Poetical Dialogues*, ed. Menner. Menner also edited the prose *Pater Noster Dialogue* in an appendix (pp. 168–71).

appearance in 'The Devil's Account of the Next World', which has led some scholars to confuse the story with the *Solomon and Saturn* texts, although they are better seen as products of a common literary milieu. Striking stylistic parallels between Vercelli IX and the *Pater Noster Dialogue*, including enumeration and extensive use of the numerical *gradatio*, link these two texts especially closely. As with Vercelli IX, there are strong indications that the Old English *Solomon and Saturn* texts have drawn on Irish sources. Several other Old English homilies and poems, including Vercelli IV and the Old English *Soul and Body* poems, share certain unusual motifs or expressions with Vercelli IX or the *Solomon and Saturn* dialogues. But Vercelli IX and the *Pater Noster Dialogue* share an unmistakable signature style that points to an Anglo-Saxon milieu influenced by Irish rhetorical models. Ælfric seems sober and restrained indeed when compared to the authors of these Old English texts.

Irish literary traditions were transmitted to Anglo-Saxon authors primarily through manuscripts containing Hiberno-Latin texts, facilitated by cultural and intellectual contacts between the Irish and the Anglo-Saxons in England both before and after Whitby, and also in the continental centres of the Anglo-Saxon and Irish missions.[130] But the Irish tradition was fundamentally macaronic: texts in Latin may be supplied with Irish rubrics, prefaces and glosses, while texts in Irish may be glossed in Latin and interspersed with Latin words and phrases.[131] The seventh-century Cambrai homily, for example – one of the oldest surviving vernacular prose texts – incorporates a Latin fragment of another triad of 'martyrdoms' that can be traced in Hiberno-Latin and Irish vernacular texts down to the end of the Middle Ages.[132] By the

[130] A striking example from a Bavarian scriptorium is the *Florilegium Frisingense*, including extensive extracts from Hiberno-Latin sources, which was copied in Freising by the Anglo-Saxon scribe Peregrinus (see below, p. 56). Hiberno-Latin texts and traditions were also transmitted to England through Wales and Brittany (see below, p. 270, n. 204).

[131] See K. McCone, 'Zur Frage der Register im frühen Irischen', in *Early Irish Literature*, ed. Tranter and Tristram, pp. 57–97, esp. 76–80; D. Dumville, 'Latin and Irish in the Annals of Ulster, A. D. 431–1050', in *Ireland in Early Mediaeval Europe*, ed. Whitelock *et al.*, pp. 320–41.

[132] On the Cambrai homily, see *BCLL*, no. 801, and below, p. 74. McNamara, 'A Plea for Hiberno-Latin Biblical Studies', pp. 350–2, notes several examples of the survival of Hiberno-Latin motifs in Irish vernacular texts from the later Middle Ages.

ninth century Irish had replaced Latin as the dominant vehicle even for works of religious instruction,[133] and Kenney believed that the vernacular literature produced in the tenth and eleventh centuries, 'characterised by an intense interest in the supernatural and the eschatological, and a constant delight in the wonderful and the bizarre', marked a significant departure from the Hiberno-Latin culture of the preceding centuries.[134] Kenney was writing before Bischoff's recovery of the bulk of early Hiberno-Latin exegesis which, if not so colourful as the later vernacular material, betrays a similar preoccupation with apocryphal lore. Also unknown to Kenney were an Old Irish poem based on the Gospel of Thomas and written in the late seventh or early eighth century, and the poems of Blathmac, written in the second half of the eighth, which also freely incorporate apocryphal material.[135] The *Nauigatio S. Brendani*, now thought to have been written in the third quarter of the eighth century,[136] is as imaginative as anything from the later period. The transition from Latin to the vernacular need not have essentially altered the character of the Irish tradition, the continuity of which has frequently been remarked.[137]

A problem in dealing with Irish vernacular texts is the lateness of many of the surviving manuscript sources. Although the situation dictates a cautious approach, it is far from hopeless, thanks to what Brian Ó Cuív (echoing Frank O'Connor) has called 'the backward look' of the Irish scribal tradition.[138] Many of the vernacular texts surviving only in the great manuscript miscellanies of the later Middle Ages are

133 See R. Sharpe, *Medieval Irish Saints' Lives: an Introduction to Vitae Sanctorum Hiberniae* (Oxford, 1991), pp. 19–26.

134 *The Sources*, p. 733.

135 These texts were unknown until their publication by J. Carney, *The Poems of Blathmac*. On the Irish Gospel of Thomas, see McNamara, *The Apocrypha in the Irish Church*, pp. 52–3 (no. 46). On apocryphal material in the Blathmac poems, see *ibid.*, p. 83 (no. 72), and Dumville, 'Biblical Apocrypha and the Early Irish', pp. 305–8.

136 On the date, see D. N. Dumville, 'Two Approaches to the Dating of "Navigatio Sancti Brendani"', *SM* 3rd ser. 29 (1988), 88–102. Lapidge and Sharpe, *BCLL*, p. 105 (no. 362), date the work to the second half of the eighth century. See also J. Strzelczyk, 'Navigatio S. Brendani abbatis – ein Werk des X. Jahrhunderts?', *Mittellateinisches Jahrbuch* 24–5 (1989–90), 507–15.

137 See F. J. Byrne, '*Senchas*: the Nature of Gaelic Historical Tradition', in *Historical Studies IX* (Belfast, 1974), 137–59, at 158.

138 'Ireland's Manuscript Heritage', *Éire – Ireland* 19 (1984), 87–110, at 89.

much earlier in origin, and in some cases Celticists are able to gauge the approximate date by linguistic means.[139] *Orgain Denna Ríg*, for example, one of the Irish tales that incorporates the Iron House motif, survives in three manuscripts, the two earliest having been written in the twelfth century, but the tale is datable on linguistic grounds to the ninth or tenth century.[140] Although much of the vernacular religious literature catalogued by Kenney post-dates the Anglo-Saxon period, there is a rather substantial body of texts that can be securely dated prior to the eleventh century, and several important works are as early as the seventh or eighth. These include both prose and poetry and represent diverse genres: homilies, prayers, didactic treatises, visions, apocrypha and penitential texts. Many of the vernacular texts which I cite as analogues of themes in Old English homilies in the next chapters belong to the earlier Middle Ages. The Old Irish *Apgitir Chrábaid* ('The Alphabet of Piety'), thought to have been composed *c.* 600, is one of the oldest.[141] One of the few surviving Old Irish homilies, edited by John Strachan, is datable on linguistic grounds to the middle of the ninth century.[142] The date of *Saltair na Rann* ('The Psalter of the Quatrains'), a vast poetic survey of sacred history from Creation to Judgement, is still disputed, but it is generally dated towards the end of the tenth century.[143] The bizarre apocryphal composition *Tenga Bithnua* ('The Evernew Tongue') survives in three recensions, the oldest of which probably dates from the tenth century.[144] *Fís Adamnán* ('The Vision of Adomnán'), the so-called 'Irish precursor of Dante', is also datable to

[139] For general discussion of the character of the manuscript record, see also Kenney, *The Sources*, pp. 1–26. On the problem of dating, see in general Carney, 'The Dating of Early Irish Verse Texts', and G. Mac Eoin, 'The Dating of Middle Irish Texts', *PBA* 68 (1982), 109–37. [140] See below, p. 195. [141] See below, p. 54.

[142] See below, p. 216.

[143] *Saltair na Rann*, ed. Stokes; *The Irish Adam and Eve Story from Saltair na Rann*, ed. Greene and Kelly (partial). For other translations of selections, see McNamara, *The Apocrypha in the Irish Church*, p. 14. The passage dating the poem to 988 is apparently an interpolation. See G. Mac Eoin, 'The Date and Authorship of Saltair na Rann', *ZCP* 28 (1960), 51–67; *idem*, 'Observations on Saltair na Rann', *ZCP* 39 (1982), 1–27. James Carney has urged an earlier dating (*c.* 870) in 'The Dating of Early Irish Verse Texts', pp. 178 and 207–16.

[144] On the three recensions of *Tenga Bithnua*, see Flower, *Catalogue of Irish Manuscripts* II, 556–9, and McNamara, *The Apocrypha in the Irish Church*, pp. 115–18 (no. 94), where editions are listed.

the tenth century.[145] The Middle Irish homily *Scéla Laí Brátha* ('Tidings of Doomsday') is probably from the eleventh century.[146] Though a mere fraction of what must once have existed – and I have mentioned only a few key texts which are important for this study – this is still a significant body of vernacular religious literature contemporary with the Anglo-Saxon period.

In some cases it is possible to confirm the antiquity of specific themes in later vernacular texts by comparison with earlier Hiberno-Latin sources.[147] The vernacular homilies in the Leabhar Breac (Dublin, Royal Irish Academy 23. P. 16; *c.* 1410), some of which may date from the eleventh century, are translated from Latin originals, most of which are copied in the same manuscript.[148] Many of these sermons have patristic and continental sources, but some, such as the homily *In cena Domini*, are based on Hiberno-Latin models of considerably earlier date.[149] Recently Martin McNamara has discovered that portions of the Leabhar Breac sermon on the Lord's Prayer correspond to the exposition of the prayer in the ninth-century compilation *Catechesis Celtica*.[150] The Leabhar Breac homily on the Temptation of Christ incorporates several themes belonging to a remarkably consistent

[145] See above, n. 94.

[146] 'Tidings of Doomsday', ed. Stokes. There is a more recent edition, without translation, in *Lebor na Huidre*, ed. Best and Bergin, pp. 77–81. The text is also ed. Walsh in *Mil na mBeach*, pp. 62–8, with notes at pp. 120–3. I cite the Irish text from the edition of Best and Bergin. Tristram, *Sex aetates mundi*, p. 33, suggests the date '10. – 11. Jh. (?)'. On a missing leaf in the sole manuscript containing the homily, see D. Dumville, '"Scéla Lái Brátha" and the Collation of Leabhar na Huidhre', *Éigse* 16 (1975), 24–8. Flower, *Catalogue of Irish Manuscripts* II, 502 n., conjectures that the homily is based on a lost apocryphal Questions of Matthew.

[147] See McNamara, 'A Plea for Hiberno-Latin Biblical Studies', pp. 350–2.

[148] F. Mac Donncha, 'Medieval Irish Homilies', in *Biblical Studies*, ed. McNamara, pp. 59–71, argues that most of the homilies are the work of Mael Ísu Ua Brolacháin (d. 1086), but Kenneth Jackson argues that the homilies are not all contemporary, and that some are perhaps a century earlier than the late-eleventh-century date implied by Mac Donncha's attribution. See Jackson, 'The Historical Grammar of Irish: Some Actualities and Some Desiderata', in *Proceedings of the Sixth International Congress of Celtic Studies, Galway, 1979*, ed. G. Mac Eoin (Dublin, 1983), pp. 1–18, at 6–7. The Leabhar Breac homilies (*BCLL*, no. 565) are partially ed. Atkinson, *The Passions and the Homilies*. For additional references, see Wright, 'Hiberno-Latin', pp. 122–3.

[149] See J. Rittmueller, 'The Hiberno-Latin Background of the Leabhar Breac Homily "In Cena Domini"', *PHCC* 2 (1982), 1–10.

[150] See below, p. 236.

Hiberno-Latin treatment of the pericope which, as I have shown elsewhere, was also available to the Anglo-Saxon author of Blickling Homily III.[151]

Both Hiberno-Latin and Irish vernacular texts, therefore, are complementary sources of evidence for reconstructing the distinctive features of Irish Christian literature. I cite vernacular as well as Hiberno-Latin texts as evidence for these features, and also as analogues of motifs in Old English literature, but without implying that Anglo-Saxon authors necessarily drew directly on Irish vernacular texts. Such influence, of course, was by no means impossible, especially when the Irish missionary presence was at its height. Bede tells us that both Oswald and Oswiu gained a fluent knowledge of the Irish language during their stays in Ireland.[152] The bilingual King Aldfrith, whose mother was Irish, was reputed to have composed poetry in Irish.[153] Although there is little other direct evidence, David Dumville has suggested that a significant level of bilingualism would have been necessary to maintain the close political and cultural relationships between the two nations.[154]

The characteristics of Irish Christianity and of Irish Christian literature which I have outlined above may serve as a partial answer to a fundamental and controversial question: to what extent, and in what ways, was the Irish learned tradition in the early Middle Ages original or idiosyncratic, or even heterodox?[155] In matters of dogma or

[151] 'Blickling Homily III'.

[152] *HE* III.3 (Oswald): 'linguam Scottorum iam plene didicerat'; *HE* III.25 (Oswiu): 'illorum etiam lingua optime inbutus'.

[153] According to later medieval Irish sources, Aldfrith was known in Ireland by the name Flann Fína, but Dumville does not think the tradition is authentic ('"Beowulf" and the Celtic World', p. 114, n. 30; 'Two Troublesome Abbots', *Celtica* 21 (1990), 146–52, at 151–2). For Irish poetry later attributed to Aldfrith, see V. Hull, 'The Wise Sayings of Flann Fína', *Speculum* 4 (1929), 95–102.

[154] '"Beowulf" and the Celtic World', pp. 111–15.

[155] G. V. Murphy has recently argued for 'a formal Irish learning tradition that was unorthodox, eclectic, speculative and peculiar to Ireland' ('The Place of John Eriugena in the Irish Learning Tradition', *Monastic Studies* 14 (1983), 93–107, at 94). But see the reply (with which I am in complete agreement) by J. F. Kelly, 'Christianity and the Latin Tradition in Early Mediaeval Ireland', *Bulletin of the John Rylands Library of Manchester* 68 (1986), 410–33. Bradshaw, 'The Wild and Woolly West', in a much more subtle argument than Murphy's, also contrasts Celtic Christianity with 'Latin Orthodoxy', but on the basis of differences in organization

interpretation of Scripture, cases of heterodoxy such as the Irish heretic Clement[156] are rare and scarcely reflect the essential character and quality of Irish learning and theology.[157] It would be easy to compile a list of a few cranks and heretics from other nationalities in the early Middle Ages, but no one would argue that such a list proved anything about an inherent propensity for heresy among, say, the Franks or the Spanish. As for John Scottus Eriugena, who was certainly no crank, elements of his philosophical and theological system may have been judged heterodox by his contemporaries, but his philosophy was developed on the Continent and does not, according to the best recent scholarship, represent a development of an indigenous Irish learned tradition. John Contreni, who finds 'nothing patently Irish in Eriugena's work', concludes that this great master 'fits more comfortably the rubric "Carolingian" than "Hiberno-Latin"'.[158]

The citation of heretical authors in Irish exegesis is not necessarily an indication of sympathy for heretical doctrines. The Irish drew from Theodore of Mopsuestia simply as a source of literal commentary on the psalms. They also made surprisingly free use of Pelagius's commentaries on the Pauline Epistles, but did not adopt his heretical views on grace and free will, and it would be misleading to suggest that Pelagianism was a significant or conscious tendency of Irish theology.[159] Nor should

and spirituality rather than theology. Bradshaw argues that 'Irish heterodoxy lay in the realm of praxis, not of doctrine' (p. 10); but it seems to me that 'heterodoxy' and 'orthodoxy' are inappropriate labels for the contrasts which Bradshaw develops.

156 On Clement, see J. Russell, 'St Boniface and the Eccentrics', *Church History* 33 (1964), 235–47.

157 Boniface also opposed an Irishman named Samson, who denied the efficacy of baptism (Gougaud, *Christianity in Celtic Lands*, pp. 164–5). Kenney (*The Sources*, p. 550) refers to Ratramnus's 'refutation of the doctrine of monopsychism expounded by an Irishman named Macarius' (see also J.-P. Bouhot, *Ratramne de Corbie* (Paris, 1976), p. 58).

158 'Carolingian Biblical Studies', p. 76 and n. 16. Bradshaw states similarly that John's 'lonely eminence serves only to emphasize the absence of a Celtic philosophical–theological tradition with which he might be associated' ('The Wild and Woolly West', p. 20).

159 See Kelly, 'Pelagius, Pelagianism and the Early Christian Irish', *Mediaevalia* 4 (1978), 99–124; Ó Cróinín, '"New Heresy for Old"'; B. R. Rees, *Pelagius: a Reluctant Heretic* (Woodbridge, 1988), pp. 120–2. Inevitably, Jerome's inaccurate but witty put-down of Pelagius (as overfed on *Scottorum pultes*) was retailed in later controversies; see Gougaud, *Christianity in Celtic Lands*, p. 289.

the mere use of apocrypha be too hastily equated with heresy, particularly in the early Middle Ages, when the status of much apocryphal literature was vaguely defined.[160] Not every library held a copy of the Gelasian decree, and not every monk was as well informed (or as discriminating) as Bede and Ælfric.[161] In any case, not all apocryphal works contain heretical doctrines, and even when they do, the heretical content may be embedded in a fabulous narrative whose doctrinal implications might not be obvious to a reader some centuries removed from the controversies which generated it.[162] As I have suggested, the Irish consulted apocryphal works as sources of literal information, eschatological and cosmological lore, and exotic and miraculous legends, and not as catecheses of long-dead heresies.

If 'Ireland was odd in the early middle ages', as an often-cited remark of Kathleen Hughes puts it,[163] its oddity had little to do with heresy. The Irish had received from Britain and from the Continent essentially the same faith and Christian-Latin heritage which the Anglo-Saxons later received from the Roman mission, and it is only against this background of essential uniformity of faith and intellectual heritage that such distinctive characteristics of Irish learning and literary style as do exist can be highlighted. But if Irish theological tradition was not genuinely heterodox, how is one to account for the periodic complaints against Irish 'heretics' voiced by ecclesiastical authorities in England and on the Continent? To begin with, much antagonism towards the Irish was due to their unusual customs in matters of observation, discipline and ecclesiastical organization. In Anglo-Saxon England, the controversial issues were the dating of Easter, the Celtic tonsure and the presence of Irish 'wandering bishops' (*episcopi uagantes*). Theodore,

[160] On the problem of the biblical canon in Ireland, see Dumville, 'Biblical Apocrypha and the Early Irish', pp. 332–3; see also the study of canonicity and apocrypha in the early church and the British Isles in Hall, 'Apocryphal Lore and the Life of Christ', pp. 10–37.

[161] On Ælfric's attitude towards apocrypha, see below, pp. 228–9.

[162] A docetic hymn from the Acts of Thomas is, however, quoted in a seventh-century Irish sacramentary (see Dumville, 'Biblical Apocrypha and the Early Irish', p. 329). On the other hand, the redactor of an Irish version of an Infancy gospel 'has expunged the offensively docetic sections' (*ibid.*, p. 328).

[163] 'Sanctity and Secularity in the Early Irish Church', in *Studies in Church History* 10, ed. D. Baker (Cambridge, 1973), pp. 21–37, at 21.

archbishop of Canterbury, sent by Rome to supervise the organization of the English Church, was uncompromising in his rejection of Irish bishops 'qui in Pascha uel tonsura catholici non sunt, adunati ecclesiae non sunt',[164] requiring that any English bishop who had been ordained by them be confirmed by a 'Catholic' bishop, and that any English church consecrated by them be reconsecrated. From the point of view of the Romanist party, these issues represented serious threats to unity in the English church, and for that reason the Irish were accounted 'heretics'. Nevertheless, it is essential to distinguish between irregularities of observance and custom such as the calculation of Easter and the Celtic tonsure – however gravely men such as Theodore, Aldhelm and Wilfrid viewed them – and heresy in matters of faith.[165] Despite the polemics of the Romanists, the evidence suggests that the overwhelming majority of Irish scholars and missionaries who came to England were theologically orthodox. Bede, himself a Romanist but a more fair-minded witness, acknowledges their learning and sanctity even as he deplores their stubbornness. The disputes over matters of discipline and ecclesiastical organization were mostly resolved by the time Bede wrote his *Historia ecclesiastica*; but the controversies which came to a head at Whitby inevitably left a legacy of bad feeling and suspicion.

Precisely because of their reputation for irregularity both in England and on the Continent, Irish *peregrini* may have attracted closer scrutiny from heresy hunters. Irish *episcopi uagantes* and ascetics had long since worn out their welcome in some quarters. Given a long-standing (and unjustified) rumour of Irish Pelagianism, only a few real or supposed cases of heresy would be sufficient to confirm the suspicions of antagonistic ecclesiastics.[166] St Boniface, for example, brought about

[164] *Councils and Ecclesiastical Documents*, ed. Haddan and Stubbs III, 197: 'who are not Catholic with respect to Easter and the tonsure and are not united to the Church' (trans. J. T. McNeill and H. Gamer, *Medieval Handbooks of Penance* (New York, 1938), p. 206).

[165] The Irish attempted to defend themselves on this very ground, as Aldhelm's letter to Geraint reveals (*Aldhelm: the Prose Works*, trans. Lapidge and Herren, pp. 159–60). Aldhelm scornfully rejected such 'wily' and 'clever' excuses, but his remarks implicitly concede the distinction.

[166] Ó Cróinín, '"New Heresy for Old"', pp. 515–16, makes the important point that pope-elect John IV, and later Ceolfrith and Bede, associated Pelagianism with Quartodecimanism, the method of calculating Easter which they mistakenly believed the Irish were advocating.

the formal condemnation of Clement, and later accused Virgil of Salzburg of heresy for his views concerning the existence of the Antipodes. Clement's audacious claims were clearly in opposition to the teachings of the church, but Virgil's cosmological theories, however much they alarmed Boniface and Pope Zachary, were not unambiguously heretical, and did not prevent him from being consecrated bishop of Salzburg in 767 and remaining in that see until his death in 784.[167] Boniface had come into conflict and competition with Irish missionaries and bishops in his attempt to organize the church in the Frankish kingdoms in accordance with Roman ecclesiastical structures, and his accusations should be evaluated in this historical context.[168] Yet, as Virgil's case suggests, Irish scholars do seem to have been given to speculation in arcane matters, especially concerning cosmology and eschatology, which more conservative authorities deemed better left alone. Irish *curiositas*, as it has been called, should not be confused with wilful opposition to church teachings in well-defined areas of theology and dogma, but the line separating speculation and heterodoxy was sometimes a fine one, and was differently drawn by different authorities.

The inquisitive nature and sometimes obscure sources of Irish learning and scholarship in the early Middle Ages earned for the Irish a mixed reputation. On the Continent, Irish scholars met with admiration or antagonism, but rarely indifference. Their reputation for learning, epitomized by the well-known anecdote of the two Irish scholars who arrived on the coast of France, selling wisdom as their wares,[169] seems

[167] V. Flint, 'Monsters and the Antipodes in the Early Middle Ages and Enlightenment', *Viator* 15 (1984), 65–80, points out that the Antipodes were dismissed as an absurd fable by such authorities as Augustine and Isidore. Flint shows that belief in 'the existence of races not descended from Adam and probably monstrous' had serious theological implications, but that neither Augustine nor Isidore branded it heretical. For the possible connection between Virgil's theories and Irish speculation regarding the existence of a sinless otherworldly race, see above, p. 27. In Irish texts these races are not depicted as monstrous.

[168] See J. M. Wallace-Hadrill, 'A Background to St Boniface's Mission', in his *Early Medieval History* (Oxford, 1975), pp. 138–54, at 146–7; P. Ó Néill, 'Bonifaz und Virgil: Konflikt zweier Kulturen', in *Virgil von Salzburg*, ed. Dopsch and Juffinger, pp. 76–83.

[169] Notker of St Gallen, *De gestis Karoli Magni*, ed. G. H. Pertz, MGH, Scriptores 2 (Hannover, 1879), 731–63, at 731; see Kenney, *The Sources*, p. 533 (no. 339). Other medieval testimonies to the learning of the Irish are cited by Gougaud, *Christianity in Celtic Lands*, p. 310. E. James, 'Ireland and Western Gaul', p. 381, characterizes

to have been matched by a reputation for obscurantism and pedantry. Some, including Benedict of Aniane, who warned against their *syllogismus delusionis*, were deeply suspicious of their methods.[170] The author of the eighth-century *Chronicon Palatinum* referred caustically to the loquacity of Irish scholars, 'qui sapientiam se existimant habere et scientiam perdederunt'.[171] Others simply mocked their pretensions to learning. Theodulf of Orléans made fun of one *Scotellus*, whom Bischoff has identified as the scholar Cadac-Andreas, with a sarcastic *Quis primus* question after the Irish manner: 'Who was the first among the Irish to have painted his face at a funeral?'[172]

A like mixture of admiration and antagonism characterized the English attitude towards Irish learning. Bede reported, with obvious appreciation, how in the previous century many English had gone to Ireland 'uel diuinae lectionis uel continentioris uitae gratia'.[173] Some of these Anglo-Saxon pilgrims, he recalled, cultivated the monastic life, while others 'magis circueundo per cellas magistrorum lectioni operam dare gaudebant. Quos omnes Scotti libentissime suscipientes, uictum eis cotidianum sine pretio, libros quoque ad legendum et magisterium gratuitum praebere curabant.'[174] Bede even refers, I think without

the ambivalence as 'a conflict between the popular view of the Irish and the official ecclesiastical one'.

170 PL 103, 1413. See Kenney, *The Sources*, p. 537 (no. 343).

171 *Cronica Minora* III, ed. T. Mommsen, MGH, Auct. antiq. 13 (Berlin, 1898), 424–37, at 427: 'who consider themselves to possess wisdom but who have squandered knowledge'. Ludwig Traube thought that the author's barbs may have been directed at Bede (for references, see Levison, *England and the Continent*, p. 170, n. 1).

172 See Bischoff, 'Theodulf und der Ire Cadac-Andreas', in his *Mittelalterliche Studien* II, 19–25; *idem*, 'Turning-Points', p. 88. The pedantry encountered in Irish exegesis, and ridiculed by Theodulf, was characteristic of much Irish Latinity and scholarship. Louis Gougaud has spoken of 'the decided bent of Celtic clerics and monks who had some smattering of letters for all that was uncommon, difficult, and esoteric. They were singularly attracted by unusual combinations of ideas and words, enigmas, acrostics, cryptology and cryptography' (*Christianity in Celtic Lands*, p. 252).

173 *HE* III.27: 'either for the sake of religious studies or to live a more ascetic life'.

174 *Ibid.*: 'preferred to travel round to the cells of various teachers and apply themselves to study. The Irish welcomed them all gladly, gave them their daily food, and also provided them with books to read and with instruction, without asking for any payment'. Alcuin testifies that Willibrord went to Ireland 'quia in Hibernia scholasticam eruditionem uiguisse audiuit' (*Vita S. Willibrordi*, cited by Kenney, *The Sources*, p. 233, n. 234).

irony, to the reputed curative powers of scrapings from Irish parchment.[175] Moreover, he seems to have drawn on Irish exegesis, though chiefly for minor details.[176] Yet his opinion of Irish scholarship was not wholly favourable, for (like Theodulf of Orléans) he derided a typically Irish exegetical method (a comparison using *more*, an Irish symptom, in a pseudonymous Hiberno-Latin commentary on the Catholic Epistles).[177] The establishment of Canterbury as a centre of sacred studies by Theodore and Hadrian had awakened the pride of English students in English learning, and inevitably fostered rivalry with their former masters. Aldhelm complained in his letter to Heahfrith that many English students were still flocking to Ireland when they could now find superior wisdom at home. In florid diction designed to surpass the rhetorical displays for which the Irish were famed, Aldhelm extolled the scholarship of Theodore and Hadrian:

Quamuis enim praedictum Hiberniae rus discentium opulans uernansque, ut ita dixerim, pascuosa numerositate lectorum, quemadmodum poli cardines astriferis micantium uibraminibus siderum, ornetur: ast tamen ... Britannia ... uerbi gratia ceu solis flammigeri et luculento lunae specimine potiatur, id est Theodoro infula pontificatus fungenti ab ipso tirocinio rudimentorum in flore philosophicae artis adulto necnon et eiusdem sodalitatis cliente Hadriano dumtaxat urbanitate enucleata ineffabiliter praedito![178]

175 *HE* I.1. Mayr-Harting, *The Coming of Christianity*, p. 50, makes the provocative suggestion that Bede meant to imply that 'the Irish were filling rather too many leaves of parchment with learning, not all of it entirely free from pedantry or wild fantasy'. But see J. F. Kelly, 'Books, Learning and Sanctity in Early Christian Ireland', *Thought* 54 (1979), 253–61, at 253–4.

176 On Bede's relation to Irish learning, see C. Jones, *Bedae Opera de Temporibus* (Cambridge, MA, 1943), pp. 105–22, and D. Ó Cróinín, 'The Irish Provenance of Bede's Computus', *Peritia* 2 (1983), 170–84; for his debt to Irish exegesis, see J. F. Kelly, 'The Venerable Bede and Hiberno-Latin Exegesis', in *Sources of Anglo-Saxon Culture*, ed. Szarmach, pp. 65–76.

177 See Bischoff, 'Turning-Points', p. 143. The commentary is pseudo-Hilary, *Expositio in VII epistolas catholicas* (*BCLL*, no. 346; Wright, 'Hiberno-Latin', no. 35). See also Bieler, 'Ireland's Contribution', p. 218, who cites a passage from Bede's *Hexaemeron*, critical of those who wonder which of the three languages God used to name the day and the night, as Bede's response to 'the excessive *curiositas* of Irish exegetes'.

178 *Aldhelmi Opera*, ed. Ehwald, pp. 492–3: 'Although the aforesaid opulent and verdant country of Ireland is adorned, so to speak, with a browsing crowd of scholars, just as the hinges of heaven are decorated with stellar flashings of twinkling stars, yet nonetheless, Britain ... possesses, for example, the luculent

Aldhelm goes on to proclaim the victory of Theodore, 'hemmed in by a mass of Irish students, like a savage wild boar checked by a snarling pack of hounds', and suggests that his correspondent's infatuation with Irish scholars ('whose bejewelled honeycomb of doctrine your Wisdom has somewhat over-employed') has been misguided.[179] Elsewhere Aldhelm warns another correspondent of the seductive dangers of Irish classical scholarship – and 'bawdy houses'.[180]

In addition to the inquisitive bent of Irish scholars, who occasionally strayed into controversial areas, the intense asceticism of Irish hermits led to excesses. In the seventh century Irish hermits such as Fursa were still held in high esteem, and their visions were considered to be an index of their holiness. The incident recorded in the *Anglo-Saxon Chronicle* concerning the three Irishmen who arrived at the court of King Alfred, having set out in a boat without a rudder on a pilgrimage for the love of God, shows that the reputation of Irish ascetics for holiness was still powerful and affecting in the ninth century.[181] But already by the eighth the extravagant claims of some Irish ascetics were met with suspicion. In his *Vita S. Guthlaci*, Felix described how the English hermit was visited by a certain Wigfrith, who had encountered in Ireland both men of holiness as well as 'pseudo-anchorites':

Dicebat enim inter Scottorum se populos habitasse et illic pseudo-anachoritas diuersarum religionum simulatores uidisse, quos praedicere futura et uirtutes alias facere, quocumque numine nesciens conperit. Alios quoque illic fuisse narrabat uerae religionis cultores signis uirtutibusque plurimis pollentes, quos ille crebro adloqui, uidere frequentareque solebat.[182]

likeness, as it were, of the flaming sun and moon, that is, Theodore, who discharges the duties of the pontificate and was from the very beginnings of his apprenticeship mature in the flower of the arts of learning, and his colleague of the same sodality, Hadrian, equally endowed with ineffably pure urbanity' (trans. Lapidge and Herren, *Aldhelm: the Prose Works*, p. 163).

179 *Ibid.* See also S. Gwara, 'Aldhelm's *P*s and *Q*s in the *Epistola ad Ehfridum*', *NQ* 234 (1989), 290–3, on Aldhelm's 'ironic posture and caustic remarks on Irish learning' (p. 293).

180 *Aldhelm: the Prose Works*, trans. Lapidge and Herren, pp. 154–5 (Letter to Wihtfrith).

181 *Anglo-Saxon Chronicle*, s.a. 891; see below, p. 267.

182 *Felix's Life of Saint Guthlac*, ed. B. Colgrave (Cambridge, 1956), p. 142: 'For he said he had lived amongst the Irish, and there had seen false hermits and pretenders of various religions, whom he found able to predict the future and perform other miracles, but he knew not by what power. He said that there were others there who

In the dark years of the Irish church following the Viking invasions, there must have been similar 'pseudo-anchorites' and charlatans. We know of one, an Irish deacon named Niall, who claimed to have once been dead for five (or seven) weeks.[183] Reports of his revelations and prophecies (accompanied by an apocryphal text, the Sunday Letter) made their way into England in the early ninth century and were being spread, along with certain heretical opinions,[184] by an English priest named Pehtred, whose book (now lost) was condemned by Ecgred, bishop of Lindisfarne. Since the archetype of the Old English 'Niall' Sunday Letter sermons used material from Vercelli IX, these two Irish-influenced texts must have been transmitted in a common milieu. But what Vercelli IX has in common with the Niall Sunday Letter sermons is not heretical doctrine, but reliance on apocryphal materials transmitted through Irish sources.

were followers of the true religion and abounded in many signs and miracles, whom he had been accustomed to speak with frequently, to see, and often to visit' (trans. Colgrave, p. 143). See now the remarks on this passage by Sims-Williams, *Religion and Literature*, p. 247. That the Irish-trained Wigfrith is subsequently shown up by Guthlac is as revealing of Felix's English pride as of his attitude towards the Irish. Equally revealing is the fact that, despite the apparent hostility to the Irish, the *Vita* is clearly indebted to Irish hagiographical traditions. See Earl, 'Literary Problems in Early Medieval Hagiography', and Kelly, 'Irish Influence in England', pp. 41–2.

183 For a detailed discussion, see below, pp. 221–2.

184 Ecgred specifically condemns the belief that the devil was created as a devil, and the attempt to fix the day or hour of the Last Judgement (his letter is ed. Whitelock, 'Bishop Ecgred, Pehtred and Niall', pp. 48–9). I can find no evidence that the first view was held by any Irishman in the Middle Ages; it is specifically opposed in the Hiberno-Latin St Gallen Commentary on the Creation and Fall (St Gallen, Stiftsbibliothek, 908, p. 11). As for the day or hour of Judgement, if Ecgred is opposed to fixing a precise date, there is again no evidence, so far as I am aware, of such a heresy in Ireland. On the other hand, Irish sources frequently do state that Judgement will take place on a Monday, or (as in the Sunday Letter and Sunday lists) on a Sunday. Another apocryphal tradition transmitted by the Irish was the view that Judgement would take place at Easter, an opinion shared by several Old English sources, including *Christ III* and Blickling Homily III, where Irish influence is likely (see Biggs, *The Sources of Christ III*, pp. 6–7, and Wright, 'Blickling Homily III', p. 134 and n.15). Although this tradition was mentioned by Jerome (see Biggs), the Irish probably found it in the apocryphal Gospel of the Hebrews, which is cited in several Hiberno-Latin commentaries. In the *Catechesis Celtica* the tradition is specifically attributed to that apocryphal gospel (in *Analecta Reginensia*, ed. Wilmart, p. 58; the passage is trans. Hennecke and Schneemelcher, *New Testament Apocrypha* I, 150–1).

By the end of the eighth century and beginning of the ninth there is some evidence of what Edmund Bishop called a 'recoil from Irishry'. In 816 the English Council of *Celchyth* (Chelsea) forbade all wandering clerics *de genere Scottorum* from exercising any ecclesiastical functions.[185] Bishop went so far as to suggest that

> if we find in England at the end of the eighth century or in the early decades of the ninth, religious or devotional pieces bearing marked evidence of a piety Spanish or Irish in character, the actual composition of these may, on general grounds, be attributed with greater probability to the turn of the seventh and eighth centuries than to that of the eighth and ninth.[186]

But as Kathleen Hughes pointed out, the canon of *Celchyth* 'also proves conclusively that Irish clerics had been ministering, and presumably in sufficient numbers, to provoke opposition'.[187] Irish literary and devotional influences need not, in any case, have been directly tied to the wavering reputations and political fortunes of Irish clerics;[188] and after

[185] *Councils and Ecclesiastical Documents*, ed. Haddan and Stubbs III, 581. See Bishop's discussion, *Liturgica Historica*, p. 172, with references to similar continental legislation against *clerici uagi*.

[186] *Ibid.*, p. 173. This is one reason Bishop preferred to identify the bishop Ethelwold named in the Book of Cerne with Ætheluald of Lindisfarne rather than Æthelwald of Lichfield (*ibid.*, p. 175). Bishop's identification has been supported by D. Dumville, 'Liturgical Drama and Panegyric Responsory from the Eighth Century? A Re-examination of the Origin and Contents of the Ninth-Century Section of the Book of Cerne', *JTS* ns 23 (1972), 374–406; for the origin of the central section of the manuscript, see Dumville, p. 382: 'written in an English scriptorium south of the Humber, in a centre under Mercian influence'.

[187] 'Some Aspects of Irish Influence', p. 61; see also Hughes, 'Evidence for Contacts', pp. 64–7. Bishop noted that the Book of Cerne is itself 'an evidence of reviving or active Irishry' (*Liturgica Historica*, p. 174). The evidence of the Book of Cerne would, of course, be stronger if its compilation were associated with Æthelwald of Lichfield, but the fact that what Kenneth Sisam characterized as 'Old-fashioned and out-of-the-way texts' were still being copied in the ninth century is itself significant (quoted by Dumville, p. 396).

[188] Dumville, '"Beowulf" and the Celtic World', p. 116, speaking of the influence of the Irish in the formative period of the English church, points out that 'Formative influences are not such as are easily suppressed or allowed to disappear. And in Northumbria we have little reason to believe that ecclesiastical outlook changed, where essentials are concerned, before the eleventh century'. Cf. D. A. Bullough's remark in connection with Irish influence in Anglo-Saxon private prayer ('The Missions to the English and the Picts and their Heritage (to c. 800)', in *Die Iren und Europa*, ed. Löwe I, 80–98, at 94–5): 'Books, the old Easter Tables excepted, were

some two centuries of active 'Irishry', the reception of Irish learning and literary traditions into Anglo-Saxon literary culture had already been accomplished, especially in Northumbria and Mercia. And it is precisely in the ninth and tenth centuries, and apparently in Mercia, that the latent 'Irishry' in Anglo-Saxon literary culture manifested itself in the Old English homiletic tradition.[189]

Any study that arrives at certain positive conclusions, however limited and qualified, regarding the distinctiveness and influence of the Irish learned tradition in the early Middle Ages will likely be suspected of what Johannes Duft has called 'Iromanie'.[190] Romantic impulses and nationalistic biases have sometimes contributed to an exaggerated estimation both of the intellectual achievements of medieval Irish scholars and of their role in the formation of Christian culture on the Continent. Once credited with an extensive knowledge of Greek and of classical literature, the Irish were viewed as the bearers of the torch of learning through the Dark Ages, the 'Light from the West', according to the title of one recent popular history of the Irish mission to the Continent.[191] On the other hand, the reaction against *Iromanie* has generated an equally distorted view – *Irophobie* – which denies any distinctiveness to the Irish and dismisses all suggestion of Irish influence. I have tried to avoid these extremes. The Irish were neither heterodox nor outlandish, but they did synthesize patristic, apocryphal and native traditions in imaginative and idiosyncratic formulations of Christian themes and doctrines. Irish influence on Old English literature was neither pervasive nor profound – not every weird motif or baroque feature of style in Old English is an Irish symptom – but where such influence can be traced, particularly among the anonymous homilies, it can be manifested in vivid and grotesque eschatological motifs and extravagant rhetorical formulations. Although the contrast is rarely so

not put on a local index in 664 or 710 or any other date; and familiar thought-worlds and their forms of expression are only slowly and reluctantly abandoned for new ones.'

189 See below, pp. 266–70.

190 'Iromanie – Irophobie: Fragen um die frühmittelalterliche Irenmission exemplifiziert an St. Gallen und Alemannien', *Zeitschrift für schweizerische Kirchengeschichte* 50 (1956), 241–62.

191 A serious blow to this view has been dealt by M. Lapidge, 'The Authorship of the Adonic Verses *Ad Fidolium* Attributed to Columbanus', *SM* 3rd ser. 18 (1977), 815–80.

sharply drawn, the Irish tradition informing Vercelli IX and the *Prose Solomon and Saturn Pater Noster Dialogue* could scarcely be more alien to the tradition represented by Ælfric and Wulfstan. One might be tempted to dismiss Vercelli IX and the Irish-influenced milieu to which it belongs as an aberrant tradition – the 'Celtic fringe' of Old English literature – but to judge from the surviving manuscripts, these texts found a large audience in Anglo-Saxon England during the tenth and eleventh centuries.[192] If they bear upon them 'some of the darkest thumb-marks of the Middle Ages', as Henry Wadsworth Longfellow said of one *Solomon and Saturn* dialogue,[193] it must be allowed that they were, after all, heavily thumbed.

[192] Scragg, *The Vercelli Homilies*, p. 157, remarks that 'Englishmen continued to be fascinated by the ideas in homily IX throughout the eleventh century. The text of E was annotated and altered by a number of hands until long after the Norman Conquest, and echoes of the piece appear in a number of late compilations.' On the manuscripts of Vercelli IX and its exemplum, see the Appendix, pp. 273–4.

[193] 'Anglo-Saxon Literature', *North American Review* 47 (1838), 90–134, at 130.

2

The 'enumerative style' in Ireland and Anglo-Saxon England

The structure of Vercelli IX, according to Paul Szarmach, is common to a number of the homilies in the Vercelli Book: a 'formula of introduction, an appropriate number of preparatory motifs, a central narrative episode or exposition, and a closing'.[1] In Vercelli IX the preparatory motif section is given structural weight equal to the central narrative episode, 'The Devil's Account of the Next World'. The homily, then, consists of these two major parts, framed by an introduction and a conclusion. The preparatory motif section consists of a series of enumerations 'be deaðes onlicnesse 7 be helle gryre',[2] arranged in ascending order: three deaths and lives, four separations and five likenesses of hell. Although the homilist's immediate source has not been recovered, parallels in Hiberno-Latin and Irish compilations suggest that he has culled these numerical themes from a florilegium of Irish origin or inspiration. In the following pages I shall describe several Hiberno-Latin florilegia, dialogues and homily collections that transmit a common stock of numerical motifs, some of which found their way from Irish compilations into Old English homilies.

THE IRISH 'ENUMERATIVE STYLE'

The numerical apophthegm is, of course, a widespread and ancient literary form. As a recurrent stylistic feature of biblical (especially Old Testament) and apocryphal literature,[3] it naturally was cultivated by

[1] 'The Vercelli Homilies: Style and Structure', p. 244.

[2] *The Vercelli Homilies*, ed. Scragg, p. 161, lines 32–3: 'concerning the likeness of death and the terror of hell'.

[3] See W. Roth, *Numerical Sayings in the Old Testament* (Leiden, 1965), and J. T. Davis, *Biblical Numerology* (Grand Rapids, MI, 1968), pp. 93–102. For enumeration in

patristic and medieval authors.[4] Indeed, Jean Leclercq regards the use of enumerations as a method of composition characteristic of monastic authors.[5] Leclercq, however, was chiefly concerned with texts dating from the twelfth century and later, when the practice of enumerating the points of a sermon and structuring didactic treatises upon numerical themes was given impetus by the logical and rhetorical methods of scholasticism.[6] But this type of composition was less common, if by no means rare, in preceding centuries. Isolated numerical themes, drawn directly from the Bible or inherited from classical and patristic authorities, did gain great currency, and provided the theme of many a sermon and didactic treatise: the three temptations, the three theological and four cardinal virtues, the six ages of the world, the seven (or eight) deadly sins, the seven gifts of the Holy Spirit and so on. These enumerative motifs are part of the shared inheritance of Christian literary culture throughout Europe in the early Middle Ages. But in general it seems fair to say that, prior to the eleventh and twelfth centuries, most authors who used numerical themes confined themselves to a relatively limited stock of well-worn favourites. The Irish, however, were not satisfied with the common run of numerical themes. In comparison with most continental authors, they were nearly obsessive in their zeal for collecting every odd enumeration they could

Rabbinic texts, see W. Towner, *The Rabbinic 'Enumeration of Scriptural Examples'* (Leiden, 1973), and for an extensive collection or Rabbinic numeral apophthegms, see A. Wünsche, 'Die Zahlensprüche in Talmud und Midrasch', *Zeitschrift der deutschen morgenländischen Gesellschaft* 65 (1911), 57–100 and 395–421; 66 (1912), 414–59.

4 See E. R. Curtius, *European Literature and the Latin Middle Ages*, trans. W. Trask (Princeton, NJ, 1953), pp. 510–14. A fair sampling of numerical motifs in medieval Latin literature can be had simply by consulting the index to *Lateinische Sprichwörter und Sentenzen des Mittelalters und der frühen Neuzeit in alphabetischer Anordnung*, ed. H. Walther, 8 vols. (Göttingen, 1963–83), under *tria*, *quattuor*, etc.

5 J. Leclercq, *The Love of Learning and the Desire for God*, trans. C. Misrahi (New York, 1977), pp. 210–11; cited by Szarmach, 'The Vercelli Homilies: Style and Structure', p. 242.

6 On the use of numerical themes to distinguish the formal *diuisiones* of sermons in the later Middle Ages, see Owst, *Preaching in Medieval England*, pp. 321–2; *idem*, *Literature and Pulpit in Medieval England* (Cambridge, 1933), pp. 67–8. As Owst shows (*Preaching in Medieval England*, pp. 310–13), late medieval preachers were conscious that the formal method of *diuisiones* was a departure from the ancient 'method of the Saints', *sine diuisionibus thematum* (see p. 311).

find in the Fathers,[7] to which they added further either by reformulating as numerical themes non-enumerative lists and sequences from biblical and patristic texts, or by inventing new ones.[8] As Kathleen Hughes has pointed out, the late-eleventh-century parody of Irish literary style, *Aislinge Meic Con Glinne* ('The Vision of Mac Con Glinne'), which 'reduces to absurdity many of the scholar's techniques', travesties the Irish preoccupation with numerical themes.[9] As a trick to get food from Cathal, king of Munster, who is possessed by a demon of gluttony, Mac Con Glinne rattles off a string of enumerations, each of which compels the king to give him another apple: '"Ferr déda hó oín i nd-ecna", ar Mac Con Glinne. Snedis aroli dó. "Umir na Trínóti", or Mac Con Glinne. Cuiris oen dó. "Cethair leba[i]r in ts[h]oscéla iar timna C[h]ríst". Tidnais óen do. "Coic lebair Móysi iar ndeich timnai Rechta". Cuiris oen dó.' This goes on through thirteen, 'in buaid ós buadu 7 in umir f[h]orpthi, Críst for a aspalu', after which the exasperated king exclaims, 'no-m ísa dia-nom lena ní as mó!'[10]

Biblical and patristic models were undoubtedly an important stimulus for the Irish habit of couching fact, lore and wisdom in numerical form,

[7] Jerome, Gregory the Great and Isidore of Seville were among the most important sources for numerical themes. The *Verba seniorum* and *Apophthegmata patrum* provided various didactic enumerations. See the index of sources in McNally, *Der irische Liber de numeris*, pp. 200–2.

[8] Such a judgement is necessarily relative and impressionistic, but a fair comparison can be made with Defensor's *Liber scintillarum*, ed. H. Rochais, CCSL 117 (Turnhout, 1957), perhaps the most extensive and influential early medieval florilegium (an Old English glossed version of the *Liber scintillarum* is ed. E. W. Rhodes, *Defensor's Liber Scintillarum*, EETS os 93 (London, 1889)). Among its hundreds of entries, culled from a wide range of patristic sources, I count scarcely a dozen enumerations – a poor ratio when compared to the Irish compilations described below.

[9] 'Irish Monks and Learning', pp. 84–5. On the date of the Leabhar Breac version of the tale, see Jackson, *Aislinge Meic Con Glinne*, pp. xx–xxvi.

[10] *Ibid.*, p. 20, lines 610–14 and 625–8: '"Better two things than one in learning", said Mac Con Glinne. He flung him another. "The number of the Trinity!" [said Mac Con Glinne.] He gave him another. "The four books of the Gospel, according to the testament of Christ!" He threw him one. "The five books of Moses, according to the Ten Commandments of the Law!" He flung him one. "The triumph beyond triumphs and the perfect number, Christ with his Apostles" ... "You will devour me, if you pursue me any further"' (trans. Meyer, *Aislinge Meic Conglinne*, pp. 49–51).

as several scholars have argued.[11] Pádraig P. Ó Néill, following Kuno Meyer, identifies the biblical sapiential books as a model for the triads and heptads in the Old Irish *Apgitir Chrábaid*.[12] Yet the characteristic incremental form of Old Testament numerical apophthegms is scarcely ever imitated in Irish enumerations.[13] The influence of native Celtic traditions should not be discounted. Patrick Sims-Williams, who notes that Irish exegetical works employ enumerations 'to an extent surprising even by medieval numerological standards', suggests that this is so 'perhaps because the mnemonic techniques of the secular learned classes were borrowed for the presentation of religious material'.[14] Irish authors worked enumerations into secular texts of all kinds, and even constructed whole texts out of them. A well-known example is *The Triads of Ireland*.[15] The triad, of course, is the Celtic numerical genre *par excellence*,[16] but Irish secular literature affords abundant examples of other forms.[17] The law tracts, for example, resort to enumerations constantly, including duads through enneads; one tract is made up entirely of heptads.[18]

[11] See Meyer, *The Triads of Ireland*, pp. xii–xiii; McNally, *Der irische Liber de numeris*, pp. 23–4. McNally mentions the Bible and the Fathers as influences, and remarks that numerical organization is 'eine typisch schulmäßige Gedächtnishilfe'.

[12] 'The Date and Authorship of *Apgitir Chrábaid*', pp. 208–9. On the contents of *Apgitir Chrábaid*, see further below.

[13] See W. Roth, 'The Sequence x/x+1 in the Old Testament', *Vetus Testamentum* 12 (1962), 302–7. All the examples which Ó Néill cites from Proverbs and Sirach for comparison with *Apgitir Chrábaid* show this characteristic form. There are no such enumerations in *Apgitir Chrábaid*, nor have I encountered any in Irish or Hiberno-Latin texts, apart from direct quotations of biblical enumerations.

[14] 'Thought, Word and Deed', p. 78. Sims-Williams argues that 'It is unlikely that the influence was *vice versa*, for although later triads show Christian influence ... the early triads ... are remarkably free from both Christian and Latin influence' (p. 78, n. 2).

[15] *The Triads of Ireland*, ed. Meyer. Concerning the triads, Meyer remarks, 'I am not aware that this kind of composition has ever attained the same popularity elsewhere as in Wales and Ireland, where the manufacture of triads seems at times almost to have become a sport' (p. xv). He cites some didactic triads from various sources on pp. viii–ix.

[16] See R. Smith, 'The Six Gifts', pp. 103–4.

[17] In his introduction (p. xii), Meyer notes that the triad 'is but one of several similar enumerative sayings common in Irish literature'. For a listing of some numerical themes, see T. P. Cross, *Motif-Index*, pp. 529–32.

[18] For a list of the enumerations in the first volume of *The Ancient Laws of Ireland*, see *The Triads of Ireland*, ed. Meyer, p. xii, n. 2. D. A. Binchy reported that Rudolf Thurneysen 'more than once commented on the ingrained tendency of the Irish

Whatever the relative weight of the influences of the Christian-Latin and native Celtic traditions, in Irish religious literature, and not only in biblical commentaries, enumerations are ubiquitous.[19] André Wilmart characterized Irish liturgical style as 'à la fois biblique et énumératif',[20] and Sims-Williams has echoed this judgement in speaking of the Irish 'enumerative style'.[21] When we look for florilegia and similar compilations from the early Middle Ages that contain sequences of enumerations, or that are made up largely or even entirely of numerical motifs – the type of florilegia, that is, which the Vercelli homilist must have consulted – we find that these are almost invariably Irish.

As Joan Turville-Petre has pointed out, 'the pool of moral excerpts had been intensively used and developed by Irish and Anglo-Saxon scholars during the seventh and eighth centuries, particularly in compilations associated with their continental missions'.[22] Among

jurists to substitute enumeration for definition' ('Semantic Influence of Latin in the Old Irish Glosses', in *Latin Script and Letters A. D. 400–900*, ed. J. J. O'Meara and B. Naumann (Leiden, 1976), pp. 167–73, at 169). N. Patterson sees a 'fusion of native jural traditions with symbols from the repertoire of Christian imagery' in certain distributive schemes in Old Irish law, particularly the scheme three plus four, which she would attribute to Christian influence: 'Kinship Law or Number Symbolism? Models of Distributive Justice in Old Irish Law', *PHCC* 5 (1985), 49–86, at 71; 'Brehon Law in Late Medieval Ireland: "Antiquarian and Obsolete" or "Traditional and Functional"?', *CMCS* 17 (Summer 1989), 43–63.

19 On the frequency of enumeration in Irish exegesis, see Bischoff, 'Turning-Points', p. 84. R. E. McNally, speaking of the Irish fondness for *Zahlensprüche*, concluded that 'While it is not possible in view of the evidence to say that this literary form is an original creation, for it is found both in Holy Scripture and as well in other ancient literatures, its repeated occurrence in Irish works makes it characteristic' ('Old Ireland, Her Scribes and Scholars', p. 133).

20 In Wilmart *et al.*, *The Bobbio Missal: Notes and Studies*, p. 34 (cited by Sims-Williams, 'Thought, Word and Deed', p. 99). Wilmart uses the term 'énumératif' to refer in general to the litanic or iterative style, especially in liturgical books. Most scholars have seen Irish influence in the iterative style; an exception is F. di Capua, 'Lo stile commatico in alcune preghiere del periodo carolingio', in *Miscellanea liturgica in honorem L. Cuniberti Mohlberg*, 2 vols. (Rome, 1948–9) II, 209–21 (I owe this reference to Dr Sims-Williams).

21 'Thought, Word and Deed', p. 90.

22 'Translations of a Lost Penitential Homily', p. 62. Alcuin's *De uirtutibus et uitiis*, discussed by Turville-Petre, is one important florilegium by an English author. Other English authors who compiled florilegia include Bede (his *Collectaneum* on the Pauline Epistles is drawn from the works of Augustine), and Boniface, who promised his correspondent Bugge a florilegium of scriptural texts (referred to as *congregationes aliquas sanctarum scripturarum* or *conscriptio sententiarum*); see H. Schüling,

these she mentions specifically the Irish treatise *De duodecim abusiuis saeculi*,[23] the Irish canonical compilation known as the *Collectio Canonum Hibernensis*[24] and the *Collectaneum* of Sedulius Scottus.[25] These compilations, together with other Irish dialogues, homily collections and biblical commentaries, bear witness to the industry with which the Irish combed patristic texts for enumerations, or simply manufactured their own.[26] To suggest the extent of this stylistic preference of Irish scribes and scholars, I will describe briefly several of these compilations.

Three particularly important florilegia, each a mine of numerical motifs, are the Old Irish *Apgitir Chrábaid*, the *Collectanea Bedae* and the *Liber de numeris*. *Apgitir Chrábaid* ('The Alphabet of Piety') contains a variety of questions and answers, didactic proverbs and lists.[27] In the thirty-eight sections its editor distinguishes occur twenty-four numerical motifs; seventeen sections consist entirely of enumeration, with or without elaboration. They are for the most part randomly organized, but there are some numerical groupings: section 19 and the beginning of 20 are triads, followed by tetrads in sections 20–8. These are almost

'Die Handbibliothek des Bonifatius', *Archiv für Geschichte des Buchwesens* 4 (1963), 286–349, at 298–9. Asser informs us that King Alfred made such a collection; see the *Life of Alfred*, chs. 24 and 88–9, trans. Keynes and Lapidge, *Alfred the Great*, pp. 75 and 99–100 (see their note, p. 268). Lapidge and Herren, *Aldhelm: the Prose Works*, p. 58, characterize Aldhelm's prose *De uirginitate* as a florilegium.

23 *Pseudo-Cyprianus de xii abusivis saeculi*, ed. S. Hellmann; see *BCLL*, no. 339. See also H. H. Anton, 'Pseudo-Cyprian De duodecim abusivis saeculi und sein Einfluss auf den Kontinent, insbesondere auf die karolingische Fürstenspiegel', in *Die Iren und Europa*, ed. Löwe II, 568–617.

24 *BCLL*, nos. 612–13; the text is presently available only in the defective edition of Recension A by Wasserschleben, *Die irische Kanonensammlung*. See M. P. Sheehy, 'The *Collectio Canonum Hibernensis* – a Celtic Phenomenon', in *Die Iren und Europa*, ed. Löwe I, 525–35; Reynolds, 'Unity and Diversity', pp. 99–135.

25 On this text, see below, pp. 56–8.

26 Of the Irish florilegia mentioned by Turville-Petre, the *De duodecim abusiuis saeculi* is, of course, structured upon a numerical theme, and the *Collectio Canonum Hibernensis* contains frequent enumerations.

27 'Apgitir Chrábaid', ed. Hull. Ó Néill, 'The Date and Authorship of *Apgitir Chrábaid*', concludes on linguistic and stylistic grounds that the text was composed *c.* 600, and that the evidence is consistent with the attribution in most of the manuscripts to Colmán maccu Béognae (d. 611). J. Carney, 'Aspects of Archaic Irish', *Éigse* 17 (1978–9), 417–35, at 424–5, suggests Fursa as a possible author; O'Dwyer, *Céli Dé*, pp. 177–8, would attribute the text to a later author, Mocholmóc Ua Liatháin (d. 730).

all didactic motifs of a very general kind, such as the four salvations of the soul, or the four hardships of sinners.[28] The *Collectanea Bedae* has been aptly described as 'a jumble of Latin apocryphal and sub-ecclesiastical bric-à-brac'.[29] It contains riddles, legends, biblical lore, *sententiae* and more, in no discernible order. Much of it is question-and-answer dialogue of the *Joca monachorum* genre.[30] Enumerations are frequent in both declarative and interrogative forms; most are biblical, such as the four rivers of Paradise, or didactic, such as the three things by which the soul is ordered.[31] The Hiberno-Latin *Liber de numeris* is more systematic.[32] The author's intention, we learn from the prologue, was to treat the numbers one to twenty-four, but in fact the work extends only to the number eight. Despite the author's promise to write 'de numero et eius mistico mysterio', it is not really a treatise on number, but rather a collection of numerical motifs arranged in numerical order: 'Quid unum dicit', 'Quid duo dicit' and so on.[33] Each section contains enumerations of the most miscellaneous nature

[28] 'Apgitir Chrábaid', ed. Hull, pp. 60 and 72. For a series of similar didactic enumerations, all triads, see 'Mac Eclaise', 'Fragment from "Leabhar Breac" – II', *The Irish Ecclesiastical Record* 4th ser. 28 (1916), 292–3.

[29] P. Kitson, 'Lapidary Traditions in Anglo-Saxon England: Part II', *ASE* 12 (1983), 73–123, at 100. Kitson dates the compilation to the last quarter of the seventh century, and suggests that it may be associated with the circle of Virgilius Maro Grammaticus. Lapidge, 'Latin Learning in Dark Age Wales', pp. 100–2, notes other Hiberno-Latin features in the *Collectanea* but tentatively suggests that the compilation may have originated in Wales. For a Hibernicism in the *Collectanea*, see my article, 'The Three "Victories" of the Wind' (summarized below, pp. 253–5). The *Collectanea* (*BCLL*, no. 1257) is in PL 94, 539–62. There is no surviving manuscript, but see Sims-Williams, *Religion and Literature*, p. 335, n. 29, for references to copies noted in Bale's *Index Brittanniae Scriptorum* and in a Saint-Bertin catalogue of *c.* 1104. An edition by Michael Lapidge and others is forthcoming in SLH.

[30] On the *Joca monachorum* and related *Adrianus et Epictitus* dialogues (consisting of riddling questions, mostly biblical, and often including enumerations), see Daly and Suchier, *Altercatio*; Suchier, *Adrian und Epictitus*.

[31] PL 94, 543D and 541C. For the latter enumeration, see Sims-Williams, 'Thought, Word and Deed', p. 88.

[32] *BCLL*, no. 778; Wright, 'Hiberno-Latin', no. 39. A portion of the text (up to the number three) is in PL 83, 1293–1302, but it has not been fully edited. For a full analysis of the contents, see McNally, *Der irische Liber de numeris* (references follow McNally's numbering of motifs).

[33] See *ibid.*, p. 24: 'Der *Liber de numeris* stellt keine Zahlensymbolik oder -mystik dar'.

imaginable: biblical, exegetical, pseudo-scientific and didactic. The section, 'Quid quattuor adserit', for example, includes items such as the four letters of the name of God (IV.1), the four seasons (IV.4), the four births of Christ (IV.21) and the four kinds of questions (IV.33), in addition to didactic motifs such as the four things that stain the soul (IV.51). The *Liber de numeris*, then, represents the Irish penchant for collecting enumerations taken to its logical extreme: a treatise consisting entirely of numerical themes, arranged in numerical order.

To the *Collectanea Bedae* and *Liber de numeris*, which have long been regarded as Irish compilations, may now be added the recently published *Florilegium Frisingense* in Munich, Bayerische Staatsbibliothek, Clm. 6433 (s. viii^{ex}).[34] The florilegium, characterized by the editor as 'eine fast durch und durch von irisch beeinflußten Vorlagen abhängige Sammlung',[35] was written in Freising by the Anglo-Saxon scribe Peregrinus.[36] Somewhat surprisingly, the twenty-one rubricated sections, which in addition to standard authorities include citations from the Insular favourites Pelagius and Virgilius Maro Grammaticus, contain scarcely an enumeration. As if to make up for the lack, however, a sequence of fifteen enumerations is included among the miscellaneous items following (items 418–33). Nearly all of these enumerations are paralleled in other Hiberno-Latin florilegia and commentaries, including the *Collectanea Bedae* and *Liber de numeris*.[37] Typical also is the numerical formulation of a non-enumerated list from the Bible.[38]

Also published recently for the first time is the *Collectaneum* of Sedulius Scottus,[39] an extensive compilation chiefly of classical and patristic excerpts, including one florilegium (section XIII) of forty headings mostly on virtues and vices, and another (section XXV) of

[34] In *Florilegia*, ed. Lehner, pp. 1–39.
[35] *Ibid.*, p. xxxvi.
[36] On Peregrinus, active during the time of Bishop Arbeo (d. 783), see Bischoff, *Schreibschulen*, pp. 61–3 and 73–5; E. Kessler, *Die Auszeichnungsschriften in den Freisinger Codices von den Anfangen bis zur karolingischen Erneuerung*, Denkschriften der Österreichischen Akademie der Wissenschaften, phil.-hist. Klasse 188 (Vienna, 1986), 64–77. Bischoff identifies the script as Anglo-Saxon, more particularly Northumbrian. On the manuscript, see also *CLA* IX, no. 1283.
[37] For details, see below, p. 61, n. 67.
[38] *Florilegia*, ed. Lehner, p. 34 (no. 418), which prefaces Eph. IV.31 with the numerical tag, 'Sex sunt uitanda ut apostolus ait...'
[39] *Sedulii Scotti Collectaneum Miscellaneum*, ed. Simpson, with a *Supplementum*, ed. Dolbeau; see *BCLL*, no. 686.

thirty-one headings, closely related to the *Collectio Canonum Hibernensis*. Enumerations are scattered throughout the non-classical sections of the collection. These include many paralleled only in other Hiberno-Latin compilations, especially the *Collectio Canonum Hibernensis*,[40] but there are also parallels with the *Collectanea Bedae*, *Liber de numeris* and *Florilegium Frisingense* (including the motif of the four keys of wisdom, which occurs in all four of these collections),[41] and with other compilations discussed below, including the *Catechesis Celtica*,[42] the *Prebiarum*[43] and the florilegium in Zurich, Zentralbibliothek, Rheinau 140.[44] There are also striking parallels with *Apgitir Chrábaid* and *Saltair na Rann*.[45] Of

[40] These occur chiefly in section XXV, e.g. XXV.ii.10, 12–13 etc.; see Reynolds, 'Unity and Diversity', p. 118.

[41] The four keys of wisdom (II.7, ed. Simpson, p. 11) occurs in the *Collectanea Bedae* (PL 94, 541A), *Liber de numeris* (IV.25, see McNally, *Der irische Liber de numeris*, pp. 82–3), and *Florilegium Frisingense*, in *Florilegia*, ed. Lehner, p. 36 (no. 439). On the theme, see McNally, 'Old Ireland, Her Scribes and Scholars', p. 138, who notes an Irish vernacular example in London, BL, Add. 30512 (citing Flower, *Catalogue of Irish Manuscripts* II, 488–9); Sims-Williams, *Religion and Literature*, pp. 334–7. See also H. D. Emanuel, 'The Seven Keys of Wisdom: a Study in Christian Humanism', *SC* 5 (1970), 36–47, at 40–1. Another parallel with the *Liber de numeris* is the enumeration of the seven sins of Cain (XXV.viii.10, ed. Simpson, p. 166); see McNally, *Der irische Liber de numeris*, p. 113; Cross, 'Identification', pp. 81 and 91; M. Lapidge, 'The Study of Greek at the School of Canterbury in the Seventh Century', in *The Sacred Nectar of the Greeks: the Study of Greek in the West in the Early Middle Ages*, ed. M. Herren, King's College London Medieval Studies 2 (London, 1988), pp. 169–94, at 175–7.

[42] The enumeration of the four reasons why speech is given to man (XIII.xxx.47, ed. Simpson, p. 108) occurs in the *Catechesis Celtica* (*Analecta Reginensia*, ed. Wilmart, p. 46). This parallel is not noted by Simpson or Dolbeau.

[43] The three reasons a prologue is written (LXXIII.37, ed. Simpson, p. 300), paralleled in the *Prebiarum* (in *Scriptores Hiberniae Minores I*, ed. McNally, p. 162). This parallel is not noted by Simpson or Dolbeau.

[44] The Zurich manuscript (36v) also contains the motif of the four keys of wisdom, as McNally noted, and has further parallels (at 34r and 33v) for the motifs of the four wheels (*rotae*) of the church (XV.8, ed. Simpson, p. 132) and (with differences of detail) the four kinds of ordination (XXV.xix.2, *ibid.* p. 177).

[45] The four virtues by which man is saved (XIII.xx.13, ed. Simpson, p. 90), paralleled in *Apgitir Chrábaid*, ed. Hull, pp. 60–1, as noted by Simpson, but also in the *Florilegium Frisingense*, in *Florilegia*, ed. Lehner, p. 35 (no. 428); the five things which are known by the wise (I.i.52–3, ed. Simpson, pp. 7–8), paralleled in *Saltair na Rann*, ed. Stokes, pp. 4–5, lines 261–8, and in the *Senchas Már* (passage cited by F. J. Byrne, 'Irland in der europäischen Geisteswelt des 8. Jahrhunderts', in *Virgil von Salzburg*, ed. Dopsch and Juffinger, pp. 45–51, at 45).

special interest is the opening section entitled *Prouerbia Grecorum*, a collection of *sententiae* particularly on wisdom and kingship, many of which are couched in numerical form.[46] Several other early medieval manuscripts, all with Insular connections, contain statements identified as *Prouerbia Grecorum*, many of which occur in Sedulius's *Collectaneum*; their dissemination, as Dean Simpson has pointed out, 'suggest[s] that knowledge of them was limited to Irish and British scholars'.[47] Connections with Irish culture and even with Irish law point to an Irish origin for these proverbs.[48] One enumeration, of the six ways man's soul was made in the likeness of God, has contacts with Hiberno-Latin exegesis of Genesis.[49]

In addition to these florilegia, we have several homily collections or *catecheses* whose contents are partially or largely Hiberno-Latin. The first of these, the so-called *Catechesis Celtica*,[50] may have been put together in its present form in Brittany, and contains some extracts of continental origin. Much of the collection, however, is Hiberno-Latin, as all

[46] See *BCLL*, no. 344; Simpson, 'The *Proverbia Grecorum*'. On the Irish *Cesta Grega*, see below, n. 142. James Carney, describing the 'Irish flavour' of a passage based on the *Prouerbia Grecorum* in Sedulius's *De rectoribus christianis* (*BCLL*, no. 685), notes particularly 'the numerical categorization' ('Sedulius Scottus', in *Old Ireland*, ed. McNally, pp. 228–50, at 247–8).

[47] 'The *Proverbia Grecorum*', p. 5. As Simpson notes, a booklist from Lincoln Cathedral library dating to *c.* 1160 includes an item 'Librum prouerbiorum grecorum inutilem'; see now R. M. Thompson, *Catalogue of the Manuscripts of Lincoln Cathedral Chapter Library* (Woodbridge, 1989), p. xiv.

[48] See Simpson, 'The *Proverbia Grecorum*', p. 6.

[49] This motif, identified as a *prouerbium grecorum* in the *Collectio Canonum Hibernensis*, occurs elsewhere in Sedulius's *Collectaneum* (LXVIII.6, ed. Simpson, p. 271), within a section headed *Ex Libro Lactantii.* Simpson, 'The *Proverbia Grecorum*', p. 4 and n. 16, has found an ultimate source for the motif in Origen's *Homeliae in Genesim*, but it occurs in the same numerical form in the pseudo-Bede *Expositio in primum librum Mosis* (PL 91, 201C; see Wright, 'Hiberno-Latin', no. *5), where it is attributed to 'Faustinus'. A closely related discussion, though not cast in numerical form, occurs in the St Gallen Commentary on the Creation and Fall (St Gallen, Stiftsbibliothek, 908, p. 22), attributed to the lost work *Agustinus in libris de gradibus celi* (on which see Wright, 'Apocryphal Lore', pp. 124–5 and 132–3).

[50] *Analecta Reginensia*, ed. Wilmart, pp. 29–112 (partial). See *BCLL*, no. 974; Wright, 'Hiberno-Latin', no. *44. I have been able to consult a typescript edition by the late R. E. McNally, provided for me by Professor Joseph Kelly. The manuscript is Vatican, Biblioteca Apostolica, Reg. lat. 49 (Brittany, s. ix/x), 1r–53r.

authorities since Grosjean have agreed.[51] The *Catechesis Celtica* is an extensive collection of homiletic and exegetical extracts, together with isolated commonplaces. Among the latter are many numerical motifs, such as the four reasons man has speech and the five places souls rest before Judgement. Many of the homiletic and exegetical pieces, too, elaborate on enumerative themes.[52]

Four other homiletic florilegia considered Hiberno-Latin are the Verona and Linz homily collections, the Cracow homily collection, and the homilies *In nomine Dei summi*. In the Verona homily collection[53] and Linz homily collection[54] enumerations are sporadic, but they are more frequent in the Cracow homily collection,[55] which contains a variety of numerical motifs paralleled in other Hiberno-Latin texts, such as the three refuges of Christ.[56] The homilies *In nomine Dei summi*[57] include a

[51] See Grosjean, 'A propos du manuscrit 49'; Ó Laoghaire, 'Irish Elements in the *Catechesis Celtica*'; McNamara, 'The Irish Affiliations'. Some further Irish connections have been noted by Stancliffe, 'Red, White and Blue Martyrdom', pp. 24–7. J. Rittmueller has recently shown that one of the supposed Carolingian sources, Paschasius Radbertus, was himself drawing on earlier Hiberno-Latin sources also used by the compiler of the *Catechesis Celtica*: 'The Gospel Commentary of Máel Brigte Ua Máeluanaig and its Hiberno-Latin Background', *Peritia* 2 (1983), 185–214, at 201–2.

[52] Ó Laoghaire, 'Irish Elements in the *Catechesis Celtica*', p. 163, remarks that 'There is one characteristic in CC which is common to other such texts considered to be of Irish origin, the fondness for litanic modes of expression and enumeration'.

[53] *BCLL*, no. 804. The collection, which is unpublished, survives in Verona, Biblioteca Capitolare, LXVII (64) (s. viii/ix), 33r–81v.

[54] Bibliothek der philosophisch-theologischen Hochschule der Diözese Linz, A I/6 (Bavaria, s. ix^{in}), fols. 71–101. The collection contains six items identified as Hiberno-Latin by R. Etaix, 'Un manuel de pastorale de l'époque carolingienne (*Clm* 27152)', *RB* 91 (1981), 105–30, at 126–30, with an edition of one item. See Wright, 'Hiberno-Latin', no. *46 (not in *BCLL*).

[55] 'Un recueil de conférences monastiques irlandaises', ed. David (partial). See *BCLL*, no. 802; Wright, 'Hiberno-Latin', no. 45. The manuscript is Cracow, Biblioteca Capitolare, 140 (olim 43) (Italy, s. viii/ix), 1r–100v.

[56] 'Un recueil de conférences monastiques irlandaises', ed. David, p. 77. The *refugia* of Christ are also enumerated in the *Questiones Sancti Hysidori* (see below) and in three Hiberno-Latin commentaries (on which see Bischoff, 'Turning-Points', p. 117). The motif also occurs in a fragment ed. A. Wilmart, 'Extraits d'*Acta Pauli*', *RB* 27 (1910), 402–12, at 405.

[57] 'Seven Hiberno-Latin Sermons', ed. McNally. See *BCLL*, no. 803; Wright, 'Hiberno-Latin', no. 47. McNally selected the sermons from a larger collection which survives in three manuscripts (see below, p. 111).

version of the Three Utterances sermon,[58] a piece enumerating the seven signs that have saved the world[59] and two pieces that adapt, but do not explicitly enumerate, themes found in enumerative form in the *Liber de numeris* and other Irish texts.[60]

Most of the florilegia which I have discussed include some numerical motifs in question-and-answer form. In the *Liber de numeris* and *Collectanea Bedae* especially there are many of these, which have obviously been borrowed from scholastic and catechetical dialogues.[61] The question-and-answer dialogue was a common genre in patristic literature, especially for exegesis and polemics,[62] and a great favourite with Irish schoolmasters.[63] Yet question-and-answer dialogues from Irish schools are seldom vehicles for dialectic – they rarely pursue a train of thought, much less an argument – but instead are repositories of miscellanea, frequently in numerical form. A good example of what might be termed an interrogatory florilegium is the *Prebiarum de multorium exemplaribus*.[64] Like the *Collectanea Bedae*, the *Prebiarum*

[58] 'Seven Hiberno-Latin Sermons', ed. McNally, pp. 134–6 (McNally's Document I). This version does not explicitly enumerate the utterances, but the Irish version and one of the Old English versions do. On the Three Utterances, see below, pp. 215–18.

[59] *Ibid.*, p. 143. On this motif, see McNally, *Der irische Liber de numeris*, pp. 117–18; *Thesaurus Palaeohibernicus*, ed. Stokes and Strachan I, 670 (Wb. 26d 9); and below, n. 74.

[60] For the numerical themes adapted in McNally's Documents IV and VI (both also found in the *Liber de numeris* and other Irish sources), see McNally's discussion, 'Seven Hiberno-Latin Sermons', pp. 128–9 and 131. The first of these, based on Matth. VII.7 and incorporating the 'thought, word and deed' triad (see McNally, *Der irische Liber de numeris*, pp. 58–9), is found also in the Cracow homily collection ('Un recueil de conférences monastiques irlandaises', ed. David, p. 82) and the *Florilegium Frisingense*, in *Florilegia*, ed. Lehner, p. 36 (no. 432) and see also pp. xxvii–xxviii. In 'The Irish "Enumerative Style"', p. 38, n. 63, I referred to Jerome, *Ep.* xxxix (PL 30, 277–8) as a possible patristic source, but this letter is spurious (see Dekkers and Gaar, *Clavis Patrum*, p. 145).

[61] L. Daly, in Daly and Suchier, *Altercatio*, p. 19, points out how easily questions from catechetical dialogues pass into florilegia.

[62] For a survey of the historical development of the genre, see *ibid.*, pp. 25–38.

[63] See McNally, *Der irische Liber de numeris*, pp. 147–9. McNally cites Kenney's remark that the question-and-answer form was 'the favourite Irish form of a catechism'.

[64] *Scriptores Hiberniae Minores I*, ed. McNally, pp. 161–71. See *BCLL*, no. 777; Wright, 'Hiberno-Latin', no. 42. McNally suggests that the work originated in the circle of Virgil of Salzburg. The manuscript, Munich, Bayerische Staatsbibliothek,

conflates standard *Joca monachorum* items with other miscellaneous questions. Of its ninety-three questions, numbers 7–37 require enumerative responses. Questions 7–20 (except for item 18) are of the type 'Quibus modis ... ?'; questions 21–37 are of the type, 'Quot sunt ... ?'. Some of these are 'scientific' or exegetical, but there are didactic motifs as well, such as item 30, which lists the four deceptions of man after the departure of the soul from the body.

A similar dialogue is the pseudo-Isidorian *Questiones Sancti Hysidori de uetere et nouo testamento.*[65] This brief text (fifty-three questions or items) contains some eighteen enumerations. In spite of its title, it includes a variety of non-exegetical questions, such as the three (or four) kinds of belief in God, found also in the *Prebiarum*, the *Liber de numeris* and a Hiberno-Latin commentary on the Catholic Epistles.[66]

The distinctive and common stock of numerical motifs characteristic of these Irish works[67] makes it possible to identify other anonymous florilegia and dialogues which, if not themselves Hiberno-Latin, have certainly been compiled from Hiberno-Latin sources. These not only draw from the same stock of numerical motifs as the texts surveyed above, but display more precise textual agreement in some particular sequences of enumerations.

J. E. Cross and Thomas D. Hill have remarked that 'we may surely

Clm. 6302 (Freising, s. viii^{med}; *CLA* IX, no. 1267), contains four other works of Irish origin (see McNally, p. 155).

65 *Scriptores Hiberniae Minores I*, ed. McNally, pp. 197–205. See *BCLL*, no. 779; Wright, 'Hiberno-Latin', no. 2.

66 *Scriptores Hiberniae Minores I*, ed. McNally, p. 199. For parallels, see *ibid.*, p. 162, note to *Prebiarum* no. 12.

67 In his source analysis of the *Liber de numeris* (*Der irische Liber de numeris*, pp. 141–4, under the heading 'Besondere Parallelen'), McNally identified nineteen parallels with the *Collectanea Bedae* and twenty with the *Catechesis Celtica*, plus many more with other Irish texts, including eighteen from one gospel commentary alone (pseudo-Jerome, *Expositio quatuor euangeliorum*; *BCLL*, no. 341). According to McNally, these four works, together with the *Prebiarum*, 'in einem ganz besondere Verhältnis zu einander stehen' (p. 141). Of the sequence of fifteen enumerations in the *Florilegium Frisingense*, no fewer than twelve are paralleled in other Hiberno-Latin texts, including the *Liber de numeris* (five parallels), the *Collectanea Bedae* (four parallels), the *Prebiarum* (three parallels), pseudo-Hilary, *Expositio in VII epistolas catholicas* (*BCLL*, no. 346; three parallels) and the homilies *In nomine Dei summi* (one parallel). See the source notes to Lehner's ed., *Florilegia*, pp. 34–6, and his introduction, pp. xx–xxiv and xxvii–xxviii.

assume that the *Prebiarum* is only one representative of its kind'.[68] On the basis of extensive parallels with the *Prebiarum* and other Hiberno-Latin texts, we may add three unpublished dialogues as examples of the kind. The first of these occurs in a ninth-century manuscript, Cologne, Dombibliothek, 15.[69] This manuscript contains Smaragdus's *Expositio libri comitis*, followed by a series of miscellaneous theological texts, including a brief exposition of the gospels showing contacts with Hiberno-Latin exegesis of the four evangelists and the Magi (fol. 82), and excerpts from a Hiberno-Latin Apocalypse commentary (95v–96v).[70] The latter extract is preceded on fol. 95 by a version of an apocryphal narrative on the creation and naming of Adam, headed *De plasmacione Adami*, which I have discussed elsewhere,[71] and by two versions of the Adam Octipartite theme (Adam's creation from eight parts or *pondera*).[72] Roger Reynolds has noted a text of the Ordinals of Christ, in the Hibernian Chronological version (93v–94r), followed by a tract *De uirtutibus uel tollerancia Saluatoris*, which Reynolds compares with the list of the events in Christ's life in the Hiberno-Latin *Liber de ortu et obitu patriarcharum*.[73] There is also a brief list *De septem sigilla* [*sic*] (93r) which correlates the seven signs of the Apocalypse with seven events in Christ's life, similar but not identical to one in the homilies *In nomine Dei summi*.[74] The dialogue begins on 88v (although the scribe does not begin marking the questions and answers with *interrogatio* and *responsio* until 89v) and continues up to 90v. It consists chiefly of numerical motifs, including ten parallels with the *Prebiarum* (items 1, 16, 22, 23, 28 and 29–33 in McNally's edition), and three with the *Questiones*

[68] Cross and Hill, *The Prose Solomon and Saturn*, p. 9.

[69] P. Jaffé and G. Wattenbach, *Ecclesiae Metropolitanae Coloniensis codices manuscripti* (Berlin, 1874), pp. 6–7.

[70] *BCLL*, no. 781; Wright, 'Hiberno-Latin', no. 36.

[71] See Wright, 'Apocryphal Lore', pp. 140–4; on the Adam Octipartite theme, see below, n. 135.

[72] The second of these is ed. W. Suchier, *L'Enfant sage* (*Das Gespräch des Kaisers Hadrian mit dem klugen Kinde Epitus*), Gesellschaft für romanische Literatur 24 (Dresden, 1910), p. 279.

[73] Reynolds, *The Ordinals of Christ*, p. 72. Reynolds prints this brief tract (n. 11), and points out that it also occurs in London, BL, Arundel 213, fol. 85 (on this manuscript, see below, n. 111). For the *Liber de ortu et obitu patriarcharum*, see *BCLL*, no. 780.

[74] McNally's Document VII, p. 143. The Cologne list ends, 'hec sunt septem dona spiritus sancti'. See above, n. 59.

Sancti Hysidori (items 31, 32 and 54 in McNally's edition).[75] The manuscript context of the dialogue in the Cologne manuscript suggests that it, like the *Prebiarum*, with which it shares so many items, may also be an Irish production, although it has certainly been transmitted in a continental milieu where a Romance language was spoken.[76]

The second dialogue, entitled *Disputatio philosophorum*, is found in Munich, Bayerische Staatsbibliothek, Clm. 5257 (Chiemsee, s. xi).[77] The dialogue, on 24r–26r, has extensive parallels with Hiberno-Latin texts, including, for example, the theme of the three martyrdoms.[78] The third dialogue, which shares some ten items with the *Disputatio philosophorum*, occurs in the *Carmen ad Deum* manuscript in Munich, Bayerische Staatsbibliothek, Clm. 19410 (Tegernsee, perhaps Passau, s. ix^{med}).[79] The manuscript contains a dialogue consisting of a standard *Joca monachorum* text supplemented by a lengthy series of additional questions, nearly all of which are numerical (pp. 13–23).[80] Later the

75 On 91v–92v occurs another dialogue, headed 'Incipit de proprietate sermonum uel differenciarum. Agustini dicta ad omnes docendos', which is ed. W. Suchier in Daly and Suchier, *Altercatio*, pp. 118–21.

76 A. Franz, *Die kirchliche Benediktionen des Mittelalters*, 2 vols. (Freiburg, 1909) II, 587–96, who prints the exorcisms at the end of the manuscript, states that the scribe's Latin 'läßt auf westfränkischen Ursprung der Hs. schließen' (p. 587, n. 2). For other texts in Cologne, Dombibl., 15, see below, pp. 69–70.

77 The contents are described by C. Halm and G. Laubmann, *Catalogus codicum latinorum Bibliothecae Regiae Monacensis* 1.3 (Munich, 1873), 2. This dialogue follows the *Disputatio puerorum* ascribed to Alcuin, but the catalogue fails to distinguish it as a separate item. The dialogue contains a version of the 'Ordinals of Christ' ed. Reynolds, *The Ordinals of Christ*, p. 81. According to Reynolds, 'The Chiemsee Ordinal is largely a type of Hiberno-Gallican Hierarchical version ... with several dominical sanctions resembling the Hibernian Chronological version.'

78 See below, pp. 74–5.

79 On the manuscript, see Bischoff, *Schreibschulen*, pp. 163–4, and 'Paläographische Fragen', p. 102; R. Derolez, *Runica Manuscripta: the English Tradition*, Rijksuniversiteit te Gent, Werken uitgegeven door de Faculteit van de Wijsbegeerte en Letteren 118 (Brugge, 1954), 206–12. For English connections in another part of the manuscript, see P. Sims-Williams, 'Milred of Worcester's Collection of Latin Epigrams', *ASE* 10 (1982), 21–38, at 37–8.

80 The *Joca monachorum* portion of the dialogue is ed. Suchier, *Adrian und Epictitus*, pp. 114–19 (from Einsiedeln, Stiftsbibliothek, 281, with variants from Clm. 19410, Suchier's 'F'). Immediately preceding the *Joca monachorum* dialogue in the manuscript (pp. 1–13) is another popular catechetical dialogue (some of the manuscripts are listed by Suchier, p. 41). A few of the additional numerical motifs

manuscript contains another series of enumerations, though not in question form (pp. 32–3). Among the enumerations in the dialogue I count seven parallels with the *Collectanea Bedae*, eight with the *Prebiarum* and twelve with the *Liber de numeris*.

Despite the extensive agreement between these dialogues and the Irish florilegia and dialogues which I have surveyed, it would be rash without further evidence to label them 'Hiberno-Latin'. Once these numerical themes had begun to circulate, a continental scribe, particularly in a centre of Insular influence, could piece together a numerical dialogue as well as an Irishman. But the parallels do suffice to show that the compilers of these texts, whatever their nationality, drew heavily on Hiberno-Latin sources. The enumerations they transmit, especially when specifically paralleled in Hiberno-Latin texts, are further witnesses to the Irish 'enumerative style'.

One particular sequence of enumerations in Cologne, Dombibl., 15, Clm. 19410 and Clm. 5257 shows close agreement with three florilegia associated with Irish traditions on various grounds. The first of these is a homiletic florilegium in Karlsruhe, Badische Landesbibliothek, Aug. perg. 254 (Novara, s. viii^{ex}), 72r–212r, which contains a compilation of homiletic pieces headed *Incipit collectario de diuersis sententiis* (153r–172v).[81] De Bruyne edited a series of texts from this portion of the

were printed by K. Rockinger (*Gelehrter Anzeigen der königlichen Akademie der Wissenschaften* 58 (1857), col. 466, n. 2). Within the *Joca monachorum* section is a version of the 'Ordinals of Christ', not printed by Suchier and unknown to Reynolds. It is essentially a sub-type of the Hibernian Chronological version, without the explanatory interlude between presbyter and doorkeeper, as discussed by Reynolds, *The Ordinals of Christ*, pp. 72–3. On pp. 63–5 (part of an older bifolium: see Bischoff, *Schreibschulen*, p. 163) is a brief sermon whose author identifies himself as 'effrem miser' (see Siegmund, *Überlieferung*, p. 70). The sermon does not correspond to any of the six sermons in the known corpus of 'Ephraem Latinus', but according to Steinmeyer and Sievers, *Die althochdeutschen Glossen* IV, 568, it is a translation of the homily *De iudicio* in *Sancti Ephraem Syri Opera Omnia quae exstant ... Graece et Latine*, 3 vols., ed. J. S. Assemani (Rome, 1732–46) II, 50. The conclusion corresponds to the opening lines of one of the homilies *In nomine Dei summi* ('Seven Hiberno-Latin Sermons', ed. McNally, p. 140, lines 2–7), a popular Hiberno-Latin theme based on Matth. VII.7 (see above, n. 60).

[81] For this composite manuscript, see *CLA* VIII, no. 1100. For a description of its contents, see Holder, *Die Reichenauer Handschriften*, pp. 573–9. The manuscript was written at Novara, according to E. Cau, 'Scrittura e cultura a Novara (secoli VIII–IX)', *Ricerche Medievali* 6–9 (1971–4), 1–87, at 29–32.

manuscript, the so-called *Apocrypha Priscillianistica*.[82] Scholars have generally abandoned the theory of Priscillianist origins, but the connections with Irish traditions in this part of the manuscript are marked, as M. R. James and later scholars have pointed out.[83] Several of the pieces in the collection contain numerical motifs, but the most important is the fifth, headed *De parabolas*[84] *Salomonis fili Dauid*, which contains the following series of enumerations (164v–165r):

1. Septem scala sunt quibus ascenditur ad regna celorum...
2. Septem modis redimitur anima...
3. Sanctus gregorius ait: hec sunt que in hoc seculo abuse fiunt...
4. Trea sunt que deducunt hominem ad profundum[85] inferni...
5. Item alia trea sunt que deducunt hominem ad regna celorum...
6. Trea sunt que non remittuntur nec hic nec in futuro...[86]

Immediately following this series is a homiletic piece on the *cibus corporis* and *cibus anime* (fol. 165), versions of which occur also in the *Liber de numeris* and in the homilies *In nomine Dei summi*.[87] Later, on 185v–187r, appears a version of the Hiberno-Latin Three Utterances sermon. Shortly thereafter, on fol. 193, the first three enumerations from the earlier series recur, this time followed by a pair of extracts *de ebrietate* and

[82] 'Fragments retrouvés'. See *BCLL*, no. 1252, and Wright, 'Apocrypha Priscillianistica'. Much of this material is also found in Einsiedeln, Stiftsbibliothek, 199 (*CLA* VII, no. 875). De Bruyne's item 4, which includes a Judgement dialogue paralleled in an Old English Rogationtide homily, occurs also in Clm. 19410 and in Salisbury, Cathedral Library, 9 (see below, pp. 225–6).

[83] M. R. James, 'Irish Apocrypha', p. 16, and *Apocryphal New Testament*, p. 480; for further references, see Wright, 'Apocrypha Priscillianistica'.

[84] De Bruyne silently corrects to *parabolis*.

[85] De Bruyne prints 'p*ro*fondum'.

[86] 'Fragments retrouvés', ed. De Bruyne, pp. 329–30 (I number them for ease of reference): (1) 'There are seven steps by which one ascends to the kingdoms of heaven...'; (2) 'The soul is redeemed in seven ways...'; (3) 'Saint Gregory says: these are the things which happen improperly in the world...'; (4) 'There are three things which lead a man down to the depth of hell...' (bad thoughts, words and deeds); (5) 'There are also three things which lead a man to the kingdoms of heaven ...' (good thoughts, words and deeds); (6) 'Three things are not forgiven here or in the next life...'

[87] McNally, *Der irische Liber de numeris*, p. 38; 'Seven Hiberno-Latin Sermons', p. 131 and p. 142, lines 2–11. Close parallels occur in a pseudo-Augustinian sermon in PL 40, 1351 (Machielsen, *Clavis*, no. 1192), and in St Gallen, Stiftsbibliothek, 682, pp. 397–9. A late example from an English manuscript (London, BL, Arundel 507) is ed. Horstmann, *Yorkshire Writers* I, 439. For a slight parallel in Old English, see Wright, '*Docet Deus, Docet Diabolus*', p. 453, n. 14.

de subrietate, considered Hiberno-Latin by McNally, which occurs also in the *Liber de numeris*,[88] *Collectanea Bedae*[89] and the *Testimonia diuinae scripturae*.[90] Finally, a piece headed *Incipit de septenario* (194r–195r) associates each of the seven gifts of the Holy Spirit with a particular patriarch, a theme which occurs in the *Collectanea Bedae*, the *Liber de numeris*, the *Catechesis Celtica*, Clm. 22053, 46r–47r and two Hiberno-Latin commentaries, in addition to the pseudo-Alcuinian *De septem sigillis*.[91]

In short, there are strong indications that the Karlsruhe florilegium originated in an Irish milieu. The series of enumerations is particularly suggestive. Item 3 of the series is the familiar Irish theme of the twelve abuses; items 4 and 5 contrast *in malo* and *in bono* the equally familiar Irish triad 'thought, word and deed'.[92] Moreover, in Hiberno-Latin texts this pair of triads is frequently grouped together with item 6, the three things not forgiven. The same group occurs, for example, in the *Liber de numeris*.[93] Patrick Sims-Williams, who was able to add several further examples of the group in his thorough study of the 'thought, word and deed' triad, concluded that 'The indications are thus in favour of an Irish origin for this little collection of triads.'[94]

88 McNally, *Der irische Liber de numeris*, pp. 43–4.

89 PL 94, 548C-D.

90 In *Florilegia*, ed. Lehner, pp. 55–127, at 124–5. See Wright, 'Hiberno-Latin', no. *41. This work has now been tentatively attributed to Eligius of Noyon by E. Dekkers, 'Een onbekend Werk van Sint Eligius?', *Ons Geestelijk Erf* 63–4 (1989–90), 296–308.

91 See Wright, 'Hiberno-Latin', no. *37. This theme occurs in the Latin treatise on number in *Byrhtferth's Manual*, ed. S. J. Crawford, EETS os 177 (London, 1929), p. 212. Another piece from the Karlsruhe manuscript, *De camara Christi* (191v), is ed. B. Bischoff, *Anecdota Novissima*, Quellen und Untersuchungen zur lateinischen Philologie des Mittelalters 7 (Stuttgart, 1984), 89–90.

92 Item 2, which occurs with minor variations in the *Poenitentiale Bigotianum* (*The Irish Penitentials*, ed. Bieler, p. 202; *BCLL*, no. 614), is ultimately from Origen, *Hom. in Leuiticum* II.iv, as Bieler notes; it is also found in Cassiodorus, *Expositio Psalmorum*, ed. M. Adriaen, CCSL 97 (Turnhout, 1958), pp. 71–2. For other Irish examples, see the Commentary on the Catholic Epistles (*BCLL*, no. 340) in *Scriptores Hiberniae Minores I*, ed. McNally, p. 25, and *Florilegia*, ed. Lehner, p. 36 (no. 431). See also two Latin sermons (Dekkers and Gaar, *Clavis Patrum*, nos. 1760–1) ed. A. E. Burn, 'Neue Texte zur Geschichte des apostolischen Symbols', *Zeitschrift für Kirchengeschichte* 19 (1901), 128–37, at 131 and 136–7.

93 See McNally, *Der irische Liber de numeris*, pp. 64–5.

94 Sims-Williams, 'Thought, Word and Deed', p. 87. To Sims-Williams's examples of the group may be added one from a late English manuscript (Oxford, Bodleian

This sequence of enumerations had indeed a wide circulation. Clm. 19410, pp. 32–3, has the last three items of the series, but the entire series occurs in question-and-answer form in the dialogue in Clm. 5257 (25r), except that the first two enumerations in the Karlsruhe florilegium come at the end of the series in the dialogue. Furthermore, as both De Bruyne and McNally noted,[95] the group of triads in the Karlsruhe manuscript also appears in Zurich, Zentralbibliothek, Rheinau 140 (probably Switzerland, s. viii^2), a collection of homilies and patristic excerpts.[96] The manuscript contains two series of enumerations. Most enumerations in the first series, in a brief miscellany headed *Testimonium Sancti Hyeronimi* (33r–36v), find parallels in Hiberno-Latin texts.[97] This series also includes a lengthy antithesis on the theme *refectio carnis* and *refectio anime*, similar to a sequence in the Karlsruhe florilegium.[98] Next (38v–41r) come two more lists, one contrasting the *uia peccatorum* and *uia sanctorum*, the other listing the virtues of the soul, both of which occur as enumerations in the *Liber de numeris.*[99] The second series of enumerations (123r) includes the 'Irish' group of triads discussed above, as in the Karlsruhe florilegium and elsewhere in Irish sources, except that the first of the pair of 'thought, word and deed' triads is

Library, Rawl. C. 285), ed. Horstmann, *Yorkshire Writers* I, 128 (here the sequence is expanded with the three martyrdoms motif). One of the vernacular Irish examples noted by Sims-Williams is ed. B. Ó Cuív, 'Tréidhe sa Nua-Ghaeilge', *Éigse* 9 (1959–60), 180. For an Icelandic example, see Marchand, 'The Old Icelandic *Joca Monachorum*', pp. 122–3.

95 *Der irische Liber de numeris*, p. 207. De Bruyne, 'Fragments retrouvés', printed the variants from the Zurich manuscript.

96 For the manuscript, see *CLA* VII, no. 1021. A. Bruckner, *Scriptoria Medii Aevi Helvetica*, 8 vols. (Geneva, 1935–55) IV, 38, suggests a North Italian origin, probably Bobbio. For an analysis of its contents, see L. C. Mohlberg, *Katalog der Handschriften der Zentralbibliothek Zürich*, I: *Mittelalterliche Handschriften* (Zurich, 1932), pp. 228–30.

97 McNally, *Der irische Liber de numeris*, pp. 37–8 and 207, identified several of these. For parallels with the *Collectaneum* of Sedulius Scottus, see above, n. 44.

98 'Fragments retrouvés', ed. De Bruyne, p. 322, where the antithesis is *refectio carnis / refeccio spiritus.* The items listed, however, do not match.

99 See McNally, *Der irische Liber de numeris*, pp. 41–2 and 37–8. On the first theme, see also McNally's remarks in 'Isidorian Pseudepigrapha', p. 313: 'Irish in spirit and style'.

missing owing to defective transmission.[100] Moreover, as De Bruyne and McNally also noted, the triads in the Zurich florilegium are followed by the same homiletic piece on the *cibus corporis* and *cibus animae* that appears in the Karlsruhe florilegium and the homilies *In nomine Dei summi*.[101] In Cologne, Dombibl., 15, the correspondences with the Karlsruhe florilegium are more extensive. Essentially the same sequence of motifs occurs in the Cologne manuscript, fol. 90, where it interrupts the question-and-answer series of the dialogue. Here, however, the first two motifs in the Karlsruhe sequence are followed by an enumeration of the six ages of the world and of man, but the sequence is then resumed with the motifs of the twelve abuses (attributed to Gregory as in the Karlsruhe manuscript), the second of the two 'thought, word and deed' triads, and the three things not forgiven, followed again by the *cibus corporis* and *cibus anime* theme. The sequence in the Cologne manuscript, in other words, is identical to that in the Karlsruhe florilegium except for the intrusion of the six ages motif and the omission of the first of the pair of thought, word and deed triads.

These textual correspondences are not limited to the Karlsruhe and Zurich florilegia. Closely related material is found in Munich, Bayerische Staatsbibliothek, Clm. 22053 (s. ix), the famous *Wessobrunner Gebet* manuscript,[102] which includes a miscellany headed *Incipit sententia Sancti Gregorii* (35v–57r).[103] McNally pointed out that the manuscript 'contains ... a number of items which are ordinarily found in the Irish

[100] No lacuna is indicated at this point by Lowe or Mohlberg, but there is an abrupt change of hands from 122v to 123r, which begins in mid-sentence with the words, 'sunt que ducunt hominem ad regna celestia'. Cologne, Dombibl., 15, also lacks the first triad of the pair.

[101] 'Fragments retrouvés', ed. De Bruyne, p. 330; McNally, *Der irische Liber de numeris*, p. 207. By oversight McNally lists the Zurich manuscript for this item only in his index, but does not mention it in his text or in his edition of the homilies. For other examples of the theme, see above, n. 87.

[102] On the manuscript, see Bischoff, *Schreibschulen*, pp. 18–21; *idem*, *Kalligraphie in Bayern: achtes bis zwölftes Jahrhundert* (Wiesbaden, 1981), p. 25; Bauerreis, 'Das frühmittelalterliche Bistum Neuburg', pp. 424–38; and especially Schwab, *Sternrune*. A facsimile is ed. A. von Eckhardt and C. von Kraus, *The Manuscript Containing the Wessobrunn Prayer* (Leiden, 1923). For a full analysis of its contents, see Bauerreis, pp. 433–8.

[103] Portions of the miscellany, but not the enumerations, are ed. Schwab, *Sternrune*, pp. 79–109, and G. A. Waldman, 'Excerpts from a Little Encyclopaedia – the Wessobrun Prayer Manuscript Clm. 22053', *Allegorica* 2 (1977), 9–26.

biblical literature of the eighth century'.[104] Among these is a description of the three Magi, versions of which occur in the *Collectanea Bedae*, the Leabhar Breac and in several Irish vernacular texts.[105] A piece on the eight capital sins is taken directly from a work attributed to Columbanus.[106] There are many numerical motifs,[107] most of which are paralleled in the *Liber de numeris* and *Collectanea Bedae*.[108] But the most striking correspondences are with the Karlsruhe and Zurich florilegia. Romuald Bauerreis and Ute Schwab have drawn attention to the textual parallels between Clm. 22053 and the Karlsruhe florilegium,[109] but neither was familiar with the Zurich florilegium. On fol. 49 of Clm. 22053 occurs the now-familiar group of triads found in both the Karlsruhe and Zurich florilegia. Moreover, the first three items in the Karlsruhe series of enumerations occur here too, though not in the same order, and here too we find the selection *de ebrietate* and *de sobrietate* (56r–57r), as well as the theme of the gifts of the Holy Spirit and the patriarchs (46r–47r), both of which appear in the Karlsruhe florilegium. The sequence of enumerations in Clm. 22053 agrees further with the dialogue in Clm. 19410, for both include in the sequence a triad on the three ways the devil lures one into false security ('Tribus modis diabolus securitatem promittit ...').[110]

There are further parallels between Clm. 22053 and Cologne, Dombibl., 15, in addition to the enumerations which both share with the Karlsruhe florilegium. These include another pair of enumerations,

[104] McNally, 'Isidorian Pseudepigrapha', p. 313, n. 61.

[105] Schwab edits this piece (*Sternrune*, pp. 99–100), with references to the Hiberno-Latin parallels. See also Dumville, 'Biblical Apocrypha and the Early Irish', pp. 316–17, and McNamara, *The Apocrypha in the Irish Church*, pp. 54–6 (no. 48).

[106] Ed. Schwab, *Sternrune*, pp. 101–5, with the parallel passage from *De VIII uitiis principalibus*, in *Sancti Columbani Opera*, ed. Walker, pp. 210–12 (for the attribution, see p. lxii).

[107] R. Bauerreis, in *Kirchengeschichte Bayerns*, 3 vols. (St Ottilien, 1949) I, 165, notes that at least twenty-one of sixty-eight items begin with an enumeration, and remarks that the anthology was the work of a monk 'der eine Vorliebe für Zahlen hatte'.

[108] McNally, *Der irische Liber de numeris*, p. 206, lists thirteen parallels with Clm. 22053. Schwab, *Sternrune*, p. 111, compares the 'numerisch gefasste Lehren' in the *Liber de numeris* and *Collectanea*.

[109] Bauerreis, 'Das frühmittelalterliche Bistum Neuberg', pp. 428–9; Schwab, *Sternrune*, pp. 18–19.

[110] For other Latin, Irish and Old English versions of this theme, see below, pp. 81–4.

De septem damnaciones peccatorum and *De septem muneraciones iustorum* in the Cologne manuscript (91r), which occurs again in Clm. 22053 (fol. 50).[111] Cologne, Dombibl., 15 also contains a slightly expanded version of the extract *de ebrietate* (92v–93r). Both manuscripts also contain a brief Genesis commentary titled *Incipit de principio celi et terre et omnis firmaciones mundi* (Cologne, Dombibl., 15, 94r–95r; Clm. 22053, 37v–40v). This same commentary occurs in another Karlsruhe manuscript, Aug. perg. 229 (Southern Italy, the Abruzzi region, s. ix[in]), 62r–69v, where it is called *Chronica Sancti Hieronimi de principio celi et terre*,[112] and with a similar title in Sélestat, BM, 1 (1093) (s. viii), beginning on 67r.[113]

111 This pair of enumerations also occurs in a florilegium surviving in three manuscripts: Zurich, Zentralbibliothek, C. 64 (Switzerland, s. ix[in]), 149v; London, BL, Arundel 213 (s. ix; provenance Würzburg), 84v; and London, BL, Cotton Nero A. ii, fols. 37–42 (North Italy, s. viii/ix), fol. 40. Cotton Nero A. ii, which contains an Irish tract on the canonical hours (see *BCLL*, no. 785), was copied from an Irish exemplar (*CLA* II, no. 186). On Arundel 213, see also A. Gwynn, 'The Continuity of the Irish Tradition at Würzburg', in *Herbipolis jubilans: 1200 Jahre Bistum Würzburg* (Würzburg, 1952), pp. 57–81, at 63 and 75. On this florilegium, see Levison, *England and the Continent*, pp. 302–7. D. A. Bullough, 'Games People Played: Drama and Ritual as Propaganda in Medieval Europe', *Transactions of the Royal Historical Society* 5th ser. 25 (1974), 96–122, at 106, n. 19, points out that the portion of the sermon 'Venus, a Man' edited by Levison from Cotton Nero A. ii was also ed. Holder, *Die Reichenauer Handschriften*, pp. 447–8, from Karlsruhe, Badische Landesbibliothek, Aug. perg. 196, 190v–191v. Unedited portions of this sermon contain material closely paralleling the Hiberno-Latin St Gallen Commentary on the Creation and Fall (see the forthcoming edition of the commentary by M. Gorman and C. Wright).

112 On this manuscript, see Holder, *Die Reichenauer Handschriften*, pp. 521–7; Schwab, *Sternrune*, pp. 16–21 and 117–18, n. 46; B. Bischoff, 'Italienische Handschriften des neunten bis elften Jahrhunderts in frühmittelalterlichen Bibliotheken ausserhalb Italiens', in *Il Libro e il testo*, ed. C. Questa and R. Raffaelli (Urbino, 1984), pp. 171–94, at 179. Schwab points out that this manuscript has several items in common with Clm. 22053. The manuscript also contains the probably Irish prayer *Oratio Sancti Gregorii* (Schwab, *Sternrune*, p. 20), on which see M. Lapidge, 'A New Hiberno-Latin Hymn on St Martin', *Celtica* 21 (1990), 240–51, at 241–2; Sims-Williams, *Religion and Literature*, p. 281.

113 *CLA* VI, no. 829. According to Lowe, the method of ruling in this manuscript is an Insular symptom. The manuscript, a lectionary which has both Milanese and Gallican liturgical connections, also contains the apocryphal *De plasmatione Adam* (ed. Förster, 'Das älteste mittellateinische Gesprächbuchlein', *Romanische Forschungen* 27 (1910), 342–8, repr. PLS 4, 938–41; see Wright, 'Apocryphal Lore', p. 140), as well as a *Joca monachorum* dialogue (ed. E. Wöllflin-Troll, 'Joca

Schwab, unaware of the Cologne and Sélestat manuscripts, noted that McNally had identified several parallels between the pseudo-Hieronymian *Chronica* and the *Liber de numeris*, but concluded cautiously that 'irische Herkunft dieses in beiden Hss. in verwildeter Form überlieferten Genesiskommentars scheint nicht ausgeschlossen'.[114] I cannot resolve the problem of the origins of the pseudo-Hieronymian *Chronica* but can introduce a further complication. The *Chronica* also appears as part of a larger work in several manuscripts to which François Dolbeau has recently drawn attention.[115] Cologne, Dombibl., 85 (s. ix) and Paris, BN, lat. 2175 (s. viii/ix) contain a common collection of texts, which survives also, but supplemented with further items, in Orléans, BM, 313 (s. ix) and Paris, BN, lat. 10612 (s. ix). Among the texts in this collection is a compilation headed *Quaestiones de litteris uel singulis causis* (I refer to Cologne, Dombibl., 85, fols. 103–18), beginning 'Quia uideo te de scripturis uelle contendere...' After an opening series of questions on the alphabet, the remainder of this text focuses on Genesis (*Incipit quaestio de libro Genesis*, 109r–114v), followed by a briefer series of questions on Exodus and the prophets (114v–118v). The Genesis commentary begins with a brief discussion of the presence of the Trinity in the initial verses of Genesis, but then continues with the pseudo-Hieronymian *Chronica*, headed *Hieronimus ait de principio caeli et terre creationis omnem firmationis mundi* (110r). As Dolbeau points out, the manuscripts containing this collection are continental. But the collection also includes a Hiberno-Latin commentary, the pseudo-Gregorian *Expositio sancti euangelii* (Recension II of pseudo-Jerome, *Expositio*

monachorum, ein Beitrag zur mittelalterlichen Rathsellitteratur', *Monatsberichte der kgl. Preußischen Akademie der Wissenschaften zu Berlin aus dem Jahre 1872* (Berlin, 1873), 106–15, at 116–18, with only the title of the *Chronicon*, at 115).

114 Schwab, *Sternrune*, p. 85 (cf. p. 19). For the parallels with the *Liber de numeris*, see the entries for Karlsruhe 229 in McNally's index. These include an exposition of the colours of the rainbow (see McNally, *Der irische Liber de numeris*, pp. 87–8), which is related to the tract on the rainbow in Cologne, Dombibl., 15, fol. 100. Schwab (*Sternrune*, unnumbered *Nachträge* to pp. 17–19 and 85 at the front of the volume) questions Siegmund's identification (*Überlieferung*, p. 89, n. 1) of the *Chronica* in Karlsruhe 229 with the *Liber generationis I*. The identification appears groundless (the *Liber generationis I* is in *Chronica minora* I, ed. T. Mommsen, MGH, Auct. antiq. 9 (Berlin, 1892), pp. 89–140).

115 'Du nouveau sur un sermonnaire de Cambridge', *Scriptorium* 42 (1988), 255–7.

quatuor euangeliorum),[116] and all the manuscripts contain texts of the Ordinals of Christ in the Hibernian Chronological version.[117] Moreover, McNally has stated that a dialogue with the same *incipit* in Venice, Biblioteca Nazionale Marciana, XLVI (2400) (s. x^{in}), 131v–134r, 'is actually an Irish *collectaneum*'.[118] Unfortunately McNally did not specify his reasons for the identification, other than stating that the text 'shows the usual Irish symptoms', but noted that the Venice manuscript also contains a Hiberno-Latin Apocalypse commentary and several extracts corresponding to the *Liber de numeris*. It is clear at least that both works circulated in collections containing other Hiberno-Latin material.[119] But to confirm or deny McNally's identification will require much closer study of the pseudo-Hieronymian *Chronica* as well as the *Quaestiones* which incorporate it.

The textual parallels between these florilegia and dialogues are summarized in table 2.1.[120] From these parallels it is clear that the florilegia have drawn ultimately from some of the same sources, and from the parallels with the *Liber de numeris*, *Collectanea Bedae*, and other Hiberno-Latin works, it is clear that the enumerations they transmit derive from the Irish tradition.

Joyce Bazire and J. E. Cross have described the *Liber de numeris* as an example of a collection of 'mnemonic lists for those who wished to

116 *BCLL*, no. 341. Part of this collection occurs also in Paris, BN, lat. 614A (s. ix/x), which includes one of the recensions of the Hiberno-Latin Reference Bible (see Bischoff, 'Turning-Points', no. 1C).

117 Reynolds, *The Ordinals of Christ*, pp. 70–1, n. 9.

118 'Isidorian Pseudepigrapha', p. 308; see also Stegmüller, *Repertorium*, nos. 5263–4. McNally's attribution is accepted by Kelly, 'A Catalogue of Early Medieval Hiberno-Latin Biblical Commentaries (I)', p. 547. In *Der irische Liber de numeris*, McNally cited eight parallels from the Karlsruhe manuscript of this work (see his index, p. 205).

119 A fragment of the dialogue occurs also in Cesena, Biblioteca Malatestiana, Plut. XXI.5, from which it was printed by J. M. Mucciolus, *Catalogus codicum manuscriptorum Malatestianae Caesenatis Bibliothecae*, 2 vols. (Cesena, 1780–4) II, 249–51. Here the dialogue follows the Hiberno-Latin Three Utterances sermon (see Mucciolus, p. 144).

120 I have numbered the sequences of enumerations for each manuscript to indicate the order of the items in each. The numbering for Clm. 22053 follows Bauerreis's analysis of the contents; the references for the *Liber de numeris* follow McNally's edition.

Karlsruhe 254	Clm. 22053	Cologne 15	Clm. 5257	Zurich 140	Clm. 19410	*Liber de numeris*
				uia sanctorum uia peccatorum		II.18 uia sanctorum uia peccatorum
1. vii scala	24. vii scalae	1. vii scale	5. Quot sunt scale?			
2. vii modis redimitur anima	23. vii modis redemitur anima	2. vii modis redemitur anima	6. Quibus modis redimitur anima?			
3. xii que abuse fiunt	4. xii qui abuse fiant	4. xii qui abuse fiant	1. Quot sunt que abusiue fiunt?			
	20b. iii modis diabolus securitatem				1. iii modis diabolus securitatem	
4. iii deducunt ad profundum inferni	19a. iii qui ducunt in infernum		2. Quot sunt … ad profundum inferni?		2. iii ducunt in infernum	III.40 iii ducunt ad profundum inferni
5. iii deducunt ad regna celorum	19b. iii quae ducunt ad regnum	5. iii que ducunt ad regna celorum	3. Quot sunt … ad regnum caelorum?	1. [iii] ducunt ad regna celestia	3. iii ducunt ad regna caelorum	III.40 iii ducitur in altitudinem regni
6. iii non remittuntur	20a. iii non remittuntur	6. iii non remituntur	4. Quot sunt … non remittuntur?	2. iii non remetuntur	4. iii non remittuntur	III.41 iii non remittuntur
7. cybus corporis cybus anime		7. cibus corporis cibus anime		3. cibus corporis cibus anime		II.15 cibus corporis cibus animae
	21. vii dampnatio peccatorum	vii damnaciones peccatorum				
	22. vii muneratio sanctorum	vii muneraciones sanctorum				
de ebrietate	28. de ebrietate	[de ebrietate]				
de subrietate	29. de sobrietate					
	6. de principio celi et terre	de principio celi et terre				

make numerological connections in sermons',[121] and indeed the florilegia I have surveyed would have been most useful for preaching. Joan Turville-Petre has stressed the importance of such florilegia as sources – whether direct or indirect – of vernacular homilies in both Old English and Old Icelandic.[122] Inevitably, numerical themes that circulated in Irish florilegia, homily collections, dialogues and commentaries found their way into vernacular sermons in both Ireland and England.

Relatively few early Irish sermons in the vernacular have survived, yet it is remarkable how often these do employ distinctively Irish (or Insular) enumerative themes. The earliest vernacular homily in Irish, for example, the seventh-century Cambrai homily,[123] distinguishes 'white, blue and red' martyrdoms ('bánmartre ocus glasmartre ocus dercmartre'), a distinction by colour that occurs in a variety of Irish and Hiberno-Latin texts.[124] In the Cambrai homily the three martyrdoms motif is accompanied by a Latin tag, *castitas in iuuentute*, *continentia in habundantia* (here the homily breaks off). McNally recognized this as a fragment of a triad preserved in the *Prebiarum*: 'Quod sunt genera martyri preter mortem? Id, tres. Continentia in habundantia, largitas in paupertate, castitas in iuuentute.'[125] But the Zurich florilegium (34r) and the *Disputatio philosophorum* in Clm. 5257 (24r) also have this triad, and

[121] *Rogationtide Homilies*, p. 12. For a list of numerical themes in the Pembroke Homiliary, several of which are paralleled in the *Liber de numeris*, see Cross, *Cambridge Pembroke College MS 25*, p. 60.

[122] 'Translations of a Lost Penitential Homily'. Turville-Petre was able to reconstruct the Latin source of portions of several vernacular sermons by piecing together extracts from florilegia. The 'lost' penitential homily has since been discovered, in the Pembroke Homiliary. See H. Spencer, 'Vernacular and Latin Versions of a Sermon for Lent: "A Lost Penitential Homily" Found', *MS* 44 (1982), 271–305; Cross, *Cambridge Pembroke College MS 25*, pp. 124–6. See also Turville-Petre's earlier article, 'Sources of the Vernacular Homily in England, Norway and Iceland', *Arkiv för nordisk Filologi* 75 (1960), 168–82.

[123] *Thesaurus Palaeohibernicus*, ed. Stokes and Strachan II, 244–7; see *BCLL*, no. 801. A recent discussion of the homily is P. P. O'Neill, 'The Background to the *Cambrai Homily*', *Ériu* 32 (1981), 137–47.

[124] See above, p. 19.

[125] *Scriptores Hiberniae Minores I*, ed. McNally, p. 163: 'How many are the kinds of martyrdom other than death? That is, three. Continence in abundance, generosity in poverty, chastity in youth'. On the motif, see also Stancliffe, 'Red, White and Blue Martyrdom', pp. 37–8.

the sequence survives to a much later date in Irish vernacular manuscripts.[126]

Later Irish treatises and homilies also transmit many numerical motifs, some found only in the vernacular. In Middle Irish we have a treatise on the two sorrows of the kingdom of heaven, which also enumerates the three cries of the world; both motifs are found in other Irish texts.[127] The Middle Irish *Betha Coluim Cille* ('Life of St Columba') prefaces the narrative with expositions of the three kinds of vocation and the three ways of leaving one's homeland.[128] Again, another Middle Irish homily enumerates the six kinds of mercy, the six chief things through which hell is attained and the three locks of sinners.[129] The Leabhar Breac homilies frequently employ enumerations, many of which are familiar from other sources.[130]

THE ENUMERATIVE STYLE IN OLD ENGLISH HOMILETIC LITERATURE

Enumerative themes of Irish origin that were especially popular in Anglo-Saxon England include the twelve abuses of the world[131] and the

[126] For some examples, see Flower, *Catalogue of Irish Manuscripts* II, 493, and P. Grosjean, 'Two Religious Pieces', *ZCP* 18 (1929–30), 299–303, at 302, lines 42–4 (part of a lengthy series on the qualities befitting a cleric).

[127] See Dottin, 'Les deux chagrins' (English translation in Herbert and McNamara, *Irish Biblical Apocrypha*, pp. 19–21). On the two sorrows motif, see below, pp. 77–8; the three cries are enumerated in the Book of Lismore (see D. Hyde, 'Trí Gáire an Domhain', *ZCP* 17 (1927–8), 111–12), and in *Duan in choícat cest*, ed. Meyer, 'Mitteilungen', p. 237.

[128] Ed. M. Herbert, *Iona, Kells, and Derry: the History and Hagiography of the Monastic Familia of Columba* (Oxford, 1988), pp. 219–20 (trans. at 248–9). The enumeration of the three kinds of vocation is based on Cassian, *Conlationes* III.4 (see Herbert, pp. 270–1). The three ways of leaving one's homeland (based on Gen. XII.1) correspond to the three renunciations enumerated in Zurich, Rh. 140, fol. 34. Cf. the extract *De Abraham* in Clm. 22053, 48r, and *Questiones Sancti Hysidori* (*Scriptores Hiberniae Minores I*, ed. McNally, pp. 198–9).

[129] 'Tidings of Doomsday', ed. Stokes, pp. 248 and 252.

[130] For example, the three kinds of remedy for sin (*The Passions and the Homilies*, ed. and trans. Atkinson, pp. 220 and 458) occur in the *Collectanea Bedae* (PL 94, 542C). Sims-Williams, 'Thought, Word and Deed', p. 83, n. 32a, cites the same triad from Apponius.

[131] For the Irish tract *De duodecim abusiuis saeculi*, see above, n. 23. Ælfric translated part of this tract and also used the theme in a homily; for references, see Pope, *Homilies*

three utterances of the soul,[132] each of which provided the basic framework for vernacular homilies in Old English. Apocryphal themes based on numerical conceptions transmitted in the west primarily by the Irish include the seven heavens, the subject of another anonymous Old English homily,[133] the fifteen signs before Doomsday[134] and the theme of Adam Octipartite, which occurs in the *Prose Solomon and Saturn* and the Durham Ritual.[135]

Other numerical themes from Irish sources were borrowed to illustrate specific points: for example, in his *Institutes of Polity*, Wulfstan lists eight columns which bear up a just kingdom, taken from Sedulius Scottus's *De rectoribus christianis*, followed by seven things which are necessary for a righteous king, from the *Collectio Canonum Hibernensis*.[136] These two motifs are followed by the theme of the three orders (*oratores*, *laborantes* and *bellatores*), which makes its first appearance in Anglo-Saxon texts.[137] An enumeration in an Old English Rogationtide homily which lists three spiritual births (baptism, confession and communion) in addition to physical birth appears to be an 'ill-remembered' version

of Ælfric I, 373–4. For examples of the theme in Old English, Icelandic and Welsh, see M. Förster, 'Kleinere mittelenglische Texte', *Anglia* 42 (1918), 145–224, at 148, n. 2. For an allusion to the first four items of the list in an Old English homily, see Bazire and Cross, *Rogationtide Homilies*, p. 92.

132 See Willard, *Two Apocrypha*, pp. 31–149, and below, pp. 215–18.

133 On the Seven Heavens apocryphon, see *ibid.*, pp. 1–31, and below, pp. 218–21.

134 See Heist, *The Fifteen Signs*; McNamara, *The Apocrypha in the Irish Church*, pp. 132–8 (nos. 104A–I). For the Old English homily on this theme, see *Early English Homilies from the Twelfth Century Ms. Vesp. D. XIV*, ed. R. D.-N. Warner, EETS os 152 (London, 1917), 89–91; Heist, pp. 125–7.

135 See Tristram, 'Der "homo octipartitus"'; McNamara, *The Apocrypha in the Irish Church*, pp. 21–3 (no. 4); Cross and Hill, *The Prose Solomon and Saturn*, pp. 67–70. Tristram, however, concludes that the examples in Old English and Irish derive independently from continental sources.

136 See K. Jost, *Die 'Institutes of Polity, Civil and Ecclesiastical'*, Schweizer anglistische Arbeiten 23 (Bern, 1950), 52–4. The *octo columnae* motif, ultimately from the *Prouerbia Grecorum*, occurs also in Cathulf's letter to Charlemagne (*BCLL*, no. 1181); see Simpson, 'The *Proverbia Grecorum*', p. 2. Wulfstan may also have used a triad, ultimately from Gregory, in a formulation transmitted through Hiberno-Latin sources; see Cross, 'Wulfstan's *Incipit de Baptismo* (Bethurum VIII A): a Revision of Sources', *NM* 90 (1989), 237–42, at 241–2.

137 For an attempt to trace the origins of this theme to Ireland, see D. Dubuisson, 'L'Irlande et la théorie médiévale des "trois ordres"', *Revue de l'histoire des religions* 188 (1975), 35–63.

of the theme of the *quattuor natiuitates* in the *Liber de numeris* (*secundum carnem*, *in baptismo*, *in penitentia*, *in resurrectione*).[138] Didactic numerical themes are among the items in the Old English *Adrian and Ritheus* derived from Irish tradition, including item 27 on the four wings of the soul, for which Cross and Hill found a close parallel in the *Prebiarum*.[139] This motif also occurs in the Zurich florilegium (36v) and Clm. 22053 (46r)[140] as well as the dialogue in Clm. 5257 (24v). Item 38, which names the four mute letters (mind, thought, writing and fear), is an expanded version of a triad found in the *Collectanea Bedae* and the *Prebiarum*, as Cross and Hill point out. It also occurs in Cologne, Dombibl., 15, 88v, where it is further explained, but in very corrupt form:

Quid [*sic*] sunt trea muta que docent hominem? Respondit. Oculus, littera, mens. Docet oculos litter[a], [oculus] autem docet mentem, mens autem lingua[m] docere uidetur. Littera namque indicat misteria scripturarum ocul[i]s et mentibus pers[c]rutantibus ea que fuerunt et qu[e] sunt et qu[e] erunt.[141]

The triad also occurs in the Irish *Cesta Grega* ('Greek Questions'): 'Caidi iat na tri dūili amlabra dobeir fiss do chāch? Ni ansa, .i. rosc, menma, liter.'[142] Item 19, which names the two men in Paradise who

[138] See Bazire and Cross, *Rogationtide Homilies*, p. 68, who tentatively suggest the parallel. For the motif of the four births, see McNally, *Der irische Liber de numeris*, pp. 83–4. It also occurs in variant form in Cologne, Dombibl., 15, 91v, and in Clm. 19410, p. 13 (where the fourth 'birth' is *in caritate*). There may be a reminiscence of this theme in the Old English *Vision of Leofric*, in which the visionary's presence in heaven is justified by a guide who says, 'He mot beon mid us, he is niwan gefullod þurh dædbote, 7 he cymð to us on þære þriddan gebyrtide' ('An Old English Vision of Leofric, Earl of Mercia', ed. A. S. Napier, *Transactions of the Philological Society 1907–1910* (London, 1910), p. 182, lines 21–2). If 'baptism through penitence' is the second 'gebyrtide' (an apparent conflation of two 'births'), the first would be physical birth and the third resurrection.

[139] See Cross and Hill, *The Prose Solomon and Saturn*, p. 150. On the contacts with Irish traditions in these two dialogues, see *ibid.*, pp. 8–11.

[140] Noted by Schwab, *Sternrune*, p. 19.

[141] 'What are the three mute things which instruct a man? One answers: Eye, letter, mind. The letter instructs the eyes, the eye instructs the mind, and the mind seems to instruct the tongue. For the letter reveals the mysteries of the Scriptures to the eyes and to minds which investigate these mysteries which were and are and shall be.'

[142] 'Irish Riddles', ed. W. Stokes, *The Celtic Review* 1 (1904), 132–5, at 132: 'What are the three dumb creatures that give knowledge to everyone? Easy (to say): an eye, a mind, a letter' (trans. Stokes, p. 134). On the *Cesta Grega*, see Flower, *Catalogue of Irish Manuscripts* II, 520–2.

'continually weep and are sorrowful' (Enoch and Elias), is related to the Irish theme of the two sorrows of the kingdom of heaven.[143]

Of course, enumerations in Old English texts often derive from patristic authorities. Sometimes, however, even these have not been taken directly from the patristic source, but have been transmitted through Irish or Anglo-Saxon florilegia.[144] In other cases non-enumerative themes or sequences culled from patristic authorities are reformulated specifically as enumerations, and circulate independently in Irish sources in this form. A good example is the enumeration of the three reasons Christ went into the desert, which appears in Blickling Homily III:

For þrim þingum Hælend eode on westen; forþon þe he wolde deofol gelaþian to campe wiþ hine, & Adam gefreolsian of þam langan wræce, & mannum gecyþan þæt se awyrgda gast æfestgaþ on þa þe he gesyhþ to gode higian.[145]

The ultimate source is Ambrose's comment on Luke IV.1:

Plenus igitur Iesus spiritu sancto agitur in desertum consilio, ut diabolum prouocaret – nam nisi ille certasset, non mihi iste uicisset – mysterio, ut illum Adam de exilio liberaret, exemplo, ut ostenderet nobis diabolum ad meliora tendentibus inuidere.[146]

143 Cross and Hill, *The Prose Solomon and Saturn*, pp. 142–4. Cross and Hill identify the parallels in the Irish texts *Dá Brón Flatha Nime* and *Fís Adamnán*. It also occurs in *Duan in choícat cest*, ed. Meyer, 'Mitteilungen', p. 237. See further McNamara, *The Apocrypha in the Irish Church*, pp. 24–7 (no. 9).

144 Such is the case, for example, of the enumeration of the four ways in which judgement is perverted in Assmann XII, ultimately from Isidore's *Sententiae* III.54 (see Turville-Petre, 'Translations of a Lost Penitential Homily', pp. 63–4), but which the homilist had third hand, by way of a Pembroke homily, from Alcuin's *De uirtutibus et uitiis* (see Cross, *Cambridge Pembroke College MS 25*, pp. 226–7). This enumeration also occurs in *Hib.* XXI.13 (*Die irische Kanonensammlung*, ed. Wasserschleben, p. 66).

145 *The Blickling Homilies*, ed. Morris, p. 29, lines 18–22. I alter slightly Morris's translation: 'For three reasons the Saviour went into the desert – because he wanted to summon the devil to fight against him, and to free Adam from the long exile, and to show men that the cursed spirit envies those he sees hasten to good.' For the following, see Wright, 'Blickling Homily III'.

146 *Expositio euangelii secundum Lucam*, ed. M. Adriaen, CCSL 14 (Turnhout, 1957), 111: 'Jesus therefore, filled with the Holy Spirit, was led into the desert as a stratagem, that he might challenge the devil (for if he had not fought, He would not have conquered for me), as an allegory, that he might free Adam from exile, and as an example, that he might show us that the devil envies those striving for the better.'

The Blickling homilist did not take the motif directly from Ambrose, however, for it had already been excerpted and simplified, and reworked as a triad introduced by a numerical tag. It survives in this form in two Hiberno-Latin Matthew commentaries. One of these has only a fragment of the enumeration (the reference to the envy of the devil has dropped out), but another preserves the motif intact, and both introduce it with a numerical tag ('Tribus causis ...') as does the Blickling homily ('For þrim þingum ...').[147] The Blickling homilist's immediate source was probably a Hiberno-Latin commentary or exegetical homily rather than a florilegium, since there are a series of significant parallels and verbal echoes with several Hiberno-Latin commentaries in the opening section of the homily.[148]

As Sims-Williams has shown, the 'thought, word and deed' triad had scattered patristic antecedents, but the Irish made it their own.[149] The triad also occurs frequently in Old English, both in the homilies and in the poetry.[150] The sequence is common in unnumbered lists,[151] but occurs also as a numbered triad. Although, as Sims-Williams states, this triad 'proved so widely popular that its Irish connections soon became obscure',[152] in several Old English homilies it occurs in contexts that suggest the immediate influence of Irish sources. The same Rogationtide homily that lists the three births, for example, also has the 'thought,

[147] The commentaries are the Vienna Commentary on Matthew (*BCLL*, no. 772; Wright, 'Hiberno-Latin', no. 24) and the Würzburg Commentary and Glosses on Matthew (*BCLL*, no. 768; Wright, 'Hiberno-Latin', no. 25). On the Würzburg Commentary, see now D. Ó Cróinín, 'Würzburg, Universitätsbibliothek, M.p.th.f. 61 and Hiberno-Latin Exegesis in the VIIIth Century', in *Lateinische Kultur im VIII. Jahrhundert*, ed. Lehner and Berschin, pp. 209–16. The relevant passages are quoted in Wright, 'Blickling Homily III', p. 133, n. 12.

[148] For details, see *ibid.*

[149] Sims-Williams cites Latin patristic examples from Gregory and Apponius only, but he informs me that he now has a few more examples from Jerome, Pelagius and Cassiodorus, which do not, however, affect the general picture.

[150] E.g., *Judgment Day II*, in *The Anglo-Saxon Minor Poems*, ed. Dobbie, pp. 61–2, lines 135–40; *A Prayer*, *ibid.*, p. 96, lines 64–5; *Christ III*, in *The Exeter Book*, ed. Krapp and Dobbie, pp. 31–2, lines 1036–8 (cf. Biggs, *The Sources of Christ III*, pp. 17–18); and *Elene*, in *The Vercelli Book*, ed. Krapp, p. 101, lines 1281b–1286a (see Wright, 'The Pledge of the Soul').

[151] E.g., Vercelli XII, in *Vercelli Homilies*, ed. Szarmach, p. 24, line 42; Vercelli XVII, *ibid.*, p. 53, line 109). Napier XXIX, in *Wulfstan*, ed. Napier, p. 137, lines 28–31, is based on the poem *Judgment Day II* (see preceding note).

[152] 'Thought, Word and Deed', p. 110.

word and deed' triad as 'three things through which we can maintain all God's decree (*dom*)'.[153] Blickling Homily III, indebted to Hiberno-Latin sources for several passages in the opening of the homily, interpolates the 'thought, word and deed' sequence, eked out to a tetrad to conform to the context, into a later passage which otherwise follows its Gregorian source quite closely.[154] Vercelli Homily V, which depends on a source closely related to the *Catechesis Celtica* for its discussion of the miracles associated with the birth of Christ,[155] has a confused enumeration of three ways men had to pay tribute in Caesar's days, linked tropologically with three ways we must pay God the tribute of true faith (words, thoughts and deeds). The enumeration and the link with the 'thought, word and deed' triad are paralleled in two Hiberno-Latin sources. In the Reference Bible the three characteristics of the Caesarian tax are identical to those in the Vercelli homily, but here the 'thought, word and deed' triad is applied instead to the three *denarii* exacted. In the Linz homily collection, the same three characteristics (with some variation in wording) are enumerated as three wonders, followed by the 'thought, word and deed' triad as in Vercelli V. From these two Hiberno-Latin texts the Vercelli homilist's source can be fairly closely approximated:

Vercelli V:	Reference Bible:
Ðrim wisum ungelice wæron mannum beboden on þæs caseres dagum: þæt is þonne, þæt æghwylc man sceolde gaful gildan, 7 ealle men sceoldon hit	Item tria habuit hic census, quod omnis homo in toto mundo reddidit eum, et quod eiusdem ponderis siue diues siue pauper, et quod a nullo [*corr. from* nulla]

[153] *Rogationtide Homilies*, ed. Bazire and Cross, p. 74, lines 186–9. The homily also alludes to 'likenesses' of heaven and hell, apparently an echo of the Irish theme discussed below in connection with the 'five likenesses of hell' in Vercelli IX. See below, p. 102.

[154] See Wright, 'Blickling Homily III', pp. 136–7. As I point out there, the homilist's addition of 'will' to the triad as a list of the four ways man sins, associated numerically with Christ's forty-day fast, is paralleled in a Hiberno-Latin commentary on Luke.

[155] See Cross, 'Portents and Events at Christ's Birth', pp. 209–13.

gildan, ge rice he heane, 7 ðam gafole mon ne onfeng æt ænegum men butan in his swæsum eðle.

accipitur nisi in sua patria.[156]

On þan wæs getacnod, þæt we sculon in þrim wisum Gode rihtes ge-leafan gaful agildan: þæt is on wordum 7 on geþohtum 7 on dædum.[157]

Linz homily:
Nobis autem conueniunt quod necesse est unicuique censum trinum ... quia tres requiret deus ab homine: uerbum bonum, opus bonum, cogitationes bonas.[158]

Particularly striking is a sequence of enumerations in an anonymous Old English homily, Napier LVII, which incorporates the 'Irish' group of triads identified by Sims-Williams, as in the Karlsruhe and Zurich florilegia, together with the additional enumeration of the three ways

[156] Paris, BN, lat. 11561, 163v: 'This tax also had three characteristics, that every man in the entire world paid it, and paid the same amount, whether rich or poor, and that it was not received from anyone except in his own homeland'. Compare a passage in the *Apocrypha Priscillianistica*, in 'Fragments retrouvés', ed. De Bruyne, p. 332: 'quiad res [*read* quia tres] argentioles exigit deus ab homine, id est, cogitationem bonam, et uerbum bonum, opus bonum'.

[157] *Die Vercelli-Homilien*, ed. Förster, p. 117–18, lines 101–7: 'In three ways dissimilarly they were demanded from men in the days of that Caesar: that is, that each man had to pay tribute, and all men had to pay it, both wealthy and poor, and the tribute was not received from any man except in his own homeland. By that was signified that we ought to pay to God the tribute of true faith in three ways: that is, in words and in thoughts and in deeds.'

[158] Bibliothek der philosophisch-theologischen Hochschule der Diözese Linz A I/6, 71v (see above, n. 54): 'But they apply to us to the extent that a threefold tax is necessary for each person ... because God requires three from man: good word, good deed, good thoughts.' The 'thought, word and deed' interpretation is repeated later (72v), followed by the statement 'debemus tributum soluere deo credulitatis' (compare 'we sculon ... Gode rihtes ge-leafan gaful agildan'). The three wonders of the Caesarian tax are enumerated in Irish in the Leabhar Breac biblical history. See the facsimile edition, *Leabhar Breac: the Speckled Book*, p. 132b, and see also Flower, *Catalogue of Irish Manuscripts* II, 536. Elements of the motif also occur in Irish versions of an Infancy gospel (see *The Irish Nennius*, ed. Hogan, p. 40; *Irish Biblical Apocrypha*, ed. Herbert and McNamara, p. 27), and in a Middle Irish account of the wonders of the night of the Nativity (*ibid.*, p. 35).

the devil lures one into false security, as in Clm. 19410, Clm. 22053, and in an Irish homily in the Leabhar Breac. J. E. Cross has identified a further example of the sequence in Munich, Clm. 14364 (St Emmeram, s. ix[1]), fol. 37.[159] I cite from this manuscript, which is verbally closest to Napier LVII:

Napier LVII:	Clm. 14364:
ac þencð se unwara on his geþance, eallswa deofol hine lærð, þe ælc yfel of cymð. þæt is, ærest he hine lærð, þæt he his synna ne andette, forþam þe he jung is; eft he cwæð to þam men: 'oðre syngodon hefelicor, þonne þu, and þeahhwæðere hig leofedon lange hwile'. he cwyð þryddan siðe: 'do swa yfele, swa þu do, godes mildheortnys is swiðe mycel, and he wyle þe forþy þine synna forgifan'. and þurh þas unwærnysse he gebringð hine on helle.	Tribus modis diabolus securitatem in mente hominis mittit. Primum suggerit hominem ut non det confessionem, 'quia iuuenis es tu'. Secundo dicit, 'quia alii grauius peccauerunt quam tu et diu regnauerunt'. Tercium, 'tu pecca quia magna clementia et misericordia dei indulget tibi peccata tua'; et per hanc securitatem ducit e[u]m ad infernum.
ðreo þing syndon, þe gebringað þone ungesæligan on helle grunde: þæt is, unclæne geþanc and idele word and yfele dæda.	Tria sunt que deducunt hominem ad profundum inferni, id est, cogitatio inmunda, uerbum alienum, opus prauum.
and oðre þreo þing syndon, þe gebringað þone gesæligan to	Tria sunt que deducunt hominem ad regna celestia, id est, cogitatio

[159] On Clm. 14364, see Bischoff, *Schreibschulen*, pp. 239–40. Cross drew attention to the sequence in Napier LVII in a paper read at the Twenty-Second International Congress on Medieval Studies, Kalamazoo, Michigan, in May 1987. I am grateful to Professor Cross for allowing me to consult his notes on these manuscripts, and for providing me with a transcript of the sequence in Clm. 14364. Cross points out that the first enumeration in the sequence occurs singly in Einsiedeln, Stiftsbibliothek, 281 (s. viii/ix; *CLA* VII, no. 875), which has one reading (*uixerunt* for *regnauerunt*) closer to the Old English (*hig leofedon*). The entire sequence occurs in a twelfth-century *Adrianus et Epictitus* dialogue, in *Adrian und Epictitus*, ed. Suchier, p. 36, which also reads *uixerunt*, and where the reading *quia iuuenis est* corresponds to the Old English *forþam þe he jung is*.

heofenan rice: þæt is, halig geþanc and god spæc and fullfremed worc.

sancta et uerbum bonum, opus perfectum.

and þreo þing syndon, þe ne beoð forgifene ne on þissere worulde ne on þam toweardan life: an is, þæt man god to tale habbe; oðer, þæt man ærestes ne gelyfe; þrydde, þæt man ortruwige godes mildheortnysse.[160]

Trea sunt que non remittuntur hic [nec] in futurum, id est, qui plasphemat deum et qui desperat de misericordia dei et qui non credit resurrectionem.

The motif of the three ways the devil lures a man into false security occurs also within a section headed *De timore Dei* in Oxford, Bodleian Library, Laud Misc. 129, 109r (Main region, s. ix^{1}).[161] An Irish version is incorporated in the Leabhar Breac homily on repentance:

Aslach diabuil tra, fodera do nech cen aithrige do dénum, ar is ed atbeir fris-in duine ic aslach uilcc fair: – 'na déna aithrige indossa, or diabul, uair bid fota do shaegul; ar is suaill in t-olcc do-rígnis, 7 is sochaide do-róine ulcu bud móu in-

[160] *Wulfstan*, ed. Napier, p. 298, line 32 – p. 299, line 16 (I print each enumeration beginning on a separate line for ease of reference, and translate the Old English only): 'But the unwary one thinks in his mind just as the devil, from whom every evil comes, persuades him. That is, first he persuades him, that he not confess his sins, because he is young; next he says to the man: "Others have sinned more gravely than you, and yet they lived for a long time." He says the third time: "Do as evilly as you may, God's mercy is very great, and he will therefore forgive you your sins." And through this unwariness he leads him to hell.' 'There are three things that bring the unhappy one to the bottom of hell: that is, unclean thought and idle words and evil deeds.' 'And there are three other things that bring the blessed one to the kingdom of heaven: that is, holy thought and good speech and perfected deed.' 'And there are three things which will not be forgiven either in this world or in the next life: one is, that one blasphemes against God; the second, that one does not believe in resurrection; the third, that one despairs of God's mercy.'

[161] This manuscript, written in Anglo-Saxon script, contains sermons and theological extracts, many of which are related to Irish tradition, including one sermon found in the Linz homily collection (see Wright, 'Hiberno-Latin', no. *46), and a fragment of another corresponding to a piece in the Cracow homily collection (see Wright, 'Hiberno-Latin', no. 45). I hope to analyse the contents of this manuscript in a future study.

datt, or diabul; uair is dirím méit trocaire Dé, 7 íccfaid-side cách di-a cintaib', ol se.[162]

A part of the same theme, with an elaborated version of the first of the devil's lures, occurs in a pseudo-Augustinian sermon which was translated by another Old English homilist:

We secgað eac to soðan þæt hit is yfel wise þæt monige, men þa leofestan, syndon on þisum life swa þæt hig syndon beswicene ðurh deofles lare ealles to swiðe; þurh þæt þonne ðe man þencð swiðe unwislice on him sylfum and þus cwyð: 'Ic eom me ead geongman, and ic hæbbe me lange tid onto plegenne and fela þinga to onginnenne on minum geogeðhade. Ic wylle, eft ðonne ic to ylde becume, don dædbote and behreowsunga þæra misdæda þe ic ær geworhte on minum geogeðhade'. Hwæt, he lyt geþencð on his mode, þæt he nah anre tide fæces geweald be his lifes lenge.[163]

Certe multi audacia diabolica decipiuntur, et securitate propria, quam sibi fingunt, decipiuntur. Dicunt enim, iuuenis sum; dum est mihi tempus, et interim quod floret in me iuuentus, fruar mundo; cum ad senectute uenero, et amplius quæ uolo exercere nequiuero, tunc poenitentiam agens abstinebo. Et non cogitat ille miser, quod non habet certum unius horae uel momenti spatium, seu etiam potestatem de uita sua. Eia, charissimi fratres; non uos decipiat aut seducat ista pessima securitas: quæ non securitas, sed potius periculum dici potest.[164]

[162] *The Passions and the Homilies*, ed. Atkinson, p. 221: 'It is the temptation of the devil that causes people not to repent at all; for he says to a man, in tempting him to evil: – "Do not repent now, for thy life will be long; trifling is the evil thou hast done; and many there are that have done worse evils than thou hast. Then the extent of the mercy of God is incalculable, and He will pardon everybody his crimes"' (trans. Atkinson, p. 459).

[163] *Nuove omelie anglosassoni*, ed. Fadda, p. 145, lines 9–17: 'We also declare truly, beloved men, that many are in an evil state in this life so that they are utterly deceived through the devil's teaching; in this way a man thinks very unwisely to himself and says thus: "I am a young man, and I have a long time to enjoy myself and many things to accomplish in my youth. When I reach old age, I will do penance and show remorse for the misdeeds which I formerly committed in my youth." Lo, he little considers in his mind, that he does not have the power of a single moment's time over his life's span.'

[164] *Sermo ad fratres in eremo LXVIII*, PL 40, 1355 (see Machielsen, *Clavis*, no. 1195),

An enumeration which appears to be distinctively Irish is the theme of the three 'households' or companies of heaven, hell and earth. In the *Catechesis Celtica* it occurs several times: Christ is the *princeps familiae caeli et terrae et inferni*; he judges *coram tribus famili<i>s caeli et terrae et inferni*.[165] According to Paul Grosjean, the term *familia* corresponds to Irish *muinter*,[166] and one finds the equivalent allusion to *na teora muntera .i. muinter nime ⁊ talman ⁊ ifirn* in Irish vernacular sources, including the Tripartite Life of St Patrick, *Airdena inna Cóic Lá nDéc ria mBráth* ('The Fifteen Tokens of Doomsday'), *Betha Maignenn* ('Life of St Maignenn'), a homily in the Leabhar Breac and an early Irish devotional poem.[167] In

trans. Allen and Calder, *Sources and Analogues*, p. 148, with slight alterations: 'Many men are certainly deceived by diabolical audacity, and by their own (false) security which they invent for themselves; for they say, "I am young; while I have the time and youth blossoms in me, I will enjoy the world. When I reach old age and can no longer do what I want, then I will be abstinent and do penance." The wretched man does not know that not one hour or moment is guaranteed him, nor even power over his own life. Alas, dearest brothers, do not let this wicked security deceive or seduce you; it cannot be called security, but rather danger.' This source for the Old English homily was noted by Willard, 'The Address of the Soul to the Body', p. 960.

165 *Analecta Reginensia*, ed. Wilmart, pp. 46 and 110–11; cf. p. 77, lines 116–18. Two of the three *familiae* are mentioned again, p. 47, and in an unpublished portion of the commentary, on 7v.

166 See Grosjean, 'A propos du manuscrit 49', p. 121; J. Pokorny, 'Zur irischen Wortkunde', *ZCP* 10 (1914–15), 202–4. See also Ó Laoghaire, 'Irish Elements in the *Catechesis Celtica*', p. 152, and cf. the sentence 'Castris celestibus, terrestribus et infernalibus imperat [*scil.* Creator]' in the Hiberno-Latin *De ortu et obitu patriarcharum*, ed. McNally, '"Christus" in the Pseudo-Isidorian "Liber de ortu et obitu patriarcharum"', p. 178. The theme was probably suggested by Phil. II.10 ('ut in nomine Iesu omne genu flectatur caelestium, terrestrium, et infernorum ...'), though the context in Scripture is not Judgement. A related theme is that of the three *mansiones* or *habitacula* (heaven, earth and hell), for which see below, p. 101 and n. 220.

167 *The Tripartite Life of St Patrick*, ed. W. Stokes, 2 vols. (London, 1887) I, 119; 'The Fifteen Tokens of Doomsday', ed. Stokes, pp. 316–17; *Betha Maignenn*, in *Silva Gadelica*, ed. O'Grady I, 45 and II, 45; *The Irish Nennius*, ed. Hogan, p. 34; B. Ó Cuív, 'Some Early Devotional Verse in Irish', *Ériu* 19 (1962), 1–24, at 7. Another Irish saint's life (*Lives of Irish Saints*, ed. Plummer I, 234 and II, 227) incorporates a verse referring to God as the 'King of the three companies' (*na ttri muinnter*). *Saltair na Rann* also lists them, without a numerical tag: 'muinter nimi noebarbar, / muinter thalman iss ifeirnn' (ed. Stokes, p. 121, lines 8255–6). The phrase *muinter nime ⁊ talman* occurs as early as the Würzburg glosses (for citations, see *DIL*, s.v.

Old English the motif of the three companies at Judgement is widespread. Many of the examples are associated with a penitential motif identified by Malcolm Godden in some fifteen Old English texts, including penitential compilations and homilies.[168] In Godden's paraphrase, the motif states that 'it is better to be shamed for one's sins before one man (the confessor) in this life than to be shamed before God and before all angels and before all men and before all devils at the Last Judgement'.[169] Most of these texts list the three hosts as *heofonwaru and eorðwaru and helwaru.*[170] An Old English poem, *The Lord's Prayer II*, also lists the three companies in connection with the Judgement.[171] Godden considered the motif of the three hosts a specifically Anglo-Saxon (and vernacular) one, since it occurs so frequently in Old English and since he was able to identify Latin parallels only in Alcuin and in a homily attributed to St Boniface.[172] The motif may have developed as an elaboration of a passage in Gregory's *Homilia XII in Euangelia*, which warns:

'muinter' (d)). Grosjean, 'A propos du manuscrit 49', p. 121, nn. 2–3, cites several examples of the phrases *muinter nime ⁊ talman*, and one of *muinter ifirn*, from the Leabhar Breac homilies. Henry, *The Early English and Celtic Lyric*, p. 214, cites several of these examples as a possible model for the phrase *eorðan bearnum* in *Caedmon's Hymn*. Other Irish sources name the three companies with the terms *slúag* ('host') or *fir* ('men'). See E. G. Quin, 'Ochtḟoclach Choluim Chille', *Celtica* 14 (1981), 122–53, at 144; J. G. O'Keeffe, 'A Poem on the Day of Judgment', *Ériu* 3 (1907), 29–33, at 29–31; 'Les deux chagrins', ed. Dottin, p. 380. A gloss in the Leabhar Breac version of *Amra Senáin* uses the term *teglach*. See L. Breatnach, 'An Edition of *Amra Senáin*', in *Sages, Saints and Storytellers*, ed. Ó Corráin *et al.*, pp. 7–27, at 11 (gloss 16).

168 'An Old English Penitential Motif', pp. 221–39.

169 *Ibid.*, p. 222.

170 This is a regular feature of the seven texts comprising Godden's Group A, but is also found in a homily of Ælfric in Godden's Group B. Godden points to other examples in Blickling VII, a Wulfstan homily, and a 'less explicit' reference in Vercelli V.

171 *The Anglo-Saxon Minor Poems*, ed. Dobbie, p. 73, line 95 (noted by Godden, p. 239): 'heofonwaru and eorðwaru, helwaru þridde'. See also *Christ I*, in *The Exeter Book*, ed. Krapp and Dobbie, p. 11, lines 285–6.

172 Godden, 'An Old English Penitential Motif', pp. 238–9. The parallel which Godden cites from Alcuin (p. 235) mentions only two of the hosts; it occurs, significantly, in his letter to the monks of Ireland. As Godden notes, 'the usual representation of the Last Judgement in Continental works (as in Alcuin's letter) has the angels and all mankind present, and sometimes the devil as prosecutor, but not the whole host of devils'.

Pensate, fratres charissimi, ante conspectum tanti iudicis qui in illo die terror erit quando iam in poena remedium non erit, quae illa confusio cui reatu suo exigente continget in conuentu omnium angelorum hominumque erubescere.[173]

Thus a sermon by Eligius of Noyon stresses the shame that will be felt in the sight of God and all men and angels at Judgement by the sinner who does not wish to be observed by even one man in this life:

Perpendamus, qualis [*var.* quales] erimus in die iudicii Dei in conspectu eciam angelorum presentandi, quando opera nostra nobis sunt ante oculos ponenda; qualis illa erit confusio, cui contingerit pro peccatis suis in conspectu Dei omniumque hominum et angelorum tunc erubescere, qui hic nec unum quidem hominem in se peccantem uult nunc inspicere.[174]

Neither Gregory nor Eligius, however, mentions the presence of the host of devils. The Anglo-Saxon homilies, then, would appear to owe the triadic formulation to Irish sources. In some Old English texts we find terms corresponding to the Irish phrase *tria familia* / *na teora muntera*, including *heregas þreo* in Napier XLIX and its analogue Vercelli X,[175] and a reference to the *þrym hiwscipum* in an anonymous homily for Easter recently edited by Clare Lees.[176] Further evidence of the Irish

[173] PL 76, 1120–1: 'Consider, dearest brothers, what terror there shall be on that day in the sight of so great a judge, when there will be from then on no remedy in punishment, what embarrassment there will be to the one who will have to blush when his own guilt demands it in the assembly of all men and angels.'

[174] *Sermo de supremo iudicio*, in *Vita S. Eligii*, ed. B. Krusch, MGH, SS rer. Merov. 4 (Hannover and Leipzig, 1902), 751–61, at 755: 'Let us consider in what condition we shall have to be presented on the day of Judgement, in the sight of God and of angels as well, when our works are to be placed before our eyes; what embarrassment there will be to the one who, on account of his sins, will then have to blush in the sight of God and of all men and angels, who now (in this life) wishes not even one man to observe him sinning here.'

[175] For these examples, see Godden, pp. 237–8 (Vercelli X omits one of the three hosts, the devils). As Godden points out, 'The Latin source for this part of the homily contains no reference to the three hosts' (p. 238).

[176] Ed. Lees, in 'Theme and Echo', p. 123, line 162. Lees (p. 138) cites two additional examples of Old English homilies which refer to the hosts at Judgement (one of these lists all three, the other only two). For further examples which mention the three hosts, see Napier XLII, in *Wulfstan*, ed. Napier, p. 202, lines 22–3 and p. 203, lines 5–6; *The Blickling Homilies*, ed. Morris, p. 83, lines 9–10; and *Old English Homilies of the Twelfth Century*, ed. Morris, p. 53, line 36 and p. 69, lines 3–4. Two other examples mention two of the hosts, the *heofonwara* and *helwara* (the presence of

background of the triadic formulation of the motif is provided by the Latin homily attributed to Boniface, the closest Latin analogue for the entire penitential motif, which uses the distinctively Irish phrase *coram tribus familiis, coeli terraeque, et inferorum*.[177]

THE ENUMERATIONS IN VERCELLI HOMILY IX

Although it is not possible to illustrate the sources for the numerical preparatory motifs in Vercelli IX so precisely as the sequence of triads in Napier LVII, parallels and analogues from Irish sources, both Latin and vernacular, demonstrate that the Vercelli homilist was also indebted to florilegia from the Irish tradition.

The three deaths and the three lives

The preparatory motif section begins with a pair of opposing triads, contrasting three deaths and three lives:

Đonne syndon þry deaðas liornode on bocum: þæt is þonne se æresta deað her on worulde þæt se man mid manegum synnum oferhealden bið; þonne is se æftera deaþ þæra sawle gescead ⁊ lichoman; þonne is se þridda deað þæt þa sawla sculon eardigan on helle, þær nis nænig man þætte mæge his scippend herigan for ðam sare þe him onsitet. Emne swa ða þry deaðas syndon fyrenfulra, swa þænne syndon þreo lif be ðam soðfæstum: an lif is þæt he bið on flæsce; þonne is oðer lif ðæt [he] bið on god[um] w[eorc]e; ⁊ þridde lif is on þære toweardan worulde mid eallum halgum.[178]

the *eorðwara* being understood); see *Nuove omelie anglosassoni*, ed. Fadda, p. 133, lines 80–1, and Blickling Homily I, in *The Blicking Homilies*, ed. Morris, p. 11, lines 3–4; a third, on the contrary, refers to *þæm miclan þreate heofonwarena ⁊ ealra eorðwarena*; see H. Logeman, 'Anglo-Saxonica Minora', *Anglia* 12 (1889), 497–518, at 511, lines 1–2.

177 See Godden, 'An Old English Penitential Motif', pp. 235–6. As Godden points out, the authenticity of the sermons attributed to Boniface has been questioned. If this particular sermon is not Hiberno-Latin, it has probably drawn on Irish sources.

178 *The Vercelli Homilies*, ed. Scragg, p. 162, lines 32–40: 'Then there are three deaths learned from books. The first death here in the world is that a man is overcome with many sins; the second death is the separation of the soul and body; the third death is that the souls must dwell in hell, where there is no man who can praise his Creator on account of the suffering that oppresses him. Just as there are three deaths of the sinful, so then there are three lives with regard to the righteous: one life is that in the flesh; the second life is that in good work; and the third life is in the future world with all the saints.'

The motif of the three deaths is a departure from the biblical and patristic norm, although the individual items do have authority in the Scriptures and the Fathers. That sin is a kind of 'death' was deduced by ecclesiastical authors from several New Testament passages that associate sin and death (John VIII.24; Rom. V.12; I Cor. XV.56; Eph. II.1, 5; I John V.16). Isidore of Seville, for example, succinctly explained how sin is a kind of death of the soul.[179] Separation of body and soul, here numbered the second death, was the standard definition of physical death in ecclesiastical writers. That dwelling in hell is yet another 'death' derives, of course, from the Apocalypse: 'in stagno ardente et sulphure quod est mors secunda' (XXI.8; cf. II.11, XX.6, 14). But if the parts of this list may conform to biblical thought, their sum does not conform to biblical reckoning. The Bible sanctions, as a numerical pattern, not three deaths but two: a first death, of the body, and a second, of the soul. Two 'deaths', then, is the standard formulation, which patristic and medieval authors constantly repeat. Ælfric, as always, followed the mainstream:

> Twegen deaðas synd, swa swa us secgað béc:
> an is ðæs lichaman deað, þe eallum mannum becymð,
> oðer is ðære sawle déað, þe ðurh synna becymð,
> na eallum mannum, ac þam mánfullum anum,
> and heora sawul lósað from þam écán life,
> and ne swelt ðeah næfre on ðære hellican susle,
> ac bið æfre geedniwed to þam ecum witum.[180]

The triad departs from the biblical formulation not only in number but also in sequence: eternal death is no longer *mors secunda*, as the

[179] *Sententiae* III.xiv (PL 83, 617). For the background, see P. Courcelle, 'De Platon à saint Ambrose par Apulée', *Revue de philologie* 35 (1961), 15–28, at 23, n. 4.

[180] *Homilies of Ælfric*, ed. Pope I, 421: 'There are two deaths, as books tell us: one is the death of the body, which comes to all men, the second is the death of the soul, which comes through sin, not to all men, but to the sinful alone, and their soul perishes from eternal life, yet it never dies in the torment of hell, but is always renewed to eternal pains.' Szarmach suggests this comparison in 'The Vercelli Homilies: Style and Structure', p. 264, n. 6. Ælfric does, however, distinguish three degrees of spiritual death (*Homilies of Ælfric*, ed. Pope I, 319, lines 160–9; see Grundy, *Books and Grace*, p. 221). For a discussion of the distinction between physical death and spiritual death in Old English homilies, see J. Hill, 'Figures of Evil in Old English Poetry', *Leeds Studies in English* ns 8 (1975), 5–19, at 13–15.

Apocalypse would have it, but *se þridda deað*. A triadic scheme does, however, appear in several works of St Ambrose, conveniently summarized by F. Homes Dudden:

Three kinds of death may be distinguished – *mors spiritalis* or *mystica*, whereby man dies to sin but lives unto God; *mors naturalis*, whereby the soul is set free from the body; and *mors poenalis*, whereby the soul dies to God through sin. The second of these – *mors naturalis* – is defined as *absolutio animae et corporis et quaedam hominis separatio*, or *animae corporisque secessio.*[181]

Ambrose's triad of deaths, however, is an imperfect parallel for Vercelli IX, not only because the sequence differs – *mors poenalis* or death through sin is the third, not the second death – but because the first death, *mors spiritalis*, is a death *in bono*.

Despite Ambrose's authority, triadic enumerations of 'deaths' seem to be rare in early medieval commentators.[182] I find two examples, however, which correspond to Vercelli IX in the essential sequence. A pseudo-Augustinian treatise *De praedestinatione Dei* informs us, 'Mors ... non tantum dupliciter, sed etiam tripliciter intelligi potest.' These are listed as follows: 'Mors ergo anime, peccatum; mors carnis, dissolutio elementorum; mors animae et carnis, poena infernalis'.[183] Alcuin, commenting on Apoc. II.11, attempted lamely to reconcile the twofold and threefold schemes:

Cum sacra Scriptura tres mortes ponere solita sit: unam scilicet peccati, alteram carnis, aliam uero damnationis, cur hoc loco ultima damnatio non tertia, sed secunda mors appellatur, nisi quia illae hic poni uidentur quae nocere

[181] *The Life and Times of St Ambrose*, 2 vols. (Oxford, 1935) II, 650, summarizing passages from *De excessu fratris* II.36, 37; *De bono mortis* II.3; *Expositio euangelii secundum Lucam* VII.35; and *De paradiso* 45. Ambrose's triadic scheme derives from Origen; see J. Longère, *Oeuvres oratoires de maîtres parisiens au xiie siècle*, 2 vols. (Paris, 1975) I, 188 and 143, n. 1.

[182] Freytag, *Kommentar*, pp. 91–2, lists several examples of three- and fourfold enumerations, but notes that compared with the two deaths, 'Die Unterscheidung von drei und vier Toden ist weniger streng gefaßt.'

[183] PL 45, 1679–80: 'Death can be understood not only in two ways, but also in three ... The death therefore of the soul, sin; the death of the flesh, dissolution of matter; the death of the soul and the flesh, infernal torment'. Klaus Gamber's attribution of this treatise to Nicetas of Remesiana (d. after 414) in his *Niceta von Remesiana*, p. 28, is not accepted by Frede (see *Kirchenschriftsteller*, pp. 160 [PS-AU prae] and 461).

probantur? Mors scilicet peccati, et mors aeterni supplicii, ad quarum comparationem, ista quae carnis est, mors dicenda non est.[184]

These examples are isolated, however, and the triad clearly could not compete in exegesis with the biblically sanctioned twofold reckoning.[185] Yet it does seem to have found a home in Hiberno-Latin tradition, where it occurs most often in question-and-answer form, but with a numerical tag and in wording similar to Vercelli IX. The *Prebiarum* asks,

Quod sunt mortes? III. Prima, in peccato; secunda, in exitu animae de corpore; tertium, in <i>ntrando in paenam.[186]

The dialogue in Cologne, Dombibl., 15 (88v) also has the motif:

Qu[ot sunt] mort[e]s? Id, III. Prima in peccato, secunda [in] exitu a[ni]me de corpore, tercia in abitacione [ignis] eterne.[187]

The *Disputatio philosophorum* (Clm. 5257, 24r) has a closely similar version of the triad:

Quot sunt mortes que in hoc mundo leguntur? Tres. Que prima mors in peccato, secunda in exitu anime de corpore, tertia in habitatione gehenne ignis eterne.[188]

184 PL 100, 1104: 'Since Holy Scripture is accustomed to count three deaths (that is, one of sin, another of the flesh, and another of damnation), why in this passage is the last, damnation, called not the third but the second death, if not because (only) those deaths are understood to be counted here which are proven to do harm: namely, the death of sin and the death of eternal torment, in comparison to which that of the flesh is not to be called death?'

185 For a twelfth-century example, see below, n. 195. A fourfold scheme, which usually incorporates the three 'deaths' enumerated in these examples, and which seems to have originated in exegesis of Genesis II.17, is rather more common. See Freytag, *Kommentar*, p. 91; McNally, *Der irische Liber de numeris*, p. 91; Cross, *Cambridge Pembroke College MS 25*, p. 80.

186 *Scriptores Hiberniae Minores I*, ed. McNally, p. 163: 'How many deaths are there? Three. The first, in sin; the second, in the departure of the soul from the body; the third, in entering into torment.'

187 'How many deaths are there? That is, three. The first, in sin; the second, in departure of the soul from the body; the third, in the habitation of eternal fire.'

188 'How many deaths are read of in this world? Three, of which the first death is in sin, the second in the departure of the soul from the body, the third in the habitation of the eternal fire of hell.'

The compiler of the dialogue in Clm. 19410 (p. 19), however, has capped the triad with a fourth 'death':

Quot modis fit mors? .iiii. Mors in peccat[o], mors in exitu anime, mors in gehenna, mors sine penitentia.[189]

Lists of this kind are, of course, commonly subject to extension. The simple triad, in declarative rather than interrogative form, is attested in the so-called 'Liber Commonei' or 'codex Oxoniensis prior' in St Dunstan's Classbook, in a brief (unprinted) treatise on Colossians II.14 which R. W. Hunt and Michael Lapidge have compared to Irish exegetical tradition:

Quod est decretum quod hic dicit? Id est, trinam difinitionem quam inuenimus a diabulo pro commercio, id est mors corporis, mors peccati, mors poenae.[190]

In the *Collectaneum* of Sedulius Scottus, however, the customary three deaths are stretched to six:

Prima mors corporis, .ii. mors animae in peccato, .iii. mors animae a peccato, .iv. mors in supplicio, .v. diabolus, .vi. mors corporis et animae in supplicio.[191]

[189] 'Death is spoken of in how many ways? Four: Death in sin, death in the departure of the soul, death in hell, death without penitence.' The Cologne dialogue and both Munich dialogues distinguish between the two (or three) deaths that can be redeemed and the one that cannot, but Clm. 5257 seems to identify the unredeemable one as natural death ('ut dictum est Ade, de terra es et in terram ibis'), while Clm. 19410 identifies it as death *in gehenna*. The Cologne dialogue does not specifically identify them.

[190] Oxford, Bodleian Library, Auct. F. 4. 32 (SC 2176), 19r–36r (Wales, s. ix[1]), 21v; cited from the facsimile, *St Dunstan's Classbook from Glastonbury*, ed. R. W. Hunt, Umbrae Codicum Occidentalium 4 (Amsterdam, 1961): 'What is the decree which he speaks of here? It is the threefold definition which we have received from the devil because of our commerce with him, that is death of the body, death of sin, death of torment.' The *commercium* with the devil is explained as follows: 'Adam uendidit uitam pro morte, longeuitatem pro breuitate, incorruptionem pro corruptione, regnum pro morte.' On the text *De questione apostoli* (*BCLL*, no. 88; Wright, 'Hiberno-Latin', no. *33), see Lapidge, 'Latin Learning in Dark Age Wales', pp. 93–4.

[191] *Sedulii Scotti Collectaneum Miscellaneum* XVII.17, ed. Simpson, p. 136: 'The first death of the body, the second the death of the soul in sin, the third the death of the soul by sin, the fourth death in torment, the fifth the devil, the sixth the death of the body and the soul in torment.'

It is evident that the fourth 'death' in Clm. 19410 is also a mere supplement to the original triad, especially since this dialogue, like the *Prebiarum* and the dialogue in Clm. 5257, pairs the four deaths with *three* lives – or rather three life forms, for the latter triad is based upon biological rather than moral distinctions (vital and rational, as man; vital and sensible, as a beast; non-vital and non-rational, as a tree).[192] This triad of lives makes a poor match for the three deaths, and one suspects that it has supplanted a more appropriate triad of moral lives such as the Vercelli homily transmits. Fortunately, one collection, the *Collectanea Bedae*, preserves both triads intact:

Dic mihi quot uitae sanctis leguntur? Tres: uita praesens, uita in bonis operibus, et uita aeterna futura.
Dic mihi quot mortes peccatoribus reputantur? Mors in peccato, et separatio animae et corporis, et mors poenae.[193]

In the *Collectanea Bedae*, as in the dialogues, the motif is transmitted in question-and-answer form, but it none the less provides the closest parallel yet discovered for the three deaths and the three lives in Vercelli Homily IX,[194] and the only parallel for the pairing of the two triads.[195] Unfortunately, the moral triad of lives apparently gave way to another popular but in context ill-fitting triad of lives in the tradition attested in the *Prebiarum* and the Munich dialogues. An Old Irish *lorica* does have

[192] *Scriptores Hiberniae Minores I*, ed. McNally, p. 163. The motif occurs also in the *Liber de numeris* (see McNally, p. 53).

[193] PL 94, 542D: 'Tell me how many lives are read of for the saints? Three: the present life, the life in good works, and the eternal future life. Tell me how many deaths are reckoned for sinners? Death in sin, and the separation of body and soul, and the death of torment.'

[194] The formulation is generally closer to the Old English as well, since the *Collectanea*, like Vercelli IX, specifies that the three deaths are the deaths of sinners (*peccatores*/*fyrenfulra*), the three lives the lives of the holy (*sancti*/*soðfæstra*). For the second life, Scragg's emendation of A's *on Godes wuldre* to *on god*[*um*] *w*[*eorc*]*e* (E has *godes weorc*, L *on Godes willan*) accords better with the Latin *in bonis operibus*.

[195] A twelfth-century homily by Radolphus Ardens (PL 155, 1486) juxtaposes within a more elaborate discussion three deaths with three lives, which are given as *mors* (*uita*) *spiritualis*, *mors* (*uita*) *corporalis* and *mors* (*uita*) *aeterna et misera* (*beata*). The Verona homily collection (Verona, Biblioteca Capitolare, LXVII (64), 73v–74r; see above, n. 53), juxtaposes two deaths and one resurrection of sinners with two deaths and two resurrections of the just.

the tantalizing phrase, 'Let the three deaths be taken from me, the three lives be given to me.'[196] But the *lorica* does not list these 'deaths' and 'lives', and the three deaths may reflect a different tradition, the widespread Celtic motif of the 'threefold death' (burning, wounding and drowning).[197] Some reworking of Ambrose or another yet unidentified authority may be the ultimate source for the basic conception of the three deaths motif, but the parallels for the motif in the dialogues, together with the parallel for both triads in the *Collectanea Bedae*, suggest that the pair of triads was transmitted to the Vercelli homilist in a Hiberno-Latin florilegium.[198]

After the three deaths and three lives comes a rather lengthy description of the qualities of death, which is elaborated in list form although not formally an enumeration. The homilist explains that death is to be feared because it is ubiquitous: death is high and low, multiple and terrible, youthful and old, freeborn and servile, happy and sad. The essential ideas behind the homilist's list of the qualities of death – that death is inescapable, and no respecter of persons – could hardly be more commonplace, but their elaboration and rhetorical expression is striking. Possible models include Ps. CXXXVIII.7–10 and Amos IX.2–4, each of which employs a sequence of conditional statements to emphasize that God's presence or vengeance is inescapable, however far one might flee, up to heaven, down to hell or to the depths of the sea.[199]

[196] 'Trī bās ūaim rohuccaiter! / trī āes dom dorataiter!' (in *Miscellanea Hibernica*, ed. K. Meyer, University of Illinois Studies in Language and Literature 2.4 (Urbana, IL, 1916), 19); trans. Greene and O' Connor, *A Golden Treasury of Irish Poetry*, p. 33 (repr. in *Sources and Analogues II*, trans. Calder *et al.*, p. 187).

[197] See J. N. Radner, 'The Significance of the Threefold Death in Celtic Tradition', in *Celtic Folklore and Christianity*, ed. Ford, pp. 180–200.

[198] The three deaths motif survived into the late Middle Ages in England. See *The Pricke of Conscience*, ed. R. Morris (Berlin, 1863), lines 1682–5. A rather different elaboration of the triad of deaths is found in an early Middle English homily in *Old English Homilies of the Twelfth Century*, ed. Morris, p. 169. Four deaths are enumerated in *Jacob's Well*, ed. A. Brandeis, EETS os 115 (London, 1900), 146.

[199] The homilist's statement that death is both 'niðerlic' and 'uplic', low and high, in the deepest cave and the highest forest, has an intriguing but very late parallel in a passage from one of a class of Irish poems known as *Aighneas an pheacaigh risan mbás* ('The Sinner's Argument with Death'), described by S. H. O'Grady, *Catalogue of Irish Manuscripts in the British Museum* I (London, 1926), p. 593, in which Death describes itself in the following terms: 'I at the one instant am both here and there, upon the sea I am and upon land; I am high up, I am low down, I'm in the forests

The homilist's list of the qualities of death is followed by another enumeration (textually corrupt) of four 'separations' of the soul (from friends, from the body, from earth-dwellers and from earthly glory). I am aware of no precise or approximate source (Irish or otherwise) for this particular tetrad, although again the ideas are commonplace. An elaboration of the fourth separation, however, which explains how death 'shuts up' (*betyneð*) the senses and then shuts up the sinner in hell, is reminiscent of an Irish enumeration of the 'three (or four) locks of the sinners', in which we find a similar juxtaposition of the 'shutting' (*íadad*) of the senses (represented by the eyes) with the shutting of hell.[200]

The five likenesses of hell

The homilist's next enumeration, of five images or 'likenesses' of hell, is a theme that can be traced in a variety of Irish sources, both Latin and vernacular.

Þonne is leornod on bocum þæt on þysse worulde syn fif onlicnessa be helle gryre. Sio æreste onlicnes is nemned wræc, for ðan se wræc bið miceles cwelmes ælcum þara þe he tocymeð, for ðan hine sona ne lysteð metes ne drynces, ne him ne bið læten gold ne seolfor, ne ðær ne bið ænig wuldor mid him þæt he fore wynsumige, þeah him syndon ealle wuldordreamas to gelædde. Þonne is þære æfteran helle onlicnes genemned oferyldo, for þan him amolsniað þa eagan for ðære oferyldo ða þe wæron gleawe on gesyhðe, 7 þa earan adimmiað ða ðe ær meahton gehyran fægere sangas, and sio tunge aw[l]is[p]að þe ær hæfde gerade spræce, 7 þa [fet] aslapað þe ær wæron ful swifte [7 hræde] to [gange], 7 þa handa aþindað þe ær hæfdon ful hwate fingras, 7 þæt feax af[ealle]ð þe ær wæs on fullere wæstme, 7 þa teð ageolewiað þa þe [ær] wæron hwite on hywe, 7 þæt

haunted by the gentle fairy folk' (trans. O'Grady, p. 594). With the homilist's assertion that a man cannot escape death, even if he were in a city surrounded by his kindred and a hundred thousand men, compare the similar numerical hyperbole from a tenth-century Irish poem on the inevitability of death, in *A Golden Treasury of Irish Poetry*, ed. and trans. Greene and O'Connor, p. 161: 'Cia no beinn tríchait cét / don ócbaid tét, tenna a cnis, / dia tí caingen in báis brais / ní fhil daingen gabas fris' ('Even if I had thirty hundred hot youths with stout skins, when the call of swift death comes there is no fortress that holds out against it').

200 This enumeration occurs in *Apgitir Chrábaid*, ed. Hull, pp. 72–3; 'Tidings of Doomsday', ed. Stokes, pp. 252–3; 'The Fifteen Tokens of Doomsday', ed. Stokes, pp. 318–19; and *Betha Maignenn*, in *Silva Gadelica*, ed. and trans. O'Grady I, 45 and II, 45.

oroð afulað þe wæs ær swete on stence. Đonne is þære þriddan helle onlicnes her on worulde deað genemned, for þan þonne se man sceal sweltan, þonne swyrceð him fram þæs huses hrof ðe he inne bið; þonne nis nænig strengo þæt hine arære, for ðan he ne bið gelustfullod metes, ne he ne gymeð þysses eorðlican rices torhtnessa. Đonne is ðære feorðan helle onlicnes byrgen nemned, for þan þæs huses hrof bið [gehnæg]ed þe him onufan ðam breostum siteð, 7 him mon þonne deð his gestreona þone wi[r]sestan dæl, þæt is þæt hine [mon siw]eð on anum [hræg]le. Hafað him þonne syððan þry gebeddan, þæt is þonne greot 7 molde 7 wyrmas. Þonne is þære fiftan helle onlicnes tintrega genemned, for ðan þænne nis nænig man þæt mæge mid his wordum asecgan hu mycel þære fiftan helle sar is.[201]

J. E. Cross[202] has drawn attention to a Latin parallel for this enumeration in the *Catechesis Celtica*:

V inferni sunt: I dolor, II senectus, III mors, IIII sepulcrum, V pena. Dolor comparatur inferno, quia si habuisset homo omnes substantias quibus homines in hoc mundo uti solent letus fieri non potest, ut dicit filius Serac *non est census super censum salutis corporis* [Ecclus. XXX.16]. – II. Senectus assimilatur quando V sensus in exitum exeunt. Nam oculi caliginant, aures sordescunt, gustus non bene discernit, odoratus uitiatur, tactus rigescit; sed et dentes

201 *The Vercelli Homilies*, ed. Scragg, p. 166, line 84 – p. 168, line 108: 'It is learned from books that there are five likenesses of hell-torment in this world. The first likeness is called pain, because pain is a great torment to each of those it afflicts, because at once food and drink do not please him, nor do gold and silver remain for him, nor is there any glory with him that he might rejoice in, even if all glorious pleasures were brought before him. The second likeness of hell is called old age, because the eyes weaken from old age, which had been keen in sight; and the ears grow dull, which had been able to hear fair songs; and the tongue lisps, which once had skilful speech; and the feet are paralysed, which had been very quick and swift to walk; and the hands swell up, which once had very nimble fingers; and the hair falls out, which had been in fuller growth; and the teeth yellow, which had been white in colour; and the breath stinks, which once had smelled fresh. The third likeness of hell here in the world is called death, because when a man must die, the roof of the building in which he lies grows dark before him; then there is no power that can raise him, for he has not delighted in food, nor does he care for the splendours of this earthly realm. The fourth likeness of hell is called the grave, for the roof of the house that sits upon his breast is bent down, and the meanest portion of his treasures is taken from him, that is someone sews it up in a bag. Thereafter he has three bedfellows, that is earth, dust and worms. The fifth likeness of hell is called torment, because there is no man who can express with his words how great the fifth pain of hell is.'

202 'The Literate Anglo-Saxon', pp. 95–6.

denudantur, lingua balbutiat, pectus licoribus grauatur, pedes tremore et tumore tumescunt, manus ad opus debilitantur, canities floret, et corpus omne infirmatur, sed sensus diminuitur. – Sepulcrum etiam infernus est: ubi terra terrae redditur; cibi [*read* ubi] cadauer uermibus exhauritur; ubi limo caro miscetur; ubi aures et os et oculi III impletionibus replentur: primo cruore, II uermibus, III humo; ubi ossa arida redatis [*read* redactis] pulueri carnibus remanent.[203]

The five 'hells' in the Latin correspond exactly to the Old English (*dolor/wræc*; *senectus/oferyldo*; *mors/deað*; *sepulcrum/byrgen*; *pena/tintrega*). There are also close correspondences in the elaboration of three of the five (the Latin lacks elaborations of *mors* and *pena*). Thus the Vercelli homilist's explanation of *wræc*,[204] that a man suffering pain cannot enjoy glory 'even if all glorious pleasures were brought before him', is closely paralleled by the Latin, 'quia si habuisset homo omnes substantias quibus homines in hoc mundo uti solent letus fieri non potest'.[205]

The litany of the parts of the body decaying with age, the second likeness of hell, is again similar to the Latin, but there are important differences as well. The Old English adds the phrase, 'þe (ær) wæron' to each item of the list, and alters some of the items in the inventory: there is nothing to correspond to the Latin *gustus*, *tactus* or *pectus*, and the teeth are merely yellow, whereas they had fallen out in the Latin. But (alas) the

203 *Analecta Reginensia*, ed. Wilmart, p. 44: 'There are five hells: (1) suffering, (2) old age, (3) death, (4) the grave, (5) torment. Suffering is compared to hell, because if a (suffering) man had all things which men are accustomed to use in this world he could not be made happy, as the son of Sirach says, "there is no riches above the riches of the health of the body" [Ecclus. XXX.16]. (2) Old age is likened to hell, when the five senses pass away at the end of life. For the eyes grow blurry, the ears grow deaf, the sense of taste distinguishes poorly, the sense of smell is corrupted, the sense of touch becomes numb; and also the teeth are revealed, the tongue stutters, the chest grows heavy with fluid, the feet swell with tumors and shaking, the hands are crippled for work, the grey hair grows, and the whole body is weakened, and perception is diminished. The grave also is hell, where earth is given unto earth; where the corpse is hollowed out by worms; where flesh is mixed with slime; where the ears and mouth and eyes are filled with three surfeitings: first with blood, second with worms, third with earth; where dry bones remain when flesh has been reduced to dust.'

204 I take *wræc* as a metathesized form of *wærc*, the reading of E (L has *worc*).

205 The phrase *omnes substantias ... in hoc mundo* has a closer equivalent in L: *he ne wunsumaþ þisses woruldlican þrymmes* (*The Vercelli Homilies*, ed. Scragg, p. 167, line L.70). In the Vercelli text *wuldordreamas* is perhaps an error for *woruldreamas*.

hair falls out instead, when it had only gone grey in the Latin. Of course, a compiler could easily excerpt and adapt a list of this kind for use in varying contexts.[206] As Cross points out, a very similar list occurs in the Irish tract *De duodecim abusiuis saeculi*:

Dum oculi caligant, auris grauiter audit, capilli fluunt, facies in pallorem mutatur, dentes lassi numero minuuntur, cutis arescit, flatus non suauiter olet, pectus suffocatur, tussis cachinnat, genua trepidant, talos et pedes tumor inflat, etiam homo interior qui non senescit his omnibus aggrauatur, et haec omnia ruituram iam iamque domum corporis cito pronuntiant.[207]

The same passage, apparently taken directly from the *De duodecim abusiuis*, turns up in the *Collectanea Bedae*.[208] The nature of the subject makes parallels between this list of the signs of old age and the list in the *Catechesis Celtica* inevitable,[209] but the correspondences are significant enough to suggest a distant relationship. While the first items in both lists are verbally identical (*oculi calig(in)ant*), the other matching items are synonymous: *aures sordescunt* / *aures grauiter audit*; *odoratus uitiatur* / *flatus non suauiter olet*; *dentes denudantur* / *dentes lassi numero minuuntur*; *pectus*

[206] The author of the composite homily Napier XXX used this passage (*Wulfstan*, ed. Napier, p. 147, line 29 – p. 148, line 7). See Scragg, 'Napier's "Wulfstan" Homily XXX', p. 207.

[207] *Pseudo-Cyprianus de xii abusivis saeculi*, ed. Hellmann, pp. 34–5: 'When the eyes grow dark, the ears hear with difficulty, the hair falls out, the face becomes pallid, the decayed teeth diminish in number, the skin dries up, the breath does not smell sweet, the chest is congested, there is a hacking cough, the knees buckle, a tumor swells the ankles and feet, and even the interior man which does not grow old is burdened by all these ills, and all these things immediately proclaim that the house of the body is on the very point of collapse.'

[208] PL 94, 544.

[209] The *Vita Tertia* of St Patrick has a briefer variation of the theme: 'Nam omnes sensus tui defecerunt: oculi non bene uident, aures non bene audiunt, lingua non bene loquitur, dentium numerus *inminutus* est, similiter et cetera membra' (*Four Latin Lives of St. Patrick*, ed. L. Bieler, SLH 8 (Dublin, 1971), 139). Compare the following phrases from a prayer in the Lambeth Psalter: 'Iam pertrahit me deuictum senectus ad occasum, floret uertex, hebet uisus, crescit dolor capitis, ruunt dentes, remunt membra, decidunt tote uires', partially glossed in Old English as 'heafod, deorcaþ gesihð, wecsð sar heafdes, feallaþ teþ, cwaciaþ lima, hreosað ealle' (ed. M. Förster, in 'Die altenglischen Beigaben des Lambeth-Psalters', *Archiv* 132 (1914), 328–35, at 328). For a survey of the topos of the signs of old age, see R. Woolf, *The English Religious Lyric in the Middle Ages* (Oxford, 1968), pp. 102–3; G. R. Coffmann, 'Old Age from Horace to Chaucer', *Speculum* 9 (1934), 249–77.

licoribus grauatur / pectus suffocatur; *pedes ... tumore tumescunt / pedes tumor inflat*). It looks as if both lists are independent translations of a vernacular original, which would account for the correspondences in sense but divergence in wording. Whether or not a vernacular original actually existed, the lists are reminiscent of the well-known lists of the parts of the body found in many Irish and Hiberno-Latin prayers, notably in the *loricae* and in penitential prayers; the presence of such anatomical lists in prayers in Anglo-Saxon manuscripts such as the Book of Cerne has long been recognized as a sign of Irish influence.[210]

In the elaboration of the fourth likeness of hell, the grave, Vercelli IX adds the metaphor of the grave as a house whose roof lies upon one's chest, which occurs later in the early Middle English poems *The Grave* and *The Worcester Fragments*.[211] Vercelli IX also incorporates another enumeration, the three 'bedfellows' (*gebeddan*): earth, dust and worms. This too departs from the Latin version of the theme in the *Catechesis Celtica*, which speaks of three 'surfeitings' (*impletiones*) of the ears and mouth and eyes: blood, worms and earth. The homilist (or his immediate source) appears to have adapted the motif in accordance with a metaphor common in the Bible and in Old English, the 'bed of death'.[212]

In the *Catechesis Celtica* we thus have only an approximation of the Vercelli homilist's source, but obviously the homilist had access to a closely similar variant text. Professor Cross concludes that we can only say that Vercelli IX and the *Catechesis Celtica* preserve 'two examples of the theme'.[213] For my purposes this is sufficient, for pinpointing an exact source is less important than demonstrating a pattern of occurrence in specifically Insular environments. For the same reason, other recognizable variations on the theme of 'likenesses' of hell in Irish

[210] See Kuypers, *The Book of Cerne*, pp. xxiv–xxv; Hughes, 'Some Aspects of Irish Influence', p. 53; Sims-Williams, 'Thought, Word and Deed', p. 90, n. 77; Frantzen, *The Literature of Penance*, pp. 85–9 and 171; F. Liebermann, 'Zur angelsächsischen Exkommunikation', *Archiv* 119 (1907), 176. For speculations on the origins of this motif, see Herren, *The Hisperica Famina: II*, pp. 24–31 and 201–4.

[211] See Heningham, 'Old English Precursors', p. 305.

[212] This modification may have been suggested by Job XVII.13–14: 'si sustinero infernus domus mea est in tenebris straui lectulum meum / putredini dixi pater meus es mater mea et soror mea uermibus.'

[213] 'The Literate Anglo-Saxon', p. 96.

and Hiberno-Latin texts, even if quite divergent in detail, are valuable evidence for its Irish background.

One example of the theme in Old Irish comes from *Apgitir Chrábaid*, where four 'hells' are opposed to four 'heavens':

Cethōra flaithi duini isin chentur .i. oītiu 7 soinmige, sláine 7 sochraite. Cethair ifirn duini isin centur .i. galar 7 sentu, bochta 7 dochraite.[214]

Of the four 'hells' the first two, *galar 7 sentu*, sickness and old age, correspond to the first two likenesses of hell in the Old English, *wræc* and *yldo* (*dolor* and *senectus* in the Latin). But the motif was obviously fluid, and those who used it felt free to substitute some of their own 'hells'.[215] The example from *Apgitir Chrábaid* shows that the motif, like the three deaths, could be accompanied by an opposing series, in this case of four 'heavens'.

We find the same kind of opposition, but again with some different 'heavens' and 'hells', in one of the few surviving Old Irish homilies:

Ataat dano cosmuiliusa flatha nime 7 iffirn isin bithso. Cosmuilius iffirnn dano and cétamus .i. gaimred 7 snechtae, sín 7 úacht, áes 7 chríne, galar 7 bás. Cosmailius flatha nime and immurgu, samrad 7 soinenn, bláth 7 bile, áilde 7 óitiu, fleda 7 tomalta, sóinmige 7 imbed cach maithiusa.[216]

[214] 'Apgitir Chrábaid', ed. Hull, p. 74: 'The four heavens of mankind in this world: Youth, prosperity, health and friendship. The four hells of mankind in this world: Sickness, old age, poverty and friendlessness' (trans. Hull, p. 75). The Irish examples of the theme were collected by B. Grogan, 'The Eschatological Doctrines of the Early Irish Church' (unpubl. PhD dissertation, Fordham Univ., 1972), pp. 142–3. The theme has also been discussed recently by Ó Laoghaire, 'Irish Elements in the *Catechesis Celtica*', p. 157. To the Irish examples adduced by Grogan I add only a late occurrence of the motif, apparently excerpted from the *Apgitir Chrábaid*, in a fragment ed. Meyer, 'Mitteilungen', p. 234; see also Flower, *Catalogue of Irish Manuscripts* II, 278.

[215] Ó Laoghaire, 'Irish Elements in the *Catechesis Celtica*', p. 157, cites Clare Stancliffe's remark that, 'while the Irish loved categorizing their material at a superficial level, beneath this they were often happy to live with two or more variants'.

[216] 'An Old-Irish Homily', ed. Strachan, p. 5: 'There are, moreover, likenesses of the kingdom of heaven and of hell in this world. The likeness of hell therein, first, i.e. winter and snow, tempest and cold, age and decay, disease and death. The likeness of the kingdom of heaven therein, however, summer and fair weather, blossom and leaf, beauty and youth, feasts and feastings, prosperity, and abundance of every good' (trans. Strachan, p. 9). Tristram, *Sex aetates mundi*, p. 137, n. 7, citing Cross, also compares this passage with the theme in the *Catechesis Celtica* and Vercelli IX, but is unaware of the additional examples cited here.

Here the theme is no longer explicitly numerical, and the homilist has become carried away with his 'heavens', listing two more of these than there are 'hells'. This example, however, unlike the *Catechesis Celtica* or *Apgitir Chrábaid*, preserves the term 'likeness' (*cosmailius*), corresponding to the Old English *gelicnes*.[217] The specific correspondences are *áes*, *galar* and *bás* (age, sickness and death), equivalent to the Old English *yldo*, *wræc* and *deað*.[218] The idea survives in reduced form in a bardic poem by Gofraidh Fionn Ó Dálaigh (d. 1387):

> Dá ionsamail aca soin,
> dá teagdais iarsma Adaim,
> 'n-a hoidce a-tá [an] treab oile
> an lá i dteag na trócoire.[219]

A final example of the theme comes from the treatise *De tribus habitaculis* of Patrick, bishop of Dublin (d. 1084). Describing the three 'abodes' (*habitacula*) of heaven, hell and earth, he defines earth as the middle place, which has 'likenesses' to the highest and the lowest:

Medium autem nonnullam habet similitudinem ad extrema. Unde lucem et tenebras habet, frigus et calorem, dolorem et sanitatem, letitiam et merorem, odium et amorem, bonos et malos, iustos et iniustos, dominos et seruos, regnum et subiectionem, famem et satietatem, mortem et uitam et innumera huiusmodi. Quorum omnium pars una imaginem habet regni dei, pars altera inferni. Commixtio nanque malorum simul et bonorum in hoc mundo est. In regno autem dei nulli mali sunt, sed omnes boni; at in inferno nulli boni sunt, sed omnes mali: et uterque locus ex medio suppletur.[220]

217 The idea, of course, is contained in the verbs *comparo* and *assimilo* in the *Catechesis Celtica*, but the Latin text does not have a phrase such as *similtudines inferni* corresponding to *onlicnessa be hellegryre* or *cosmuiliusa flatha iffirn*.

218 A Welsh poem about Llywarch Hen has what appears to be a variation of the theme: 'The four things I have always hated most / Have converged on me at the same time: / A cough and old age, disease and grief' (*The Poetry of Llywarch Hen*, trans. P. K. Ford (Berkeley, CA, 1974), pp. 80–1). In a note Ford compares *The Seafarer*, in *The Exeter Book*, ed. Krapp and Dobbie, p. 145, lines 68–70: 'Simle þreora sum þinga gehwylce, / ær his tid aga, to tweon weorþeð; / adl oþþe yldo oþþe ecghete fægum fromweardum feorh oðþringeð.'

219 *Aithdioghluim Dána*, ed. L. McKenna, 2 vols., ITS 37 and 40 (Dublin, 1939–40) I, 265. McKenna translates (II, 162): 'There are two similitudes for the two houses of Adam's race; day shines in the House of Mercy, the other abode (Hell) is as night.'

220 *The Writings of Archbishop Patrick*, ed. Gwynn, p. 106: 'But the middle abode has many likenesses to the two extremes. Whence it has light and darkeness, cold and

The specific correspondences here are only *dolor* (= *wræc*) and *mors* (= *deað*), but like the Old Irish homily the Latin has the equivalent term *similitudo*, corresponding to Old English *gelicnes*. Another Old English homilist, who alludes to 'þa gelicnysse þe se witega cwæð be heofona rice and be helle', appears to have been familiar with a list of likenesses of both heaven and hell, but unfortunately he does not go on to enumerate them.[221]

The three deaths and three lives, the four separations and five likenesses of hell make up the preparatory motif section of Vercelli IX, but one more motif must be treated briefly, a list of the qualities of heaven in 'The Devil's Account' which, though not explicitly numerical, demonstrably derives from a Hiberno-Latin numerical motif.

The joys of heaven

'The Devil's Account' includes a list of six characteristics of heaven in the form 'x without y':

heat, suffering and health, happiness and sadness, hate and love, the good and the bad, the just and the unjust, lords and slaves, kingship and servitude, hunger and satiety, death and life and countless things of this sort. Of all these things, one half has the likeness of the kingdom of God, the other half of hell. For there is commingling of evil and good persons together in this world. But in the kingdom of God there are no evil persons, but only good; and in hell there are no good, but only evil: and each place is filled from the middle.' On this text, see *BCLL*, no. 309. There is a version of this theme in the *Collectanea Bedae*, but without the term *similitudines*: 'Tres principales mansiones constituit Deus: coelum, et terram, et infernum: et in illis tribus tres principales res. In coelo constituit pacem et aeternitatem; in terra autem constituit fidem et poenitentiam, et remissionem peccatorum; in inferno constituit timorem et aeternam poenam, et nullam remissionem. De terra autem, quae in medio posita est, replebitur coelum et infernus' (PL 94, 542C). See also *The Irish Liber Hymnorum*, ed. Bernard and Atkinson I, 89. McNally, *Der irische Liber de numeris*, pp. 42–3, compares the above passage from *De tribus habitaculis* with another theme in the *Liber de numeris* entitled *de duobus infernis*.

221 *Rogationtide Homilies*, ed. Bazire and Cross, p. 71, lines 44–5: 'the likenesses which the wise man spoke of concerning the kingdom of heaven and hell'. The homilist does, however, list a series of miseries which do not exist in heaven. A closely parallel passage in another homily does not use the word *gelicnysse* (*ibid*., p. 113, line 126).

Ðær bið lif butan deaþe 7 god butan ende 7 yld butan sare 7 dæg butan nihte, and þær bið gefea butan unrotnesse 7 rice butan awendednesse.[222]

This pattern is common in rhetorical descriptions of heaven in Irish and Anglo-Saxon sources.[223] The nouns filling out the basic antithetical pattern vary somewhat from text to text, but one particular pattern, listing seven antitheses with a tag such as 'Septem sunt miracula qui non inueniuntur in hoc saeculo',[224] was particularly well established. This motif is found in many Hiberno-Latin sources, including the *Liber de numeris*, the *Collectanea Bedae* and the *Catechesis Celtica*,[225] and in florilegia

222 *The Vercelli Homilies*, ed. Scragg, p. 178, lines 173–5: 'There will be life without death and good without end and old age without pain and day without night, and there will be joy without sadness and kingdom without change.'

223 On this rhetorical pattern, see Tristram, *Sex aetates mundi*, p. 334, n. 61; *idem*, 'Stock Descriptions', pp. 104–5. Vercelli IX also includes a sequence of five antitheses in the same form describing hell (*The Vercelli Homilies*, ed. Scragg, p. 172, lines 132–4). See D. Johnson, 'The Five Horrors of Hell: an Insular Homiletic Motif', forthcoming in *ES*.

224 'There are seven miracles which are not found in this world.'

225 See McNally, *Der irische Liber de numeris*, p. 116; Ó Laoghaire, 'Irish Elements in the *Catechesis Celtica*', p. 147. Bazire and Cross, *Rogationtide Homilies*, p. 12, note two further Latin examples in pseudo-Augustinian sermons. Marchand, 'The Old Norwegian Christmas Homily', p. 30, who cites similar examples in Old High German, describes the theme as a 'patristic commonplace', but neither of his examples is patristic (one is pseudo-Augustine, *Sermo ad fratres in eremo* 64, PL 40, 1351; cf. PL 40, 1353). The secondary references he cites (nn. 3–4) also provide no genuine patristic examples, but rather the sermons attributed to Boniface, and a few anonymous sermons and falsely attributed works. Only one is from an identifiable Carolingian author, Emmo (Hemmo), *Liber de qualitate caelestis patriae ex sanctorum patrum opusculis excerptus* (PL 118, 878; for the attribution, see A. Wilmart, 'Lettres de l'époque Carolingienne', *RB* 34 (1922), 236). No doubt the theme became generally popular (for an example in a tenth-century Fulda manuscript, see Steinmeyer and Sievers, *Die althochdeutschen Glossen* IV, 435), but the early Latin examples are mostly from texts with Insular connections. A sermon first ed. W. Scherer, 'Eine lateinische Musterpredigt aus der Zeit Karls des Grossen', *Zeitschrift für deutsches Altertum* 12 (1865), 436–46, which corresponds largely to a homily ed. G. di S. Teresa, 'Ramenta Patristica 1: Il florilegio pseudoagostiniano palatino', *Ephemerides Carmeliticae* 14 (1963), 195–241, at 238–41 (see Wright, 'Hiberno-Latin', no. *49) has a form of the motif: 'ubi lux sine tenebris et uita sine morte, ubi est laetitia et gaudium sine fine, ubi iuuentus laeta sine meta senectutis, ubi salus sine egritudine, ubi securitas sine timore, ubi regnum inmutabile' (ed. Scherer, p. 441). K. Gamber, *Niceta von Remesiana*, pp. 176–81, seeks to identify this sermon (known to him only in the defective Vienna manuscript) as part of the *Instructio ad competentes*

such as the *Collectaneum* of Sedulius Scottus and the *Florilegium Frisingense*, as well as the dialogue in Clm. 19410 (p. 20).[226]

Thomas D. Hill and other scholars have drawn attention to several reflexes of this theme in Old English homilies and in *Christ III*.[227] None of the Old English examples includes a tag announcing a specific number; as a result, the motif is unstable, yet there are enough common items to reveal its ultimate derivation from the Hiberno-Latin theme. The following chart shows the correspondences between the list in Vercelli IX and the *Liber de numeris*:

Liber de numeris:	Vercelli IX:
1. uita sine morte	1. lif butan deaðe
2. iuuentus sine senectute	3. (yld butan sare)
3. lux sine tenebris	4. dæg butan nihte
4. gaudium sine tristitia	5. gefea butan unrotnesse
5. pax sine discordia	
6. uoluntas sine iniuria	
7. regnum sine commutatione	6. rice butan awendednesse

The Latin has no equivalent for the second antithesis in Vercelli IX, *god butan ende*, while Vercelli IX has no equivalent for the fifth and sixth

of Nicetas (d. after 414). If the identification is correct, this work would have to be regarded as an ultimate source for the motif in Hiberno-Latin texts. But Gamber was unaware of Scherer's attribution of the sermon to the Carolingian period, and Frede, *Kirchenschriftsteller*, p. 461, in his listing for the *Instructio* (NIC frg) does not follow Gamber in adding to the previously identified fragments of that work.

226 Sedulius lists 'octo beatitudines quae in caelesti regno deputantur' (*Sedulii Scotti Collectaneum Miscellaneum* XVIII.21, ed. Simpson, p. 139). See also the *Florilegium Frisingense*, in *Florilegia*, ed. Lehner, pp. 35–6 (no. 430). Clm. 19410 (p. 32) lists five items as 'dona ... regni dei'.

227 Thomas D. Hill, 'The Seven Joys of Heaven in "Christ III" and Old English Homiletic Texts', *NQ* 214 (1969), 165–6. Other examples have been noted by P. Szarmach, 'Vercelli Homily XX', *MS* 35 (1973), 1–26, at 26, and by Bazire and Cross, *Rogationtide Homilies*, pp. 11–12. Variations on the list, with varying numbers of items, occur in Vercelli Homilies V, IX, XIX, XX, and XXI, Napier XXIX, Bazire and Cross no. 1, and in the Old English Apocalypse of Thomas homily ('A New Version of the Apocalypse of Thomas', ed. Förster, p. 18). For examples in the Leabhar Breac homilies, see *The Passions and the Homilies*, trans. Atkinson, pp. 391, 400, 413, 418 and 430. For Welsh examples, see *Vita S. Kebii*, in *Vitae Sanctorum Britanniae et Genealogiae*, ed. A. W. Wade-Evans (Cardiff, 1944), p. 248; *The Welsh Life of St David*, ed. D. Simon Evans (Cardiff, 1988), p. 14.

items in the Latin. The third item in the Vercelli Book text of the homily, *yld butan sare*, appears to be a conflation of readings preserved in L's *iugoð butan yldo* (*iuuentus sine senectute*) and *hælo butan sare* (corresponding to *sanitas sine dolore*, as in the *Catechesis Celtica*).[228]

This study of the numerical preparatory motifs in Vercelli IX has not identified any 'sources' in the strict sense of the word. Certainly, the homilist did not directly consult any of the surviving Hiberno-Latin florilegia I have surveyed, at least not in the forms in which they have come down to us. But we are not likely to find the actual florilegium the Vercelli homilist consulted. Only those florilegia with a specific and fixed organization, like the *Liber scintillarum*, or even the *Liber de numeris*, would be copied and recopied in relatively unaltered form. Most florilegia were haphazard collections of whatever material the compiler had at hand; they were not intended as self-sufficient 'texts' to be maintained in their integrity, but rather were commonplace books to be plundered and modified according to the practical needs of the preacher.

None the less, we can draw certain conclusions about the Vercelli homilist's florilegium. Certainly, a substantial part must have consisted of numerical motifs. Some of these were mere lists, as in the Karlsruhe and Zurich florilegia, but perhaps organized in numerical order as in the *Liber de numeris*. Such an arrangement may well have suggested the numerical structure of the preparatory motif section: *three* deaths and lives, *four* separations and *five* likenesses of hell. But other numerical motifs in the florilegium were probably already elaborated as homiletic set pieces, as in the *Catechesis Celtica* or in the sermons *In nomine Dei summi*. But whatever its exact form and organization, the homilist's florilegium transmitted much material from the Irish tradition.

[228] See Scragg, *The Vercelli Homilies*, note to lines 173–5. See also Bazire and Cross, *Rogationtide Homilies*, p. 15, n. 42.

3

The *Visio S. Pauli* and the Insular vision of hell

The fifth 'likeness' of hell, torment (*tintrega*), affords the Vercelli homilist an opportunity to elaborate on the pains of hell through a series of motifs culminating in the devil's account of hell. Echoing his earlier claim that no man can express the good things that God has prepared in heaven, the homilist states that 'nænig man ... mæge mid his wordum asecgan hu mycel þære fiftan helle sar is'.[1] He then amplifies the theme of inexpressibility with three motifs that frame the central exemplum – the Hanging Sinner, the Men with Tongues of Iron and the Monster of Hell. These motifs derive ultimately from interpolations characteristic of the short redactions of the Apocalypse of Paul, but each developed in distinctive ways in Insular tradition.

THE *VISIO S. PAULI* IN IRELAND AND ANGLO-SAXON ENGLAND

Composed in Greek perhaps as early as the third century,[2] the Apocalypse of Paul was the most influential apocryphal vision in the Middle Ages. Two Long Latin versions have survived, as well as a series of redactions.[3] The redactions of the *Visio S. Pauli* (as the Latin versions

[1] *The Vercelli Homilies*, ed. Scragg, p. 168, lines 107–8: 'no man ... can express with his words how great the pain of the fifth (likeness of) hell is'.

[2] On the date and origin of the Apocalypse, see R. P. Casey, 'The Apocalypse of Paul', *JTS* 34 (1933), 1–32, and T. Silverstein, 'The Date of the "Apocalypse of Paul"', *MS* 24 (1962), 335–48.

[3] The definitive edition and study of the Latin versions is Silverstein, *Visio Sancti Pauli*. This edition contains the St Gallen text (Recension L^1) and Vienna fragment (Recension L^2) of the Long versions, together with seven of the eight redactions (I–III and V–VIII) which Silverstein had then distinguished. Silverstein omitted the

are called) eliminate much of the Long Latin text, including the episode of the going-out of souls and the entire vision of heaven, focusing instead on Paul's guided tour of hell, which they embellish with lurid interpolations.[4] Theodore Silverstein was able to identify some eleven separate redactions.[5] Apart from the distinctive Redaction VI, which survives in two ninth-century manuscripts, the earliest manuscripts of these redactions are only eleventh century, but reflexes of three interpolated motifs peculiar to these redactions in Blickling Homily XVI and Vercelli Homily IX – the Hanging Sinner, the Men with Tongues of Iron and the Dragon Parthemon – suggest that a redaction circulated in England in some form in the tenth century.[6]

Paris text of the Long version (Recension L[1]), previously ed. James, *Apocrypha Anecdota*, pp. 11–42, as well as the important Redaction IV, of which several texts had been printed previously (for these editions, see below, n. 14). Silverstein later identified two more manuscripts of Recension L[2], and additional manuscripts of the redactions, including three new redactions (IX, X and *Br*). See Silverstein, 'The Graz and Zürich Apocalypse of Saint Paul: an Independent Medieval Witness to the Greek', in *Medieval Learning and Literature: Essays presented to Richard William Hunt*, ed. J. J. G. Alexander and M. T. Gibson (Oxford, 1976), pp. 166–80; *idem*, 'New Links and Patterns'. Another partial text of L[1], overlooked by Silverstein and later scholars, was printed from Escorial, Real Biblioteca, A. II. 3 (s. x^{ex}) by P. G. Antolín, 'Opúsculos desconocidos de San Jerónimo', *Revista de Archivios, Bibliotecas y Museos* 20 (1909), 60–80, at 75–80. This version corresponds to James's text, sections 18–23 and 25–33 (p. 21, line 3 – p. 28, line 33), but with considerable corruption. For English translations based chiefly on James's Latin text, see James, *Apocryphal New Testament*, pp. 526–55, and Hennecke and Schneemelcher, *New Testament Apocrypha* II, 759–98. For translations of Greek, Syriac and other versions, see Silverstein, *Visio Sancti Pauli*, pp. 98–9. French translations of Armenian versions have been published by L. Leloir, *Écrits Apocryphes sur les Apôtres*, Corpus Christianorum Series Apocryphorum 3 (Turnhout, 1986), 112–72.

4 These are '(1) the infernal rivers and the enumeration of the torments, (2) the dragon, (3) the burning trees upon which sinners hang, (4) the furnace with its flames of divers colors, (5) the fiery wheel, (6) the dangerous bridge across the stream of Hell, and (7) the granting of respite for the damned souls' (Silverstein, *Visio Sancti Pauli*, p. 64). Redaction VI has its own peculiar series of interpolations (see *ibid.*, pp. 82–90).

5 For the textual tradition of the redactions, see *ibid.*, pp. 40–63, and Silverstein, 'New Links and Patterns', pp. 224–5.

6 See Silverstein, *Visio Sancti Pauli*, pp. 6–12, where the author discusses briefly Blickling XVI and the Hanging Sinners, Napier XLIII (which has part of 'The Devil's Account') and the Men with Tongues of Iron, as well as passages from

The Old English adaptations of motifs from the *Visio S. Pauli* in the Blickling homilies and elsewhere, which have been conveniently catalogued by Antonette diPaolo Healey,[7] reflect the important role of Anglo-Saxon England in the early history and transmission of the apocalypse. Aldhelm's disparaging allusion to a Long Latin version of the *Visio* in his prose *De uirginitate*[8] testifies to its availability in England in the late seventh century, and Ælfric's condemnation of the work near the other end of the Anglo-Saxon period only confirms its continued popularity.[9] A fragmentary Old English translation of a Long Latin text survives,[10] and there are significant connections with England in the manuscript tradition of the redactions. Twenty-one of the fifty-six known manuscripts of the redactions are English,[11] a fact 'which points', in Silverstein's words, 'if not to the origin of the abbreviated versions, at least to their special popularity in England'.[12] Regarding

Napier XLVI on the assembly of the devils and angels before God at sunrise and sunset and the going-out of souls. Silverstein also refers to an English version of the *Visio* in the Lambeth homilies, in *Old English Homilies and Homiletic Treatises*, ed. Morris, pp. 40–7. This homily is based on Redaction III but has certain details showing contamination from Redaction IV (Silverstein, *Visio Sancti Pauli*, pp. 97–8, n. 54; 'New Links and Patterns', p. 224). On the Lambeth homily and the *Visio S. Pauli*, see also van Os, *Religious Visions*, p. 139.

[7] Healey, *The Old English Vision*, pp. 41–57; see also her summary of the evidence in *Sources of Anglo-Saxon Literary Culture*, ed. Biggs *et al.*, pp. 66–7.

[8] *Aldhelmi Opera*, ed. Ehwald, p. 256, trans. Lapidge and Herren, *Aldhelm: the Prose Works*, p. 81: 'does [Paul] not, because of the privilege of his pure integrity, traverse the third heaven contemplating the secrets of the heavenly citizens with chaste vision, and exploring the mysteries of the celestial army with (his) ineffable account of events, even though the so-called *Revelatio Pauli* says foolishly that he came to the delights of flowering Paradise in a golden ship? But divine law forbids the followers of the catholic faith to believe more, in any respect, than what the judgment of canonical truth promulgates, and the decrees of the orthodox fathers in decretal writings have sanctioned the utter rejection and complete banishment of the other absurdities of the apocrypha as being a cacophonous thunder of words.'

[9] *Ælfric's Catholic Homilies: the Second Series*, ed. M. Godden, EETS ss 5 (London, 1979), p. 190, lines 14–16: 'Humeta rædað sume men. ða leasan gesetnysse. ðe hí hatað paulus gesihðe. nu hé sylf sæde. þæt he ða digelan word gehyrde. þe nán eorðlic mann sprecan ne mót.' See Godden's remarks in 'Ælfric and the Vernacular Prose Tradition', p. 101.

[10] *The Old English Vision*, ed. Healey. On the relationship of the Old English version (in Oxford, Bodleian Library, Junius 85/86) to the Latin texts, see *ibid*, pp. 26–30.

[11] The figures are Healey's, *ibid*, p. 20, n. 8.

[12] Silverstein, *Visio Sancti Pauli*, p. 10.

Redaction IV, 'the version which was most frequently translated into the vernaculars and through which the Visio Pauli chiefly left its mark on the general body of vision literature of the later Middle Ages',[13] Silverstein remarked on the 'evidence of a special currency in England (perhaps even its origins there)'.[14] In Rudolf Willard's opinion, 'The formation of this version must have been accomplished in the British Isles, under Celtic influence; surely it is through insular channels that certain of the interpolations peculiar to this redaction became incorporated in the vision.'[15]

The *Visio S. Pauli* was also well known in medieval Ireland. Themes identified by Healey as having been furnished to Anglo-Saxon authors by the *Visio* are also prominent in Irish literature, including the going-out of souls and the respite of the damned.[16] The *Visio* exerted a profound influence on Irish visionary texts such as *Fís Adamnán*, the *Nauigatio S. Brendani*[17] and the *Visio Tnugdali*,[18] as well as the *Purgatorium S. Patricii*, which Silverstein regards as the 'English-Irish pendant' of

[13] *Ibid.*, p. 52.

[14] Silverstein, 'New Links and Patterns', p. 212. On Redaction IV, see *idem*, *Visio Sancti Pauli*, pp. 52–6. Silverstein does not print this redaction, which must be consulted in Brandes's edition, *Visio S. Pauli*, pp. 75–80. For other texts of Redaction IV, see PL 94, 501–2, and P. Meyer, 'La descente de Saint-Paul en enfer', *Romania* 24 (1895), 365–75 (repr. van Os, *Religious Visions*, pp. 264–6).

[15] Willard, 'The Latin Texts', p. 157. Two stylistic features of Redaction IV suggest Irish influence. The distinctive opening sentence, 'Dies dominicus dies est electus, in quo gaudebant angeli et archangeli maior diebus ceteris' (*Visio S. Pauli*, ed. Brandes, p. 75), is reminiscent of the refrain 'Dies dominicus dies beatus, in qua ...' of Recension II of the Hiberno-Latin treatises *Dies Dominica* (*Scriptores Hiberniae Minores I*, ed. McNally, pp. 185–6; see *BCLL*, nos. 903–5; Wright, 'Hiberno-Latin', no. *4). See also Recension II, 'Dies dominicus, dies letus, dies beatus, dies uenerabiles ... ' (*Scriptores Hiberniae Minores I*, ed. McNally, p. 183) and Recension I, 'in ceteris diebus omnium dierum dominicus maior est' (*ibid.*, p. 181). Similarly, the question 'quis primus rogauit ut animae haberent requiem in inferno ...?' recalls the 'quis primus' questions that Bischoff identified as an Irish symptom in exegetical texts ('Turning-Points', p. 102).

[16] On the going-out of souls, see Seymour, 'The Bringing Forth of the Soul in Irish Literature'; *idem*, 'Notes on Apocrypha in Ireland', p. 108; McNamara, *The Apocrypha in the Irish Church*, pp. 107–13 (nos. 91C, 91E and 91F). On the respite of the damned, see Gougaud, 'La croyance au répit périodique', pp. 63–72; Silverstein, *Visio Sancti Pauli*, pp. 12 and 95, n. 28.

[17] See G. Orlandi, *Navigatio Sancti Brendani: Introduzione* (Milan, 1968), pp. 124–9.

[18] See Spilling, *Die Visio Tnugdali*, p. 57.

the *Visio S. Pauli*.[19] Just as Redaction IV has special connections with England, so Redaction VI, which differs strikingly from the other redactions, has special connections with Ireland. Silverstein stresses its 'numerous and obvious' similarities with Irish vision literature,[20] an observation confirmed by David Dumville, whose investigation of its influence on *Fís Adamnán* concludes that Redaction VI 'was composed, if not in Ireland, at any rate in an Irish continental centre retaining the closest links with the home culture'.[21] Dumville notes further points of contact between the *Visio S. Pauli* and the Seven Heavens apocryphon transmitted in *Fís Adamnán*, Recension III of *Tenga Bithnua* and in the *Apocrypha Priscillianistica* in the Karlsruhe florilegium, whose Irish connections I have outlined in the preceding chapter.[22]

In addition to Redactions IV and VI, which both appear to have taken shape in an Insular milieu, another unique redaction, recently published by M. E. Dwyer,[23] also has Insular connections. This redaction provides crucial evidence for reconstructing the development of the motif of the Hanging Sinner in Old English texts, in particular for the topographical setting of the vision of hell attributed to Paul in Blickling Homily XVI, with its striking parallels to the description of Grendel's mere in *Beowulf*. Unlike the redactions identified by Silverstein, Redaction XI (as Dwyer has designated this new text) preserves in abbreviated form Paul's tour of heaven as well as his tour of hell. Wholly independent of the other redactions, it lacks their characteristic interpolations, except for a brief scene that combines elements from the Hanging Sinner and the Bridge of Hell. The author of Redaction XI has taken considerable liberties in abbreviating a Long Latin text of the *Visio*, not only by omission and conflation, but also by addition of substantial and apparently original scenes.

[19] Silverstein, *Visio Sancti Pauli*, pp. 3 and 14. A later Irish vision influenced by the *Visio S. Pauli* is *Fís Merlino* (see McNamara, *The Apocrypha in the Irish Church*, p. 109, no. 91D).

[20] Silverstein, *Visio Sancti Pauli*, p. 89; on Redaction VI, see pp. 58–9 and 82–90. Silverstein believed that 'the Irish visions and Redaction VI are independent debtors to a third and non-extant work' that drew upon the Apocalypse of Peter (pp. 89–90).

[21] 'Towards an Interpretation of *Fís Adamnán*', p. 70. See also Silverstein, 'Dante and the Legend of the *Mi'rāj*', p. 78.

[22] 'Towards an Interpretation of *Fís Adamnán*', pp. 67–9. On the *Apocrypha Priscillianistica*, see above, pp. 64–5.

[23] 'An Unstudied Redaction'.

I have argued elsewhere for an Insular, probably Irish origin of Redaction XI.[24] As Dwyer noted, both Redaction XI and Redaction VI 'are extant in manuscripts of the ninth century, and both have Irish or Anglo-Saxon connections'.[25] Redaction XI survives in a single manuscript, Vatican, Biblioteca Apostolica, Pal. lat. 220 (Middle or Upper Rhineland, s. ix^{in}), written in Anglo-Saxon script.[26] Dwyer was unaware that McNally had published from the same manuscript the homilies *In nomine Dei summi*, which he regarded as Hiberno-Latin. Pal. lat. 220 also contains the interpolated version of the Apocalypse of Thomas,[27] an apocryphon which was known in Ireland and was translated in Anglo-Saxon England,[28] as well as a recension of another Hiberno-Latin text, *Dies Dominica*, which had previously been edited by McNally.[29] Immediately following Redaction XI (and immediately preceding the tract *Dies Dominica*) occurs an enumerative motif encountered in several Hiberno-Latin compilations.[30] In short, the manuscript has significant connections with Irish traditions and is a valuable witness to apocryphal texts known to the Irish as well as to the Anglo-Saxons,[31] including material now considered to be of Celtic origin.

[24] Wright, 'Some Evidence for an Irish Origin of Redaction XI'.

[25] Dwyer, 'An Unstudied Redaction', p. 136.

[26] See Bischoff, 'Lorsch im Spiegel seiner Handschriften', in *Die Reichsabtei Lorsch: Festschrift zum Gedenken an ihre Stiftung 764*, ed. F. Knöpp, 2 vols. (Darmstadt, 1973–7) II, 7–128, at 49, with further references at 108–9. The manuscript was at Lorsch in the tenth century, when the *Lorscher Bienensegen* was added in the margin of one of the folios (58r) containing part of Redaction XI of the *Visio*; see Bischoff, 'Paläographische Fragen', p. 88, and n. 27 for reference to a facsimile of this folio.

[27] Variants from Pal. lat. 220 are included in the edition by D. P. Bihlmeyer, 'Un texte non interpolé de l'Apocalypse de Thomas', *RB* 28 (1911), 270–82 (Bihlmeyer's Text P). Bihlmeyer (pp. 278–81) drew attention to parallels with the Seven Heavens apocryphon from the *Apocrypha Priscillianistica* in the Karlsruhe florilegium.

[28] See McNamara, *The Apocrypha in the Irish Church*, pp. 119–21 (no. 96); Heist, *The Fifteen Signs*; Förster, 'A New Version of the Apocalypse of Thomas'; M. McC. Gatch, 'Two Uses of Apocrypha in Old English Homilies', *Church History* 33 (1964), 379–91; and the entry by F. Biggs in *Sources of Anglo-Saxon Literary Culture*, ed. Biggs *et al.*, pp. 68–9.

[29] See above, p. 109, n. 15.

[30] McNally, 'Seven Hiberno-Latin Sermons', p. 132, n. 39, noted that the enumeration *septem scale sunt quibus ascendentur regna celorum* is found in Hiberno-Latin tradition, but gave no references. For some examples, see above, p. 73.

[31] The sermons in the manuscript transmit a core of texts used in some form by Old

In addition to the manuscript context, certain linguistic features of Redaction XI are also consistent with an Irish origin.[32] But the most compelling internal evidence for an Irish connection is the quotation of verses 4–6 of the *Te Deum*. The Irish texts of this hymn provide an excellent illustration of what Edmund Bishop called the Irish 'tinkering method'.[33] There are several quite distinctive readings in the Irish text tradition, including in the lines quoted by Redaction XI, which read 'incessabili uoce proclamant dicentes SANCTUS SANCTUS SANCTUS, dominus deus sabaoth, pleni sunt celi ET uniuersa terra honore glorie tue'.[34] These lines (closely paralleling the Sanctus of the Mass liturgy)[35] follow the Irish textual tradition of the hymn, which regularly inserts the word *uniuersa*; the phrase '*honore* glorie tue' is similarly characteristic of Irish texts of the hymn (where the Milan and Ordinary or Roman recensions read *maiestatis* instead of *honore*).[36] The English texts all agree

English homilies in Oxford, Bodleian Library, Junius 85/86; London, BL, Cotton Faustina A. ix; and Cambridge, Corpus Christi College 302. See Wright, '*Docet Deus, Docet Diabolus*', p. 452, and below, pp. 215–16 and 244–5. See also Cross, *Cambridge, Pembroke College MS 25*, pp. 245–7, for another anonymous sermon in the collection, where the text of Pal. lat. 220 is closer to the version used by the Pembroke homilist than the one printed by Migne.

32 For details, see Wright, 'Some Evidence for an Irish Origin of Redaction XI'.

33 Bishop, *Liturgica Historica*, p. 166; cf. p. 84, n. 6 and p. 86, n. 19. Wilmart, *The Bobbio Missal: Notes and Studies*, p. 57, n. 1, quotes a remark by Bishop that in liturgy the Irish 'respect nothing, but disfigure every scrap they can lay their hand on'.

34 'An Unstudied Redaction', ed. Dwyer, p. 127 (sect. ix, lines 12–14): '[two angels] proclaim with unceasing voice, "Holy, Holy, Holy, Lord God of hosts, heaven and all earth are full of the honour of your glory"'.

35 The subject of an exhaustive study by Cagin, *L'Euchologie*; see especially pp. 58–109.

36 See Bernard and Atkinson, *The Irish Liber Hymnorum* II, 139. The text printed by Bernard and Atkinson (I, 59) agrees exactly with Redaction XI, including the addition of *dicentes*. The readings of five Irish texts, together with the English texts from the Book of Cerne and Book of Nunnaminster, can be consulted in M. Frost, 'The Irish Text of the *Te Deum*', *The Church Quarterly Review* 203 (1926), 136–41. For a table comparing the Irish, Milan, Ordinary and Greek recensions of the *Te Deum*, see the article by J. Wordsworth in J. Julian, *Dictionary of Hymnology* (London, 1908), pp. 1120–1; for a table comparing two Irish texts of the hymn with the version of the Roman breviary, see F. E. Warren, *The Antiphonary of Bangor*, 2 vols. (London, 1895) II, 93–5 (Warren also included the text of London, BL, Harley 7653, under the assumption that it was Irish). The reading *uniuersa* is also found in the Sanctus of the Stowe Missal (see Cagin, *L'Euchologie*, pp. 377 and 401). The reading *dicentes*, paralleled in the Sanctus in several early missals (*ibid.*, p. 108 and n. 4), is found in

with the Milan and Ordinary recensions against the Irish.[37] The cumulative weight of this evidence suggests that Redaction XI was compiled by an Irish monk or nun, probably on the Continent.

Redactions IV, VI and XI bear witness to the important role played by the Irish and Anglo-Saxons in disseminating variant and interpolated versions of the *Visio S. Pauli*. As Dwyer noted, both Redactions VI and XI 'stand apart from the main body of the medieval Latin redactions. They are unique in their connection to the Long Latin version, and their authors exercise much more freedom in their use of the Long Latin original.'[38] The *Visio* was a seminal text to which Insular authors turned for memorable descriptions of hell, one they felt free to embellish in distinctive ways. Of particular interest is Dumville's suggestion that the *Visio S. Pauli* and *Fís Adamnán* 'shared eschatological motifs which may well have belonged to a common stock available to Irish ecclesiastical writers of the earlier Middle Ages'.[39] Part of this common stock are distinctive elaborations of three eschatological motifs deriving from the *Visio* – the Hanging Sinner, the Men with Tongues of Iron and the Dragon Parthemon – which appear in a variety of Irish and Anglo-Saxon texts, including Vercelli IX.

THE HANGING SINNER

On the authority of 'holy books', the homilist informs us that *helle hus* is twice as deep as from the roof of heaven to the earth, and that it is filled with terrible fire and extreme cold.[40] Although the torments of hell are inexpressible, the homilist attempts to suggest their horror by positing a grotesque hypothetical torment:

three of the Irish versions of the *Te Deum* collated by Frost, and is also attested in citations in the commentary to the *Amra Coluim Cille* and Prayer of Adomnán (see Bernard and Atkinson, *The Irish Liber Hymnorum* II, 139).

37 The five Irish versions collated by Frost all agree against the two English texts in the readings *uniuersa* and *honore*. A prayer in another English manuscript (London, BL, Harley 7653, s. viii/ix) quotes these lines from the *Te Deum*, omitting *uniuersa* and *honore* (the script of Harley 7653 was once thought to be Irish, but is instead Anglo-Saxon; see *CLA* II, no. 204). For English texts of the *Te Deum*, see A. S. Cook, 'The Old English Glosses of the *Te Deum*', *Archiv* 122 (1909), 263–8.

38 'An Unstudied Redaction', p. 136.

39 'Towards an Interpretation of *Fís Adamnán*', p. 70.

40 *The Vercelli Homilies*, ed. Scragg, p. 170, lines 114–22.

For ðan gif hwylc man bið on hell ane niht, þonne bið him leofre, gif he þanon mot, þæt he hangie siofon þusend wintra on þam lengestan treowe ufeweardum þe ofer sæ standeð on þam hyhstan sæclife,[41] [7 syn þa fet gebundene to ðam hehstan telgan 7 þæt heafod hangige ofdunrihte 7 þa fet uprihte, 7 him sige þæt blod ut þurh þone muð, 7 hine þonne gesece ælc þæra yfela þe æfre on helle sy, 7 hine ælc yð gesece mid þam hehstan þe seo sæ forðbringð, 7 þeah hine ælc tor gesece þe on eallum clyfum syndon, þonne wile he eall þis luflice þrowian wið ðan þe he næfre eft helle ne gesece.[42]

The description draws its force not merely from its gruesome detail, but from the implication that such tortures are mild in comparison to those of hell.[43] None the less, the substance of the description derives from apocryphal visions of hell. The hanging punishment is a topos of infernal descriptions from Plato's *Gorgias* to early Christian apocalypses. Of the Christian visions that include it, most noteworthy are the Greek Apocalypse of Peter and Acts of Thomas, the Apocalypse of Paul and the fragmentary Elijah apocalypse.[44] In all these visions the hanging

[41] At this point a lacuna in the Vercelli Book text is supplied from E.

[42] *Ibid.*, p. 170, lines 122–30: 'For if any man were in hell for a single night, thereafter it would be more agreeable to him, if he could escape from there, that he should hang for seven thousand years atop the tallest tree that stands on the highest seacliff, [and that his feet should be bound to the highest branch, and his head should hang upside down and his feet upright, and the blood flow out through the mouth, and every evil that ever existed in hell should afflict him, and every wave with the highest the sea produces, and even if every rock from all cliffs should beset him, yet will he endure all this provided that he should never again visit hell.' The version in L (ed. Scragg, p. 171, lines L.97–8) introduces a motif concerning the length of Doomsday: 'then he will gladly endure all this, though he have to be (there) six thousand years and also the thousand on which Doomsday takes place, provided that he never again visit hell'. The thousand-year duration of Doomsday (based on a literal understanding of II Pet. III.8) occurs in another Old English homily showing Irish influence, an Easter homily ed. Lees, 'Theme and Echo', pp. 122–3, lines 159–61 (cf. Lees, p. 138, n. 71). The idea is found in several Irish sources as well, including the *Catechesis Celtica*, in *Analecta Reginensia*, ed. Wilmart, p. 56; 'Tidings of Doomsday', ed. Stokes, p. 252; and *Saltair na Rann*, ed. Stokes, p. 123, lines 8389–92.

[43] The motifs of the hypothetical torment and the single night in hell occur again later in the devil's account of hell, and can be paralleled in Latin and Irish tales. See below, pp. 190–1 and 207–9.

[44] The hanging punishment in apocryphal literature is surveyed by Himmelfarb, *Tours of Hell*, pp. 84–92.

punishment (often accompanied by immersion) exemplifies the principle of measure for measure. As the Elijah fragment expresses it, 'by the limb with which a man sinned, by the same limb will he be punished'.[45] Slanderers and blasphemers hang by their tongues, thieves by their hands and so on.

The hanging punishment remains a prominent feature in the Long Latin versions of the *Visio S. Pauli* as well as the redactions. Seven of the redactions (II – IV, VII – IX and X) include an interpolated passage which Silverstein labels the Hanging Sinners:

Et postea Paulus ductus ad portas inferni. Et uidit ibi arbores igneas, in quarum ramis peccatores cruciati pendebant: quidam per capillos, alii per pedes, alii per manus, alii per lingwas, alii per colla, alii per brachia, alii per membra diuersa.[46]

Unlike most visions that include the hanging punishment, the *Visio S. Pauli* does not specify the particular sins for which the sinners hang. But its grouping of the sinners through a list of the members by which they hang is paralleled in the Acts of Thomas and the Elijah apocalypse.[47]

A list of hanging sinners based on the *Visio S. Pauli* occurs in an anonymous Old English homily, transmitted indirectly by way of a Latin sermon in the Pembroke homiliary:

And eft hi gesawon synfulra manna sawla on witum earmlice fram deoflum gewriðene ... Sume þær hangiað be þam fotum, þæs þe us halige gewritu onwrigen habbað, and sume þær hangiað be þam handum, and sume þær hangiað be þam sweorum ... and	Et iterum: Viderunt animas peccatorum in poenis miserabiliter a daemonibus alligatas ... Alii enim pendunt ibi ex pedibus, alii ex manibus, alii ex uerticibus, alius ad genua, alius ad umbilicum, aliusque ad labia, alii usque ad capillos

[45] Quoted by Himmelfarb, p. 35. See her table, 'Measure-for-Measure Hanging Punishments', p. 87.

[46] Quotation from Redaction II, in *Visio Sancti Pauli*, ed. Silverstein, p. 156: 'And afterwards Paul was led to the gates of hell. And he saw there fiery trees, in whose branches tormented sinners were hanging: some by the hair, others by the feet, others by the hands, others by the tongue, others by the neck, others by the arms, others by various members.' See Silverstein's discussion of this motif, *ibid.*, pp. 69–72; for variant readings in manuscripts of Redaction IV, see p. 113, n. 43. For Redactions IX and X, see Silverstein, 'New Links and Patterns', pp. 238–9 and 244.

[47] See Silverstein, *Visio Sancti Pauli*, p. 70.

sume þær hangiað be heora feaxe capitum eorum.[49]
on þam þuruhhatan fyre.[48]

There can be little doubt of the influence of the *Visio* here, but the simple list of hanging sinners in the *Visio* hardly accounts for the more elaborate scene in Vercelli IX, and one might reasonably doubt whether the scene in the *Visio* can be considered more than a remote analogue, especially since, as Martha Himmelfarb has shown, 'Almost all the tours of hell contain some hanging punishments, but many of these punishments consist not of hanging by the sinful limb but simply of hanging or hanging upside down.'[50] Only in the *Visio S. Pauli*, however, do sinners hang from the branches of trees, as in Vercelli IX.[51] Still, this detail alone does not prove a relationship, since the idea of a tree as the instrument of the hanging punishment suggests itself readily enough,[52] and since the tree in Vercelli IX is not fiery, as are the trees in all known versions of the *Visio*. Nor does this detail account for the topographical setting of the hanging punishment in Vercelli IX, where the tree grows atop a great cliff overlooking the ocean.

Compelling evidence that the description of the Hanging Sinner in Vercelli IX is indeed a development of a version of the *Visio S. Pauli* comes from another Old English homily, Blickling XVI. This homily records a vision of hell in which sinners hang from trees that grow, like

[48] *Vier altenglische Predigten*, ed. Tristram, p. 168: 'And afterwards they saw the souls of sinful men in torment miserably bound by devils ... Some hung there by the feet, as holy writings have revealed to us, and some hung there by the hands, and some hung there by the neck ... and some hung by their hair in the exceedingly hot fire.' See also Tristram's discussion in 'Stock Descriptions', pp. 109–10.

[49] Ed. Cross, *Cambridge Pembroke College MS 25*, pp. 192–3.

[50] *Tours of Hell*, p. 86.

[51] Silverstein considers the fiery trees one of two 'distinctive characteristics' of the hanging punishment in the redactions (*Visio Sancti Pauli*, p. 69). In three other visions (the Vision of Alberic, the Greek Apocalypse of Mary and the Ethiopic Apocalypse of Baruch) sinners hang from trees, but all of these are thought to have been influenced by the Apocalypse of Paul. For the first two see *ibid.*, p. 71; for the last, see Himmelfarb, *Tours of Hell*, p. 101.

[52] One thinks immediately of Germanic analogues, including Othin's hanging. On death by hanging in ancient and Germanic tradition, see Himmelfarb, *Tours of Hell*, pp. 82–5, and H. R. Ellis Davidson, *Gods and Myths of Northern Europe* (New York, 1964), pp. 50–1.

the tree in Vercelli IX, from a great cliff overlooking the ocean. This scene, we are told, was witnessed by St Paul:

Swa sanctus paulus wæs geseonde on norðanweardne þisne middangeard þær ealle wætero niðergewítað 7 he þær geseah ofer ðæm wætere sumne hárne stán 7 wæron norð of ðæm stáne awexene swiðe hrimige bearwas 7 ðær wæron þystrogenipo 7 under þæm stáne wæs niccra eardung 7 wearga 7 he geseah þæt on ðæm clife hangodan on ðæm ísgean bearwum manige swearte saula be heora handum gebundne 7 þa fynd þara on nicra onlicnesse heora gripende wæron swa swa grædig wulf 7 þæt wæter wæs sweart under þæm clife neoðan 7 betuh þæm clife on ðæm wætre wæron swylce twelf mila 7 ðonne ða twigo forburston þonne gewitan þa saula niðer þa þe on ðæm twigum hangodan 7 him onfengon ða nicras.[53]

This passage has been celebrated for its striking similarities to the description of Grendel's mere in *Beowulf*, to which Richard Morris first drew attention.[54] In the poem, the monsters' abode and its surrounding landscape are described first by Hrothgar, the morning after the attack by Grendel's mother:

Hie dygel lond
warigeað wulfhleoþu, windige næssas,
frecne fengelad, ðær fyrgenstream
under næssa genipu niþer gewiteð,
flod under foldan. Nis þæt feor heonan
milgemearces, þæt se mere standeð;

[53] Text as printed from the manuscript by Collins, 'Blickling Homily XVI', p. 62: 'So St Paul was looking at this northern [part of the] world, where all waters go down, and there he saw over the water a grey rock, and to the north, grown exceedingly out of the rock, were frosty groves, and in that place were mists and darkness, and under the rock was the abode of water-monsters and wolves. And he saw that on the cliff many black souls were hanging on the icy groves, bound by their hands; and the (hellish) enemies of those (black souls), in the likeness of water-monsters, were taking hold of them even as a greedy wolf (would do); and the water was black under the cliff from beneath. And between the cliff and the water were such (black souls) for twelve miles, and when the boughs broke, then the souls that were hanging on the boughs went down and the water-monsters took them' (trans. Malone, 'Grendel and His Abode', pp. 304–5, with slight alterations). The homily is numbered XVII in Morris's edition, where the passage occurs at p. 209, line 29 – p. 211, line 5. Morris had numbered as Homily XVI a fragment which properly belongs with Homily IV; see R. Willard, *The Blickling Homilies*, EEMF 10 (Copenhagen, 1960), pp. 38–40, esp. n. 82.

[54] *The Blickling Homilies*, pp. vi–vii.

ofer þæm hongiað hrinde bearwas,
wudu wyrtum fæst wæter oferhelmað.
Þær mæg nihta gehwæm niðwundor seon,
fyr on flode. No þæs frod leofað
gumena bearna, þæt þone grund wite.
Ðeah þe hæðstapa hundum geswenced,
heorot hornum trum holtwudu sece,
feorran geflymed, ær he feorh seleð,
aldor on ofre, ær he in wille,
hafelan [beorgan]; nis þæt heoru stow!
Þonon yðgeblond up astigeð
won to wolcnum þonne wind styreþ,
lað gewidru, oð þæt lyft drysmaþ,
roderas reotað.[55]

Later, the poet describes the rugged approach as the Danes and Geats, following the tracks of Grendel's mother, arrive at the terrible place:

Ofereode þa æþelinga bearn
steap stanhliðo, stige nearwe,
enge anpaðas, uncuð gelad,
neowle næssas, nicorhusa fela;...
oþ þæt he færinga fyrgenbeamas
ofer harne stan hleonian funde,
wynleasne wudu; wæter under stod
dreorig ond gedrefed.[56]

[55] *Beowulf*, ed. Klaeber, pp. 51–2, lines 1357b–76a: 'They dwell in a land unknown, wolf-haunted slopes, wind-swept headlands, perilous marsh-paths, where the mountain stream goes down under the mists of the cliffs, – a flood under the earth. It is not far hence, in miles, that the lake stands over which hang groves covered with frost: the wood, firm-rooted, overshadows the water. There may be seen each night a fearful wonder, – fire on the flood! Of the sons of men none lives so wise as to know the bottom. Although, pressed by the hounds, the ranger of the heath, the hart strong in its horns, may seek the forest, chased from far, he will give up his life, his being, on the brink, sooner than he will plunge in it to save his head. That is no pleasant spot. Thence rises up the surging water darkly to the clouds, when the wind stirs up baleful storms, until the air grows misty, the heavens weep' (trans. J. R. Clark Hall, *Beowulf and the Fight at Finnsburg*, rev. ed. C. L. Wrenn (London, 1940), pp. 89–90).

[56] *Beowulf*, ed. Klaeber, p. 53, lines 1408–11 and 1414–17a: 'Then the son of nobles went over the steep, rocky slopes, the narrow ways, the thin, lone paths – an unknown course, – the beetling crags, many homes of water-monsters... till

The significant verbal parallels between the homily and the poem may be listed as follows:[57]

Blickling XVI	*Beowulf*
þær ealle wætero niðergewítað	ðær fyrgenstream niþer gewíteð (1359b–60b)
ofer ðæm wætere sumne hárne stán	fyrgenbeamas ofer harne stan (1414b–15a)
of ðæm stáne awexene swiðe hrimige bearwas	ofer þæm hongiað hrinde bearwas (1363)
ðær wæron þystrogenipo	under næssa genipu (1360a)
niccra eardung	nicorhusa fela (1411b)
7 þæt wæter wæs sweart under þæm clife neoðan	wæter under stod dreorig ond gedrefed (1416–17)

It is immediately clear that there is a close relationship between the two texts. Has one author borrowed directly from the other? If so, is the homilist indebted to the poet or the poet to the homilist? Or have both authors drawn independently on a third, intermediary source? All three possibilities have found advocates. Carleton Brown, the first to investigate the textual evidence in detail, concluded with Morris that the author of Blickling XVI had borrowed distinctive phrases from the poem.[58] Brown's argument seems to have convinced Klaeber, who had earlier preferred to attribute the verbal parallels between the two texts to a common source,[59] and until quite recently Brown's opinion was generally accepted.[60] Of course, so long as *Beowulf* was firmly anchored

suddenly he found mountain trees hanging over a grey rock – a dismal wood. The water was below, blood-stained and turbid' (trans. Clark Hall, p. 92).

57 The following list is based on Brown, '*Beowulf* and the *Blickling Homilies*', p. 908.

58 *Ibid.*, p. 909. Morris (*The Blickling Homilies*, p. vii) had considered the passage in the homily 'probably a direct reminiscence' of the poem.

59 Klaeber had suggested 'the use of the same or a very similar source' in the note to lines 1357ff. in his first edition (1922) of the poem (*Beowulf*, p. 183; see also his 'Die christlichen Elemente im *Beowulf*', *Anglia* 36 (1912), 169–99, at 185–7). But the note in his First Supplement (p. 456) appears to approve Brown's conclusions. Two other scholars, Hoops and Westlake, writing before Brown's article, had also argued for a common source; for references see Collins, 'Blickling Homily XVI', p. 64, n. 1.

60 P. Clemoes, however, sees 'no evidence compelling us to think that there was any direct link between the wording of the description in *Beowulf* and the wording of the

in the Age of Bede, it was not possible to argue that the poet had borrowed from a tenth-century homily. But in 1984, with the poem unmoored and adrift in the wake of *The Dating of Beowulf*, the late Rowland Collins argued just that.[61]

The problem of the relationship of these two Old English texts is further complicated by a third text, the *Visio S. Pauli*. As Silverstein first pointed out, the homilist's description of the souls hanging from icy trees is reminiscent of the description of the Hanging Sinners in the *Visio*. According to Silverstein, the Hanging Sinners scene was in fact the 'main foundation' of the description in the Blickling homily, while *Beowulf* 'furnished merely a transforming suggestion' to the homilist.[62] But this general parallel, unsupported by any distinctive verbal echoes, was the only direct connection adduced by Silverstein between the homily and the apocryphon. Furthermore, the trees in the *Visio* are fiery, not icy, a discrepancy which suggests that the homilist adapted that source quite freely, or else had access to a version substantially different from the extant redactions of the *Visio*. No one doubts,

homily itself', but thinks instead that the 'homily derived its depiction of the mouth of hell from a source which either suggested features in the scenery of Grendel's mere or was similar to one that did' ('Style as the Criterion for Dating the Composition of *Beowulf*', in *The Dating of Beowulf*, ed. C. Chase (Toronto, 1981), p. 181 and n. 27). N. K. Chadwick, 'The Monsters and Beowulf', in *The Anglo-Saxons: Studies in Some Aspects of their History and Culture presented to Bruce Dickins*, ed. P. Clemoes (London, 1959), pp. 171–203, at 177, states that 'A common literary tradition would seem to be the only tenable explanation' for the similar descriptions of the home of the monsters in Norse and English texts. C. L. Wrenn allows for the possibility 'that both the *Beowulf* poet and the Blickling Homilist were drawing independently from a common source among material now lost concerning Hell', but thinks that the homilist 'knew *Beowulf* well, and thought this passage an apt illustration and source for descriptive material suggested to him by the *Visio Pauli*' (*Beowulf with the Finnesburg Fragment* (London, 1953), p. 210).

61 Collins's chief evidence for reversing the conventional chronology is that the words '*þystrogenip* and *hrimige* are more nearly typical of the language of Homily XVI (because used both in the *Visio Pauli* section *and* outside it) than their analogues, *næssa genipu* and *hrinde bearwas* are of *Beowulf*' ('Blickling Homily XVI', p. 66). Collins did not believe, however, that his theory of the influence of Blickling XVI upon *Beowulf* requires a late dating of the poem, since the relevant passage could have been a late 'textual modification' of an earlier poem (*ibid.*, p. 69).

62 *Visio Sancti Pauli*, p. 11. Silverstein states that the flaming trees were added by the hypothetical Redaction β, itself derived from the archetypal Redaction α (*ibid.*, pp. 60–1).

however, that some version of this apocryphon must have influenced the Anglo-Saxon homilist, since trees are the instrument of the hanging punishment in both texts, and since the homilist does, after all, name Paul as the visionary.[63]

Evidence for the *Beowulf*-poet's knowledge of the *Visio S. Pauli*, on the other hand, is much less compelling. According to Carleton Brown, 'the descriptions in the *Visio* and *Beowulf* are wholly independent – except that trees occur in both – while the description in the Homily presents a fusion of elements in the other two'.[64] Brown's opinion on this point has also been accepted by most later scholars, including Healey, who cites Brown's argument in support of the cautiously phrased position 'that we cannot state with any certainty that the *Beowulf* poet knew the *Vision* and drew upon it'.[65]

Close comparison between Blickling XVI and all the surviving redactions of the *Visio S. Pauli* – a comparison which surprisingly seems never to have been made – reveals significant verbal parallels previously overlooked. These parallels show that the essential features of the description of hell in Blickling XVI derive from two separate scenes in the redactions that must have been conflated in the homilist's source, together with certain other stock elements of descriptions of hell, most of which can be found in the *Visio* itself. Moreover, the recently discovered Redaction XI, whose Irish characteristics I have detailed above, shows that some of the crucial features of this composite scene had indeed been combined in a Latin text at least a century prior to the composition of the Blickling homily. A similar comparison between *Beowulf* and the redactions of the *Visio* is unfortunately less conclusive, but does reveal at least one likely borrowing from the *Visio* that cannot have been derived from the homily. Because the relationship between the *Visio* and these two Old English texts is crucial to an understanding of the hanging torment in Vercelli IX, we must leave its hapless hypothetical victim hanging while this old problem is re-examined in the light of new evidence.

[63] Collins states simply that the passage in the homily 'is, without question, derived from the *Visio Pauli*' ('Blickling Homily XVI', p. 68). So far, however, only the motif of sinners hanging from trees has been shown to be derived from the *Visio*, leaving considerable detail unaccounted for.

[64] Brown, '*Beowulf* and the *Blickling Homilies*', p. 908.

[65] *The Old English Vision*, p. 52.

Blickling Homily XVI and the Visio S. Pauli

Silverstein's identification of the Hanging Sinners interpolation as 'the main foundation' of the description of hell in Blickling XVI – essentially correct if somewhat overstated – seems to have prevented him and subsequent scholars from examining more closely the remaining scenes of hell in the redactions for further parallels. In the *Visio*, hell is described in a series of isolated scenes linked only by phrases such as 'Vidit in alio loco... ' or 'Postea uidit...' One such scene, preserved in Redaction IV and four of its derivatives, describes a horrible river into which sinful souls plunge from a bridge overhead to be devoured by diabolical beasts in the water below:

Postea uidit flumen orribile, in quo multe bestie dyabolice erant quasi pisces in medio maris, que animas peccatrices deuorant sine ulla misericordia quasi lupi deuorant oues. Et desuper illud flumen est pons, per quem transeunt anime iuste sine ulla dubitacione, et multe peccatrices anime merguntur unaqueque secundum meritum suum. Ibi sunt multe bestie dyabolice multeque mansiones male preparate, sicut dicit dominus in ewangelio: 'Ligate eos per fasciculos ad comburendum; id est similes cum similibus, adulteros cum adulteris, rapaces cum rapacibus, iniquos cum iniquis.'[66]

As Silverstein has shown, this scene, an interpolation he labels the Bridge of Hell, has borrowed the bridge motif from a description in Gregory's *Dialogi* of a bridge which separates the wicked from the just.[67] According to Silverstein, however, the bridge motif itself 'was

[66] *Visio S. Pauli*, ed. Brandes, p. 76: 'Afterwards he saw a horrible river, in which were many demonic beasts like fish in the middle of the sea, who devour the sinful souls without any mercy as wolves devour sheep. And above that river is a bridge, which just souls cross without any hesitation, and many sinful souls sink, each according to its deserts. There are many demonic beasts and many evil dwellings prepared there, as the Lord says in the gospel: "Bind them in bundles to burn [Matth. XIII.30]; that is like with like, adulterers with adulterers, the violent with the violent, the iniquitous with the iniquitous."' The bridge scene also appears, with variations, in Redactions V (*Visio Sancti Pauli*, ed. Silverstein, p. 198), VIII (*ibid.*, p. 209), IX ('New Links and Patterns', pp. 239–40) and X (*ibid.*, p. 244).

[67] *Visio Sancti Pauli*, pp. 78–9. For Gregory's description, see PL 77, 385. Silverstein considered the allusion to the mansions of hell in the *Visio*, with the accompanying quotation of Matth. XIII.30, decisive proof of Gregory's influence, since Gregory

not part of the older forms of the Vision, nor did it occur in the mediaeval redactions, Latin or vernacular, until the author of Redaction IV added it some time before the twelfth century'.[68] Silverstein apparently regarded the entire Bridge of Hell scene as an invention of the author of Redaction IV, which he suggests was probably composed before the year 1100.[69] But the evidence of the Blickling homily shows that the infernal setting of the Bridge of Hell scene was already in place by the second half of the tenth century, for what remains when the bridge is removed from the scene is a terrible river filled with diabolical beasts plying the waters like fish – features that were certainly part of the version known to the Blickling homilist. The verbal echoes are precise: the *fynd ... on nicra onlicnesse* answer to the *multe bestie dyabolice ... quasi pisces in medio maris*. Further, just as these demonic water monsters seize the souls that drop into the water *swa swa grædig wulf*, so too the demons in the *flumen orribile* devour the sinful souls *quasi lupi deuorant oues*.[70] The biblical image of wolves devouring sheep may be com-

had earlier described these mansions in similar terms, citing the same biblical passage (PL 77, 380–1). But Owen, 'The *Vision of St Paul*: the French and Provençal Versions', pp. 38–9 and n. 16, believes this passage is a later addition to the bridge scene, and that Gregory need not have been the inspiration for the bridge itself.

[68] 'New Links and Patterns', pp. 220–1. The bridge motif was, however, exceptionally popular in eschatological visions. See P. Dinzelbacher, *Die Jenseitsbrücke im Mittelalter*, Dissertationen der Universität Wien 104 (Vienna, 1973); P. Dinzelbacher and H. Kleinschmidt, 'Seelenbrücke und Brückenbau im Mittelalterlichen England', *Numen* 31 (1984), 242–87; Silverstein, 'Dante and the Legend of the *Mi'rāj*', pp. 95–6. Gregory's vision of the soldier influenced not only the *Visio S. Pauli*, but also the Old English *Vision of Leofric*. See Silverstein, 'The *Vision of Leofric* and Gregory's *Dialogues*', *RES* 9 (1933), 185–8, and P. Pulsiano, 'Hortatory Purpose in the OE *Visio Leofrici*', *MÆ* 54 (1985), 109–16. A similar vision occurs in the letter of Wynfrith (Boniface) to Eadburg, for which see below, p. 124.

[69] No manuscript of Redaction IV earlier than the twelfth century has survived. But Silverstein argues that Redaction VII, which survives in an eleventh-century manuscript, is 'directly dependent on a form of IV', and this fact, together with the existence of an English version drawing on Redaction IV in a collection (the Lambeth homilies) that probably goes back to the eleventh century, leads Silverstein to argue 'that IV itself had been written and even rendered in the vernacular before the year 1100' ('New Links and Patterns', p. 224).

[70] Closely similar phrases occur in Redactions V, IX and X. Redaction IX, which mentions the beasts but does not have the comparison to wolves, describes the sinful souls as those 'qui non egerunt penitentiam in hoc mundo', a slight and perhaps coincidental parallel with Blickling XVI, which describes the black souls as those

monplace, but the mixed metaphor shared by the homily and the apocryphon (demons like fish devouring souls as wolves would do), and of course the shared context, virtually precludes coincidence.

It appears, in short, that the source of Blickling XVI had conflated the Hanging Sinners and Bridge of Hell scenes, retaining the infernal setting from the latter but replacing the bridge itself with the (fiery?) trees of the hanging punishment, so that the sinners drop into the clutches of the diabolical beasts in the water below not from a bridge, but from the branches of the trees, which now grow around the water. The trees thus perform the same mechanical function as the bridge, even though they do not fulfil the same purpose, since they do not separate good souls from bad. As a purgatorial motif, the hell-gate bridge is no longer appropriate for what has now become a punishment of hell proper.[71] But it is just possible that a vision such as that of the monk at Wenlock, where the bridge is a *lignum* ('an treow ofer þa éa on brycge onlicnysse' in the Old English version),[72] might have suggested the modification of the hanging punishment so that the souls drop from the branches of *trees* into the water below.

The significance of Redaction XI is that it represents the only known version of the *Visio S. Pauli* that combines the fiery trees with the beast-filled river. Although it is not the lost source of Blickling XVI or *Beowulf*, it does confirm that these very features of the scene, including at least some of the crucial phrasing, were indeed part of a unified scene composed over a century prior to the Blickling homily. Although it lacks nearly all the characteristic interpolations of the other redactions, it does preserve – if only in the barest form – a composite scene in which the fiery trees of the Hanging Sinners interpolation have been transplanted to the beast-filled river of the Bridge of Hell scene:

Vidit multos arbores igneos in circuitu fluminis ignis. Vidi bestias in medio aque maris quasi pisces in medio maris.[73]

who 'her on worlde mid unrihte gefyrenode wæron, & ðæs noldan geswican ær heora lifes ende' (*The Blickling Homilies*, ed. Morris, p. 211, lines 5–7). Redaction VIII does not mention the beasts.

[71] Unlike the bridge, which is usually purgatorial, the river can serve equally as a purgatorial or infernal motif; see Silverstein, 'The Passage of the Souls to Purgatory in the *Divina Commedia*', *Harvard Theological Studies* 31 (1938), 53–63, at 56–8.

[72] Sisam, *Studies*, pp. 218–19: 'a tree over the water like a bridge'.

[73] 'An Unstudied Redaction', ed. Dwyer, p. 126 (sect. iv): 'He saw many fiery trees

The infernal scenery is all in place here, but there are no souls hanging from these trees and dropping from them into the fiery river, whose beasts are uncharacteristically idle. Moreover, this composite scene is apparently not part of hell proper, since it is only *after* Paul views the scene that the angel bids him, 'ueni seque me et ostendam tibi paenam impiorum'.[74] As the passage stands in Redaction XI, the fiery trees and aquatic beasts are blind motifs. But they are unlikely to have been invented merely for scenery; rather, they must originally have been instruments of torment, as indeed they are in all other versions. One suspects that the intended victims have simply been abbreviated out of existence – a kinder fate than awaited their less fortunate cousins in the more fully developed redactions.

Oddly enough, however, there is a group of souls hanging from trees in the passage immediately preceding this one in Redaction XI. In front of the gates of paradise, in what is apparently a different stand of trees (they are not fiery), hang the souls of those who refused to give alms:

ET uidi singulos arbores ante portas ciuitates [*sic*] paradisi non habentes fructum nisi folia tantum. Vidi multos homines suspensos in arboribus. ET interrogaui ad angelum: domine, domine, qui sunt hii fili[75] hominum suspensi in arboribus? Respondit mihi angelus et dixit mihi: hii sunt domni [*sic*] filiorum hominum qui non fecerunt elimosinas in uita eorum. ET respiciunt in fructu arborum et non manducauit [*read* manducant] in eis fructos.[76]

around a river of fire. I saw many beasts in the middle of the water of the sea like fish in the middle of the sea'. On the alternation of first and third person forms in the account of the vision (*uidit/uidi*), see below, n. 80.

74 *Ibid*: 'Come, follow me and I shall show you the torment of the impious.' Dwyer (p. 122) believes that the *flumen igneum* in which sinners are immersed to varying degrees in the section immediately following (section v) is the same river of fire described here. But the angel's invitation to show Paul the pains of the impious suggests that the river of section iv is part of a distinct scene, vaguely located but not within hell. Moreover, no other redaction combines the beast-filled river with the river of the immersion punishment.

75 So ms.; Dwyer mistakenly prints *filii*. On the significance of this form and other Vulgar Latin features, see Wright, 'Some Evidence for an Irish Origin of Redaction XI', p. 36.

76 'An Unstudied Redaction', ed. Dwyer, p. 126 (sect. iii): 'And I saw several trees before the gates of the city of paradise bearing no fruit but only leaves. I saw many men suspended in the trees. And I asked the angel: "Master, master, who are these sons of men suspended in the trees?" The angel responded and said to me: "these

This passage is a variant of a scene in the Long versions of the *Visio*, known in some form to the author of Blickling IV, in which those who were proud and who failed to fast are found in great trees before the gates of paradise.[77] Brandes thought that this scene from the Long versions may have provided the suggestion for the fiery trees at the gates of hell in the redactions.[78] However, while in the Long versions these souls are vaguely situated in the trees (*uidi paucos uiros dispersos in medio arborum*), in Redaction XI they are hanged (*suspensos*), as are the sinners in the fiery trees in the redactions. It is just possible that the reading *suspensos* in Redaction XI represents a genuine variant from a lost Long version, which in turn provided the suggestion for the Hanging Sinners interpolation in the redactions.[79] But it seems equally possible that the reading *suspensos* is itself due to the influence of a redaction that included some form of the Hanging Sinners interpolation, and that the author of Redaction XI has transferred the hanging motif to the earlier scene.[80]

are the lords of the sons of men who did not give alms in their lives. And they gaze upon the fruit of the trees but do not eat fruit from them."'

77 *Apocrypha Anecdota*, ed. James, p. 24, line 25 – p. 25, line 2. For the parallel in Blickling IV (*The Blickling Homilies*, ed. Morris, p. 41, lines 33–6), see Silverstein, *Visio Sancti Pauli*, p. 7, and Healey, *The Old English Vision*, pp. 51–2.

78 *Visio S. Pauli*, p. 27; but see Silverstein, *Visio Sancti Pauli*, p. 71. Silverstein doubted the influence, since according to his reconstruction 'the interpolation was probably added to *Paul* by the author of Redaction β, and there is no evidence that he knew any of the Long texts of the Apocalypse, in which alone the trees of the City of Christ occur'. But Dwyer suggests 'that the author of β could have had access not to a Long Latin version but to Redaction XI or its source, in which the *fiery* trees are added and placed in proximity to the sinners suspended in the *fruitless* trees before the City of Christ' ('An Unstudied Redaction', p. 135).

79 Dwyer argues that Redaction XI is 'either to be derived from the source of β, a source which already had the fiery trees, or to be itself the source of β for this interpolation', and suggests that the fiery trees' 'proximity to the hanging sinners in the fruitless, leafless trees outside the gates of Paradise (and also perhaps to the fiery river with its souls immersed to varying levels) may well have been the stimulus for the merging of these features, which is presumed to have been one of the major contributions of β to the development of the later Latin redactions' (*ibid.*, pp. 134–5).

80 The frequent confusion of first and third person in Redaction XI could also be attributed to the redactor's familiarity with another redaction, since the other surviving redactions are all related in the third person, whereas the type of Long version followed by the author of Redaction XI (L^1) is related in the first person

Whatever the case, in the later redactions the hanging punishment is consistently associated with the fiery trees, and in this respect they transmit a closer approximation of the homilist's source than Redaction XI. On the other hand, like Blickling XVI, Redaction XI omits the bridge,[81] and instead places the trees around a body of water filled with water monsters – a configuration of elements which in the later redactions are found only in separate scenes, but which must also have been combined in the homilist's source.[82]

These basic elements of the description, at least, were not the invention of the homilist, but have their ultimate source in a lost version of the *Visio S. Pauli*. As for the remaining details which embellish the homilist's account, nearly all are traditional in apocryphal descriptions of hell, and some could have been suggested by other passages in the *Visio* itself.[83] The location of the hanging punishment 'where all the waters go down' (*þær ealle wætero niðergewítað*) was probably derived from the *Visio*, though this apocryphon merely transmits a much more ancient conception. The location of hell at the confluence of all waters, specifically the world-river Oceanus, the source of all waters, is traditional. This is where Socrates fixes Hades in the *Phaedo*:

One of the chasms of the earth is greater than the rest, and is bored right through the whole earth; this is the one which Homer ... and many other poets have called Tartarus. *For all the rivers flow together into this chasm* and flow out of

throughout. However, as Dwyer notes (*ibid.*, p. 130), the Long Latin versions *F* and *Gz* of type L² are related in the third person.

81 The bridge is also omitted in two manuscripts of Redaction IV (London, BL, Harley 2851 and Arundel 52), apparently by scribal error: see Brandes, *Visio S. Pauli*, p. 76, n. 1, and Ward, *Catalogue of Romances* II, 402. A Middle English version, 'The XI Pains of Hell' (Jesus College manuscript), in *An Old English Miscellany*, ed. Morris, pp. 147–55, also includes the beast-filled river apart from the bridge motif (at p. 149, line 75 – p. 150, line 118). The Vernon and Douce manuscripts of the poem, however, do mention the bridge.

82 Dwyer argues that the scene with the beast-filled river 'was already in β, and that another version of III existed which contained the interpolation and passed it on from β to IV, IX and X' ('An Unstudied Redaction', p. 136).

83 Collins claims that in 'Redaction II, sections 4–5 ... one finds the dark water, the deep pit, the trees ... on a precipice from which the unrepentant sinners are hanging' ('Blickling Homily XVI', p. 63). The (fiery) trees are there (section 4), and there is an abyss in 'another place' (section 5), but there is no dark water and the trees are not located on a precipice. (Redaction II does *not* contain the Bridge of Hell scene.)

it again, and they have each the nature of the earth through which they flow.[84]

Chief among these rivers, as Socrates enumerates them, is Oceanus, commonly the boundary of the Otherworld in classical tradition.[85] The same conception appears in apocryphal cosmology. Thus in I Enoch the seer traces his itinerary to the ends of the earth and to Sheol:

And I saw all the great rivers and reached to the great darkness and went into the place where all flesh must walk cautiously. And I saw the mountains of the dark storms of the rainy season and from where the waters of all seas flow. And I saw the mouths of all the rivers of the earth and the mouth of the sea.[86]

The *Visio S. Pauli* also preserves this ancient conception. As Silverstein explains,

At the threshold of Hell lies the world-encircling river Oceanus, placed there by the primitive third-century text and handed on by means of λ to Redaction α. Beside this great water α placed the four rivers of the classical Hades, each with its name, as is shown by the separate testimony of Redactions I and VII.[87]

One of the redactions (VIII) places the river spanned by the bridge of hell in the same vicinity as Oceanus, at the very spot where the rivers of hell flow together:

Et interrogauit Paulus quis esset fluuius. Et dixit angelus, 'Hic est Occeanus, super quem girant sydera celi, et circuit orbem terrarum.' Et uidit ibi locum terribilem, et non erat lumen in illo, sed tenebre, mesticie et suspiria. Et erat flumen igneum et feruens; fluctus autem eius exaltat se super usque ad nubes et ad celum. Et nomen illius Cochiton. Et alia tria que confluunt sicut in eum et grauiora erant stillicidio super peccatores, et ut mons magnus igneus.[88]

84 Cited by Patch, *The Other World*, p. 20 (emphasis mine).

85 As in the eleventh book of the Odyssey (cited by Patch, *ibid.*, pp. 19–20).

86 I Enoch XVII.6–8, trans. E. Isaac in Charlesworth, *Old Testament Pseudepigrapha* I, 22. In the Ethiopic version the place is located where 'the waters are gathered together' (*The Ethiopic Book of Enoch*, ed. and trans. M. A. Knibb, 2 vols. (Oxford, 1978) II, 105, note to Enoch XVII.10).

87 Silverstein, *Visio Sancti Pauli*, p. 65. See also T. D. Hill, 'Apocryphal Cosmology and the "Stream uton Sæ": a Note on *Christ and Satan*, Lines 4–12', *PQ* 48 (1969), 550–4.

88 *Visio Sancti Pauli*, ed. Silverstein, pp. 209–10: 'And Paul asked what river that was. And the angel said, "This is Ocean, above which revolve the heavenly bodies, and it encircles the orb of the earth". And he saw there a terrible place, and there was

The location of hell in the north is commonplace.[89] In classical tradition Oceanus is commonly located in the west, but already in I Enoch the confluence of the rivers appears to be located in the north.[90] The direction is not specified in the *Visio*, although the Long versions and several of the redactions of the *Visio* do imply a north or a northwest direction for the *puteus inferni*.[91]

Some additional details of the Blickling homilist's description are not yet accounted for. A minor detail is that in the homily, but not in the *Visio*, the Hanging Sinners are described as 'black' souls. This would be easy enough to credit to the homilist's own ingenuity, particularly since very little ingenuity would be required. That damned souls are black is perhaps too common an idea to document meaningfully. As a popular item in early medieval question-and-answer dialogues has it, 'Quid nigrius coruo? Anima peccatorum in inferno.'[92] Nevertheless, in the *Visio*, although the Hanging Sinners are not themselves described as black, there are several groups of 'black' sinners in other scenes.[93]

no light in it, but darkness, sorrows, and sighs. And there was a fiery and boiling river; its wave-surge mounts up to the clouds and to the heavens. And its name is Cochiton. And three other rivers flowed together into it and they were more heavy than a shower over the sinners, and like a great fiery mountain [read *fons*, 'fountain'?].' This passage occurs immediately after the bridge scene, but here without the beast-filled river.

89 Is. XIV.13 (*ponam sedem meam ad aquilonem*) was particularly important in establishing the idea in Christian tradition. It occurs in the Vision of Laisrén: 'Thereupon he is let down northward into a great glen' (in 'Stories and Songs from Irish MSS.', trans. Meyer, pp. 17–18). John Carey has kindly sent me a transcription of the following question and answer from Dublin, National Library of Ireland, G. 1, 51r: 'Cia bhail dorus iffirn? Nī ansa: isin tuaiscert; ⁊ is aire-sin is ōn tuaiscert tigid na huile olc ⁊ doraigh' ('Where is the door of hell? Not difficult: in the north; and that is why all evils and hardships come from the north'). According to Snorri's *Prose Edda*, 'niðr ok norðr liggr helvegr' (cited by Malone, 'Grendel and His Abode', p. 297, n. 1).

90 According to J. T. Milik, *The Books of Enoch: Aramaic Fragments of Qumran Cave 4* (Oxford, 1976), pp. 38–9.

91 See Silverstein, 'New Links and Patterns', p. 211, n. 59; T. D. Hill, 'Some Remarks on "The Site of Lucifer's Throne"', *Anglia* 87 (1969), 303–11, at 310; Healey, *The Old English Vision*, pp. 55–6.

92 *Adrian und Epictitus*, ed. Suchier, p. 37: 'What is blacker than a raven? The soul of sinners in hell.'

93 See, e.g., Redaction II, in *Visio Sancti Pauli*, ed. Silverstein, p. 157, line 14: 'Et iterum uidit ... uiros et mulieres nigros'. Likewise the water into which the souls fall

One detail for which the surviving Latin versions of the *Visio* afford no parallel is the grey rock (*har stan*) which in the homily (and in *Beowulf*) looms out over the water and from which grow the frosty trees. In the *Visio* there is a deep pit, as Collins noted,[94] but the trees do not grow around it, and although many sinners are confined within, the text does not actually describe any falling in from above. Cliffs are frequently part of the infernal landscape, however, as in the Apocalypse of Peter, which describes 'a great rock' or precipice from which sinners are cast down.[95] A strikingly similar description occurs in a thirteenth-century French translation of Redaction IV, which describes a 'great rock' one thousand fathoms high, with one thousand ledges, each with a different torment. A thousand devils cast a thousand souls a day into a ditch below filled with serpents who feed on them. D. D. R. Owen argued for 'the ultimate identity' of the rock torment in the French text and the Apocalypse of Peter, suggesting that the translator was following a lost Latin version in which the rock episode had been interpolated from that apocryphon.[96] Although the details of the episode do not closely parallel the description in Blickling XVI, both texts suggest that some lost versions of the *Visio* incorporated a rock torment, possibly derived from the Apocalypse of Peter.[97]

The Blickling homily also specifies the distance between the cliff and the water as about twelve miles, an oddly precise figure, tantalizingly paralleled in a slightly different context by the Old English *Christ and Satan*, which says that the weeping and gnashing of teeth in hell may be heard from the same distance.[98] In the *Visio* (Redactions I, III, VIII and X) the angel tells Paul that the abyss has no measure, a biblical notion contradicted by some redactions which do specify a figure (30,000

is *sweart*, a natural enough description, but cf. Redaction IIIc-d, *ibid.*, p. 173, line 11, which describes a 'flumen niger ardens'. In the Middle English version cited above, n. 81, the water of the beast-filled river itself is described as 'Blakkure þan þe swarte pich'.

[94] See above, n. 83.

[95] *Apocryphal New Testament*, trans. James, p. 510.

[96] 'The *Vision of St Paul*: the French and Provençal Versions', pp. 45–6.

[97] The Apocalypse of Peter seems a likely ultimate source for the rock torment. According to Fadda, *Nuove omelie anglosassoni*, pp. 40–1, a description in an Old English homily on the going-out of souls based on the *Visio S. Pauli* recalls details of the Apocalypse of Peter as well (the text actually names Peter as the visionary, rather than Paul).

[98] In *The Junius Manuscript*, ed. Krapp, p. 146, lines 337–8.

cubits).[99] I am aware of no exact parallel for the distance specified by the homily, but the number twelve is a recurrent figure of distance and measurement in apocryphal descriptions of hell, including Hebrew visions and the various versions of the Seven Heavens apocryphon.[100]

The most striking discrepancy is, of course, that the trees in the homily are frosty, not fiery, a detail echoed by *Beowulf*. A different kind of alteration may be seen in the Greek Apocalypse of Mary, where the sinners hang not from fiery trees but from an iron tree.[101] But the change from fiery to icy trees is a logical corollary of the northern setting of the punishment in the homily, and it is characteristic of hell that fire and ice are coexisting (sometimes alternating) torments.[102]

The evidence of Redaction XI, together with a close examination of the previously edited redactions, allows us to reconstruct the source of Blickling Homily XVI from surviving texts in greater detail than has hitherto been possible. It combined the trees from the Hanging Sinners scene with the fiery river and demonic beasts from the Bridge of Hell, locating this composite scene at the confluence of Oceanus. It efficiently employed the trees of the hanging punishment as the mechanism for dropping souls into the demon-infested waters from a cliff, this last feature interpolated from another source, perhaps the Apocalypse of Peter. It compared the demonic beasts plying the waters to fish, but also to wolves devouring souls.

The homilist's source was clearly not as spare as Redaction XI, which provides the only surviving textual evidence for such a composite scene in the Latin versions. The trees in the Blickling homilist's source, for example, obviously had sinners hanging from them. For this crucial

99 Redaction II, section 5, mentioned by Collins (see n. 83) is one of these.

100 See Willard, *Two Apocrypha*, pp. 18–19 and n. 95.

101 On this text see Himmelfarb, *Tours of Hell*, pp. 23–4 and 159–60.

102 As in the *Visio* (e.g., Redaction IV, in *Visio S. Pauli*, ed. Brandes, p. 77, lines 13–14, or Redaction II, in *Visio Sancti Pauli*, ed. Silverstein, p. 157, lines 19–20). For Old English examples, see Tristram, 'Stock Descriptions', p. 111, n. 37, and *Christ and Satan*, in *The Junius Manuscript*, ed. Krapp, p. 140, line 131. For examples in Celtic sources, see Gougaud, *Christianity in Celtic Lands*, p. 296, n. 2, and J. Vendryes, 'L'enfer glacé', *RC* 46 (1929), 134–42. A late Irish version of the *Visio* describes a band of sinners 'up to their chins in cold frosty water of the colour of coal'; the water is filled with reptiles (trans. Hyde, *The Religious Songs of Connacht* II, 343). Cf. the passage from the Irish *Fís Adamnán* quoted by L. Whitbread, 'Grendel's Abode: an Illustrative Note', *ES* 22 (1940), 64–6.

feature, and for some, if not all, of the remaining details, we must look the later redactions. But because scholars have focused solely on the Hanging Sinners scene, they have not appreciated the extent to which the description in the homily is indebted to the *Visio*.

Beowulf *and the* Visio S. Pauli

As early as it is, the corrupt text of Redaction XI suggests that it represents a relatively late and debased stage of transmission; the ninth-century Vatican text is hardly an original or archetypal version. An abbreviated text of the *Visio* must thus have been in existence at least by the late eighth century, perhaps earlier. Moreover, Redaction XI shows that specific scenes and phrases attested only in much later redactions might well preserve readings older by some two to three centuries. These findings would place the question of direct influence upon *Beowulf* by a redaction of the *Visio* much more securely in the realm of possibility and reasonable conjecture than has hitherto been the case, especially if verbal parallels between the poem and surviving versions could be identified.

Although Lawrence and other earlier scholars believed that the famous analogue in the Icelandic *Grettissaga* preserved 'the original conception of the dwelling of the demons' in *Beowulf*,[103] most recent scholarship concurs that the *Beowulf*-poet has adapted conventional features of hell for his description. Klaeber already conceded that 'manifestly conceptions of the Christian hell have entered into the picture as drawn by the poet'.[104] Kemp Malone was more emphatic on this point: 'the poet gives us not a confused and distorted description of natural scenery but a consistent and carefully-wrought picture of a hell on earth, an imaginative construction based on traditional Christian ideas about hell'.[105] As for the corresponding scene in *Grettissaga*,

[103] W. W. Lawrence, 'The Haunted Mere in *Beowulf*', *PMLA* 27 (1912), 208–45, at 232. See also Lawrence's *Beowulf and Epic Tradition* (Cambridge, MA, 1930), pp. 183–7. For the *Grettissaga* passage and other folktale analogues, see Klaeber, *Beowulf*, pp. xiii–xxi, and R. W. Chambers, *Beowulf: an Introduction to the Study of the Poem*, 3rd ed. (Cambridge, 1959), pp. 451–85. Both Brown ('*Beowulf* and the *Blickling Homilies*', p. 909) and Chambers (pp. 451–3) approved Lawrence's theory.

[104] In his note on the passage, *Beowulf*, p. 183.

[105] 'Grendel and His Abode', p. 306.

Malone conceded a relationship but considered 'the hellish setting for the adventure as the original'.[106] Hildegard Tristram agrees that the description 'is wholly traditional and probably borrowed from homiletic writings'.[107]

Brown's opinion that 'the descriptions in the *Visio* and in *Beowulf* are wholly independent – except that trees occur in both' has already been quoted. One cannot, it is true, piece together a composite approximation of Grendel's mere from two passages in the redactions of the *Visio*, as it is possible to do for the description of hell in the Blickling homily. That is hardly surprising, since poetry is more allusive than prose and tends to transform its sources more freely to conform to its own purpose. And in *Beowulf* the purpose is not quite the same as in the Blickling homily and the *Visio*, both of which are describing the same thing – hell. *Beowulf* is describing something different, however much it may owe to the same tradition.

The poem does, however, preserve the essential configuration of the composite scene reconstructed above from the redactions of the *Visio*: the trees grow from a great rock over a body of water infested by water monsters, at a place where a great river descends.[108] All these features, of course, could be accounted for by assuming that *Beowulf* has borrowed from the Blickling homily, especially since *Beowulf* also preserves, in strikingly similar language, some of the additional features or alterations which distinguish the homily from the surviving Latin texts of the *Visio*: the trees are frosty, not fiery, and grow from a *har stan*, just as in the homily; and both texts mention the dark mists below the cliff. On the other hand, these similarities could as well be accounted for by assuming that the common source from which both Anglo-Saxon writers borrowed was not a Latin but a vernacular version of the *Visio*. This would explain verbal as well as conceptual parallels. Furthermore, in one of these features, the poem is more precise than the homily, for

[106] *Ibid.*, p. 307.

[107] 'Stock Descriptions', p. 111.

[108] D. K. Fry has argued that the description incorporates several recurrent elements of an oral-formulaic 'type-scene', including 'cliffs, serpents, darkness, and deprivation, and occasionally wolves and wind': 'The Cliff of Death in Old English Poetry', in *Comparative Research on Oral Traditions: a Memorial for Milman Parry*, ed. J. M. Foley (Columbus, OH, 1987), pp. 213–33, at 215 (see pp. 218–25 for his discussion of Grendel's mere). See also Tristram, 'Stock Descriptions', p. 113.

the homily locates the scene at the place where 'all waters' (*ealle wætero*) go down, while *Beowulf* specifically mentions the *fyrgenstream*, which Kemp Malone has identified as the world-river Oceanus (the word's regular poetic meaning).[109] As we have seen, the redactions agree in placing Oceanus at the threshold of hell.[110]

Other conceptual details in the poem could reflect independent knowledge of a common source, though these possible connections are tenuous and inconclusive. The poet's reference to a 'fire on the flood' (line 1366) may reflect the fiery quality of the beast-filled *flumen igneum*. Again, speaking of the deep waters, Hrothgar tells Beowulf that 'of the sons of men none lives so wise as to know the bottom' (1366b–67), a statement reminiscent of the angel's comment to Paul, 'Abyssus mensuram non habet'.[111]

Still, if the *Beowulf*-poet did draw independently on the same source as the Blickling homily – that is, on a vernacular version of the *Visio* – then one might reasonably expect to discover some distinctive verbal echo between *Beowulf* and the *Visio*. There does appear to be at least one. In six of the redactions, the river (Cochiton) which flows into Oceanus at the confluence of the waters in the *locus terribilis* is described as a 'flumen igneum et feruens; fluctus autem eius exaltat se super usque ad

[109] 'Grendel and His Abode', p. 298. The poet's conception of the mere into which the *fyrgenstream* flows is apparently ambiguous, since the terms he uses could designate the sea or a lake. See R. Frank, '"Mere" and "Sund": Two Sea-Changes in *Beowulf*', in *Modes of Interpretation in Old English Literature: Essays in Honour of Stanley B. Greenfield*, ed. P. R. Brown, G. R. Crampton and F. C. Robinson (Toronto, 1986), pp. 153–72. The fact that Oceanus is itself a 'river' may have contributed to this ambiguity, which also characterizes the description of the water in some versions of the *Visio*, such as Redaction IX, where the river is described as 'uelud mare largum' (Silverstein, 'New Links and Patterns', p. 239), or 'The XI Pains of Hell' (Jesus College Manuscript), where it is called a 'pool' (*An Old English Miscellany*, ed. Morris, p. 149, line 81). In the Vulgate the word *mare* refers to lakes as well as to seas, reflecting a Hebrew usage commented upon by Christian authors, including Isidore (*Etym.* XIII.14).

[110] If the parallel references to the abodes of water monsters (*nicorhusa fela* in *Beowulf*, *niccra eardung* in the Blickling homily) both derive from the phrase *Ibi sunt multe bestie dyabolice multeque mansiones male preparate*, the poet's *nicorhusa fela* is again a more precise equivalent. In the *Visio*, of course, the *mansiones* are intended for the sinners, not for the beasts, but the phrase could easily have been misconstrued (or mistransmitted) to suggest that there were 'many abodes of beasts'.

[111] *Visio Sancti Pauli*, ed. Silverstein, p. 154 (Redaction I): 'The abyss has no measure.'

nubes et ad celum'.[112] This seems to be echoed in the poet's description of the fiery, troubled waters of the mere (1416b–17a), whose 'dark wave-surge rises up to the skies':

> Þonon yðgeblond up astigeð
> won to wolcnum[113]

The image, though extravagant enough, is perhaps not so distinctive as to render borrowing beyond question.[114] But it is a close parallel all the same, and may well be the vestige of a common source not preserved by the homily. If so, the poet has rationalized the detail by ascribing it to the effects of the wind and *lað gewidru* (1374b–76a), but this has been his procedure with all the specifically 'hellish' descriptive elements of his source, whether that source was Blickling XVI itself or some version of the *Visio*. While retaining the essential configuration, he divests particular elements of their explicitly eschatological reference by literalizing them:[115] his 'hell' is still in the north, because that is where the Danes live;[116] his frosty trees, bereft of the souls that once were suspended from their branches, are left themselves to 'hang' over the water below;[117] and his water-monsters have been exorcised of their demons.

112 Quotation from Redaction VIII, *ibid.*, p. 210: 'a fiery and boiling river; its wave-surge mounts up above to the clouds and to the heavens'. This passage also occurs, with slight variations, in Redactions I (Barcelona manuscript), II, III, VII and X.

113 *Beowulf*, ed. Klaeber, p. 52, lines 1373–4a.

114 The image appears to have had a wider currency in apocalyptic and visionary texts. The Latin Seven Heavens apocryphon in the *Apocrypha Priscillianistica* describes a fiery river in similar terms: 'fluctus eius exaltatur usque ad quintum celum' ('Fragments retrouvés', ed. De Bruyne, p. 323). The following passage in the *Visio Tnugdali*, however, appears to have been influenced by the *Visio S. Pauli*: 'Euntes uero longius uiderunt stagnum amplum ualde et tempestuosum, cuius fluctus astantes non permittebat cernere celum. Inerat etiam ibi plurima multitudo bestiarum terribilium, que mugientes nil aliud poscebant, nisi ut animas deuorarent' (*Visio Tnugdali*, ed. Wagner, p. 19). The souls fall into this stream from a narrow bridge.

115 Tristram arrives at a similar conclusion: 'The *Beowulf* passage uses the descriptive elements apart from their religious context' ('Stock Descriptions', p. 111).

116 See Malone, 'Grendel and His Abode', p. 306.

117 Or did the bare trees as in Redaction XI survive in a more fully developed version known to the *Beowulf*-poet, otherwise so closely parallel to the homilist's source? It seems to me not only an unlikely development, but an unnecessary hypothesis. That the *Beowulf*-poet's trees are bare of souls is no sure indication that they were so in his source, for if the poet had found his trees hung with sinners – or black souls – he would almost certainly have removed them.

If no single one of these details proves that the *Beowulf*-poet drew independently on the *Visio S. Pauli*, the cumulative weight of the parallels I have listed (none of which occurs in Blickling XVI) supports the presumption that he did. Brown's opinion that the description in *Beowulf* is 'wholly independent' of the *Visio* can no longer be sustained. He dismissed the possibility of direct influence of the *Visio* on *Beowulf*, and hence the view that it might have been a common source for both homily and poem, on the grounds that the scene with the fiery trees was a late addition. But it is clear, in fact, that the essential configuration of the description in *Beowulf* can be derived from the same composite scene that underlies the homily, combining the trees from the Hanging Sinners interpolation with the terrible river and demonic, fish-like beasts from the Bridge of Hell scene. Redaction XI, though not itself the source for either Old English text, proves that both the trees and the beast-filled river are primitive features already combined at an early date, perhaps early enough to have influenced even an eighth-century *Beowulf* – and nothing proves that the combination could not have existed even earlier. The ninth-century Vatican manuscript shows that elements of a scene Silverstein considered an invention of the eleventh- or twelfth-century author of Redaction IV actually antedate that redaction by some two to three centuries.

The hanging sinner and the story of Cairpre Crom

The description of the hanging torment in Vercelli Homily IX is not directly related to the scene described in the Blickling homily. The hanging punishment itself is handled differently in Vercelli IX: the victim is bound by his feet instead of his hands, and blood flows from his mouth. But this gruesome posture is no doubt based upon an apocryphal source as well. In the *Visio S. Pauli* some sinners hang by their feet, others by their hands, and a redactor who wished to focus on a single victim could have it either way. Apocryphal visions often describe individual sinners hanging by different members, and it would be easy enough to elaborate on the Hanging Sinners in the *Visio* by constructing individual scenes modelled on those in similar visions. This transition, from a group of hanging sinners to a scene focusing on a single victim, can be found in a later vision that seems to be dependent on the *Visio S. Pauli*, the Greek Apocalypse of Mary. In this text Mary first sees in one place 'an iron tree and it had branches of iron, and on it there hung a multitude of men and women hanging by their tongues'. Immediately thereafter, Mary sees 'in another place a man hanging from his four extremities, and from his nails blood gushed vehemently'.[118]

The tree as the instrument of the hanging punishment in Vercelli Homily IX suggests that the scene is a similar development of the motif of the Hanging Sinners in the *Visio*, especially since the tree's setting is similar to the hellish landscape in the Blickling homily. Although there are no striking verbal parallels, the essential topographical elements of the composite scene surviving in these two texts are all there, in the same configuration: the tree from which the victim hangs is 'the tallest tree on earth' which, like the huge trees in the Blickling homily and *Beowulf*, grows from a great sea-cliff and leans out over the ocean, whose waves beat upon the victim hanging from the topmost branch. Although the description in Vercelli IX cannot be attributed to a common source, it does reflect a common tradition. Comparison of *Beowulf* and the Blickling homily shows that a vision of sinners hanging from trees in a setting constructed from elements drawn from the *Visio S. Pauli*, and incorporating the rock torment, was current in Anglo-Saxon England. But once these elements had been assembled into a unified scene they became the core of a stock description that could easily be adapted, elaborated or abbreviated.

This stock description appears in an Irish vernacular text as well. An anecdote found in four Irish manuscripts[119] relates how Cairpre Crom, bishop of Clonmacnois (d. 899), rescued the soul of Mael Sechnaill mac Maele Ruanaig, king of Tara (d. 862), from hell by dint of prayers, alms and fasting. After the end of a year the soul of the king, which had first appeared to Cairpre Crom as a black shape, re-appears 'half-speckled'. The bishop enquires into the soul's new condition: 'Cindus sin? ol in clerech. Indas maith, ol ind ainim, acht co ro lentar don cedna. Cidh on,

[118] Trans. in *Ante-Nicene Christian Library* 9 (Edinburgh, 1896), 171.

[119] The manuscripts are the Leabhar Breac (Dublin, Royal Irish Academy 23. P. 16; *c.* 1410), pp. 259b–260a; Brussels, Bibliothèque Royale, 5100–4 (written by Michael O'Clery in 1630), 76v; London, BL, Egerton 92 (s. xv), 28v; and Dublin, National Library of Ireland, G. 449 (copied in 1729). The anecdote is listed by C. Plummer, 'A Tentative Catalogue of Irish Hagiography', in his *Miscellanea Hagiographica Hibernica*, p. 206 (no. 92). The version of the anecdote in the Brussels manuscript is

cindas atai in truma do phéne anosa? ol in cleirech.'[120] Mael Sechnaill's response is couched in two difficult stanzas.[121] The text of the Leabhar Breac reads:

Et dixit in rig:
In animm is luga pian
fil a n-iathaib na n-ocian
suaill ni bud did [...] di-a bull
mad dia tisad a hifurn.

Ind chraind cruaidluim co n-gairge
os all gaibtech glasfairrge
contuilfed and, cen terce,
in aidche gairb goethsnechta.[122]

The third line of the first stanza has caused the most difficulty. The Brussels manuscript (which reverses the order of the stanzas) reads, *suaill na bad ingnad dia chunn*, which Stokes translates tentatively, 'Hardly should its body have wonder.'[123] Dottin considered the stanza incomprehensible in both manuscripts. But in the lithograph facsimile of the Leabhar Breac the three letters which Dottin transcribes as *dib*

ed. and trans. Stokes, 'Three Legends'. The Leabhar Breac version is ed. Dottin, *Manuel d'irlandais moyen* II, 119–23. The Egerton copy was noted by Flower, *Catalogue of Irish Manuscripts* II, 514–15. I have not seen the Dublin manuscript, which is indexed by Hayes, *Manuscript Sources* XI, 823. For another marginal copy of one stanza in the Leabhar Breac, see below, n. 128. A summary of the story, without the poem, is included in *The Martyrology of Donegal*, ed. J. H. Todd and W. Reeves (Dublin, 1864), p. 66.

120 'Three Legends', ed. Stokes, pp. 366–7. Stokes translates: '"What is this state?" quoth the cleric. "A good state", says the soul; "only one that goes on with the same (torments)". "What? How is the heaviness of thy punishment now?" asks the cleric.'

121 The seventeenth-century hagiographer John Colgan rendered the stanzas into Latin as follows: 'ut in summitate cuiusdam arboris, supra subiectae abyssi horrendum fastigium, sine quiete & intermissione inter uentorum flabra & algores cruciaretur; mirumque esse quempiam esse inter eos, qui ad poenas in altera uita sustinendas deputati sunt, quantumcumque sint exiguae, qui non putet se torqueri in inferno'. See *The 'Acta Sanctorum Hiberniae' of John Colgan*, Irish Manuscripts Commission, Reflex Facsimiles 5 (Dublin, 1948) [facsimile of Louvain, 1645 ed.], p. 508.

122 Ed. Dottin, *Manuel d'irlandais moyen* II, 122–3, with the alteration discussed below.

123 'Three Legends', pp. 368–9.

(followed by a gap of about three letters) are transcribed as *did*.[124] In 1984, having overlooked Flower's notice of the Egerton manuscript of the anecdote, and basing my discussion solely on the two printed versions, I compared the readings of the Leabhar Breac and the Brussels manuscripts (*did* [...] and *ingnad*) and proposed an original reading *didnad*, verbal noun of *do-dona* ('console', 'comfort'), translating the stanza as follows:

The soul whose punishment is least,
Which is in the regions of the oceans,
It would not be a small comfort to its limb
If it should come out of hell.

Rarely does one have the opportunity to test a conjectural reading by discovering an additional manuscript, but I have since been able to consult a microfilm of the Egerton manuscript, which clearly reads *didnad*.[125] The sense of the stanza, then, is that even the least of the pains of hell is such that the tormented soul would be greatly relieved by escaping it – so much so, indeed, that it would easily endure any other torment that might be devised, as the second stanza dramatically illustrates. Following the text of the Leabhar Breac and the Egerton manuscript, which have the verb *contuilfed* in the third line, this stanza may be rendered,

On top of the hard, bare tree with fierceness,
Above the dangerous cliff of the green sea,
It would sleep there without want
In the rough night of windy snow.

Stokes, working from the Brussels manuscript, printed *contulacht* instead of *contuilfed*, and translated the third line 'I [i.e. Mael Sechnaill] suffered

[124] *Leabhar Breac: the Speckled Book* [facsimile of transcript by J. O'Longan], p. 260a. The letters *did* are at the end of a line, with a gap indicated at the beginning of the next line. The gap is explained in Appendix III, 'Table of Defects in the Original Manuscript', as an 'obscure or illegible place' (p. 8).

[125] The text of the poem, as Flower commented, generally agrees with the Leabhar Breac; the only significant variant is *cund* for *bull* in the same line, which agrees with the Brussels manuscript, but does not materially affect my interpretation of the stanza.

there without stint.'[126] But *contulacht* is obscure, and Stokes's translation, as he admits, is only a guess.[127] On the other hand, *contuilfed*, the reading of the other two manuscripts, makes perfect sense, and the third-person singular secondary future affords better continuity with the first stanza (the second in the Brussels manuscript): the hypothetical soul (*in animm*) fortunate enough to escape the 'least' of the torments of hell would be so relieved (stanza 1) that it would sleep through the torment described in stanza 2. The poem derives its impact through a rhetoric of inexpressibility in which the tree torment serves precisely the same function as it does in Vercelli Homily IX. The soul of Mael Sechnaill cannot adequately describe even the least of the tortures of hell itself, but to impart an indirect sense of their severity he posits a grandiose hypothetical torment which, however terrifying it may seem to someone in this world, would easily be endured by a soul that had escaped from hell.[128] The hanging punishment in Vercelli Homily IX is a hypothetical torment as well, one that obliquely but dramatically impresses its readers through a kind of lurid *uia negatiua*. For gruesome as the tree torment may be, a soul that could escape from hell (*gif he þanon mot / mad dia tisad a hifurn*) would easily endure it (*þonne wile he eall þis luflice þrowian / contuilfed and cen terce*).[129]

126 Stokes, 'Three Legends', pp. 368–9.

127 Stokes analyses the form as '1st sg. t-pret. of *con-to-longim?' As Stokes prints the word, the first and last syllables must be abbreviated in the manuscript. The abbreviation for *co(n)* is too distinctive to be mistaken, but one wonders if the final *-acht* is an error, or if Stokes has correctly expanded the abbreviation mark. John Carey points out to me that the abbreviation for *-acht*, a tall *s* with a suspension mark (i.e., the nota for Latin *sed*), could easily be confused with an abbreviation for *-fad* or *-fed*. The first two syllables (*contul-*), at any rate, agree with the Leabhar Breac reading.

128 A marginal copy of stanza 2 in the Leabhar Breac (facsimile ed., p. 115, top margin), hitherto overlooked, is corrupt: 'id cen tercca / i n-agaid gairb gothsnechta / a mbeind lommain co n-gairde / os all gaibthech glasfairrge'. The note accompanying the marginal copy of the stanza shows that it occurred in a different context: 'Spirut Fathad Chanand cecinit, er tuaruscbail pheini h-iffern' ('The spirit of Fotha Chanand cecinit, describing the pains of hell'; see p. 34 of the facsimile ed.).

129 The hyperbole in the Irish version, 'it would sleep there without stint' compares closely to that in 'The Devil's Account', in which another hypothetical torment is so light compared to hell that 'the soul that was earlier in hell for a single night could not wake up'. See below, p. 189.

Even with the textual difficulties of these stanzas one can easily recognize a variation of the stock description in Vercelli Homily IX. The similarities in the topographical configuration of the torment are striking, whatever readings one adopts, and in fact Stokes himself was reminded of this Old English exemplum, which he knew from Kemble's *The Dialogue of Solomon and Saturnus*.[130] Although we are not told that the soul hangs from the tree, it is similarly positioned at the top (*ind chraind* / *on þam lengestan treowe ufeweardum*). And here too the tree as the instrument of torment is placed upon a cliff overlooking the sea (*os all gaibtech glasfairrge* / *ofer sæ ... on þam hyhstan sæclife*), where the victim must endure the harsh elements (*in aidche gairb goethsnechta*) just as the hanging victim in Vercelli Homily IX is exposed to the waves of the sea. Two further details are reminiscent of the scene described in the Blickling homily and *Beowulf*. The location of the 'least' torment itself is specified as 'the regions of the oceans' (*a n-iathaib na n-ocian*), recalling the location of the torment at the confluence of the ocean, and the wintry environment (*goethsnechta*) recalls the frosty trees in these two texts.

The isolation of the victim on a cliff overlooking the ocean is reminiscent of another scene from Irish literature, the passage in the *Nauigatio S. Brendani* in which Brendan and his monks encounter Judas, stranded on a rock in the ocean:

Igitur sanctus Brendanus cum nauigasset contra meridiem iter septem dierum, apparuit illis in mare quedam formula quasi hominis sedentis supra petram, et uelum ante illum a longe quasi [mensura] unius sagi, pendens inter duas furcellas ferreas, et sic agitabatur fluctibus sicut nauicula solet quando periclitatur a turbine ... et unde ex omni parte quando effluebant ad illum, percuciebant eum usque ad uerticem, et quando recedebant, apparebat illa petra nuda in qua sedebat infelix ille. Pannum quoque, qui ante illum pendebat, aliquando uentus minabat a se, aliquando percuciebat eum per oculos et frontem.[131]

130 'Three Legends', p. 367, n. 3.

131 *Navigatio Sancti Brendani*, ed. Selmer, p. 65: 'When Saint Brendan had sailed towards the south for seven days, there appeared to them in the sea the outline as it were of a man sitting on a rock with a cloth suspended between two small iron fork-shaped supports about a cloak's length in front of him. The object was being tossed about by waves just like a little boat in a whirlwind ... As the waves flowed towards him from every side, they struck him even to the top of his head. When they receded, the

The setting and manner of Judas's torment are perhaps similar enough to the hypothetical punishments described in the story of Cairpre Crom and Vercelli Homily IX to suggest a related tradition, if no more immediate relationship. Judas is also isolated on a rock in the ocean, exposed to the harsh elements and pounding waves; but there is no tree or hanging punishment, and here at least the rock is only a rock, although in a variant form of the legend, the *Vita secunda S. Brendani*, Judas is found clinging to a cliff (*scopulo herens*), from which the crashing waves threaten to strip him.[132] The similarities that do exist, however, are more intriguing in view of the similar rhetorical context. As Judas explains to St Brendan, his torment – like the torment of the hypothetical victims in the Irish and Old English legends – is actually a relief from the incomparably harsher torments of hell:

'Non mihi computatur penalis iste locus sed pro indulgencia Redemptoris propter honorem dominice resurrectionis'. Nam erat dies dominicus tunc. 'Mihi enim uidetur, quando sedeo hic, quasi fuissem in paradiso deliciarum propter timorem tormentorum que futura sunt mihi in hac uespera...'[133]

The motif of the Sunday respite of the damned, here granted to Judas,[134] appears in Prudentius and other early Christian writers, but again the *Visio S. Pauli* was probably the most important source of dissemination for the idea in both Ireland and Anglo-Saxon England, where it occurs quite frequently in vernacular sources.[135] In Gougaud's words, 'Si l'Irlande a reçu des pays continentaux la notion première de répit périodique, elle l'a renvoyée outre-mer développée, enrichie, et

bare rock where the unhappy man was sitting was exposed. The wind also sometimes drove the cloth hanging in front of him away from him, and sometimes blew it against his eyes and forehead' (trans. O'Meara, *The Voyage of Saint Brendan*, p. 56). I am grateful to John Carey for drawing my attention to this passage.

132 *Vitae Sanctorum Hiberniae*, ed. Plummer II, 285. In a vernacular version of the story quoted below, Judas sits on a 'huge rock' in an 'infernal sea'.

133 *Navigatio Sancti Brendani*, ed. Selmer, p. 66: '"This place is not reckoned as punishment but as an indulgence of the Saviour in honour of the Lord's Resurrection." That day was in fact the Lord's day. "When I am sitting here I feel as if I were in a paradise of delights in contrast with my fear of the torments that lie before me this evening"' (trans. O'Meara, *The Voyage of Saint Brendan*, pp. 56–7).

134 See P. Baum, 'Judas' Sunday Rest', *MLR* 18 (1923), 168–82.

135 For a survey of the theme in Irish sources, see Gougaud, 'La croyance au répit périodique'. For reflexes of the motif in Old English, see Healey, *The Old English Vision*, pp. 48–50.

enchâssée dans des légendes dont s'est passionné le moyen âge.'[136] The actual period of respite in both Irish and Anglo-Saxon texts varies, though it is most often sabbatical. In the story of Cairpre Crom and Vercelli Homily IX, the victims' escape from hell is not clearly defined as a periodic respite, but the hypothetical cases they describe can be interpreted as a transformation of the respite motif into an inexpressibility topos. A similar transformation occurs, for example, in the Irish *Tenga Bithnua* and in Bishop Patrick's *De tribus habitaculis*, in which an apocryphal tradition that the pains of the damned were momentarily relieved by the sight of Christ at the Harrowing of Hell[137] is phrased hypothetically:

Ata do aille 7 edrochta a ghnuisi .i. dia ndercaitis a bhfil do anmundaib ind iffirn for etrochta a ghnuisi ni airechdais saeth na pein na todernam ind iffirn.[138]	Cuius faciem si omnes carcere inferni inclusi uiderent, nullam penam nullum dolorem nullamque tristiciam sentirent: cuius presentia si in inferno cum suis habitatoribus appareret, continuo infernus in amenum conuerteretur paradysum.[139]

In both the Irish and Old English legends, the victims' torments are also posited as a relief which their victims would easily endure if they could escape from hell, but it is not clear whether their escape is periodic or permanent – or more precisely, since the situation is entirely

[136] Gougaud, 'La croyance au répit périodique', p. 70.

[137] On this tradition, see A. Cabassut, 'La mitigation des peines de l'enfer d'après les livres liturgiques', *Revue d'histoire ecclésiastique* 23 (1927), 65–70.

[138] 'The Evernew Tongue', ed. Stokes, p. 142: 'Such are the beauty and effulgence of His face that if all the souls in hell were to look on the splendour of His countenance they would not perceive trouble, nor pain, nor punishment in hell' (trans. Stokes, p. 143).

[139] *The Writings of Bishop Patrick*, ed. Gwynn, p. 116. I reproduce, with slight modifications, the sixteenth-century English translation printed by Gwynn (p. 117): 'Whose face if all people enclosed in the dungeon of hell could see they would feel no pain, no grief, and no sorrow: whose presence if it should appear in hell to the dwellers there, hell would straightway be turned into a pleasant paradise'. Bishop Patrick's apparent use of *Tenga Bithnua* here has not previously been remarked. For evidence that material from *Tenga Bithnua* was available in twelfth-century England, see P. Kitson, 'The Jewels and Bird *Hiruath* of the "Ever-New Tongue"', *Ériu* 25 (1984), 113–36, at 127–30.

hypothetical, whether the torment is to be imagined as a periodic respite of an eternally damned soul, or a purgatorial torment of a soul rescued from hell by intercession.[140] The context of the Irish tale suggests the latter, since it concerns the rescue of Mael Sechnaill's soul through the intercession of Cairpre Crom. The distinction may not be crucial, but neither is it entirely idle, since it affects an assessment of the ultimate sources and relationships of these descriptions. The stock description I have outlined, of a hanging punishment located on a cliff by the ocean, was built upon elements derived from the *Visio S. Pauli*, where the torment is clearly infernal, as it is in Blickling XVI. Even Judas's punishment appears elsewhere as simply an infernal punishment, with no question of a respite. In *Dá Apstol Décc na hÉrenn* ('The Twelve Apostles of Ireland'), which incorporates a variant form of the Brendan legend, Brendan encounters Judas not on the earthly ocean but on the sea of hell itself:

Conidh annsin atconnairc Brenainn in carraicc ndermair; is fuirre sidhe ro búi a nat-cualaidh; 7 ticcedh an muir ifernaidhe da cech aird darsin carraicc ndermair .i. tonn teinedh dubh-ruaidhe anair thairsi, 7 tonn uar, eighreta, aníar cech re fecht. Is annsin búi oen duine truagh ina shesamh forsin carraic. Iarfaighis Brenainn de, cuich é. 'Iudas Scarioth meisi', ol se.[141]

At some point, however, the torment was adapted either as a periodic respite, perhaps along the lines of Judas's torment in the *Nauigatio*, or as a purgatorial torment as in the story of Cairpre Crom, but representing in both cases an escape from the torments of hell, in comparison to which the hanging punishment is to be lightly regarded by its relieved victim.[142] Although the victim can easily be made to

[140] The deliverance of souls from hell through intercession is a recurrent theme in Irish legend. Psalm CXVIII, the *Beati*, was considered to have special power to release souls from hell; see below, pp. 240–1.

[141] *Lives of Irish Saints*, ed. Plummer I, 100: 'And then Brendan saw a huge rock, and on it was that which he had heard. And the infernal sea would wash over the huge rock on every side; a wave of black-red fire (would break) over it from in front, and a cold icy wave from behind alternately. And one wretched man was standing on the rock. Brendan asked him who he was. "I am Judas Iscariot", said he' (trans. Plummer II, 96).

[142] The motif of purgatorial punishment on a rock in the ocean survives in modern Irish folklore. See, for example, the story summarized by P. Ó Héalaí, 'Popular Morality in Irish Religious Tales', in *Irish Spirituality*, ed. M. Maher (Dublin, 1981), pp. 71–87, at 76–7, and 'The Poem of the Tor', cited below, p. 209, n. 108.

describe the hell torments he has escaped – as Judas does at great length in the *Vita secunda* – it is much more effective to leave them unexpressed. Such is the case in the story of Cairpre Crom and Vercelli Homily IX, in which the victims' torment now functions as an inexpressibility topos, whose impact is further heightened by having the entire description recast in hypothetical form.

This coincidence of rhetorical formulation is even more striking than the coincidences of descriptive detail. That variations of essentially the same stock description should serve precisely the same rhetorical function in the Irish tale and in the Old English homily can hardly be fortuitous. Just as *Beowulf* and Blickling XVI represent one distinctive development of the same stock description, so Vercelli Homily IX and the story of Cairpre Crom represent another. Apparently, both texts have preserved variations of a set piece which circulated as an exemplum *de poenis inferni*, in which the hanging punishment with its distinctive setting, originally part of a vision of hell based on the *Visio S. Pauli*, functions instead as a hypothetical torment in a new rhetorical context built on an inexpressibility topos.[143]

THE MEN WITH TONGUES OF IRON

Inexpressibility is the dominant rhetorical mode of Vercelli IX, initiated by the quotation of Psalm VI.6 in the introduction. Later, just before the

[143] A more direct connection between the two texts is perhaps not entirely out of the question, for the story of Cairpre Crom seems to have been a significant document in the alliance between the abbots of Clonmacnois and the heirs of Mael Sechnaill (Hughes, 'The Distribution of Irish Scriptoria', pp. 254–5), and some knowledge of Clonmacnois traditions in Anglo-Saxon England is evidenced by the obituary notice of Suibne mac Maele Umai of Clonmacnois in the *Anglo-Saxon Chronicle*, s.a. 891. Hughes notes that the *Chronicum Scotorum*, s.a. 904, records the apparition of Mael Sechnaill. See *Chronicum Scotorum: a Chronicle of Irish Affairs, from the Earliest Times to A. D. 1135*, ed. and trans. W. M. Hennessy, Rolls Series 46 (London, 1866), pp. 178–9. The story of Cairpre Crom, which conforms closely to the type of revelation described by Seymour, 'The Eschatology of the Early Irish Church', pp. 201–3 and J. Le Goff, *The Birth of Purgatory*, trans. A. Goldhammer (Chicago, 1984), p. 294, may of course be a much later tale, and may not have been the original setting of the poem, which was also used in at least one other context (see above, n. 128). For similar stories concerning gradual release from hell, see *Vita prima Sancti Brendani*, in *Vitae Sanctorum Hiberniae*, ed. Plummer I, 148–9; *Vita Sancti Coemgeni*, *ibid.* I, 254–5; J. Vendryes, 'Betha Grighora', *RC* 42 (1925), 119–53, at 149.

description of the Hanging Sinner, the homilist includes a variation of perhaps the most well-known inexpressibility topos in classical and medieval tradition. The Men with Tongues of Iron, part of an interpolated motif descending from the archetypal redaction Silverstein designated α, occurs in Redactions I, IV, V, VIII and X.[144] These redactions reckon the number of pains of hell at 144,000, but – as if to counter any impression that these pains, though manifold, are at least finite – conclude the inventory with an inexpressibility topos:

et si essent .c. uiri loquentes ab inicio mundi et unusquisque .c. iiii. linguas ferreas haberent, non possent dinumerare penas inferni.[145]

The ultimate source for this adynaton is Virgil's description of Hades in the sixth book of the *Aeneid*:

> Non, mihi si linguae centum sint, oraque centum,
> Ferrea uox, omnis scelerum conprendere formas,
> Omnia poenarum percurrere nomina possim.[146]

Virgil's disclaimer is itself merely a variation of a more ancient classical topos,[147] but for the Middle Ages it was the most influential formulation.

[144] On this motif, part of interpolation (1), the enumeration of torments, see Silverstein, *Visio Sancti Pauli*, pp. 65–6 (for Redaction X, see Silverstein, 'New Links and Patterns', pp. 218 and 246). For convenience I adopt Silverstein's name for the motif, even though it will be seen that it is not quite appropriate for the Old English versions.

[145] Quotation from Redaction IV (in *Visio S. Pauli*, ed. Brandes, p. 80): 'and if there were a hundred men speaking from the beginning of the world and each had a hundred and four iron tongues, they could not enumerate the pains of hell'. In Redaction I there is only a single iron tongue (*Visio Sancti Pauli*, ed. Silverstein, p. 155); in Redactions V and VIII, there are four (*ibid.*, pp. 203 and 213).

[146] *Aeneid* VI.625–7, in *Virgil, with an English Translation*, 2 vols., ed. H. R. Fairclough, Loeb Classical Library 58 (Cambridge, MA, 1935) I, 548–9. Fairclough translates: 'Nay, had I a hundred tongues, a hundred mouths, and voice of iron, I could not sum up all the forms of crime, or rehearse all the tale of torments.' The same adynaton occurs in a different context in *Georgics* II.42–4.

[147] For references, see Pöschl *et al.*, *Bibliographie*, under the headings 'Munde, hundert' (p. 256) and 'Zungen, hundert' (p. 593). The most famous example is from the catalogue of ships in *Iliad* II.489–90, a passage known to the Middle Ages through Macrobius's quotation (*Saturnalia* V.vii.16, cited by Silverstein, *Visio Sancti Pauli*, p. 117, n. 7). An early apocryphon, the Epistle of the Apostles, refers to ten thousand tongues, but without the iron voice (*Apocryphal New Testament*, trans. James, p. 500).

Pierre Courcelle has traced some two dozen Latin quotations of it in varying contexts, from patristic and medieval sources up to the twelfth century.[148] But the example from the *Visio S. Pauli* cannot really be called a quotation. For the Virgilian first-person singular the *Visio* substitutes a hundred hypothetical speakers, and instead of a hundred tongues and mouths, each has a hundred and four tongues, and it is the *tongues* that are iron, not the voice as in the *Aeneid*. And as if the Virgilian hyperbole were not sufficient, the *Visio* allows these formidable orators to speak 'from the beginning of the world'. Finally, the rhetorical formulation has been subtly altered, for the simple equative enumeration of the *Aeneid* (a hundred heads *and* a hundred mouths) becomes a reduplicating pattern (a hundred men, *each* with a hundred and four tongues).

This motif had a long and varied history in Anglo-Saxon England and Ireland. The Old English versions of the motif have been noted by several scholars, but their relationship to the *Aeneid* and to the *Visio S. Pauli*, though it has been recognized, has not been investigated in sufficient detail.[149] I begin with Vercelli IX, in which the inexpressibility topos amplifies the homilist's assertion that no man can express the magnitude of torment (*tintrega*), which is the fifth likeness of hell:

> ⁊ þeah .vii. men sien, ⁊ þara hæbbe æghwylc twa ⁊ hundsiofontig gereorda, swa feala swa ealles þysses middangeardes gereorda syndon, and þonne sy þara seofon manna æghwylc to alife gesceapen, ⁊ hyra hæbbe æghwylc siofon [heafdu, ⁊ þara heafdu ælc hæbbe siofon] tungan, ⁊ þara tungena ælc hæbbe isene stemne, ⁊ þonne hwæðre ne magon þa ealle ariman helle witu.[150]

148 'Histoire du cliché virgilien'.

149 Silverstein cited only Napier XLIII (*Visio Sancti Pauli*, p. 11). He also referred (p. 98, n. 57) to passages in Napier XXIX and XXX, but these do not have the specific elements that give the motif its identity. Other brief discussions of the Old English examples are Tristram, 'Stock Descriptions', pp. 107–8; Bazire and Cross, *Rogationtide Homilies*, p. 58; Healey, *The Old English Vision*, pp. 54–5; Sauer, 'Die 72 Völker und Sprachen', pp. 35–7; Tveitane, 'Irish Apocrypha', pp. 119 and 132. R. Hasenfratz, '*Eisegan stefne* (*Christ and Satan* 36a), the *Visio Pauli*, and *ferrea vox* (*Aeneid* 6, 626)', *MP* 86 (1989), 398–403, has recently surveyed the topos in Old English, arriving independently at some of the same conclusions I had drawn in my dissertation, but without reference to the Irish parallels; he suggests emending the phrase *eisegan stefne* in *Christ and Satan* to *isenan stefne* as a reflection of this topos.

150 *The Vercelli Homilies*, ed. Scragg, p. 168, line 108 – p. 170, line 113: 'And even if there were seven men, and each of them had seventy-two languages, as many languages as there are in this world, and then if each of those men were created with

In Vercelli IX the motif that appears in the *Aeneid* and in the *Visio S. Pauli* has been altered by substituting the number seven for one hundred and by adding a learned allusion to the seventy-two world languages.[151] But the formulation of Vercelli IX is not simply an elaboration of the *Aeneid* or the *Visio*; although it owes something to each Latin text, it does not depend exclusively on either.[152] Like the *Visio* it replaces the Virgilian first-person singular with multiple speakers and arranges the items (which do not include mouths) in a reduplicating series linked by the catchword 'each' (*unusquisque/æghwylc*). But one detail points unmistakably to the Virgilian form of the motif: Vercelli IX refers to an iron *voice* (*stemn*) as in the *Aeneid*, not to iron *tongues*, as in the *Visio*.[153] That the archetype of Vercelli IX also added heads to the anatomical list is clear from L and N. As Scragg suggests, the reference to the seven heads 'was omitted by homeoteleuton from the AE version'.[154]

eternal life, and each one of them had seven [heads, and each of the heads had seven] tongues, and each of the tongues had an iron voice, yet none the less they could not enumerate all the pains of hell.'

151 See Sauer, 'Die 72 Völker und Sprachen'. For some examples in Irish and Hiberno-Latin, see D. Ó Cróinín, *The Irish Sex Aetates Mundi* (Dublin, 1983), p. 148; *Scriptores Hiberniae Minores I*, ed. McNally, p. 197, note; Carey, 'The Heavenly City in *Saltair na Rann*', p. 101.

152 In connection with Napier XLIII (N), Silverstein remarks that 'the influence of the Redactions is clear enough, since the motif itself, in the form in which it is here presented, seems to have been brought originally into the stream of Christian vision literature by the first of the ten abbreviations of *Paul*' (*Visio Sancti Pauli*, p. 11). But Silverstein fails to recognize the difficulty in connecting the Old English directly with any surviving version of the *Visio*, especially the important detail of the iron *voice*. Marchand, 'The Old Norwegian Christmas Homily', pp. 29–30, criticizes Tveitane for referring the motif in the Norwegian homily to the *Visio S. Pauli* rather than to the *Aeneid*, since 'the same adynaton is found in so many places'. But many of the vernacular examples, as I shall show, have distinctive formulations which should not be levelled by classing them all as 'the same adynaton'.

153 In the extract from Vercelli IX in Napier XXX (O), however, the iron image is dropped, and rather than specifying the number of the tongues, their multiplicity is emphasized by hyperbole: 'ealle þa tungon, þe æfre clypedon and spræcon, syððan Adam leofode se forma mann, þe Crist ærest gescop, þeah hi gyt on þysum life wæron, and ða þe nu gyt syndon, and ða þe towearde syndon, ær domes dæg cume, ealle hi ne mihton asecgan and areccan, hu wa þam sawlum bið, þe on helle beon sceolon' (*Wulfstan*, ed. Napier, p. 147, lines 13–18).

154 'The Corpus of Vernacular Homilies', p. 247, n. 6. I adopt Scragg's manuscript sigla to refer to the different versions of Vercelli IX and other anonymous homilies.

Variations on the motif occur in four other Old English homilies. The first of these, from the Old English version of the Seven Heavens apocryphon, is not so elaborate as the others:

D: And ðeah ðe hwylc mon hæbbe .c. tungena, and ðara æghwylc hæbbe isene stefne, ne magon hi asec<g>an helle tintrego and ða fulnissa ðara dracena and ðone singalan hungor![155]

Here we have only a single hypothetical speaker rather than seven, but the combination of the single iron *voice* as in the *Aeneid* and the rhetorical expression with the catchword 'each' as in the *Visio S. Pauli* once again characterizes the Old English formulation. Another example occurs in the homily *Be heofonwarum 7 be helwarum*:

JK: þeah ænig man hæfde .c. heafda and þæra heafda æghwilc hæfde .c. tungan and hi wæron ealle isene and ealle spræcon fram frymðe þyssere worulde oð ende ne mihton hi asecgan þæt yfel þe on helle is.[156]

The iron *tongues*, as well as the reference to the duration of speaking 'from the beginning of the world' directly recall the *Visio*, as does the use of the number one hundred instead of seven; but unlike the *Visio*, there is only a single hypothetical speaker. The addition of heads to the anatomical list parallels versions L, M and N of Vercelli IX.

The two remaining Old English examples, both from Rogationtide homilies, more closely resemble Vercelli IX in its prolixity, but differ in detail (and in one case, also in context):

O: And ðær is wanunga and wita ma þonne æniges mannes earan ahlystan magon ne nanes mannes tunga nis to þam swyft: þeah þe he hæbbe XII heafdu and þæra heafdu æghwylc hæbbe XII tungan and ðæra tunga æghwylc hæbbe XII stefna and ðæra stefna gehwylc hæbbe snyttro Salomones; ne magon he

[155] *Two Apocrypha*, ed. Willard, p. 6, lines 63–6: 'And even if someone had one hundred tongues, and each of them had an iron voice, they could not relate the torments of hell and the foulness of the dragons and the perpetual hunger!'

[156] Willard did not publish this part of the homily; I cite from Callison, 'An Edition of Previously Unpublished Anglo-Saxon Homilies', p. 247 (I omit the manuscript pointing retained in this edition, except where it marks the roman numerals): 'Even if any man had one hundred heads and each of the heads had one hundred tongues and they were all iron and all spoke from the beginning of this world until its end they could not express the evil that is in hell.'

þeahhwæðere ealle þa wean and ða witu ariman ne areccan þe þa earman and þa werigan sawla geþafian and þrowian sculon.[157]

H: Men þa leofestan, þær syndon heofonas us to blisse togeanes þam hellebrogan; nu syndon ealle þa mid mærðan afylled. Ðeah þe wære twa and hundseofontig manna and hæfde ælce þara manna twa and hundsefontig heafodo and ælc þæra hæfda twa and hundseofonti tungena and ælc þære tungena hæfde twa and hundseofontig gereorda and hig swa lange spræcan þæt hi ealle wæron werige, ne mihten hi þone teoðan dæl asecgan hu feola beorhta beama is on þan seofan heofonum ne hu fela hwitra blosmena.[158]

The Rogationtide homilies are similar to Vercelli IX in adding heads to the anatomical list and in constructing a reduplicating series with the catchword 'each' (*æghwylc* or *ælc*). H, which applies the motif to the joys of heaven rather than to the pains of hell, shares an additional detail with Vercelli IX in its allusion to the seventy-two world languages. The most obvious divergences are that both Rogationtide homilies use a different number as the basis for the series (twelve in O, seventy-two in H), and that neither refers to *iron* tongues or voices. Finally, H has no reference to the duration of speaking, and O differs in this regard from both the *Visio* and Vercelli IX, having the speakers continue 'until they were all weary'.

It is clear that the motif in Old English has been reworked with elements borrowed from both the *Aeneid* and the *Visio S. Pauli*, and then circulated independently within the vernacular. D preserves the simple combination of the one hundred tongues and the voice of iron from the *Aeneid* with the reduplicating pattern ('and þara ægwhylc hæbbe...')

[157] *Rogationtide Homilies*, ed. Bazire and Cross, pp. 142–3, lines 90–5: 'And there are griefs and torments more than any man's ear may hear, nor is any man's tongue sufficiently swift: even if he had twelve heads and each of the heads had twelve tongues, and each of the tongues had twelve voices, and each of the voices had the wisdom of Solomon, still they could not recount or number all those pains and torments which the wretched and cursed souls have to endure and suffer.'

[158] *Ibid.*, p. 64, lines 85–90: 'Beloved men, for our bliss there are heavens set against the terror of hell. Now all of these are filled with delights. Even if there were seventy-two men and each of the men had seventy-two heads and each of the heads [had] seventy-two tongues and each of the tongues had seventy-two languages, and they could all speak so long that they were all weary, they could not recount the tenth part of how many bright rays or how many white flowers are in the seven heavens.'

and the omission of the Virgilian 'hundred mouths' as in the *Visio*. Vercelli IX represents the basic elaborated form of the motif.[159] H has generalized the number seventy-two throughout the series and dropped the reference to iron voices. The affiliations of O are more difficult to reconstruct. O retains the voices, but does not describe them as iron, and O differs from the other elaborated forms of the motif by including the voices in the reduplicating series (twelve voices instead of a single voice) but excluding the speakers (a single speaker instead of twelve). O is unique among the elaborated versions in alluding to the wisdom of Solomon rather than the seventy-two languages. In short, O probably does not depend directly on the formulation represented by Vercelli IX with a confusion of roman numerals (xii for vii), but is instead a separate development of the simple combined form represented by D. The motif obviously lends itself well to variation and extension, as several Middle English reflexes also attest.[160]

Commenting on the Men with Tongues of Iron motif in Vercelli IX, Hildegard Tristram noted that 'a similar phraseology is also topical in Irish prose', and referred, without further discussion, to examples in three Irish texts.[161] It must be said at the outset, however, that Irish versions of the motif do not show close agreement among themselves or with the comparatively more stable Old English formulation. But the number of examples, their varying contexts and their occurrence in Irish sources from the eighth through the sixteenth century show how popular the motif was in Ireland, and a survey of the Irish versions does reveal significant similarities with the Old English formulation.

159 Sauer, 'Die 72 Völker und Sprachen', believes that N, in which the motif is part of the exchange between the devil and the anchorite, preserves the original form. But if Scragg is right in suggesting that the original context of 'The Devil's Account' was within Vercelli IX, it is more likely that the compiler of the composite homily in N has extracted the motif from a version of Vercelli IX related to L (retaining the term *susl*, the fifth 'likeness' of hell in L), but transferred it to the exemplum from its original position as a transition between the preparatory motifs and exemplum.

160 Silverstein, *Visio Sancti Pauli*, p. 66, cites several examples from Middle English texts, in which the numbers are sometimes inflated (one thousand tongues of steel in *Sawles Warde*, one hundred thousand men and tongues of steel in the *Pricke of Conscience*). Cf. the Middle English version of the *Visio* quoted by Becker, *Medieval Visions of Heaven and Hell*, pp. 52–3.

161 'Stock Descriptions', p. 108, n. 27. See now Carey, '*Visio Sancti Pauli* and the *Saltair*'s Hell', who refers to some of the same examples.

As in England, the Latin formulations of the motif in both the *Aeneid* and the *Visio S. Pauli* were influential. Some of the Irish examples recall one or the other directly. Thus the *Visio Tnugdali* quotes twice from the *Aeneid*, virtually verbatim, but a third time the formulation with the word *unoquoque* echoes instead the *Visio S. Pauli*: 'quanta uel qualia et quam inaudita ibi uiderit tormenta, si centum capita et in unoquoque capite centum linguas haberet, recitare nullo modo potest'.[162] In vernacular poetry, the motif occurs in the eighth-century poems of Blathmac, though in reduced form and altered context:

> Ní r-aisndet, a bé co lí,
> do mac, mét a chumachtai,
> ced cét tengad labrath de;
> níbu lán int aithscéle.[163]

Saltair na Rann uses the motif twice, first in praise of God, and later in its more usual infernal context:

> Cianobeth cét tengad ndron
> frisirlabra cenairchron,
> níaisneidfind triabithsír
> cétmad adamra m'ardrig.[164]

> Cia no beth cēt mīli fer,
> cona tengthaib íarnaideib,

[162] *Visio Tnugdali*, ed. Wagner, p. 35: 'And there, what number and variety of unheard of torments he saw; even if he had a hundred heads and a hundred tongues in each head, he could not have given an account of them all' (trans. Picard, *The Vision of Tnugdal*, p. 138). The three passages from the *Visio Tnugdali* are cited by Courcelle, 'Histoire du cliché virgilien', p. 239. See also Spilling, *Die Visio Tnugdali*, p. 189.

[163] *The Poems of Blathmac*, ed. Carney, p. 68, lines 801–4. Carney translates: 'Beautiful maiden, were a hundred tongues to speak of it they could not recount the extent of your son's power: the repetition would not achieve completeness' (this example is noted by J. Carey, 'Questions of Interpolation in the Opening Cantos of *Saltair na Rann*', *PHCC* 6 (1986), 69–82, at 81, n. 15). A reduced form of the motif occurs in an earlier stanza (p. 12, lines 141–2): 'Lín fertae maic Dé bí, de / ní r-aisnedat cét ecnae' ('A hundred sages cannot tell the number of the miracles of the son of the living God').

[164] *Saltair na Rann*, ed. Stokes, p. 12, lines 825–8: 'Though I had a hundred strong tongues continually speaking without rebuking, I would not tell forever a hundredth part of the wonder of my high king.'

oenphían dib, co brāth mbrudin
ní choemstais do derbthurim.[165]

In the first example the first-person singular recalls Virgil, but the reference to the eternal duration of the speaking recalls the *Visio S. Pauli*. In the second, the multiple speakers and iron *tongues* also recall the apocryphal text.

Similar variations occur in Manus O'Donnell's *Betha Colaim Chille* ('Life of St Columba'), in which a certain Mongán reports a vision of hell and heaven to the saint:

'Ni hurassa dam a tuarascbail do tabairt uaim', ar Mongan, 'oir da mbeith mile teanga am cenn 7 saegal go la na breithe agam, ni fhedfaind uile dhuad uilc an tighe ud 7 na haitrebhe d'indisin.'[166]

'Ni heidir limsa breth do breith air', ar Mongan, 'oir da mbeith mile cenn orum 7 mile tenga in gach cenn dibh, ni thicfed dim an gloir is lugha a bflaithes De d'indisin duit.'[167]

The inflated numbers in these two examples (one thousand instead of one hundred, as in the second quotation from *Saltair na Rann*), and the addition of heads to the anatomical list in the second quotation (as in the *Visio Tnugdali*), are paralleled in Sedulius Scottus's *Collectaneum*, where a

165 *The Irish Adam and Eve Story from Saltair na Rann*, ed. Greene and Kelly, p. 16, lines 929–32: 'Though there should be a hundred thousand men, with their iron tongues, they could not, until judgment of…, recount accurately one of those pains' (trans. Greene and Kelly, p. 17). A weakened reflex of the theme occurs a few lines later (p. 19, lines 953–6).

166 *Betha Colaim Chille: Life of Columcille*, ed. A. O'Kelleher and G. Schoepperle (Urbana, IL, 1918), p. 81, lines 32–5: '"Not easy were it for me to give thee tidings thereof", saith Mongan, "for if there were a thousand tongues in my head, and if I should have life till Doomsday, I could not tell thee all the hardship of evil in that house and dwelling"' (trans. O'Kelleher and Schoepperle, p. 83).

167 *Ibid.*, p. 82, lines 3–6: '"Not easy for me to give tidings thereof", saith Mongan, "for were there a thousand heads upon me, and a thousand tongues in every head, I could not describe to thee the least of the glories of the Kingdom of God"' (trans. O'Kelleher and Schoepperle, p. 83). Manus O'Donnell wrote the Life (Kenney, *The Sources*, no. 221) *c.* 1530 using earlier materials. The story of Columba's encounter with Mongán is apparently related to an earlier (eighth- or ninth-century?) text *Imacallam Choluim Chille ocus in Óclaig* ('The Colloquy of Columcille and the Youth'), ed. K. Meyer, *ZCP* 2 (1899), 313–17; P. Grosjean, *AB* 45 (1927), 75–83. See P. Mac Cana, 'Mongán mac Fiachna and *Immram Brain*', *Ériu* 23 (1972), 102–42.

loose variation of the motif is applied to the joys of heaven: 'Nam si uox infatigata per tot tempora, per millena capita, uociferaret numerare et narrare regnum caelorum sicut est, non potuisset.'[168]

In the twelfth-century *Cogadh Gaedhel re Gallaibh* ('War of the Irish with the Foreigners') the motif occurs in a secular context:

Cid tra acht, cid cet cend cadut comcruaid iarnaidi no beith ar oen bragit, ocus cet tengad aig athlom innuar umaidi nemergdi in gach cind, ocus cet guth glortumlacha glanidi nemircradach o cach oen tengaid, ni tairesad a thuruim, no a asneis, no a arium, no a innisi [an] ro odimset gaedil uli co cotcend.[169]

The sheer prolixity of the description, which reflects a later development of Irish prose style,[170] is only superficially similar to the Old English examples of the theme. Significant, however, in addition to the (iron!) heads in the anatomical list, is the extension of the numbered items in a reduplicating series linked by *gach* ('each').

Finally, four Irish examples parallel the preference for the number seven in the Vercelli IX group. In the early-ninth-century *Félire Oengusso* ('The Martyrology of Oengus') the motif is quite reduced, and applied to the number of the saints:

Cé betis secht tengtha
im gin sóee suilgind
co bráth, mó cech delmaimm,
issed ma doruirminn.[171]

In the late Middle Irish *Accalamh na Senórach* ('Colloquy of the Old Men'), Cailte praises Find: 'uair da mbeitís secht tengtha im cind 7 secht

[168] *Sedulii Scotti Collectaneum Miscellaneum*, ed. Simpson, p. 139: 'For if an unwearied voice should speak for all time, through a thousand heads, to enumerate and recount how the kingdom of heaven is, it could not do so.'

[169] *Cogadh Gaedhel re Gallaibh: the War of the Gaedhil with the Gaill*, ed. J. H. Todd (London, 1867), p. 50: 'In a word, although there were an hundred hard steeled iron heads on one neck, and an hundred sharp, ready, cool, never-rusting, brazen tongues in each head, and an hundred garrulous, loud, unceasing voices from each tongue, they could not recount, or narrate, or enumerate, or tell, what all the Gaedhil suffered in common' (trans. Todd, p. 51).

[170] See Hughes, *Early Christian Ireland*, pp. 288–9.

[171] *Félire Oengusso Céli Dé*, ed. Stokes, p. 270: 'Though there were seven tongues in my sage, studious mouth, it is until doom – greater than any noise – if I should recount them' (trans. Stokes, p. 271). For a very similar example, applied to the 'wonders of Mary', see *Dán Dé*, ed. L. McKenna (Dublin, n.d.), p. 128.

solabarta súadh cecha tengad dib ní táirsed uaim leth na trian a maithesa fecht d'indisin ar Find'.[172] In the Middle Irish (tenth- or eleventh-century) *Togail Troí* ('The Destruction of Troy') a much-reduced version of the motif occurs when Agamemnon asks envoys for a report on Troy: '"Cía nobetís émh," ar íat, "secht tengtha i cind cech áin acanne, ní fétfaimís aisnís cech neich atchondcammar."'[173] Recension II of *Tenga Bithnua* affords a more elaborate example, with two sevenfold items linked by *gach* ('each'):

óir in tén is lúaithi & is treisi lúamhairecht fá neimh da mbeith sé ré mile bliadan ac taistel ifrinn ní budh eidir leis rimh pian ifrinn & .uii. tengtha file na chind & .uii. so-urlabra suadh in gach tengaidh dib.[174]

None of these texts provides a close parallel for the formulation of the motif in the Old English homilies, but from the diverse forms represented in Irish sources one can construct a composite that would parallel most of the peculiarities of the Old English formulation: the duration of the speaking until Doomsday (*Félire Oengusso*, *Betha Colaim Chille*); the addition of heads to the anatomical list (*Visio Tnugdali*, *Betha Colaim Chille*, *Cogadh Gaedhel re Gallaibh*, *Tenga Bithnua*); the number

[172] Ed. W. Stokes in *Irische Texte* 4.1, ed. Stokes and Windisch, p. 211: 'for were there seven tongues in my head, and seven sages' eloquence in each tongue, not half nor a third of his excellence would be uttered by me as to Find' (trans. Stokes, p. 261). For the date, see M. Dillon, *Stories from the Accalam*, MMIS 23 (Dublin, 1970), p. 23.

[173] Ed. W. Stokes in *Irische Texte* 2.1, ed. Stokes and Windisch, p. 26: '"In truth", say they, "though there were seven tongues in the head of each of us, we could not set forth everything that we beheld"' (trans. Stokes, p. 91). For the date, see G. Mac Eoin, 'Das Verbalsystem von Togail Troí (H 2 17)', *ZCP* 28 (1960–1), 73–106.

[174] 'The Second Recension of the *Evernew Tongue*', ed. Nic Énri and Mac Niocaill, p. 45 (text of ms. R, printed among the variants): 'for the swiftest and strongest-flying bird under heaven, though it be a thousand years travelling in hell, could not recount the number of pains of hell, and seven tongues were in its head and seven eloquent voices of wise men in each tongue'. Cf. the following from Recension I: 'For all the beasts under seas, and birds in the air, and cattle and [wild] animals and men on earth, and angels in the heavens, and devils in hell, though they should commence from the beginning of the world, they would not, before the Judgment, have declared one seventh of the works of God' ('The Evernew Tongue', trans. Stokes, p. 141). In 'Tidings of Doomsday', trans. Stokes, p. 255, occurs the following hyperbole: 'Now though one should be put in seven ages and though there should be a thousand years in each age of them, not more than the one and twentieth part of Hell's evils would he relate.'

seven (*Accalamh na Senórach*, *Togail Troí*, *Félire Oengusso*, *Tenga Bithnua*);[175] and the extension of the numbered items into a reduplicating series linked by the catchword 'each' (*Betha Coluim Cille*, *Cogadh Gaedhel re Gallaibh*, *Tenga Bithnua*). These common features by no means indicate a generic relationship – heads are a natural addition to the anatomical list, and seven is a universally favoured round number – but they do reflect similar literary tastes. In particular, the construction of a numerical *gradatio* or reduplicating series linked by 'each' is significant, for this is a favourite rhetorical pattern in Irish literature, and occurs elsewhere in Old English. In the next motif, the Monster of Hell, the same pattern recurs.

THE MONSTER OF HELL

At the close of 'The Devil's Account' the homilist appeals once more to his anonymous but authoritative 'books' for a final revelation of the terrors of hell:

Eala mycel is on bocum leornod 7 hit is soðlice eal gesewen; sagað hit þæt on helle sy an hund. Ne meahte hit þæt dioful þam ancran eall asecgan hu mycel þær[e] s[aw]le witu bioð þe to him bioð gescyrede. He hafað hundteontig heafda, 7 he hafað on ælcum heafde hund eagena, 7 ælc þara egena is fyre hat, 7 he hafað .c. handa, 7 on ælcre handa hundteontig fingra, 7 on ælcum fingre .c. nægla, 7 hyra is ælc on nædran wisan ascyrped.[176]

Although an erasure after the word *hund* in the Vercelli text leaves room for doubt, this grotesque creature is apparently a hound, albeit a hound with at least one dominant reptilian trait. Förster suggested supplying *wita* in the gap, taking *hund* as the numeral, thus, 'in hell there are a

[175] The number seven occurs also in a distant variant of the motif in the Old English *Solomon and Saturn II* (see below, p. 235).

[176] *The Vercelli Homilies*, ed. Scragg, p. 182, line 214 – p. 184, line 220: 'Oh, much is learned from books and it is all truly known; it says that in hell there is a hound. The devil could not tell fully to the anchorite how great are the soul's torments that are assigned to them. He has a hundred heads, and he has a hundred eyes in each head, and each of the eyes is hot as fire, and he has a hundred hands, and on each hand a hundred fingers, and on each finger a hundred nails, and each of the nails is sharpened in serpent fashion.'

hundred torments'.[177] But in E there is no gap, and the text may be translated, without emendation, 'it says that in hell there is a certain hound'. As we will see, most analogues make the beast a dragon or serpentine monster, but this is not decisive for determining the reading of Vercelli IX, especially since multi-headed hounds and dragons are equally fabled as guardians of the netherworld in ancient and medieval traditions, and could easily be confused, or as it were crossbred.[178] Cerberus, the three-headed hound of hell, was well known to the Middle Ages through Virgil's *Aeneid* (VI.417–20), but in other classical texts Cerberus has fifty heads (Hesiod) or a hundred (Pindar, Horace and elsewhere), or simply an uncountable number (Statius). And he sometimes has a mane of serpents or a serpent's tail.[179] The Hydra, like Cerberus an offspring of Echidne, is a sea-serpent with a dog-like body and eight, nine, fifty, a hundred or even a thousand heads. The Dragon of the Hesperides may likewise have two, three or a hundred heads.[180]

For the Middle Ages the definitive dragon of hell was, of course, the seven-headed, ten-horned serpent of the Apocalypse (XII.3). But the *Visio S. Pauli* has a dragon too, described in considerable detail in seven of the redactions (I–III, VII, VIII, X and *Br*), 'hence patently the lurid addition of their common source, Redaction α'.[181] Although the essential picture of the dragon remains relatively consistent in these redactions, there are significant divergences in details. I will quote from Redaction I, which Silverstein makes the basis of his discussion, and note the relevant variations.

At the beginning of the vision, after Paul has been transported over the world-river Oceanus, he approaches a *locus terribilis* through which run the rivers of hell. There lies the dragon,

centum capita habens in collo eius et mille dentes in unoquoque capite, et ut leo unusquisque dens ardebat. Et erant oculi eius quasi gladii acuti, semper ore

177 See Szarmach's note on the line.

178 For bibliography on multi-headed monsters, see Pöschl *et al.*, *Bibliographie*, under the heading 'Tiere mit meheren Häupten'.

179 For references, see *ibid.* Cerberus also appears in some of the redactions of the *Visio S. Pauli*, sometimes as the dog of the *hostiarius inferni*, sometimes as the *hostiarius inferni* himself. See Silverstein, *Visio Sancti Pauli*, pp. 44, 56–7 and 115, n. 59; *idem*, 'New Links and Patterns', p. 219, n. 90.

180 For references, see Pöschl *et al.*, *Bibliographie*.

181 Silverstein, 'New Links and Patterns', pp. 205–6. For Silverstein's discussion of this interpolation, see *Visio Sancti Pauli*, pp. 66–9.

aperto et deglucìebat animas. Et erat nomen eius Parthemon. Ab eo procedunt copie ranarum et omnia genera uermium. In ore eius mittuntur satrape omnes qui iniquitatem faciunt in terra cum principibus.[182]

Silverstein calls Parthemon 'a synthetic creature', for whose various features he finds 'numerous and scattered suggestions and parallels in the Scriptures and elsewhere in Western tradition'.[183] Silverstein refers to the dragon as 'Hydra-headed', but whether the multiple heads are a reminiscence of the Hydra, the Dragon of the Hesperides, or Cerberus, it is significant that this feature echoes classical rather than biblical tradition: Parthemon has a hundred heads in Redactions I, VII, VIII and *Br*, a thousand in Redactions III and X and three in Redaction II – never seven. The hundred-headed form matching the monster of Vercelli IX probably preserves the reading of the archetypal Redaction α, since Redactions I and *Br* both derive directly and independently from α (VII and VIII depend on I). The thousand heads of the dragon in Redaction III and its descendant X, both of which derive indirectly from α through β, probably mirror the dragon's thousand teeth, a number common to all these redactions. The reading *tria capita* of Redaction II is no doubt a reflection of the Cerberus myth.

Although Parthemon has a hundred heads like the monster of Vercelli IX, the latter beast has a series of appendages which Parthemon lacks, and the hundred heads could derive independently from classical tradition (or just possibly from Irish tradition, as I shall show presently), so they do not necessarily prove a relationship. But there are stylistic as well as physiological similarities between the two beasts. The multiple parts of both are knit together by means of the same reduplicating numerical pattern with the catchwords *unusquisque* and *ælc* that we have encountered in the Men with Tongues of Iron. And if the hound of Vercelli IX is a descendant of Parthemon (once or twice removed), the

[182] *Ibid.*, p. 153: 'having a hundred heads on his neck and a thousand teeth in each head, and like a lion each tooth gleamed. And his eyes were like sharp swords, his mouth always open and he swallowed souls. And his name was Parthemon. From him proceeded multitudes of frogs and all kinds of vermin. In his mouth were placed all the officials and princes who committed iniquity on the earth.' Silverstein supplies the words *draco igneus* from other redactions. Carey, '*Visio Sancti Pauli* and the *Saltair*'s Hell', pp. 40–1, has independently drawn attention to this passage in connection with a description of Satan in *Saltair na Rann*.

[183] *Visio Sancti Pauli*, pp. 66–7.

motif has undergone a similar stylistic development: the originally disparate numbers (*centum capita / mille dentes*) have been made equivalent, and the numerical series has been extended by additions to the anatomical list (hands, fingers and nails), linked by the catchword 'each'. In the Men with Tongues of Iron we have seen how this extended rhetorical formulation of a motif from the *Visio S. Pauli* was characteristic of a group of Old English texts, and to a lesser extent of the Irish analogues. For the monstrous beast in Vercelli IX we again have a close parallel elsewhere in Old English, and in this case the Irish vernacular analogues are strikingly similar both in detail and in rhetorical formulation.

The Old English parallel occurs in the anonymous homily *Be heofonwarum 7 be helwarum*, partially edited by Rudolf Willard as an example of the Three Utterances exemplum. In a description paralleled in the *Apocrypha Priscillianistica* and in vernacular Irish witnesses to the Seven Heavens apocryphon, the homilist describes how twelve dragons in hell swallow and discharge the damned soul, until it is brought before Satan. Satan is described in terms much like the beast in Vercelli IX:

> He is swiþe andryslic; he hæf<ð> an hund heafda, and þara hæfda gehwylc an hund tungan; and he hæfð egeslice fingras, and on ælcum fingre hund clifra. Se lið innan helle gebunden onbæc mid fyrenum raceteagum.[184]

Willard, who noted the similarity to our passage in Vercelli IX, also remarked that the 'beast is certainly very much like Behemoth [one of the many variants of Parthemon's name], the many-headed, fiery dragon of the shorter versions of the *Vision of Paul*'.[185] Here the monster has its hundred heads, and fingers equipped with a hundred claws, like the hundred fingers and nails of the monster in Vercelli IX. The hundred tongues are new, possibly an intrusion from the Men with Tongues of Iron.

In his note on the monstrous form of Satan in the Old English homily, Willard referred to a study by St John D. Seymour on the *Visio*

184 *Two Apocrypha*, ed. Willard, pp. 24–5: 'He is exceedingly terrifying; he has a hundred heads, and each of the heads a hundred tongues; and he has horrible fingers, and on each finger a hundred claws. He lies in hell bound backwards with fiery chains.'

185 *Ibid.*, p. 25, n. 121. On the variations on the monster's name, see Silverstein, *Visio Sancti Pauli*, pp. 68–9.

Tnugdali. In this influential Irish vision, Tundale sees the monster Lucifer chained to a gridiron over a great fire tended by demonic smiths:

Vidit ergo principem tenebrarum, inimicum generis humani, diabolum, qui magnitudine precellebat uniuersas, quas ante uiderat, bestias ... Erat namque prefata bestia nigerrima sicut coruus, habens formam humani corporis a pedibus usque ad caput, excepto, quod illa plurimas habebat manus et caudam. Habet quoque illud horribile monstrum non minus mille manibus et unaqueque manus in longitudine quasi centum cubitos, in grossitudine decem. Est autem unaqueque manus digitis insita uicenis, qui digiti habent in longitudine centenas palmas et in grossitudine denas, ungulas lanceis militum longiores, et ipsas ferreas, et in pedibus totidem ungulas.[186]

Seymour thought that this portrait of Lucifer owed something to the dragon Parthemon,[187] but Silverstein was doubtful. He considered Lucifer 'a direct elaboration of the description of Anti-Christ, bound in chains', from the Apocalypse of Esdras. But the description of the Antichrist in this Greek apocalypse, which Silverstein does not actually quote, is not pertinent.[188] Though Lucifer in the *Visio Tnugdali* does not

186 *Visio Tnugdali*, ed. Wagner, pp. 35–6: 'For he saw the prince of darkness himself, the enemy of the human race, the devil, who surpassed in size all the beasts he had seen before ... The beast was very black, like a raven, and had the shape of a human body from head to toe, except that it had many hands and a tail. This horrible monster had no less than a thousand hands, and each hand was about a hundred cubits in length and ten in thickness. Each hand had twenty fingers and the fingers were a hundred palms in length and ten in thickness, with nails made of iron and longer than soldiers' spears, and with just as many nails on his feet' (trans. Picard, *The Vision of Tnugdal*, p. 138, with slight alterations).

187 'Studies in the Vision of Tundal', p. 105; 'The Eschatology of the Early Irish Church', pp. 186–8.

188 See Silverstein, *Visio Sancti Pauli*, p. 117, n. 11. According to Silverstein, Lucifer's 'hands are the hands of Anti-Christ, with fingers as sharp as scythes, modified perhaps by contact with the multi-handed Briaraeus of the Aeneid.' But the detail has a more likely source in Dan. VII.19–20, as noted by D. D. R. Owen, *The Vision of Hell: Infernal Journeys in Medieval French Literature* (New York, 1980), p. 36. Owen cites a passage from the *Visio Esdrae* in which the Antichrist inhales and exhales souls like flies, but this work does not describe him in any detail (cf. Silverstein, 'Dante and the Legend of the *Mi'rāj*', p. 103). Strangely, Silverstein is willing to allow that Acheron, another monster in the *Visio Tnugdali*, 'seems related, both in function and details, to the dragon Parthemon', but Acheron certainly has less in

have a multitude of heads, his thousand hands and twenty fingers with sharp nails resemble the multiplicity if not the exact physiology of Parthemon's anatomy, and here too the anatomical list is constructed by means of the repeated *unaqueque*.

Lucifer has more in common with the redrawn version of the dragon in Redaction IX:

Vidit Paulus in capite supradicti pontis unum diabolum hostiarum uinctum cathenis manibus et pedibus, nomine Belzebut, qui cum ore prohiciebat flammas et sulfura nigra <que> in multis coloribus permutabat, et peccatrices anime degluciebat, et ita non requiescebat die noctuque <sed> semper esuriebat; cuius dentes sunt sicut e<s>t sagitta et lingua eius sic<ut> gladius acutus. Anime peccatrices in eius uentrem fiunt coloris sulfuris; cum esciunt [*read* exeunt] nigre sunt sicut carbones. Et tantum est demon orribilis credo si appareret in mu<n>do homines et mulieres pro timore et fetore inferni omnes morientur.[189]

According to Silverstein, 'Overlaid as it is with daubs from what was by then a widely familiar chromo of the devil in mediaeval vision literature, this is still the portrait of the hundred-headed dragon Parthemon–Patinot of Redactions I, II, *Br*, and III.'[190] But the portrait also approaches that of Lucifer in the *Visio Tnugdali* in certain respects: Belzebut is chained hand and foot, as Lucifer is bound *catenis ferreis ... ignitis*.[191] As he lies bound he ingests and expels the souls, as Lucifer

common with Parthemon than does Lucifer (Spilling, *Die Visio Tnugdali*, p. 74, dismisses the comparison). As for Silverstein's statement that 'Acheron appears frequently in Irish texts', he can only be referring to the monsters discussed by Seymour (see below), which Seymour and other scholars have associated with Lucifer rather than with Acheron. Silverstein's reference to the Irish *Tenga Bithnua* is not relevant, for there Acheron is the river of hell and not a monster. In short, Lucifer is not a 'direct elaboration' of Antichrist, nor is Acheron of Parthemon.

189 'New Links and Patterns', ed. Silverstein, p. 240: 'Paul saw at the head of the aforementioned bridge a demon of sacrifices, named Belzebut, bound hand and foot with chains, who when vomiting from his mouth flames and black sulphur which is changed into various colours, was devouring sinful souls at the same time, and so he never rested day or night but always hungered; whose teeth are as is the arrow and whose tongue is like a sharp sword. Sinful souls in his belly become the colour of sulphur; when they come out, they are black like coals. And the demon is so horrible, I believe if he appeared in the world all men and women would die from fear and the stench of hell.'

190 *Ibid.*, p. 220.

191 The image of the bound Satan derives ultimately from Apoc. XX.1–3.

inhales and exhales the souls in the *Visio Tnugdali*. In short, if the *diabolus hostiarium* of Redaction IX is a development of Parthemon modified by conventional imagery of Satan, the Lucifer of the *Visio Tnugdali* must be the product of a parallel evolution.

In his discussion of the *Visio Tnugdali*, Seymour stated that 'This description of the Devil's personal appearance is based on a conception that runs through Irish literature, and no doubt has been influenced by paganism.'[192] Multi-headed monsters do seem to infest early Irish literature, both religious and secular. In Irish the monster is invariably a *piast* (*péist*), a term (derived from Latin *bestia*) that usually designates a kind of sea-beast, against which Irish heroes and saints alike struggle.[193] The *piast* often has a multitude of heads and other parts, usually reckoned fifty, a hundred or multiples of these numbers. In the late tale *Aidedh Ferghusa* ('The Death of Fergus') the hero battles a fierce beast with 'trí caeca cos cruaid coimlethan as gach tóeb di ocus trí caeca ionga frithbacánach ar gach nénchois'.[194] In the *Dindshenchas* is a poem lamenting that 'Cin mná Adaim dosrat forn / am-míl cen chond cluichedrenn / ... secht fichit coss, ceithri chend'.[195] Among the many Irish saints who vanquish a serpent or *piast* are Colmán Elo, who confronts a monster with 'Caocca cos fora tarr tra, / Is cáocca ingen urghránna',[196]

[192] 'The Eschatology of the Early Irish Church', p. 187.

[193] For a list of such episodes in Irish hagiography and secular narrative, see Plummer, *Vitae Sanctorum Hiberniae* I, cxxxix, n. 5. A particularly elaborate example is in the Life of Mac Creiche, in *Miscellanea Hagiographica Hibernica*, ed. Plummer, pp. 76–8. In the context of Irish literature J. Carney insists on distinguishing between serpents and dragons on the one hand and water monsters on the other: 'Since classical antiquity it was well known that Ireland harbored no venomous creatures of the serpent, hence of the dragon, type. The only kind of monster for the hero to overcome is therefore the water-beast. A general rule may be stated: *where continental saints or heroes overcome serpents or dragons Irish heroes overcome water-monsters*' (*Studies in Irish Literature and History*, p. 123; italics Carney's). This may be to confuse natural history with literary history. Cf. A. Ross, *Pagan Celtic Britain: Studies in Iconography and Tradition* (London, 1967), pp. 345–8.

[194] *Silva Gadelica*, ed. O'Grady I, 251: 'thrice fifty equally broad hard feet on each side of it, and thrice fifty barbed claws on each single foot'.

[195] *The Metrical Dindshenchas*, ed. Gwynn III, 100: 'The sin of Adam's wife brought upon us the senseless rough-sporting beast ... [which had] seven score feet, four heads' (trans. Gwynn III, 101).

[196] *Lives of Irish Saints*, ed. Plummer I, 175: 'Fifty feet are there on its belly, and fifty hideous claws' (trans. Plummer II, 169).

and Abbán, whose prayer repels a sea-beast with 'cet cend fuirre, 7 dá cet súil, 7 da cet clúas'.[197]

Not surprisingly, these protean monsters haunt hell too, where like Parthemon and Lucifer they busy themselves devouring souls instead of warriors.[198] Seymour cited four Irish texts with similar hellish beasts. In *Immram Curaig Ua Corra* ('The Voyage of the Uí Corra's Boat') a certain Lochán sees in hell 'béist i n-ifirn co n-immad cenn 7 cos fuirri, 7 ro gébtais fir domain bás dia faicsin'.[199] This monster provides only a general parallel for the monster of Vercelli IX, but the three other texts cited by Seymour in connection with the description of Lucifer describe what is clearly the same beast, virtually head for head and limb for limb. In *Scéla Laí Brátha* hell is described as

> airm i mbia fri taíb cach uilc in pheist irdairc úathmar ilchennach co rubnib riches rúad. Ní dia tuarascbáil .i. cet muinel forri 7 cét cend for cach muineol. 7 coic .c. fiacal cach óenchind. cét lam forri. 7 c. mbas for cach láim. 7 c. n-ingen for cach bais.[200]

Here the hundred heads are supported by a hundred necks, and five hundred teeth substitute for the hundred eyes of the Vercelli IX beast. But the monster also has the hundred hands, claws and nails answering to the hundred hands, fingers and nails of his Old English cousin.

[197] *Ibid.* I, 6: 'a hundred heads, two hundred eyes, and two hundred ears' (trans. Plummer II, 6; for the Latin version, see *Vitae Sanctorum Hiberniae*, ed. Plummer I, 15).

[198] In the Welsh *Cad Goddeu* there is a description of a 'great scaly animal: a hundred heads on him ... A black, forked toad: a hundred claws on him. / An enchanted, crested snake in whose skin a hundred souls are punished' (*The Mabinogi and Other Medieval Welsh Tales*, trans. P. Ford (Berkeley, CA, 1977), p. 184).

[199] *Immrama*, ed. van Hamel, p. 98, lines 86–8: 'the Monster of Hell with abundance of heads and feet upon it, and [all] the men of the world would die of seeing it' (trans. W. Stokes, 'The Voyage of the Húi Corra', *RC* 14 (1893–4), 22–69, at 33). Van Hamel (p. 94) considers the tale early Middle Irish, perhaps eleventh century.

[200] *Lebor na Huidre*, ed. Best and Bergin, p. 80, lines 2428–31: 'A place wherein beside every evil shall be the Monster, conspicuous, awful, many-headed, with crowds of red glowing coals. Somewhat of his description, to wit: a hundred necks upon him and a hundred heads on each neck, and five hundred teeth in each head. A hundred hands upon him, and a hundred claws on each hand, and a hundred nails on every claw' (trans. Stokes, 'Tidings of Doomsday', p. 253, but I substitute 'claw' for 'palm'; cf. *DIL*, s.v. *bas* (a), ad fin.).

Another Irish text, from the Liber Flauus Fergusiorum, supplies fingers between the claws and nails:

.v. .c. cend furri 7 .v. .c. fiacail in gach cind dibhsin 7 .c. lam furri ga biathadh 7 .c. bos ar gach laim .c. mer ar gach mbhois 7 .c. inga ar gach mer re gabail 7 re congbail gacha neich.[201]

The number of heads and teeth are also inflated to five hundred in *Airdena inna Cóic Lá nDéc ria mBráth* ('The Fifteen Tokens of Doomsday'):

7 enpéist mór ann 7 .u. cét cend uirre 7 .u. cét fiacal in gach cend, 7 cét coss uirreh 7 cét mér for gach cois 7 cét inga for gach mér dhi.[202]

Seymour did not cite another example from *Saltair na Rann*, which describes Lucifer in exactly the same terms and which may be the source of the other Irish texts:

Cōic cēt cenn fri díartain tinn
cōic cet fíaccail cech oenchind,
  cēt lām, cēt bass, indel nglaiss,
  cēt n-ingen for cach oenbaiss.[203]

Considering how easily numbers and anatomical parts can be substituted in a description of this kind, it is remarkable how closely

[201] Dublin, Royal Irish Academy 23. O. 48, pt II (s. xv), 32va: 'Five hundred heads on it, and five hundred teeth in each of these heads, and a hundred hands on it feeding it, and a hundred claws on each hand, and a hundred fingers on each claw, and a hundred nails on each finger to seize and hold each person' (trans. Seymour, 'The Eschatology of the Early Irish Church', p. 187, with the same modification as in the preceding example; Seymour did not print the Irish text).

[202] 'The Fifteen Tokens of Doomsday', ed. Stokes, p. 318: 'and one great monster there, with five hundred heads and five hundred fangs in every head, and a hundred feet, and a hundred toes on every foot, and a hundred nails on every toe' (trans. Stokes, p. 319). On the text, see McNamara, *The Apocrypha in the Irish Church*, no. 104C.

[203] *The Irish Adam and Eve Story from Saltair na Rann*, ed. Greene and Kelly, p. 12, lines 885–8: 'Five hundred heads for sore wrath, five hundred teeth in every head, a hundred arms, a hundred hands – an instrument of captivity – a hundred nails on every hand' (trans. Greene and Kelly, p. 13). Carey ('*Visio Sancti Pauli* and the *Saltair*'s Hell', pp. 40–1) drew attention to the description in the Irish poem.

these Irish texts agree with each other and with the descriptions of the monster in the two Old English homilies. There are minor variations (the Irish monster has a hundred or five hundred teeth, as Parthemon has a thousand teeth, rather than a hundred eyes, as in Vercelli IX, or a hundred tongues, as in the homily printed by Willard). But the sequence of hands, fingers, palms and nails is nearly identical, except that one Irish text prefers to place the nails on a hundred feet and toes (we recall that Lucifer in the *Visio Tnugdali* had *in pedibus totidem ungulas*). In the extended and inbred family of many-headed monsters, these Insular beasts clearly belong to the same brood. Their multiple anatomies suggest some more distant relationship with Lucifer as he is depicted in the *Visio Tnugdali*, as Seymour suggested. At the same time, the hundred or five hundred heads, and the similar rhetorical formulation with the catchword 'each', allow us to trace their literary lineage and establish the hundred-headed dragon Parthemon of the *Visio S. Pauli* as their ultimate progenitor. And we may add to the comparative evidence adduced here the testimony of the Middle Irish poem *Duan in choícat cest* ('The Poem of the Fifty Questions'), which even names the monster for us:

Cía delb i fil Lucifer?
.i. delb pésti dianad ainm Prothimeon .i. cét cenn fuirri 7 cét dant cach cinn.
.i. delb na biasda dianad ainm Parthameth 7 cét cenn fuirri 7 cét tengadh gach a cind 7 cét sul.[204]

THE NUMERICAL GRADATIO

The motifs of the Men with Tongues of Iron and the Monster of Hell share a common rhetorical formulation in Old English and in Irish. Both are based on a sequence of two or more items usually assigned the

204 Text and translation from an edition in progress by C. Wright and F. Biggs: 'What is Lucifer's shape? That is, the shape of a beast whose name is Prothimeon, that is a hundred heads upon it and a hundred teeth in each head.' 'That is, the shape of a beast whose name is Parthameth, and a hundred heads upon him and a hundred tongues in each of his heads and a hundred eyes.' The poem was ed. from a single manuscript (London, BL, Egerton 1782) by Meyer, 'Mitteilungen', and Tristram, *Sex aetates mundi*, pp. 285–93. I give the answers from two manuscripts, the second of which (Dublin, National Library, G. 3) shows the substitution of a hundred tongues and eyes for the teeth, as in the Old English homilies.

same number and linked in a numerical progression using the catchword 'each' ('x of one thing, and x of another in each one of those').[205] This numerical *gradatio* is present in its simplest form already in the *Visio S. Pauli*, where two numbered items are linked by the words *in unoquoque*, although in the *Visio* the numbers are not precisely equivalent, as they usually are in the vernacular formulations. Since both motifs are probably derived from the *Visio*, however, their numerical formulation can be explained simply as an extension and development of that source. On the other hand, since the Irish and Anglo-Saxons certainly contributed to the formation of the interpolated redactions, where this pattern chiefly occurs, the possibility that the interpolations themselves reflect Insular influence cannot be dismissed. Apart from the Men with Tongues of Iron and the Dragon Parthemon, the pattern occurs in one other interpolation, which Silverstein calls the Wheel of Torment, found in Redaction IV and its derivatives V and VIII:

Timendus est nobis locus inferni ... in quo est rota ignea habens mille orbitas. Mille uicibus uno die ab angelo tartareo uoluitur, et in unaquaque uice mille anime cruciantur in ea.[206]

Silverstein finds that a similar description in the *Apocrypha Priscillianistica* 'throws important light upon the source of the interpolation'. The description occurs within the Seaven Heavens apocryphon:

In medio eius rotam et angelo tartarucho cum uirgis ferreis percutientis rotam ... Centum scintille procedit de rotam & centum pondus in uno scindule & centum anime percremant.[207]

As Silverstein recognized, the parallel is striking not only because of the similarity of the torment and the use of the rare word *tartaruchus*, but

[205] Tristram, 'Stock Descriptions', p. 108, refers to the 'characteristic stepwise structuring' in the Men with Tongues of Iron and in the devil's account of hell.

[206] *Visio S. Pauli*, ed. Brandes, pp. 75–6: 'We must fear the place in hell ... in which there is a fiery wheel with a thousand spokes. It is turned a thousand times in one day by the Tartarus angel, and a thousand souls are tormented on it each time.'

[207] 'Fragments retrouvés', ed. De Bruyne, p. 323 (without emendation): 'In the middle of it [sc. the sixth heaven] is a wheel, with the Tartaruchus angel striking the wheel with iron rods ... One hundred sparks shoot forth from the wheel, and a hundred pounds in each spark, and they burn one hundred souls.'

also because of the rhetorical formulation: 'The phrases "centum scintille", "centum pondus in uno scindule", and "centum anime percremant", indicate the relationship with Redaction IV ("mille orbitas", "Mille uicibus in uno die", "mille anime cruciantur")'.[208]

In vernacular Irish literature the frequent use of *cach* as a catchword in similar numerical patterns raises the possibility that the formulation of these two interpolated motifs in the *Visio S. Pauli* reflects an Irish feature of style.[209] I do not wish to suggest that the numerical *gradatio* was either invented by Irish authors or used exclusively by them; it can be found in certain apocryphal texts, including one passage in the Long Latin version of the *Visio S. Pauli*,[210] in Rabbinic eschatological texts,[211] and also in some arithmetical riddles ('As I Was Going to Saint

208 Silverstein, *Visio Sancti Pauli*, p. 76; see also Seymour, 'The Eschatology of the Early Irish Church', p. 188. This pattern is not found in apocryphal descriptions of the wheel torment apart from the *Visio S. Pauli* and the Seven Heavens apocryphon. Cf. the description of the iron walls of hell in the *Apocrypha Priscillianistica*, with twelve towers and twelve dragons on each tower ('et xii turres & xii dracones in uno turre'). The walls too were probably originally twelve, as in the Old English version ed. Willard (see *Two Apocrypha*, p. 6, lines 55–6).

209 For *cach* as a catchword in Irish gnomic poetry and in the law tracts, see Henry, *The Early English and Celtic Lyric*, pp. 110–11; R. Smith, 'The *Cach* Formulas in the Irish Laws', *ZCP* 20 (1935), 262–7. Although the formulas discussed by Henry and Smith do not include examples of the numerical *gradatio*, they do show that runs of parallel phrases linked by *cach* were a favoured rhetorical device in Irish literature.

210 See the description of the superabundant vines in the *terra repromissionis*: 'Vinee autem uites habebant .X. milia arbusta; in singulis autem uitibus .X. milia butriones, et .X. milia racemi in singulis butrionibus; singule autem arbores ferebant milea fructuum' (St Gallen text, in *Visio Sancti Pauli*, ed. Silverstein, p. 137). Closely similar descriptions occur in I Enoch X.19, II Baruch XXIX.5 and Irenaeus, *Adversus Haereses* V.xxxiii.3–4 (see the note on II Baruch XXIX.5 in Charlesworth, *Old Testament Pseudepigrapha* I, 630). I am grateful to Thomas Hall for drawing my attention to these examples.

211 For examples, see M. Gaster, 'Hebrew Visions of Hell and Paradise', in his *Studies and Texts in Folklore, Magic, Medieval Romance, Hebrew Apocrypha and Samaritan Archaeology*, 3 vols. (London, 1925–8) I, 124–64, at 128, 135, 140, 158 and 161. These include examples with anatomical lists very similar to the two motifs discussed above, such as the following description of the angel of the third heaven: 'He has 70,000 heads, in each head 70,000 mouths, in each mouth 70,000 tongues, and each tongue 70,000 dictions' (p. 128). See also below, pp. 251–2, for a further assessment of the possible influence of Rabbinic and Christian apocrypha on this rhetorical technique.

Ives').[212] But although the numerical *gradatio* in Irish literature may have been learned from apocryphal or other sources, or taken over from popular oral traditions such as the riddle, I am not aware that it was so common a feature of style in any other medieval literary tradition. In the case of the Men with Tongues of Iron, the modification of the Virgilian inexpressibility topos by the addition of the phrase *in unoquoque* is precisely the same made by a twelfth-century Irish translator of the *Aeneid*, who adds the phrase *in gach*,[213] as a reflex of a rhetorical formula that Kuno Meyer listed as among the most common stereotypical expressions in Irish prose.[214] Descriptive passages in Irish literature often use variations of the pattern, usually with only two numbered items linked by *cach* (or *cach áe*, 'each of them'), but sometimes extended into a series of three or more. Readers of Irish saga will recall the fantastic description in *Táin Bó Cúailnge* ('The Cattle-Raid of Cooley') of the young Cú Chulainn:

> Secht meóir cechtar a dá choss 7 secht meóir cechtar a dá lám, 7 secht meic imlessan cechtar a dá rígrosc iarum 7 secht ngemma de ruthin ruisc fo leith cech mac imlesan díb. Cethri tibri cechtar a dá grúad.[215]

212 V. Hull and A. Taylor, *A Collection of Irish Riddles*, University of California Publications, Folklore Studies 6 (Berkeley, CA, 1955), 108, state that 'Riddles that involve the repeated multiplication of the same number are rather numerous, but the number mentioned varies considerably.' For bibliography on arithmetical riddles, see A. Taylor, *A Bibliography of Riddles*, FFC 126 (Helsinki, 1939), 141–2.

213 *Imtheachta Æniasa: the Irish Æneid*, ed. G. Calder, ITS 6 (London, 1907), 88. Cf. the description of Solomon's daily provisions in the Leabhar Breac biblical history, cited by E. Gwynn in *The Metrical Dindshenchas* III, 72: '.xxx. coire do mhin-arba ann cech dia ocus .xxx. miach in cech coire' ('thirty caldrons of fine meal there every day, and thirty measures to every caldron'), where the biblical text has a simple equative formulation, 'thirty measures of fine flour, and threescore measures of meal' (III Kings IV.22).

214 *Eine irische Version der Alexandersage* (Leipzig, 1884), p. 14. This text (p. 26, lines 149–51) numbers the slain among the Persian army at 'Ceithri cét míle fer n-armach 7 deich cét in cech míle 7 cóic fichit in cech chét' ('Four hundred thousand armed men and ten hundreds in each thousand and five score in each hundred').

215 *Táin Bó Cúalnge from the Book of Leinster*, ed. C. O'Rahilly (Dublin, 1967), p. 33, lines 1199–1202: 'He had seven toes on each of his feet and seven fingers on each of his hands. He had seven pupils in each of his royal eyes and seven gems sparkling in each pupil. Four dimples in each cheek' (trans. O'Rahilly, p. 171). Cf. the description of Cú Chulainn in the mnemonic *rosc* 'Cathcarpat Serda', ed. C. O'Rahilly, *Celtica* 11 (1976), 194–202, where instead of four dimples, the hero has

The anatomical series with the repeated number seven and the catchword 'each' (*cechtar*) is quite similar to the rhetorical structure of the descriptions of the monster of hell. For obvious reasons, Cú Chulainn is not given seven feet and seven hands to go with his seven toes and fingers, or seven eyes to go with his seven pupils. The reduplication is limited to the seven sparkling gems in each of his seven pupils, which is sufficiently fantastic but does not make the hero into a literal monster.[216]

The above example is from the later Recension II of the saga in the Book of Leinster (LL; Dublin, Trinity College Library, H. 2. 18, s. xii/xiii); in the parallel description in Recension I, from the Lebor na hUidre (LU; Dublin, Royal Irish Academy 23. E. 25, before 1106), the seven toes and fingers are mentioned but not the reduplicating sequence of seven gems in each of seven pupils.[217] The reduplicating pattern does appear elsewhere in Recension I, in the description of Cú Chulainn's namesake, the hound of Culann the smith: 'Tri slabrada fair 7 triar cacha slabraide.'[218] The pattern seems to have been virtually *de rigueur* when describing a group connected by chains. In the Stowe version of the LL *Táin* occurs the following description of a leader of the Ulstermen: 'Fer dub dian temhnighe temerdha i n-airenach na buidhne sin. Seacd slabhradha ima braghait, moirseser i ccin cacha slabhraidh.'[219] Compare

'Seven dimples in each of his cheeks, seven rays of light shining from each dimple' (p. 198; Irish text at 196).

216 D. Swartz, 'The Beautiful Women and the Warriors in the *LL TBC* and in Twelfth-Century Neo-Classical Rhetoric', *PHCC* 5 (1985), 128–46, finds influence of classical *ecphrasis* in many of the descriptive passages in the *Táin*, but characterizes the sequences of toes, fingers and pupils as 'primitive details' (p. 143).

217 *Táin Bó Cúailnge Recension I*, ed. C. O'Rahilly (Dublin, 1976), p. 90, lines 2965–6.

218 *Ibid.*, p. 18, lines 572–3: 'There are three chains on him and three men holding each chain' (trans. O'Rahilly, p. 141). H. L. C. Tristram, 'Aspects of Tradition and Innovation in the *Táin Bó Cuailnge*', in *Papers on Language and Mediaeval Studies presented to Alfred Schopf*, ed. R. Matthews and J. Schmole-Rostosky, Neue Studien zur Anglistik und Amerikanistik 37 (Frankfurt, 1988), 19–38, considers Recension I a product of the tenth century.

219 *The Stowe Version of Táin Bó Cuailnge*, ed. C. O'Rahilly, p. 143, lines 4530–2: 'A black, hasty, swarthy, [dark] man in the front rank of that band; seven chains around his neck; seven men at the end of each chain' (trans. J. Dunn, *The Ancient Irish Epic Tale Táin Bó Cúalnge* (London, 1914), p. 335). This passage is cited by Chadwick, 'Intellectual Contacts', p. 192, in connection with a description of the 'cauldron of covetousness' in *Cormac's Glossary*, where a loose variation of the

the following description from *Mesca Ulad* ('The Intoxication of the Ulstermen'):

at-chonnac-sa gilla ... Trí slabraid cechtar a dá choss 7 slabrad cechtar a dá lám. Trí slabraid imma brágit 7 mórfessiur cecha slabraide, conid inund óenmórfessiur déc.[220]

The pattern is recognizable even when the numbers do not match, as in the following description of the hair of Étaín: 'Dá trilis n-órbuidi fora cind. Fige ceithri ndúal ceachtar ndé, 7 mell for rind cach dúail.'[221]

In addition to describing personal and anatomical features, the numerical *gradatio* may also be used to express natural fecundity or abundance of wealth. In *Aided Celtchair meic Uthechair* ('The Death of Celtchar mac Uthechair'), Blái Briuga of the Ulstermen is said to have owned a wealth of cattle: 'Secht n-airgeda leis. Secht fichit bó cecha airgi 7 seisred cecha airgi.'[222] A character from another story, Buchet, owned the same number:

Seacht n-āirge cond oenfiur fial
nā tuc d'oegedaib anfiad;
secht fichit bō, ba buan blad,
in cach āirge nīrb ingnad.[223]

pattern occurs: 'It has nine chains out of it ... There is a hole at the end of every chain, with nine artists standing round it, while the company sang, each with the point of his spear fixed in the hole of the chain that was next him' (trans. Chadwick, p. 191).

220 *Mesca Ulad*, ed. Watson, p. 29, lines 659–63: 'I saw a young lad ... Three chains round each leg and a chain round each arm; three chains round his neck, and seven men holding each chain, seventy-seven men in all' (trans. Gantz, *Early Irish Myths*, p. 207).

221 *Togail Bruidne Da Derga*, ed. Knott, p. 1, lines 14–15: 'On her head were two golden-yellow tresses, in each of which was a plait of four strands, with a bead at the point of each strand' (trans. W. Stokes, in Cross and Slover, *Ancient Irish Tales*, p. 94).

222 *The Death Tales of the Ulster Heroes*, ed. K. Meyer, TLS 14 (Dublin, 1906), 24: 'He owned seven herds of cattle, seven score kine in each herd, and a plough-team with each herd' (trans. Meyer, p. 25). The Death Tales seem to have been composed by the ninth century (see Thurneysen, *Die irische Helden- und Königsage*, p. 571).

223 From a poetic version of *Esnada Tige Buchet*, in *Fingal Rónáin*, ed. Greene, p. 33, lines 619–22: 'Seven herds had the one generous man, who did not give an ill welcome to guests. Seven score cows – enduring was the fame – were in each herd, it was no wonder' (trans. M. Hayden, 'The Songs of Buchet's House', *ZCP* 8 (1911), 261–73,

Not to be outdone, St Ciarán of Saiger owned even more cattle, 'ar batar .x. ndorais for lias a bó 7 .x. crái gacha dorais ... 7 batar .x. loig in gach crúo 7 .x. mbú im gach loeg'.[224] A mare of Finn had 'ocht tairberta 7 ocht serraig gacha tairberta'.[225] Here is a description from the Old Irish *Táin Bó Fraích* ('The Cattle-Raid of Froech') of the gifts given the hero by his aunt: 'coíca scíath n-argdide co n-imlib óir impu, 7 caindel rígthigi i lláim cech áe, 7 coíca semmand findruine ar cech n-áe. Coíca toracht di ór forloiscthi im cech n-áe.'[226] A lament for Lugna Fer Trí describes the richness of the house of Nia:

Trī naī miach
ised do-beirth[e]a i tech Ni[a]d:
trī naī laech, trī naī triar
issed do-beirt[he]a im gac[h] miach.[227]

The status of the numerical *gradatio* as an established feature of Irish literary style is best illustrated by *Aislinge Meic Con Glinne* ('The Vision of Mac Con Glinne'), where it is wittily parodied not one but several times. Robin Flower, who has described this text as 'one long parody of the literary methods used by the clerical scholars', remarked that 'A full commentary on the Vision from this point of view would be little short of a history of the development of literary forms in Ireland.'[228] Although the Leabhar Breac version of *Aislinge Meic Con Glinne*

at 263). Hayden (p. 261) tentatively dates the language of the poem to the first half of the eleventh century.

224 From the marginal additions to the *Félire Oengusso*, ed. Stokes, p. 88: 'for there were ten doors to the shed of his kine and ten stalls for every door ... and there were ten calves in every stall, and ten cows with every calf' (trans. Stokes, p. 89).

225 *Accalamh na Senórach*, ed. W. Stokes in *Irische Texte* 4.1, ed. Stokes and Windisch, p. 8, lines 258–9: 'eight birthings and eight foals at each birthing'.

226 *Táin Bó Fraích*, ed. W. Meid, rev. ed., MMIS 22 (Dublin, 1974), 1, lines 20–4: 'Fifty silver shields with gold rims, and a candle of a king's house in the hand of each man, with fifty rivets of white gold in each candle, and fifty coils of refined gold about each' (trans. Gantz, *Early Irish Myths*, p. 115). Gantz, perhaps unconsciously in view of the pattern established in the passage, translates 'fifty candles in the hand of each man', but the manuscripts all agree that each man holds only one candle – a small concession to realism in a generally fantastic setting! The archetype of the tale is generally dated to the eighth century (see Meid, p. xxv).

227 'A Miscellany of Irish Verse', ed. Carney, p. 240. Carney translates: 'Thrice nine measures used to be brought into the house of Nia; thrice nine warriors and thrice nine men used to be brought with every measure.'

228 *The Irish Tradition*, p. 76.

probably dates from the last quarter of the eleventh century, it parodies well-established literary techniques. I have already referred to the parody of the 'enumerative style' in this work.[229] The author also makes use of grotesque exaggeration by way of the reduplicating numerical *gradatio*, to express how replete with food is the magical land to which Mac Con Glinne sails in a coracle of lard. When a phantom appears to Mac Con Glinne in a vision, he asks him for 'tidings of food and eating'. The phantom replies of his news that 'twould be no luck for a friend who had no power of eating to come up with it'. Mac Con Glinne asks, 'How is that?'

'Ní h-annsa ém', ol in Scál, '.i. cen broind coíc-duirn comlethain cernaig cian-fhota cethar-láin cethar-ochair acca, i tallfatís na trí noí n-ithe 7 na secht n-óla imm ól nónbuir cacha díb-side, 7 na secht tomaltais 7 na noí ndíthata, 7 praind c[h]ét cacha h-ithe 7 cacha h-óla 7 cacha longthi 7 cacha díthata díb-side fo leith.'[230]

Later Mac Con Glinne describes a doorkeeper, 'co n-a s[h]echt cornib imme i n-a chind (7 bátar secht n-immaire do f[h]ír-chainnind in cach coraind díb-side fo leth); co n-a s[h]echt n-epislib do chaelánu inbi fo [a] brágait; co n-a s[h]echt mbille do blonaig bruithi for cind cacha h-episle díb-side'.[231] A doctor prescribes an elaborate remedy for Mac Con Glinne's disease, including eight kinds of grain: 'Ocht mbairgena cacha h-orbaind díb-side 7 ocht n-andlaind cacha bargine, 7 [ocht] torsnu fria cach n-andland.'[232]

229 See above, p. 51.

230 *Aislinge Meic Con Glinne*, ed. Jackson, pp. 28–9, lines 884–90: '"Indeed, it is not hard to tell", said the phantom. "Even so: unless he had a very broad, four-edged, four-times-filled belly, having corners long and lengthy, five hands in diameter, in which could be fitted thrice nine eatings, and seven drinkings (with the drink of nine in each of them), and of seven meals, and nine snacks – a dinner of a hundred being in each eating, each drinking, each meal and each snack of those separately"' (trans. Meyer, *Aislinge Meic Conglinne*, p. 75, with alterations based on Jackson's glossary).

231 *Aislinge Meic Con Glinne*, ed. Jackson, pp. 34–5, lines 1068–72: 'with seven circlets of butter on his head, in each circlet of which was the produce of seven ridges of fresh leeks separately; with his seven amulets of chitterlings about his neck, and seven seals of boiled lard on the point of every amulet of them' (trans. Meyer, *Aislinge Meic Conglinne*, p. 88, with alterations).

232 *Aislinge Meic Con Glinne*, ed. Jackson, p. 38, lines 1184–6: 'eight cakes of each grain of these, and eight condiments with every cake, and eight relishes with each condiment' (trans. Meyer, *Aislinge Meic Conglinne*, p. 98, with alterations). These three passages occur only in the expanded Leabhar Breac version of the tale.

The examples I have cited above show that the numerical *gradatio* with *cach* was a well-established rhetorical figure in Irish literature, one that reflects the fondness of Irish authors for geometrical constructs and multiplicity motifs.[233] But the numerical *gradatio* was used only as an occasional adornment, and was generally restricted to the limited number of contexts I have described. The pattern was adopted by authors of religious texts as well, but again for a few specific contexts, indeed chiefly in the variations of the motifs of the Men with Tongues of Iron and the Monster of Hell. Both motifs are essentially anatomical lists. *Saltair na Rann* has another example, in a description of the flock of birds in the Tree of Life:

> Alaind indenlaith cotngaeib,
> cechen glermaith cet n-etteib,
> canait cenbet, cogleor gle,
> cet ceol cacha oenheitte.[234]

A Middle Irish account of the miracles which occurred at the birth of Christ describes the head of a great whale, which had 'L for CCC adarc ... 7 ol L ar C in cech adairc dib side'.[235] In *Dá Brón Flatha Nime* ('The Two Sorrows of the Kingdom of Heaven'), the souls at Judgement are said to be burned in four rivers surrounding Mt Sion for 'deich míle bliadna 7 deich cét mbliadna in cach míle'.[236]

In Old English the numerical *gradatio* is rare apart from Vercelli IX and variations on the motifs of the Men with Tongues of Iron and the Monster of Hell. I know of no examples in Old English secular literature, and only three homiletic examples, one of which occurs in the Old English version of the Seven Heavens apocryphon. Immediately following the mention of the wheel of torment, the Old English version

[233] See Sayers, 'Ringing Changes on a Cosmic Motif', especially pp. 109–10 (Sayers does not discuss the numerical *gradatio*).

[234] *Saltair na Rann*, ed. Stokes, p. 10, lines 621–4: 'Beautiful the flock of birds which he keeps; each very good bird has a hundred plumes, they chant without sin, clearly, a hundred songs for each single plume.'

[235] 'The Middle Irish Apocryphal Account of "The Seventeen Miracles at Christ's Birth"', ed. V. Hull, *MP* 43 (1945–6), 25–39, at 30: 'three hundred and fifty horns ... and [there was] drink for one hundred and fifty in every horn of them' (trans. Hull, p. 35).

[236] 'Les deux chagrins', ed. Dottin, p. 378: 'ten thousand years (and there are ten hundred years in each thousand)' (trans. Herbert and McNamara, *Irish Biblical Apocrypha*, p. 19).

describes how the angel of this heaven strikes the souls with a heavy rod, employing a looser variation of the same formula applied to the wheel in the Latin version: 'of æghwelcum anum slege aspringeð .c. spearcena, in æghwylcum anum bið mannes byrðen. .C. sawla ðara synfulra sweltað and forweorðað for ðam spearcum'.[237] In a related description of the seven heavens in Recension III of *Tenga Bithnua*, an angel confronts the sinners with an iron flail having 'céad roin air gach aon dealg dá mbeit air, go ttabharthach gach deilg diobh céad creacht air gnúis gach peacaidh dhibh'.[238] In Vercelli IX we encounter it again in 'The Devil's Account', which describes Samson, who had 'xii loccas ... ⁊ an elcan locce wæs xii manna megen'.[239] The numerical *gradatio* also occurs in the poem *Solomon and Saturn II*, however, and in the bizarre *Prose Solomon and Saturn Pater Noster Dialogue* it forms the basic rhetorical structure of a large part of the text. I shall return to the *Solomon and Saturn* texts in ch. 5, which presents evidence for their Irish background and relationship to the literary milieu of Vercelli IX.

[237] *Two Apocrypha*, ed. Willard, p. 5: 'from each single stroke spring one hundred sparks, in each one of which is the weight of a man. One hundred souls of the sinful die and perish on account of those sparks.'

[238] 'Une rédaction moderne du *Teanga Bithnua*', ed. G. Dottin, *RC* 28 (1907), 277–307, at 297: 'one hundred points on each single spike, each spike inflicts a hundred wounds on the face of each sinner'. See also Willard, *Two Apocrypha*, p. 21. Seymour drew attention to this passage in connection with the description of the wheel in the *Apocrypha Priscillianistica* ('The Eschatology of the Early Irish Church', p. 188). From Irish secular narrative cf. the following from *Togail Bruidne Da Derga*, ed. Knott, p. 43, lines 1452–4, where Macc Cécht arrives with a bar of iron: '⁊ do-bert .ix. mbuilli dond inbiur iaraind ar doruss mBruidne ⁊ do-thuit nónbur cacha builli' ('At the entrance to the hostel he dealt nine blows with the iron bar, and each blow felled nine men'; trans. Gantz, *Early Irish Myths*, p. 104). Cf. also the fifteenth-century *Cath Finntrágha* ('The Battle of Ventry'), ed. C. O'Rahilly, MMIS 20 (Dublin, 1962), p. 31, lines 970–4, in which Mongach comes to battle armed with an iron flail: 'súisti imreamhar iarnaighi ana láim lesa rabhadar secht caera athleaghta iarainn ⁊ caeca slabhradh iarnaide eisti ⁊ caeca ubhall gacha slabraidh ⁊ caeca dealg neime an gach ubhall' ('a strong iron flail in his hand, with seven balls of refined iron, and fifty iron chains from it, and fifty balls on each chain, and fifty venomous thorns on each ball'; trans. Meyer, *Cath Finntrága*, Anecdota Oxoniensia, Mediaeval and Modern Irish Series 4 (Oxford, 1885), 37).

[239] *The Vercelli Homilies*, ed. Scragg, p. 177, lines M.42–3: 'twelve locks ... and in each lock was the strength of twelve men'.

4

Apocryphal cosmology and Celtic myth in 'The Devil's Account of the Next World'

To judge from the surviving copies and variant versions, 'The Devil's Account of the Next World' was among the most popular religious tales in late Anglo-Saxon England. Its genre and literary antecedents have not been fully investigated, but Fred C. Robinson has pointed in the right direction by suggesting that the tale 'resembles the narratives gathered into the so-called *Vitas Patrum*'.[1] The *Vitas patrum* is a massive and diverse collection that includes 'Lives' in the normal sense of the word, such as Jerome's *Vita S. Pauli*, together with monastic histories (including the *Historia monachorum* translated by Rufinus) and the collections of anecdotes known as the *Verba seniorum*.[2] Though of varied origins, these works are unified by a common subject: the desert fathers, the hermits and anchorites of Egypt, Syria and Palestine. The anecdotes in the *Verba seniorum* (a term which embraces more than one group of texts) are a series of disconnected vignettes, often little more than a maxim with the barest narrative framework.[3] The protagonists

[1] 'The Devil's Account of the Next World', p. 364.

[2] The basic collection is that of H. Rosweyd, *Vitae Patrum*, 2nd ed. (Antwerp, 1628), repr. PL 73–4. See W. Berschin, *Greek Letters and the Latin Middle Ages*, rev. ed., trans. J. C. Frakes (Washington, DC, 1988), pp. 57–9, and for a convenient analysis of the contents of Rosweyd's collection, Rosenthal, *The 'Vitae Patrum'*, pp. 10–21. For selections in English translation, see H. Waddell, *The Desert Fathers* (Ann Arbor, MI, 1957).

[3] The *Verba seniorum* in Rosweyd's edition (PL 73, 851–1052) combines several Latin versions of the Greek collections known as the *Apophthegmata patrum*. For a survey of recent scholarship on the Latin versions, see G. Philippart, 'Vitae Patrum: trois travaux récents sur d'anciennes traductions latines', *AB* 92 (1974), 353–65. The Greek alphabetical collection has been translated by B. Ward, *The Desert Christian: Sayings of the Desert Fathers* (New York, 1975).

are sometimes nameless, but even when they are identified no individual portrait emerges from the blank face of sanctity. Encounters with the devil are the focus of many anecdotes, and there are a number of tales (often attached to the figure of Macarius) in which a hermit receives a report or a vision of the Otherworld or of the struggle of angels and demons over the soul at death.[4] Inspired by such tales, a great many later medieval exempla also feature hermits and devils.[5] The encounter between these stock figures in 'The Devil's Account' also reflects a hagiographic motif in which a saint or apostle captures the devil and forces him to confess.[6] This motif is most familiar to Anglo-Saxonists from Cynewulf's *Juliana*, but St Margaret has a similar encounter, and in the apocryphal acts of the apostles, Thomas and Bartholomew also capture devils and force them to talk.[7]

Robinson also remarked that many eschatological tales of the kind

[4] Several of these stories will be mentioned below. For others, see PL 73, 374–5, 1014 and 1126. For the eschatological visions associated with Macarius, see in general Batiouchkof, 'Le débat de l'âme et du corps', pp. 5–17, and J. Leclercq, 'Deux anciennes versions de la légende de l'Abbé Macaire', *Revue Mabillon* 36 (1946), 64–79. F. C. Robinson has discussed the tradition of the struggle of angels and demons over the soul in 'God, Death, and Loyalty in *The Battle of Maldon*', in *J. R. R. Tolkien: Scholar and Storyteller*, ed. R. T. Farrell and M. Salu (Ithaca, NY, 1979), pp. 76–98, at 81 and n. 12.

[5] For examples, see the index in Tubach, *Index Exemplorum*, s.v. 'hermit'.

[6] This is explicit only in the separate version of the exemplum in London, BL, Cotton Tiberius A. iii. (M) and in the brief extract in Napier XLIII (N). M reads: 'Hyt gelamp hwylan æt suman cyrre þæt an ancra gefing ænne deofol þurh Godes mihte ... Þa se a[n]cra angun þrea[t]ian swyþe þone deofol, þæt he him asæde eal helle wites brogan ⁊ eac heofona rices fegernesse' (*The Vercelli Homilies*, ed. Scragg, p. 169: 'It happened once that an anchorite captured a devil through the power of God... Then the anchorite began to compel the devil sternly to tell him all the terrors of hell-torment and also the beauty of the kingdom of heaven'). According to Scragg, '"The Devil's Account of the Next World" Revisited', p. 108, the context supplied in M is a secondary elaboration (N seems to be related to M), but in Vercelli IX we are undoubtedly to imagine that the devil gives his account under compulsion.

[7] For Thomas, see Hennecke and Schneemelcher, *New Testament Apocrypha* II, 459–61; for Bartholomew, see James, *Apocryphal New Testament*, pp. 174–9. For St Margaret's capture of the devil, see *Angelsächsische Homilien und Heiligenleben*, ed. Assmann, pp. 175–7. The compiler of Cotton Tiberius A. iii, who copied the Life of St Margaret in close proximity to the separate version (M) of 'The Devil's Account' (see Ker, *Catalogue*, art. 186, items 15 and 18), was perhaps conscious of the generic affinity of the two stories.

found in the *Vitas patrum* 'were apparently given currency through Irish writings of the period',[8] but he did not pursue the possibility of Irish influence beyond this hint. Eschatological tales from the *Vitas patrum* were often adapted or imitated by both Irish and Anglo-Saxon authors. A story about Macarius and a decapitated head which reveals to him the pains (and the dimensions) of hell was adapted in an Irish saint's life,[9] and the Irish version of the Three Utterances sermon borrows its framing narrative from another eschatological anecdote in the *Vitas patrum*.[10] The fragmentary vision of Laisrén, in which the soul of the Irish anchorite is rapt from his body, fought over by angels and demons and conducted on a tour of hell, is apparently an original composition in this genre.[11] In Old English, another vision attributed to Macarius is the source of two related body-and-soul homilies.[12] Even Ælfric, who, as we might expect, expressed reservations about the *Vitas patrum*, translated two visionary anecdotes from the collection, in-

[8] 'The Devil's Account of the Next World', p. 364. For general studies of Irish visions, see the references cited above, p. 23, n. 93.

[9] The story is included in the *Verba seniorum* (PL 73, 1014), and is retold in a pseudo-Bedan homily (PL 94, 499–500; Machielsen, *Clavis*, no. 4071). The Life of St Cainnech, in *Vitae Sanctorum Hiberniae*, ed. Plummer I, 155–6, tells how the saint discovers a head which converses with him, confessing that his soul is in hell, and relating 'alias multas fabulas'. The Macarius story has been associated with a series of similar tales in Irish. See Flower, *The Irish Tradition*, pp. 7–9; J. Szövérffy, 'Heroic Tales, Medieval Legends and an Irish Story', *ZCP* 25 (1956), 183–210. Nagy, 'Close Encounters', p. 139, relates these episodes to what he considers a native Irish narrative tradition of otherworldly encounters (see below, pp. 212–13).

[10] 'The Two Deaths', ed. C. Marstrander, *Ériu* 5 (1911), 120–5; the framing story from the *Vitas patrum* is in PL 73, 1011–12 (see Seymour, 'The Bringing Forth of the Soul in Irish Literature').

[11] See Meyer, 'Stories and Songs from Irish MSS', pp. 113–19. For the identification of this Laisrén with the anchorite Laisrén of Clonmacnois, see P. Grosjean, 'Notes d'hagiographie celtique: 51. Un fragment des Coutumes de Tallaght et la Vision de Laisrén', *AB* 81 (1963), 251–9.

[12] The Old English homilies are Napier XXIX (in *Wulfstan*, ed. Napier, p. 140, line 9 – p. 143, line 5) and the 'Macarius' homily first ed. B. Thorpe, *Ancient Laws and Institutes of England*, 2 vols. (London, 1840) II, 394–400, and more recently by H. Sauer, *Theodulfi Capitula in England* (Munich, 1978), pp. 411–16. For the identification, see J. Zupitza, 'Zu "Seele und Leib"', *Archiv* 91 (1893), 369–404, at 370–8. The Latin source, ed. Batiouchkof, 'Le débat de l'âme et du corps', pp. 576–8, is trans. Allen and Calder, *Sources and Analogues*, pp. 41–4.

cluding the same story that supplied the framing narrative for the Irish version of the Three Utterances.[13]

That the protagonist of 'The Devil's Account' is an anchorite is certainly consistent with an Irish background, for Eastern monasticism and the ascetic ideals of the desert fathers exerted a strong influence on monastic spirituality in Ireland, where anchoritism was actively cultivated.[14] The *Catalogus Sanctorum Hiberniae* identifies the third order of saints as those 'qui in locis desertis habitabant'.[15] An Irish Litany of Pilgrim Saints refers to many anchorites, including 'Seven monks of Egypt in Disert Uilaig'.[16] The eremitic impulse, renewed in the eighth- and ninth-century anchorite movement associated with the Céli Dé,[17] found expression in Irish literature and hagiography,[18] which in turn influenced Anglo-Saxon hagiographic tradition. Speaking of the

[13] For Ælfric's use of the *Vitas patrum*, see Rosenthal, *The 'Vitae Patrum'*, pp. 57–62, and M. McC. Gatch, *Preaching and Theology in Anglo-Saxon England: Ælfric and Wulfstan* (Toronto, 1977), pp. 17, 70 and 181, n. 54. For the eschatological tales which Ælfric translated from the *Vitas patrum*, see *Homilies of Ælfric*, ed. Pope II, 775–9, with Pope's introduction, pp. 770–4; see also W. Temple, 'The Song of the Angelic Hosts', *Annuale Mediaevale* 2 (1961), 5–14.

[14] See especially N. K. Chadwick, *The Age of the Saints*, pp. 35–60, 86–7, 92–3 and 117–18; Mayr-Harting, *The Coming of Christianity*, pp. 78–93. A brief sketch is offered by G. MacGinty, 'The Influence of the Desert Fathers on Early Irish Monasticism', *Monastic Studies* 14 (1983), 85–91. The role of Gaul as an intermediary for the transmission of Egyptian monastic ideals is often stressed, but see Chadwick, *The Age of the Saints*, pp. 86–7, and J. F. Kelly, 'The Gallic Resistance to Eastern Asceticism', *Studia Patristica* 18 (1982), 506–10.

[15] P. Grosjean, 'Edition et commentaire du Catalogus sanctorum Hiberniae secundum diversa tempora ou De tribus ordinibus sanctorum Hiberniae', *AB* 73 (1955), 197–213 and 289–322, at 206.

[16] See K. Hughes, 'On an Irish Litany of Pilgrim Saints Compiled c. 800', *AB* 77 (1959), 305–31, at 325.

[17] On the anchorite movement, see R. Flower, 'The Two Eyes of Ireland: Religion and Literature in Ireland in the Eighth and Ninth Centuries', in *The Church of Ireland A.D. 432–1932*, ed. W. Bell and N. D. Emerson (Dublin, 1932), pp. 66–75; Hughes, *The Church in Early Irish Society* (Ithaca, NY, 1966), pp. 173–93; Henry, *The Early English and Celtic Lyric*, pp. 40–5. On the Céli Dé (anglicized 'Culdees'), see now O'Dwyer, *Céli Dé*.

[18] One thinks immediately of the so-called 'hermit poetry', but D. Ó Corráin has recently cast doubt on the traditional association of these poems with the anchorite movement ('Early Irish Hermit Poetry?', in *Sages, Saints and Storytellers*, ed. D. Ó Corráin *et al.*, pp. 251–67).

'marvelous element' in the lives of the desert fathers, Bertram Colgrave has remarked that 'the Irish lives with their extravagant wonder stories, which were derived partly though not entirely from this source, also had considerable influence on writers such as Bede and Felix and the anonymous biographer of St. Cuthbert'.[19]

If 'The Devil's Account' is modelled on the eschatological revelations of the desert fathers, the revelation itself is remarkably oblique and negative. Rather than describe heaven and hell directly, the devil posits fantastic hypothetical torments and pleasures that are dismissed as inconsequential in comparison to the realities of the next world, which remain inexpressible. But even though the devil does not actually grant the anchorite a vision or conduct him on a tour of the Otherworld, his account is furnished with a cosmological setting based on topoi from visionary literature, together with a piece of apocryphal cosmology transmitted through Hiberno-Latin sources.

THE COSMOLOGICAL SETTING

The devil prefaces his account of the next world with a cosmological digression whose relevance is not immediately apparent:

Sægeð hit eac on bocum þæt sum deofles gast sæde anum ancran ealle helle ge[ryne] ⁊ þara sawla tintrega. ⁊ he wæs cweðende þæt eall þes middaneard nære þe mare dryges landes ofer þone micclan garsegc þe man ænne prican aprycce on anum brede, ⁊ nis þes middaneard swilce se seofoða dæl ofer þone micclan garsecg, se mid micclum ormætnyssum ealle þas eorðan utan ymbligeð. ⁊ lytel dæl is under heofonum dryges landes þæt hit ne sy mid garsecge oferurnen.[20]

[19] 'The Earliest Saints' Lives Written in England', *PBA* 44 (1959), 35–60, at 41. On the Irish background of Anglo-Saxon hagiography, see also Earl, 'Literary Problems in Early Medieval Hagiography', pp. 101–10.

[20] *The Vercelli Homilies*, ed. Scragg, p. 174, lines 144–50: 'It also says in books that a certain devilish spirit told an anchorite all the mystery of hell and the torments of souls. And he was saying that all this earth would be no more of dry land beside the great Ocean than a point pricked on a tablet, and this earth is not but as the seventh part over the great Ocean which with great immensity encircles all this earth on the outside. And there is little portion of dry land under heaven that it is not covered over with the Ocean.'

Dante's Guido da Montefeltro was surprised to learn that the devil is a logician. It would appear that he is also a geographer. But what is the point of this geography lesson? No doubt the homilist and his audience would have found such information interesting for its own sake. Earlier the homilist had described the relative dimensions of hell, stating that 'emne swa mycel swa fram heofenes hrofe is to þysse eorðan ... sio hel sie swylc twa deop, ⁊ nis na ðe unwidre'.[21] But the devil's cosmological digression has a generic function. In ancient literary tradition, saints and seers who experience a revelation of the next world are generally conducted on a tour of the universe before viewing the regions of reward and punishment. In 'The Devil's Account', accordingly, the devil conducts the anchorite on a verbal tour of the heavens before his verbal revelation concerning the pains of hell and the joys of heaven. The devil's peculiar digression on Oceanus and his striking comparison of the earth to a mere mark or point (*prica*) are based upon ancient topoi of visionary literature, both classical and apocryphal.

The otherworldly guide often carries the visionary up to the great world-river Oceanus, which marks the threshold between this world and the regions of reward and punishment. In the Testament of Abraham, for example, God commands Michael to '"take up Abraham in the body and show him everything ... " Then Michael left and took Abraham up onto a cloud in the body and bore him up to the river Oceanus.'[22] The same tradition is reflected in II Enoch. Enoch describes what he sees when the angels transport him to the first heaven: 'And there I perceived the air higher up, and higher still I saw the ether. And

[21] *The Vercelli Homilies*, ed. Scragg, p. 170, lines 114–16: 'just as far as from the roof of heaven to this earth, then it is learned in holy books that hell is twice as deep and no less wide'. T. D. Hill has cited this passage in connection with the conclusion of *Christ and Satan*, in which Satan is forced to measure hell, as 'evidence of some contemporaneous interest in the dimensions of Hell' ('The Measure of Hell: *Christ and Satan* 695–722', *PQ* 60 (1981), 409–14, at 414, n. 10). The dimension given by the Vercelli homilist is simply a doubling of the relative size of Tartarus in classical tradition (*Aeneid* VI.578–9) and of hell in Christian tradition, including the *Visio Pauli*, Redaction IV: 'Et erat profunditas eius quasi de terra ad celum' (*Visio S. Pauli*, ed. Brandes, p. 78). The story of Macarius and the severed head in the *Vitas patrum* has the same information (PL 73, 1014), as does *Saltair na Rann* (see Carey, '*Visio Sancti Pauli* and the *Saltair*'s Hell').

[22] Testament of Abraham VIII.1–4, in *Old Testament Pseudepigrapha*, ed. Charlesworth I, 899.

they placed me on the first heaven. And they showed me a vast ocean, much bigger than the earthly ocean.'[23] Similarly, in the Greek Apocalypse of Baruch (III Baruch), an angel guides the seer 'to where the heaven was set fast and where there was a river which no one is able to cross'.[24]

Once again the *Visio S. Pauli* was the source through which an ancient apocryphal tradition was disseminated to the West. As we have seen in the previous chapter, in the *Visio* Oceanus borders the *locus terribilis* at the beginning of Paul's journey through the infernal regions, a detail carried over from the Long versions.[25] But in the Long versions Oceanus also marks Paul's transit to the heavenly regions:

Inde exiui primum caelum, et deduxit me in celum alium. Et iterum deduxit me de firmamento, et duxit me supra ianuas caeli. Et aperuit hostium, et erat initium eius fundatum super flumina quae erant super omnem terram. Et interrogaui angelum dei, 'Quis est hic fluuius aque?' Et dixit mihi, 'Hic est Oceanus.'[26]

From his heavenly vantage point the seer may cast a critical look back at the tiny earth.[27] Abraham, guided by Michael, 'soared over the entire inhabited world', and 'beheld the world as it was that day';[28] Zephaniah sees 'the whole inhabited world ha[nging] like a drop of wa[ter], which is suspended from a buc[ket] when it comes up from a well'.[29] Paul too has such a vision, and is struck by the inconsequential smallness of man's world: 'Et respexi de celo in terra, et uidi totum mundum, et erat quasi nihil in conspectu meo: et uidi filios hominum quasi nihil essent,

[23] II Enoch III.2–3 (*ibid.* I, 110). Compare the Testament of Levi II.7–8: 'And I entered the first heaven, and saw there much water suspended' (*ibid.* I, 788).

[24] III Baruch II.1 (*ibid.* I, 665). See the editor's note on the passage, and M. R. James, *Apocrypha Anecdota, Second Series*, Texts and Studies 5.1 (Cambridge, 1897), lvi.

[25] See above, pp. 127–8.

[26] Quotation from the St Gallen text, in *Visio Sancti Pauli*, ed. Silverstein, p. 136: 'From there I left the first heaven, and he led me to another heaven. And again he led me from the firmament, and carried me over the doors of heaven. And he opened the gate, and its beginning was founded upon rivers which were over all the earth. And I asked the angel of God, "What is this river of water?" And he said to me, "This is Oceanus."'

[27] On this theme, see Patch, *The Other World*, p. 128; J. Schwartz, 'Le voyage au ciel dans la littérature apocalyptique', in *L'Apocalyptique*, Etudes d'Histoire des Religions 3, ed. M. Philonenko and M. Simon (Paris, 1977), 91–126, at 95.

[28] Testament of Abraham X.1–2, in *Old Testament Pseudepigrapha*, ed. Charlesworth I, 887.

[29] Apocalypse of Zephaniah II.5–6 (*ibid.* I, 510).

et deficientes, et miratus sum et dixi angelo: Haec est magnitudo hominum?'[30]

The privilege of viewing the earth from the perspective of the heavens is one which these Jewish and Christian visionaries share with their pagan counterparts.[31] Indeed, it is a classical topos that provides the devil with the simile which he uses to express the smallness of the earth. That the earth viewed from the heavens is a mere point (*punctum*) is a visionary theme that stretches from Cicero to Chaucer. Its origins and dissemination in the ancient world have been traced by A.-J. Festugière, who shows how a comparison current in antique astronomical treatises became a moral topos of classical literature.[32] For the Middle Ages its most influential expressions were in Macrobius's *Commentarii in Somnium Scipionis* and Boethius's *De consolatione Philosophiae*. In Macrobius's treatise the idea appears several times: 'physici terram ad magnitudinem circi per quem sol uoluitur puncti modum obtinere docuerunt'.[33] But Macrobius stresses that Africanus's comparison of the earth to a point had an ethical purpose: 'ideo autem terrae breuitas tam diligenter adseritur, ut parui pendendum ambitum famae uir fortis intellegat, quae in tam paruo magna esse non poterit'.[34]

[30] *Apocrypha Anecdota*, ed. James, pp. 15–16 (Paris text): 'And I looked back from heaven to the earth, and I saw the entire world, and it was as nothing in my sight: and I saw the sons of men as though they were nothing, and they were perishing, and I marvelled and said to the angel: "This is the greatness of men?"'

[31] In addition to the examples discussed below, compare the legend of the flight of Alexander, who sees the earth like a threshing floor surrounded by a serpent (Oceanus). See I. Michael, *Alexander's Flying Machine: the History of a Legend* (Southampton, 1974), pp. 13–14; for an allusion to the legend in a medieval Welsh poem, see M. Haycock, '"Some Talk of Alexander and Some of Hercules": Three Early Medieval Poems from the Book of Taliesin', *CMCS* 13 (Summer 1987), 7–38, at 15–16.

[32] *La révélation d'Hermès Trismégiste*, I: *Le dieu cosmique* (Paris, 1949), pp. 442–58. Festugière shows that the motif was transmitted through late antique cosmographers. See also E. R. Dodds, *Pagan and Christian in an Age of Anxiety: Some Aspects of Religious Experience from Marcus Aurelius to Constantine* (Cambridge, 1965), pp. 7–8.

[33] *Commentarii in Somnium Scipionis*, ed. Willis, p. 66: 'Astronomers have shown us that the earth occupies the space of a point in comparison with the size of the orbit in which the sun revolves' (trans. Stahl, *Macrobius*, p. 154). Stahl's note cites several parallels in late antique authors.

[34] *Commentarii in Somnium Scipionis*, ed. Willis, p. 124: 'His reason for emphasizing the earth's minuteness was that worthy men might realize that the quest for fame should

The topos and its ethical application re-appear in Boethius's influential treatise. Endeavouring to convince the imprisoned Boethius of the vanity of worldly fame, Lady Philosophy reminds him:

Omnem terrae ambitum, sicuti astrologicis demonstrationibus accepisti, ad caeli spatium puncti constat obtinere rationem, id est, ut, si ad caelestis globi magnitudinem conferatur, nihil spatii prorsus habere iudicetur ... In hoc igitur minimo puncti quodam puncto circumsaepti atque conclusi de peruulganda fama, de proferendo nomine cogitatis, ut quid habeat amplum magnificumque gloria tam angustis exiguisque limitibus artata?[35]

Such a powerful expression of contempt for the world was bound to appeal to Christian authors. In his commentary on the first psalm, Ambrose states that in comparison to the multitude of the angels, the gentiles are like a 'drop in the bucket' (Is. XL.15), 'ut a plerisque punctum comparatione caeli terra sit aestimata'.[36] Variations on this topos occur in a number of medieval literary visions, including the famous vision of St Benedict in Gregory's *Dialogi*, in which 'omnis etiam mundus uelut sub uno solis radio collectus, ante oculos eius adductus est'.[37] From Anglo-Saxon England we may cite the letter of

be considered unimportant since it could not be great in so small a sphere' (trans. Stahl, *Macrobius*, p. 216).

[35] *De consolatione Philosophiae* II, pr. 7, ed. Bieler, 32: 'You know from astrological computation that the whole circumference of the earth is no more than a pinpoint when contrasted to the space of the heavens; in fact, if the two are compared, the earth may be considered to have no size at all ... Do you, therefore, aspire to spread your fame and enhance your reputation when you are confined to this insignificant area on a tiny earth? How can glory be great that is severely limited by such narrow boundaries?' (trans. R. Green, *The Consolation of Philosophy* (Indianapolis, IN, 1962), p. 37). For parallels in other classical texts, see Bieler's references. For a discussion of these passages from Boethius and Macrobius, see P. Courcelle, 'La postérité chrétienne du "Songe de Scipion"', *Revue des études latines* 36 (1958), 215–23.

[36] *Explanatio super psalmos xii*, ed. M. Petschenig, CSEL 64 (Vienna, 1919), 42: 'just as the earth is judged by many a point in comparison to heaven'.

[37] PL 76, 198: 'the whole world, as though gathered up under a single ray of the sun, was brought before his eyes' (trans. M. Uhlfelder, *The Dialogues of Gregory the Great Book Two: Saint Benedict* (Indianapolis, IN, 1967), p. 45). See P. Courcelle, *La Consolation de Philosophie dans la tradition littéraire : antécédents et postérité de Boèce* (Paris, 1967), pp. 355–72. For similar examples in Irish hagiography, see Plummer, *Vitae Sanctorum Hiberniae* I, clxxi, n. 10, and J.-M. Picard, 'Structural Patterns in Early Hiberno-Latin Hagiography', *Peritia* 4 (1985), 67–82, at 76.

Wynfrith (Boniface) to Eadburg, reporting a vision of a priest rapt from the body: 'þa þuhte him þæt eall þes middaneard wære gesamnod beforan his lichaman gesihðe ... And he sæde þæt hig abrudon up in þone lyft ... "and næs eall þes middaneard, þa ic hine sceawode, buton swilc he wære on anes cleowen onlicnysse"'.[38] Readers of Chaucer will recall his use of the theme in *Troilus and Criseyde*, in the famous passage which describes how the soul of Troilus, transported to the eighth sphere, looks down upon 'This litel spot of erthe that with the se / Embraced is, and fully gan despise / This wrecched world'.[39] Chaucer burlesques the visionary theme in *The House of Fame*, in which the eagle transports the terrified poet 'fro the ground so hye / That al the world, as to myn yë, / No more semed than a prikke'.[40]

The revelation of the devil (who cannot be expected to press the moral) that the earth is but a *prica* clearly belongs to this 'apotheosis tradition'. The Old English prose *Boethius* even has the same explanatory gloss that the 'point' is as if on a *bred* or (wax) tablet.[41] But I do not think that the author of 'The Devil's Account' derived the idea directly from Macrobius or Boethius. In the classical tradition represented by these authors the earth's smallness is in comparison to the universe as a whole, or to the orbit of the sun. As Macrobius makes clear, the tiny point of earth *includes* the encircling Oceanus:

item quia omnis terra, in qua et Oceanus est, ad quemuis caelestem circulum quasi centron puncti obtinet locum, necessario de Oceano adiecit *qui tamen tanto nomine quam sit paruus uides*. nam licet apud nos Atlanticum mare, licet magnum

38 *Studies*, ed. Sisam, pp. 213–14: 'Then it seemed to him that all this world was gathered before his bodily vision ... And he said that they drew up into the sky ... "and all this world, as I beheld it, was not but as the likeness of a ball".'

39 *Troilus and Criseyde* V.1814–19, ed. S. Barney in *The Riverside Chaucer*, ed. Benson, p. 584. See also A. Kellogg, 'On the Tradition of Troilus's Vision of the Little Earth', *MS* 22 (1960), 204–13, and J. M. Steadman, *Disembodied Laughter: Troilus and the Apotheosis Tradition* (Berkeley, CA, 1972). Steadman has also traced the apotheosis tradition and the earth-as-point motif in Milton; see his *Milton's Biblical and Classical Imagery* (Pittsburgh, PA, 1984), pp. 167–89.

40 *The House of Fame* III.905–7, ed. J. M. Fyler in *The Riverside Chaucer*, ed. Benson, p. 359.

41 *King Alfred's Old English Version of Boethius De Consolatione Philosophiae*, ed. W. J. Sedgefield (Oxford, 1899), p. 41: 'þisse eorðan ym[b]hwyrft ... is eal wið þone heofon to metanne swilce an lytlu price on bradum brede, oðþe rondbeag on scelde' (Alfred characteristically adds a more homely image).

uocetur, de caelo tamen despicientibus non potest magnum uideri, cum ad caelum terra signum sit, quod diuidi non possit in partes.[42]

The devil, however, does not compare the circle of the earth (including the Ocean) with the vastness of the universe, but compares the small portion of dry land on the earth with the vastness of the Ocean itself. Now Cicero and Macrobius do remark that the inhabitable parts of the earth divided by Oceanus are but small islands, and Boethius follows up the comparison of the earth and the universe by noting the yet smaller portion of the earth inhabited by living things, especially when the seas and deserts are subtracted, characterizing what remains as 'this smallest point of that other point' (*in hoc igitur minimo puncti quodam puncto*).[43] But this is still not the same as comparing the extent of the dry land to the Ocean, and there is another important difference: Boethius conceives of a four-part division of the earth based on the proportion of habitable to uninhabitable parts,[44] but 'The Devil's Account' conceives of a seven-part division based on the proportion of dry land to the waters of the Ocean.

The source of this conception is not classical cosmology but apocryphal exegesis. In a précis of creation, IV Ezra specifies that on the third day God commanded the waters to congregate in the seventh part: 'Et tertio die, imperasti aquis congregari in septima parte terrae, sex uero partes siccasti et conseruasti.'[45] Although IV Ezra was often included in medieval bibles, citations from it are relatively rare, and this detail did not become part of the mainstream of Hexaemeral exegesis.[46]

[42] *Commentarii in Somnium Scipionis*, ed. Willis, p. 124: 'Furthermore, since the whole earth, including Ocean, is but a point in comparison with any circle in the celestial sphere, Cicero was obliged to add, when speaking about Ocean, *But you can see how small it is despite its name!* Although we call it the Atlantic Sea and the Great Sea, it cannot seem great to those who behold it from the sky, since in comparison with the sky the earth is a mark that cannot be divided' (trans. Stahl, *Macrobius*, pp. 215–16).

[43] *De consolatione Philosophiae* II pr. 7, ed. Bieler, CCSL 94, 32.

[44] The Old English *Boethius*, after subtracting the seas, marshes and deserts, arrives at the figure of one tenth for the part inhabited by men.

[45] IV Ezra VI.42, in *The Fourth Book of Ezra*, ed. R. L. Bensly, Texts and Studies 3.2 (Cambridge, 1895), 23.

[46] M. R. James, in the introduction to Bensly's edition, pp. xxvii–xliii, collects the references from early sources. At a much later date, however, this verse figured in Christopher Columbus's calculations for his journey to the New World; see B. Metzger, *An Introduction to the Apocrypha* (New York, 1957), pp. 232–4.

It is, however, a regular feature of the Genesis commentaries which Bischoff identified as Irish or Irish influenced, which uniformly interpret the 'one place' of Genesis I.9 ('Congregentur aquae quae sub caelo sunt in locum unum') as the seventh part of the earth. This interpretation is found in the St Gallen Commentary on the Creation and Fall,[47] in the Munich Commentary on Genesis[48] and in the *Commemoratio Geneseos*,[49] as well as in the Genesis portion of the Reference Bible.[50]

The notion of a seven-part division of the earth based upon the proportion of dry land to the waters can only have been learned from this apocryphal tradition, which appears to have been transmitted almost exclusively in Hiberno-Latin commentaries. We know that the creation passage from IV Ezra circulated independently in an Irish milieu, since it is found, slightly abbreviated, appended to the text *Dies Dominica* in two manuscripts.[51] In 'The Devil's Account', however, the *seofoða dæl* has been transferred from the waters to the dry land. This reversal of the original ratio has been caused by the imperfect synthesis of two conflicting conceptions, one of which, the classical topos of the *punctum*, restricts the relative size of the earth, while the other, the apocryphal tradition of the seventh part, restricts the relative size of the waters. The new context, according to which the earth is but a point in comparison with the waters of the Ocean, logically demands that the dry land receive the smaller portion.

To judge from the *Commemoratio Geneseos*, which Bischoff states 'was certainly formed under Irish influence',[52] this fusion of disparate traditions had already been accomplished in an exegetical context. This commentary provides a remarkable parallel for the combination of the rare detail of the seventh part with the image of the earth as a point in comparison to the waters of Oceanus:

47 St Gallen, Stiftsbibliothek, 908 (North Italy or Switzerland, s. viii/ix), p. 17. See *BCLL*, no. 1260; Wright, 'Hiberno-Latin', no. *8.

48 Munich, Clm. 6302 (Freising, s. viii²), 51r. See *BCLL*, no. 1258; Wright, 'Hiberno-Latin', no. *6.

49 Paris, BN, lat. 10457 (s. viii/ix), 23v–24r (quoted below). See *BCLL*, no. 1259; Wright, 'Hiberno-Latin', no. *7.

50 Paris, BN, lat. 11561 (s. ix^med), 10v. See *BCLL*, no. 762; Wright, 'Hiberno-Latin', no. 1.

51 The creation passage was printed by Bischoff, 'Turning-Points', p. 145; its source was identified by McNamara, *The Apocrypha in the Irish Church*, p. 27 (see also p. 9 on the use of IV Ezra in Ireland).

52 'Turning-Points', p. 104.

Quando enim dixit 'congregentur' ac si dixisset 'fiant', non quia de regionibus congregarentur sed quia create sunt ut in unum locum essent. Aque enim iste, id est stagna et flumina et maria, terris infuse intellegende sunt. *Oceanum uero infusum esse terris non intellegimus, sed seorsum congregatum, in cuius conparationem mundus in instar puncti intellegitur esse. Aque uero iste septimam partem terrae tenuerunt, sicut Esdra testatur.*[53]

The image of the *punctum* is here reconciled with the detail of the seventh part by careful observation of the distinction between the lower waters, including the lakes, rivers and seas, and the upper waters of Oceanus gathered above the earth. But the world-encircling river Oceanus was usually considered the source of the lesser oceans, with which it was connected. Once divorced from its immediate exegetical context, the distinction was likely to collapse. This has happened in 'The Devil's Account', where the context is cosmological and visionary rather than exegetical. Whereas the commentary is at pains to stress that the waters *sub caelo* cover the earth ('aque enim iste ... terris infuse intellegende sunt'), but that the water of Oceanus *seorsum congregatum* does not ('Oceanum uero infusum esse terris non intellegimus'), the Old English text uses the same term (*garsecg*) both for the great Ocean that encircles the earth ('se mid micclum ormætnyssum ealle þas eorðan utan ymbligeð') and for the waters *sub caelo* ('under heofonum'), with which all but a little portion of dry land is flooded ('lytel dæl is ... dryges landes þæt hit ne sy mid garsecge oferurnen'). Since the dry land of the earth is but a *prica* in comparison to this now undifferentiated flood, the *garsecg* can scarcely be assigned a mere seventh part; on the contrary, the dry land must be but a seventh part in comparison to the *garsecg*, which covers all the rest ('7 nis þes middaneard swilce se seofoða dæl ofer þone micclan garsecg').

The use of the detail of the seventh part as an illustration of the smallness of the earth has a late survival in the *South English Legendary.*

[53] Paris, BN, lat. 10457, 23v–24r: 'For when he said "let there be gathered", as though he had said "let there be", (it was) not because the waters were being gathered together from (different) regions but because they were created so that they would be in a single place. For these waters, that is lakes and rivers and seas, are to be taken as having covered the earth. *But we do not take Oceanus as having covered the earth, rather as having been gathered all by itself, in comparison to which the earth is taken to be like a point. These (lower) waters, however, occupy a seventh part of the earth, as is proven by Esdra*' (emphasis mine).

In the section devoted to St Michael (Part III), a hotchpotch of cosmological and other 'scientific' lore, the poet explains that there is more water than land on earth (line 629), and that the seas of the earth are fed by the great Ocean (631–48). He then describes the relative size of the earth and the Ocean:

> Eorþe is amidde þe grete se . as a lite bal al round
> And pur helle amidde eorþe . wo so soȝte þe ground
> And ȝute as gret as eorþe þincþ . & as lite as he is
> Þare nis bote þe seueþe deol . þat men wonieþ on iwis.[54]

The Middle English poet's conception differs from the Old English homilist's, because here the seventh part refers to the proportion not of dry land to water, but rather of the habitable parts of the earth to the uninhabitable. In the north, the poet explains, it is too cold for man to live, in the south too hot and in many other places where a man might live no food grows (lines 653–8), so that 'Þer nis to wonie inne men . bote unneþe þe seueþe part' (600). Despite the different application, this passage clearly represents a development of the same cosmological motif, which has survived tenaciously in the vernacular tradition.

In the *South English Legendary* the motif is part of an odd assortment of cosmological lore, but in 'The Devil's Account' the cosmological topoi of the earth as a point and the dry land as the seventh part have a structural function. Before the devil grants the anchorite his 'revelation' of the next world, he must first be conducted on a verbal cosmological 'tour', featuring Oceanus and the spectacular view of the tiny point of earth. The cosmological setting, in turn, helps to explain why the *garsecg* figures in the bizarre hypothetical scenario which the devil invents to give the anchorite some idea of the inexpressible pains of hell.

[54] *The South English Legendary*, 'Michael III', ed. C. D'Evelyn and A. Mill, EETS os 235, 236 and 244 (London, 1956–9) II, 423, lines 649–52. The section 'Michael III' occurs separately in eight manuscripts; see C. Brown and R. Robbins, *The Index of Middle English Verse* (New York, 1943), no. 3453; R. Robbins and J. Cutler, *Supplement to the Index of Middle English Verse* (Lexington, KY, 1965), no. 3453. For a recent discussion of 'Michael III', see G. M. Sadlek, 'The Archangel and the Cosmos: the Inner Logic of the *South English Legendary*'s "St. Michael"', *SP* 85 (1988), 177–91.

THE DEVIL'S ACCOUNT OF HELL AND THE IRON HOUSE

In the Vercelli Book and in the abbreviated version of the homily in E, 'The Devil's Account' is defective; but the complete exemplum is preserved in L, and also in M, where it occurs as a separate tale. The account of hell is also partially preserved in the extract in Napier XXX (O), and in the précis of the legend in H. I shall cite the fuller version from L:

Þa cwæþ þæt deoful to þæm ancran: 'Þeah mon þone garsecg mid isernum weallum utan betyne, 7 hine þonne fyres afylle up oþ heofnes hrof, 7 hine þonne utan besette mid smiþbylium 7 heora æghwylc oðrum ætrine, 7 sy to ælcum þara man togeset and ælc þara manna hæbbe Samsones strenge (7 se Samson ealle F[i]llestina þeode gererde 7 heora duguþe afylde, 7 he hæfde twelf loccas 7 on ælcum locce he hæfde twelf manna mægen) 7 man þonne sette iserne þele ofer þæs fyres hrof 7 þæt sy eall mid mannum afylled 7 heora æghwylc hæbbe hamor on honda, 7 hit þonne aginne eal samod brastlian 7 þa bylias blawan 7 þæt fyr dynian 7 þa hamoras beatan, hweþere for eallum þyssum gedyne ne mæg seo sawl awacian seo þe wæs ær ane niht on helle.'[55]

Taken separately, most of the elements of this description can be paralleled in classical and Christian visions of hell. A river of fire (as the *garsecg* in essence becomes) in which damned souls are submerged is an especially common feature. The *Visio S. Pauli* features a *flumen igneum*.[56] A fiery furnace tended by demonic smiths is encountered in a number of visions, from Plutarch's Vision of Thespesius to the *Visio Tnugdali*.[57]

55 *The Vercelli Homilies*, ed. Scragg, p. 177, lines L.140–51: 'Then the devil said to the anchorite: "Even if the Ocean were closed up from without with iron walls, and then filled with fire up to the roof of heaven, and then surrounded by smith's bellows so that each touched the other, and a man were placed at each bellows and each of those men had the strength of Samson (and that Samson stirred up all the people of the Philistines and felled their troops, and he had twelve locks and in each lock he had the strength of twelve men) and an iron plate were then placed over the roof of the fire and it were all filled with men and each had a hammer in his hand, and then all together began to crash it, and blow the bellows and cause the fire to roar and beat the hammers, none the less despite all this commotion the soul that was earlier in hell for a single night could not wake up."'

56 On rivers of fire, see Himmelfarb, *Tours of Hell*, pp. 110–12 and 122–3. For the *Visio S. Pauli*, see above, p. 134.

57 For the Vision of Thespesius, see Becker, *Medieval Visions of Heaven and Hell*, pp. 27–9; for the *Visio Tnugdali*, see Wagner's edition, pp. 30–2. The smith of hell is a

But these similarities with traditional descriptions of hell hardly account for the configuration of the scene as a whole. Particularly striking is the emphasis on the process by which the torment is prepared. It is not a static description of an eternal and unchanging punishment. The iron chamber is not a permanent fixture but rather an *ad hoc* rhetorical construction whose hypothetical preparation is outlined step by step: the Ocean is first enclosed with an iron wall, the enclosure is then filled with fire up to the roof of heaven, the fire is then surrounded by smiths' bellows, the bellows are manned, and the fire is then stoked by the smiths. Granted the logic of conducting the stages of the procedure in this order, its detailed elaboration is none the less peculiar.

No direct sources have been discovered for the devil's remarkable hypothetical scenario, although several of its essential features, both narrative and rhetorical, can be paralleled in medieval Latin exempla of later date. Several exempla concerning purgatory, for example, stress the horror of its inexpressible torments by stating that a soul which had experienced them for a single hour or day (or comparably brief period of time) would rather suffer a specified hypothetical torment in this world for a thousand years, or until Judgement.[58] Two Latin exempla have a character state that he would rather suffer a specified hypothetical torment than be in purgatory: in one, 'a priest says he would stay in a lake of fire until Doomsday to escape purgatory'; in another, 'a dead Cistercian appears and says he would rather be flayed alive than repeat his experience in purgatory'.[59]

common figure in medieval folklore, including Irish; for references, see T. P. Cross, *Motif-Index*, no. A677.1.

58 A particularly elaborate example is from the spurious (fourteenth-century) *Epistula Cyrilli ad Augustinum de miraculis Hieronymi* (Bibliotheca Hagiographica Latina, 2 vols., Subsidia Hagiographica 6 (Brussels, 1898–1901), no. 3868; cf. Dekkers and Gaar, *Clavis Patrum*, no. 367): 'Si omnes quae in mundo cogitari possunt poenae, tormenta, afflictiones, minori quae illic habentur poenae et tormenta comparentur, solatia erunt. Mallet enim quidlibet uiuentium (si illas experientia nosceret poenas) usque ad finem mundi, omnibus his simul sine remedio cruciari poenis, quas omnes homines ab Adam hucusque sigillatim pertulerunt, quam uno die in Inferno, siue Purgatorio minori quae illic habetur poena, torqueri' (PL 22, 293). For similar examples, cf. Tubach, *Index Exemplorum*, nos. 3994, 3997, 4001 and 4004, and Coulton, *Five Centuries of Religion* I, 74–5.

59 Tubach, *Index Exemplorum*, nos. 3996 and 4007. A passage from an English sermon printed by Owst, *Preaching in Medieval England*, p. 337, is similar.

Like the homilist's earlier description of the hanging sinner, the devil's rhetorical account of hell combines both these motifs, the 'single night' in hell and the hypothetical torment which the soul would prefer to suffer. The story of Cairpre Crom has a similar hypothetical torment (suffered by a soul for a night), and several Irish tales also refer to a soul's single night in hell (or heaven) as an inexpressibility topos.[60] But these Latin and Irish parallels do not account for the elaborate and specific realization of the hypothetical torment in 'The Devil's Account', which synthesizes two other narrative models: a type of exemplum in which the devil describes what he would be willing to endure to return to heaven, and a motif known to Celticists as the 'Iron House'.

Several Latin exempla in collections dating from the thirteenth century incorporate as a hypothetical torment a fiery iron column stretching from earth to heaven and studded with knives and razors, a motif which Peter Dinzelbacher terms 'Die Messersäule'.[61] The earliest is Caesarius of Heisterbach's *Dialogus miraculorum*, compiled *c.* 1223–4. In a story which Caesarius locates at 'the church of the blessed Peter at Cologne', a demon, having taken possession of a woman, is asked what he would be willing to endure if he could return to the glory of heaven. Although another demon, in response to the same question, had answered that he would rather go back down to hell with one soul he had deceived, this one gives a contradictory response:

> Si esset, inquit, columna ferrea et ignita, rasoriis et laminis acutissimis armata, a terra usque ad coelum erecta, usque ad diem iudicii, etiam si carnem haberem, in qua pati possem, me per illam trahere uellem, nunc ascendendo, nunc descendendo, dummodo redire possem ad gloriam in qua fui.[62]

[60] These are discussed below, pp. 207–9, in connection with the devil's account of heaven, which employs a variation of the same rhetorical formula.

[61] Dinzelbacher, 'Die Messersäule'.

[62] *Caesarii Heisterbacensis monachi Dialogus miraculorum* V.10, ed. J. Strange, 2 vols. (Cologne, 1851) I, 290: '"If", he said, "there were a column of burning iron set up from earth to heaven, and if it were furnished with the sharpest razors and blades of steel, and if I were given a body capable of suffering, most gladly would I drag myself up it from now till the Day of Judgment, now climbing up a little and now slipping down again, if only I might at the last win home to the glory in which I once dwelt"' (trans. Scott and Bland, *The Dialogue on Miracles*, p. 331). Dinzelbacher, 'Die Messersäule', p. 51, n. 30, points out that Strange has unnecessarily emended the

The author of 'The Devil's Account' was probably familiar with a cognate exemplum. The rhetorical structure of the two texts is parallel: in each the devil posits a hypothetical torment, elaborated in a series of conditional clauses ('si esset ... et si ... ' / 'þeah ... ⁊ þeah ... ') whose dramatic effect depends on its victim's willingness to endure it, so long as he does not have to return to hell – or as the demon expresses it in the equivalent positive terms, if only he could return to heaven. The mechanisms of the hypothetical torments in both texts are similar as well: an iron chamber of fire in 'The Devil's Account' and a fiery column of iron in Caesarius's exemplum, both of cosmic dimensions, stretching up to heaven.[63] In view of these similarities, 'The Devil's Account' might be considered an adaptation for a slightly different context of an earlier but cognate form of the *Messersäule* exemplum.

Another version, apparently independent of Caesarius, survives in a thirteenth-century *Liber exemplorum* compiled in Ireland by an English Franciscan:

> Inter exempla Deodati uero hoc etiam exemplum super hac materia reperi, uidelicet quod demon per os cuiusdam demonici loquens, cum requisitus esset a fratre Iordano condam magistro ordinis predicatorum, quid pateretur ut posset saluari in die iudicii, respondit: 'Si totus esset mundus inflammatus ab

manuscript reading *calamis* ('quills', 'arrows') to *laminis*. A paraphrase of Caesarius's exemplum, drawn from the unpublished *Alphabetum narrationum*, occurs in the *Copia exemplorum* of Magister Matthias, ed. L. Wålin and M. Andersson-Schmitt (Uppsala, 1990), p. 29. See the Middle English version of the *Alphabetum narrationum*, in *An Alphabet of Tales*, ed. Banks I, 177–8. The passages from later German sources discussed by L. Kretzenbacher, 'Des Teufels Sehnsucht nach der Himmelsschau', *Zeitschrift für Balkanologie* 4 (1966), 57–66, may also depend on Caesarius. See also A. Gurevich, 'Santi iracondi e demoni buoni negli "exempla"', in *Santi e demoni nell'alto medioevo occidentale (secoli V–XI)*, 2 vols., Settimane di studio del Centro Italiano di studi sull'alto medioevo 36 (Spoleto, 1989), 1045–63, at 1056.

63 Dinzelbacher cites several other later medieval visions which involve a column stretching from earth to heaven. The *Messersäule* motif also appears (but as an actual torment of hell rather than a hypothetical one) in a collection of exempla compiled *c.* 1300 by Rudolf von Schlettstatt (see Dinzelbacher, 'Die Messersäule', pp. 42–3). In the *Visio Alberici* there is a great burning ladder of iron which a particular group of sinners is forced to go up and down (see Patch, *The Other World*, p. 111). The motif of the *Messersäule* may also have been influenced by the nail-studded bridge in the *Visio Tnugdali* and the cosmic ladder in the Vision of Perpetua, as Dinzelbacher (pp. 45–7) suggests.

oriente in occidentem et ab aquilone usque ad austrum, illud tormentum sustinere[m] libenter usque ad diem iudicii ad hoc quod recuperare possem quod amisi. Et si columpna ignea plena aculeis acutis esset de terra ad celum, ego septies in die ascenderem et descenderem per eam ad hoc quod possem saluus fieri in die iudicii.'[64]

Here the column is not said to be made of iron, but the devil's hypothetical conflagration, which fills the entire world with fire, is reminiscent of the cosmic conflagration posited in 'The Devil's Account'.[65] An exemplum of the *Messersäule* type, then, probably

[64] *Liber Exemplorum*, ed. Little, p. 91: 'But among the exempla of Deodatus I have also found this exemplum concerning this subject, namely that a demon speaking through the mouth of a possessed person, when he was asked by brother Jordanus, formerly head of the Dominican order, what he would undergo that he might be saved on the day of Judgement, responded: "If the entire world were set on fire from the east to the west and from the north to the south, I would freely endure that torment until the day of Judgement so that I might recover what I lost. And if there were a fiery column full of sharp spikes from earth to heaven, I would go up and down it seven times a day so that I might be saved on the day of Judgement."' On the author of this collection, see *ibid.*, pp. vi–viii. Dinzelbacher considers this to be a reworking of Caesarius's exemplum, but acknowledges that the different formulation precludes direct borrowing. But Caesarius's *Dialogus miraculorum* is not among the impressive list of sources given by Little for the *Liber exemplorum*, whose author attributes this exemplum to Deodatus, who in turn refers to 'Jordanus' (of Saxony?). Deodatus is identified in another manuscript as having been a minister of the Friars Minor in Ireland (see Little, pp. 141–2). Dinzelbacher cites a third Latin version of the *Messersäule* exemplum from another thirteenth-century Franciscan collection: 'Propter Dominum, et pro remissione malorum que in seculo feci, libenter hec facio ... si a summo celi usque in inferni profundum esset descensus, et uia plena acutissimis rasoriis, ego libenter omni die centies, si corpus haberem, descenderem per gladios illos, et facere hoc uellem usque ad centum milia annorum, dummodo penitudinem et humilitatem et contritionem habere ex hoc possem ad Deo satisfaciendum' (ed. L. Oliger, *Antonianum* 2 (1927), 203–76, at 233; cited by Dinzelbacher, p. 51, n. 33).

[65] In another exemplum in Caesarius's *Dialogus miraculorum* XII.23, a soul states, 'If one fire were made of all the wood in the world, I would rather burn in it until the day of judgment than for the space of an hour endure that' (trans. Scott and Bland, *The Dialogue on Miracles*, p. 311). Cf. also the following from a thirteenth-century sermon of Berthold of Regensburg: 'If thy whole body were of red-hot iron, and the whole world, from earth to heaven, one vast fire, and thou in the midst, that is how a man is in hell, but that he is an hundredfold worse' (cited by Coulton, *Five Centuries of Religion* I, 450).

supplied to the author of 'The Devil's Account' the basic idea of a hypothetical torment posited in a sequence of conditional clauses, as well as the realization of the torment as an *iron* structure (as in Caesarius) and cosmic conflagration (as in the *Liber exemplorum*). Despite these fundamental similarities, it is clear that this narrative material has been freely reworked. In the first place, the anecdote is now framed in a different context, modelled on the *Vitas patrum*. It is still a demon who posits the hypothetical torment, but now in response to an anchorite who would have him reveal not what he would be willing to endure in order to return to heaven, but what he knows about the pains of hell and joys of heaven. Since the information required in 'The Devil's Account' does *not* call for a hypothetical response, as does the question put to the demon in the Latin exemplum, and since the devil's hypothetical response still presumes such a question, we may infer that the later Latin *Messersäule* exemplum best preserves the original context. In keeping with the new context, however, the devil's response now concerns the hypothetical torment that any human soul would gladly endure in order to escape from the inexpressibly more horrible pains of hell.[66]

In addition to these modifications necessitated by context, the hypothetical torment itself has been modified. Instead of a fiery iron *column* reaching up to heaven, the devil describes the preparation, in a series of distinct stages, of a cosmic fiery house, made with 'walls' of iron, filled with fire up to the 'roof' of heaven and then surrounded by bellows and smiths. The cosmological topoi which I have described help to explain why the Ocean should serve as the foundation upon which this cosmic iron 'house' is superimposed. What remains to be explained is the new metaphor of the house and the new emphasis on the elaborate process of its construction and firing.

The reconfiguration of the devil's hypothetical torment in 'The Devil's Account' was inspired, I believe, by Celtic narrative tradition. Two Irish tales, *Mesca Ulad* ('The Intoxication of the Ulstermen') and *Orgain Denna Ríg* ('The Destruction of Dinn Ríg'), and the Welsh tale *Branwen* from the *Mabinogion*, preserve a narrative motif known to Celticists as the 'Iron House'. In these tales enemies are lured to a feast

[66] In a variant type of the *Messersäule* motif, the torment is expressed as either a voluntary or hypothetical penance which a pious human would undergo in order to attain God's love (see Dinzelbacher, 'Die Messersäule', pp. 44 and 49).

in a specially constructed house with walls of iron, which is stacked with fuel, surrounded by smiths and bellows and then set ablaze. The Iron House motif in these Celtic tales has been analysed in detail by Proinsias Mac Cana.[67] *Orgain Denna Ríg*, preserved in three manuscripts, probably dates from the late ninth or early tenth century.[68] The story tells of the seizing of Dinn Ríg and the kingdom of Leinster by Labraid Loingsech. To avenge the murder of his father and grandfather by Cobthach Coel, Labraid lures Cobthach to a deadly feast:

Ro-chuirestar iarum Cobthach do dēnam a menman ⁊ do airiuc thuile dó. Do-rónad teg les-seom dano ara chind Chobthaigh. Imchomnart immorro a tech; d'iurn eter fraig ⁊ lár ⁊ chomlada do-rōnad a tech. Lagin oco dēnam bliadain lāin ⁊ do-ceiled athair ar a mac ⁊ māthair ar ingin. Is de atá, Nīt lia Lagin rúni. Is and do-rónad a tech, i nDind Ríg.

Ro-cured didiu Cobthach dond irgnam ⁊ do-lluid .xxx. ríg imbi do rīgaib Hērenn. For-émdes immorro ō Chobthach dul issin tech co ndigsed máthair Labrada ⁊ a drūth. Is ed do-rroíga in drúth, bennachtu Lagen ⁊ soīri a chlainne co bráth; ar maithius dia mac do chuaid in ben. É-sseom féin .i. Labraid oc a ferthaigis ...

Tene duib, ar sē, ⁊ lind ⁊ biad isa tech.

Is cóir, ar Cobthach.

Nónbur dō for lár in taigi. Sreṅgait in slabraid baí assin chomlaid ina ndiaid conda ralsat ar in coirthe in ndorus taige ⁊ ro sétea na trī choícat bolg goband dōib immon tech ⁊ cethrur ōclách for cach bulg, combo te dont ṡluag ...

Orggthir trā Cobthach Coel secht cētaib ⁊ co .xxx. ríg imbi.[69]

[67] *Branwen*, pp. 16–23. [68] See D. Greene, *Fingal Rónáin*, pp. 16–17.

[69] *Ibid.*, pp. 21–2, lines 415–26, 433–9 and 443: 'He then invited Cobthach in order to provide for him hospitality and entertainment. He had a house built specially for Cobthach. It was a very strong house indeed, for it was made of iron, walls and floors and doors. The Leinstermen were a full year building it, and neither did father disclose it to son nor mother to daughter. Thence is the proverb, "Every Leinsterman has his secret." It was in Dinn Ríg that the house was built. Cobthach was then invited to the feast and came with a retinue of thirty of the kings of Ireland. However, Cobthach could not be prevailed upon to go into the house till Labraid's mother and his jester should go before him. The jester chose the Leinstermen's blessing and the freedom (honour) of his descendants for ever; it was for the benefit of her son the woman went. Labraid himself waited on them ... "Fire will be brought to you in the house, and food and drink", said he. "That is fitting", said Cobthach. He had nine men on the floor of the house. They pulled after them the chain that was attached to the door and fixed it to the pillar in the entrance to the

Mesca Ulad survives partially in two main manuscripts, representing two separate redactions of the tale.[70] The Iron House passage occurs in the later version in the Book of Leinster. The house is prepared for Conchobar and the Ulstermen:

Is cían atá i tairṅgiri a taidecht 7 ra fritháilit. Is é a frithálim, teg íarnaidi 7 dá thech cláraid immi et teg talman foí anís 7 lecc imdaṅgen íarnaide fair-side 7 na fríth da chrín 7 do lassamain 7 da gúalach ra timmairged issin tech talman conid for lán. Is sed ra tairṅgered dún co timmairgfitís mathi Ulad i n-óenaidchi issin tech sain. Atát secht slabraid úríairn sund fa chossaib ind leptha sa ra hairichill chengail 7 forríata; a ceṅgul do na secht coirthib failet for in fhaidchi se immuich.[71]

When the Ulstermen are invited to choose a house, their champion, Cú Chulainn, chooses the largest:

Is esede in tech íarnaide imma rrabatar in dá thech cláraid.

Táncatar lucht a frithálma chucu 7 ra hatód tor tended dermár dóib. Ra deoraintea airigthi bíd 7 lenna dóib. Cach faicsi thiced d'aidchi ra etlaitís lucht a frestail 7 a frithálma ar óenfheraib úathu cu ríacht in fer ndédenach co ro íad in comlai da éis. Co tucait na secht slabraid úríairn forsin tech et ro cenglait do na secht coirthib cloch bátar forsind fhathchi immuich. Tucait trí coícat goband cona mbolgaib goband da gressacht in tened. Tucait a trí timchúardda imman tech. Ra hadnad in tene anís 7 anúas issin tech co tánic robruth in teined trisin tech anís. Cu ra thromgairset in slúag immon tech curba thaí tastadach for Ultaib. Cu n-ebairt Bricriu: 'A Ultu, ca rét in bruth romór gabas ar cossa? Acht

house. The thrice fifty smith's bellows, which they had around the house, [with four warriors at each bellows,] were blown till it became hot for the host inside... Cobthach Coel is slain there with seven hundred men and thirty kings' (trans. Mac Cana, *Branwen*, pp. 17–18; Mac Cana omits the bracketed phrase).

70 See Watson, *Mesca Ulad*, pp. vii–viii.

71 *Ibid.*, p. 36, lines 807–16: 'Long has their coming been in prophecy, and preparation has been made for them. The preparation is a house of iron and two houses of boards about it and an earthen house below beneath it and a firm-set slab of iron thereupon; and all that could be found of faggots and firewood and coal has been gathered into the earthen house, so that it is quite full. This is what has been foretold to us, that the nobles of Ulster would gather on the same night in that house. There are seven chains of fresh iron here under the legs of this bed as a preparation for binding and closing in; they are to be made fast to the seven pillars that are outside upon this green' (trans. Watson, as quoted with alterations by MacCana, *Branwen*, pp. 18–19).

is irdarcu damsa sanas ná do neoch aile égem: dar limsa atáthar icar loscud anís 7 anúas 7 is forríata in tegdas.'[72]

Cú Chulainn attempts to break out by thrusting his sword through the house, and thereby discovers how it is constructed: '"Tech íairn and so", bar Cú Chulainn, "etir dá thech cláraid". "Messu cach main ón", bar Bricriu'.[73]

The earlier version of the tale, in the Lebor na hUidre, may be as early as the eighth century,[74] but the corresponding episode is quite different, lacking the features that make the Iron House motif distinctive. Cú Chulainn and his warriors are taken 'into an oaken house with cup-shaped roof, having a door of yew three full feet thick, in which there were two hooks of iron, and an iron bolt through these two hooks'.[75] But they escape from this house, and it is not set ablaze. The Iron House episode in the Book of Leinster version (which Mac Cana dates to the first quarter of the twelfth century) may thus be a later elaboration of the scene.[76] However, *Orgain Denna Ríg* shows that the basic motif existed

[72] *Mesca Ulad*, ed. Watson, pp. 38–9, lines 860–78: 'That was the iron house about which were the two houses of boards. There came servants to attend them, and a huge pile of a fire was lit for them. Choice portions of food and of drink were dispensed to them. As night drew on, their servants and attendants one by one stole away from them until the last: he shut the door behind him. The seven chains of fresh iron were put upon the house and made fast to the seven stone pillars that were outside on the green. Thrice fifty smiths with their smith's bellows were brought to stimulate the fire. Three circles of them were set about the house. The fire was kindled from below and from above into the house, so that the fierce heat of the fire came through the house from below. The host shouted loudly about the house, and the men of Ulster fell silent and mute. And Bricriu said: "O men of Ulster, what is this intense heat that is seizing our feet? But a whisper is clearer to me than a shout to another: me thinks we are being burned from below and from above, and the house is closed upon us"' (trans. Watson, as quoted by Mac Cana, *Branwen*, pp. 19–20).

[73] *Mesca Ulad*, ed. Watson, p. 40, lines 890–2: '"This is a house of iron", said Cú Chulainn, "between two houses of boards". Quoth Bricriu, "That is worse than every trick!"' (trans. Watson, as quoted by Mac Cana, *Branwen*, p. 20).

[74] *Ibid.*, p. 18.

[75] Trans. Watson, as quoted by Mac Cana, *Branwen*, p. 29; for the Irish text, see Watson, *Mesca Ulad*, pp. 40–1.

[76] *Ibid.*, pp. xvii–xviii. See also Watson, '*Mesca Ulad*: the Redactor's Contribution to the Later Version', *Ériu* 13 (1940), 95–112, at 111. Mac Cana concludes that '*Mesca Ulad* provides no tangible evidence of the Iron House theme before the beginning of the twelfth century' (*Branwen*, p. 20).

at least two centuries earlier, and as Mac Cana has stated, 'we cannot preclude the possibility that other versions of the theme have been lost or that the twelfth century *Mesca Ulad* was based on an earlier recension containing the Iron House'.[77]

A third Irish tale, the tenth- or eleventh-century *Bórama*, describes a house burning which Mac Cana thinks may be a reduced version of the Iron House motif, but in this story the royal house is not constructed of iron, and the procedure of the burning is not so elaborate as in the other Irish tales. Mac Cana suggests that 'it is just barely possible that the omission of the Iron House is merely accidental', but he thinks it more likely that *Bórama* provides 'an instance of the type of tale which was the immediate forerunner of the Iron House theme'.[78]

The fully developed motif of the Iron House does occur in one other text, the Welsh *Branwen Uerch Lŷr* ('Branwen Daughter of Llyr'). The Iron House episode occurs as part of the story of the magic cauldron that Bendigeidfran offers King Matholwch of Ireland in recompense for an insult. Matholwch relates that the cauldron had belonged to a giant and his wife, whom he had sheltered until they had caused so much trouble that his people threatened to rebel. They then devised a way to rid themselves of the unwanted guests:

Ac yna yn y kyuyng gynghor, y causant gwneuthur ystauell haearn oll; a gwedy bot y barawt yr ystauell, dyuyn a oed o of yn Iwerdon yno, o'r a oed o perchen geuel a mwrthwl, a pheri gossot kyuuch a chrib yr ystauell o lo, a pheri guassanaethu yn diwall o uwyt a llyn arnunt, ar y wreic, a'y gwr, a'y phlant. A phan wybuwyt eu medwi wynteu, y dechreuwyt kymyscu y tan a'r glo am ben yr ystauell, a chwythu y megineu a oed wedy eu gossot yg kylch y ty, a gwr a pob dwy uegin, a dechreu chwythu y megineu yny uyd y ty yn burwen am eu penn. Ac yna y bu y kynghor ganthunt hwy ymherued llawr yr ystauell; ac yd arhoes ef yny uyd y pleit haearn yn wenn. Ac rac diruawr wres, y kyrchwys y bleit a'e yscwyd a'y tharaw gantaw allan, ac yn y ol ynteu y wreic. A neb ni dieghis odyna namyn ef a'e wreic.[79]

[77] *Ibid.*, p. 23. See now U. Mac Gearailt, 'The Edinburgh Text of Mesca Ulad', *Ériu* 37 (1986), 155–6, who postulates an earlier version 'Q' of *c.* 1100 as a possible source of the Iron House theme in the Welsh *Branwen* (discussed below).

[78] Mac Cana, *Branwen*, p. 22. Another text that describes a house-burning in similar terms is 'Da Choca's Hostel', ed. W. Stokes, *RC* 21 (1900), 312–27, at 320–2. Gantz, *Early Irish Myths*, p. 60, compares a similar episode in *Togail Bruidne Da Derga*.

[79] *Branwen Uerch Lyr*, ed. Thomson, p. 7: 'And then, in this strait, they decided to make a chamber all of iron. And when the chamber was ready, every smith that was

Mac Cana considers this one of three 'obvious borrowings from Irish' in *Branwen*.[80] Mac Cana's argument for Irish influence in *Branwen*, however, has been disputed by Patrick K. Ford and Andrew Welsh, who stress international parallels for many of the folktale motifs in the story.[81] As for the Iron House motif itself, Kenneth Jackson[82] has drawn attention to Aarne-Thompson folktale Type 513, The Helpers, in many versions of which there is a helper called 'Freezer' who can withstand extreme heat.[83] In the Grimms' tale 'Six Go Through the Whole World' (Type 513A), this character foils a plot of a king and his daughter to kill the hero and his companions:

Then the king said to her, 'I've found a way; don't be alarmed; they won't get back home', and said to them, 'Now have a good time eating and drinking', and led them to a room with an iron floor and whose doors were also of iron and the windows guarded with iron bars. In the room was a table set with delicious food. The king said to them, 'Just go in and enjoy yourselves', and when they were inside had the door locked and bolted. Then he had the chef come and ordered him to make a fire under the room till the iron got red hot.

in Ireland was summoned there, each and every possessor of tongs and hammer. And they caused charcoal to be piled as high as the top of the chamber, and they had the woman and her husband and her offspring served with ample meat and drink. And when it was known that they were drunk, they began to set fire to the charcoal against the chamber, and to blow the bellows which had been placed around the house with a man to each pair of bellows, and they began to blow the bellows till the house was white-hot around them. Then they held a council there in the middle of the chamber floor. And he waited till the iron-wall was white, and by reason of the exceeding great heat he charged the wall with his shoulder and broke it out before him, and his wife after him. And none escaped thence save him and his wife' (trans. G. Jones and T. Jones, *The Mabinogion* (New York, 1949), pp. 30–1, as quoted by Mac Cana, *Branwen*, pp. 16–17).

80 *Ibid.*, p. 16, and see Thomson's discussion of the passage, *Branwen Uerch Lyr*, pp. xxxvi–xl. See also C. O'Rahilly, *Ireland and Wales: Their Historical and Literary Relations* (London, 1924), pp. 104–7. W. J. Gruffydd thought the Welsh version 'more primitive' than the Irish, for reasons summarized and rejected by Mac Cana, *Branwen*, p. 23, n. 1.

81 See Ford, 'Branwen: a Study of the Celtic Affinities', *SC* 22–3 (1987–8), 29–41, at 31–2; Welsh, 'Branwen, Beowulf, and the Tragic Peaceweaver Tale', *Viator* 22 (1991), 1–13, at 1–4.

82 *The International Popular Tale and Early Welsh Tradition* (Cardiff, 1961), pp. 100–1.

83 See A. Aarne, *The Types of the Folktale: a Classification and Bibliography*, 2nd ed. trans. and enlarged by S. Thompson, FFC 184 (Helsinki, 1961), 180–1.

The chef did so, and the fire started, and as they were sitting at table, the six in the room got very warm and thought it was on account of the food. When, however, it kept getting hotter and they wanted to get out and found the door and windows locked, they saw that the king had evil designs and meant to suffocate them. 'But he won't succeed', said the man with the cap, 'I'll bring a frost that will put the fire to shame and make it creep away.' Then he set his cap on straight, and at once such a frost descended that all the heat disappeared and the food in the dishes began to freeze.[84]

Though he concedes that 'its application is different', Jackson is justified in seeing a variation of the Iron House motif in this passage.[85] Still, the existence of folktale analogues more remote in time and space does not establish that the Iron House episode in *Branwen* is independent of Irish literary tradition, where the Iron House motif is attested as early as the tenth century (*Orgain Denna Ríg*).[86] Moreover, as Mac Cana notes, the immediate context of the episode in *Branwen* points unmistakably to Ireland. Bendigeidfran had told Matholwch that he obtained the cauldron from Llasar Laes Gyfnewid when the giant and his wife 'had escaped from the iron house in Ireland when it was made white-hot

[84] *The Grimms' German Folk Tales*, trans. F. P. Magoun, Jr. and A. H. Krappe (Carbondale, IL, 1960), p. 275.

[85] For a list of analogues to the tale, see J. Bolte and G. Polívka, *Anmerkungen zu den Kinder- und Hausmärchen der Brüder Grimm*, 5 vols. (Leipzig, 1913–32) II, 86–96. Jackson does not cite any analogues in which the Freezer episode is formulated in this way. Of those I have been able to consult, none provides as close an analogue for the Iron House theme as does the Grimms' tale. In some versions, the Freezer rescues the hero from a hot bath or iron cage. A. Welsh, 'The Traditional Narrative Motifs of *The Four Branches of the Mabinogi*', *CMCS* 15 (Summer 1988), 51–62, at 56–62, provides a list of 'Celtic' motifs distinguished from international ones; the Celtic motifs account for about 20 per cent of the total (Welsh's figure, p. 54). From the total he excludes thirteen motifs 'that can be verified in at least one non-Celtic context' (p. 55), among them the Iron House (K811.4) because of the parallel in the Grimms' tale.

[86] Mac Cana concedes that 'As far as textual evidence goes, there is none to show that the Iron House theme existed before the ninth or tenth century in Irish literature, but of course that is not proof that it did not, nor that it was first employed by the writer of *Orgain Denna Ríg*' (*Branwen*, pp. 22–3). A. Bruford has shown that the Iron House motif survives in Irish oral folk literature. See his *Gaelic Folktales and Mediaeval Romances: a Study of the Early Modern Irish 'Romantic Tales' and their Oral Derivatives* (Dublin, 1969), pp. 101–2. Bruford points out that in the 'leaden house' (*teach luaidhe*) episode in the Donegal versions of *Oidheadh Chloinne Uisneach* 'there seems to be an echo of the Iron House in the Old Irish *Mesca Ulad*'.

around them'. He then says to Matholwch, 'I am amazed that you do not know anything about that'. In Mac Cana's words, 'The implied comment is "You are an Irishman; you ought to know this story better than I."'[87] In this case, then, internal evidence and the context of the episode within the tale support Mac Cana's argument for a borrowing from Irish. Even Patrick Sims-Williams, who has systematically challenged many supposed cases of Irish influence on medieval Welsh literature,[88] states that 'Irish influence on the story is probable'.[89]

Fortunately, we do not have to determine the precise origin of this particular motif (which is, after all, rarely possible when dealing with a folktale motif) to see that it was fully developed, and in a highly specific and stable form, in Irish and Welsh literature at a relatively early date. *Orgain Denna Ríg* (*ODR*), *Mesca Ulad* (*MU*), and *Branwen* (*Br*) share the following essential formulation:

1. An iron house or chamber is specially constructed, to be fired when the enemies have been lured within by the offer of food and drink (*ODR*, *MU*, *Br*). In *ODR* and *Br* the entire house or chamber is made of iron ('walls and floors and doors' (*ODR*); 'all of iron' (*Br*)). In *MU* the iron house is a more complex structure, with 'two houses of boards about it and an earthen house below beneath it, and a firm-set slab of iron thereupon'.
2. When the enemies are gathered within, the iron house is secured by an iron chain fixed to a pillar (*ODR*; in *MU* there are seven chains and seven pillars). This step is lacking in *Br*.
3. The house or chamber is filled with fuel. In *Br* charcoal is 'piled as high as the top of the chamber'; in *MU* it is the earthen house below the iron house that is loaded with wood 'so that it is quite full'. This procedure is not mentioned in *ODR*.
4. A great number of smith's bellows surrounding the house are manned and blown by smiths when the house is fired. In the two Irish tales there are 'thrice fifty' smith's bellows and smiths; in *ODR*

87 *Ibid*., p. 23.

88 'The Evidence for Vernacular Irish Literary Influence'; 'Riddling Treatment of the "Watchman Device" in *Branwen* and *Togail Bruidne Da Derga*', *SC* 12–13 (1977–8), 83–117; 'The Significance of the Irish Personal Names'; 'Some Celtic Otherworld Terms', in *Celtic Language, Celtic Culture: a Festschrift for Eric P. Hamp*, ed. A. T. E. Matonis and D. Melia (Van Nuys, CA, 1990), pp. 57–81.

89 'Some Functions of Origin Stories', pp. 104 and 124, n. 34.

they are simply positioned 'around the house', but *MU* specifies that they are arranged in three circles. *Br* does not specify the number of smiths but says that 'every smith in Ireland was summoned there', and these are positioned 'with a man to each pair of bellows'.

The essential structure of the Iron House motif as outlined above is preserved in 'The Devil's Account', although the context is, of course, entirely different. First we may note that here too the iron structure is conceived as an *ad hoc* construction, built for the purpose of burning the soul subsequently placed inside. The eschatological context does not provide for the element of deception as in the Celtic tales, in which enemies must be lured to the house by the prospect of a feast: here the soul has escaped *to* the iron chamber, and has no desire to escape from it, since the unspeakable torment of hell is the alternative. One further aspect of the preparation of the iron structure is reminiscent of a detail in *Mesca Ulad* – the iron plate (*isern þel*) set over the roof of the fire may be compared to the 'firm-set slab of iron' placed over the earthen house (and therefore on the roof of the fire) in this Irish tale. The cosmological setting of the iron structure in 'The Devil's Account' reflects the cosmic dimensions of the iron column in the Latin exemplum, modified by the visionary topoi which suggested making the Ocean its framework. But it is described as if it were a house, albeit on a cosmic scale – the Ocean is enclosed by an iron *wall*, and then filled with fire up to the *roof* of heaven.[90]

There is nothing in 'The Devil's Account' to correspond to (2), the iron chain that secures the iron house in the two Irish tales; rather, the *garsecg* itself is closed up (*þeah mon ... betyne*) with the iron walls. This stage is also lacking in *Branwen*. And although this cosmic iron 'house' is not stacked to the top with fuel (3) as in *Branwen* and *Mesca Ulad* (though not in *Orgain Denna Ríg*), it is filled with fire to the 'roof' (*oþ heofenes hrof*), and this procedure is followed by the placing of the smith's

[90] The idea of making Oceanus the walls and roof of a cosmic house is not as strange as it might first appear. The metaphor of the heavens as a house is a commonplace in Christian literature, and is prominently expressed in Psalm CIII.2–3, in which God is said to stretch out the heavens 'like a pavilion', covering 'the upper rooms with water'. An Irish gloss on the Milan commentary on the Psalms explains that 'a covering is always set against a floor, so then the waters are set against the floor of the heaven' (*Thesaurus Palaeohibernicus*, ed. Stokes and Strachan I, 407 [Ml. 120d 7]).

bellows, which are then manned and blown, corresponding to (4) in the Celtic tales. Finally, as in the Celtic tales, the bellows are placed all around the house (⁊ *hine þonne utan besette mid smiþbylium*), and here too the number of bellows and smiths is pointedly exaggerated: they are set so thickly that each pair of bellows touches the other (⁊ *heora æghwylc oðrum ætrine*),[91] and a man is placed at each pair of bellows (⁊ *sy to ælcum þara man togeset*); compare the similar phrasing in *Branwen*, 'with a man to each pair of bellows' (*a gwr a pob dwy uegin*) and *Orgain Denna Ríg*, 'with four warriors at each bellows' (⁊ *cethrur oclach for cach bulg*). In the further hyperbole describing the smiths as having the strength of Samson, 'who had twelve locks, and in each lock was the strength of twelve men', we recognize once again the numerical *gradatio*. Compare the description of Brandubh and Angus in *Bórama*, who carry a barrow into the hostel before it is fired: 'uair bái nert nónbair in cach fhiur doib'.[92]

The hypothetical torment which the devil describes to the anchorite thus appears to be a reworking of an earlier version of a Latin exemplum of the *Messersäule* type, as represented by the *Dialogus miraculorum* of Caesarius and the 'Exempla Deodati' preserved in the *Liber exemplorum*, by an author familiar with the Iron House motif. He has retained the eschatological context and rhetorical formulation of the exemplum, and has also incorporated the motif of the single night in hell, which may have been in the version of the exemplum he consulted, but which he might also have found in other visions and exempla both Latin and Irish. But the description in the *Messersäule* exemplum of a hypothetical torment involving a burning iron column inspired him to evoke a popular and memorable theme from secular narrative tradition.

[91] This kind of exaggeration is common in Irish literature. Compare a description in the Irish *Cáin Adamnáin*: 'such was the thickness of the slaughter into which they came that the soles of one woman would touch the neck of another' (trans. K. Meyer, *Cáin Adamnáin*, Anecdota Oxoniensia, Mediaeval and Modern Series (Oxford, 1905), p. 5); for similar examples see *DIL*, s.v. 1 *bonn*, and Sayers, 'Ringing Changes on a Cosmic Motif', p. 110.

[92] *Bórama*, in *Silva Gadelica*, ed. O'Grady I, 372: 'in either man of the two was the strength of nine'. See also *Fled Bricrend* ('Bricriu's Feast'), ed. G. Henderson, ITS 2 (London, 1899), 122, lines 2–4: 'Ba he tra a calmatus an Muinremair hisen: nert cét cathmiled antt ⁊ nert cét cetluigh a ccechtar a dao righedh' ('Now, Muinremur had the strength of one hundred warriors, and each arm had the strength of one hundred'; trans. Gantz, *Early Irish Myths*, p. 252).

It seems reasonable to assume that this new synthesis was first accomplished in an Irish milieu, since the Iron House theme is a distinctive feature of medieval Celtic literary tradition. The synthesis of a Christian exemplum and a native Irish narrative motif is precisely the kind of syncretism of religious and secular traditions characteristic of Irish literature throughout the Middle Ages.[93] The Iron House motif lent itself easily to an infernal context. The houses of hospitality in which the enemies feast in *Orgain Denna Ríg* and *Mesca Ulad*, though they are simply called houses (*tige*), are clearly types of the mythical hostel or *bruiden* so prominent in Irish literature and folk tradition. These hostels are often, as in the later *bruidhean* tales of the Fionn cycle, places of danger associated with the Otherworld.[94] In one Irish tale, *Aided Muirchertaig meic Erca* ('The Death of Muirchertach mac Erca'), a house-burning is explicitly 'demonized'. The king is entertained in the house of Cletech with a magical feast prepared by an enchantress named Sín ('Storm'). After sapping his strength with magic wine and a sleeping charm, the enchantress conjures a host of demons to surround and fire the house:

An fat tra ro bi sin isin colladh sin eirgid Sin ⁊ coirgis gae ⁊ slegha na slog ar indill aigh i ndoirsib in tighi ⁊ a renna uili c[h]um an tighi. Iar sin delbaidh si tra il-imud ⁊ sochaidi a timc[h]ill an dúnaidh. Téit fein istech ⁊ scailid in teine ar gach aird fon tech ⁊ fona fraightibh ⁊ teit isin lebaid.

Ba hand sin dano do muscail in ri asa c[h]olladh. 'Créd sin?' ar an ingen. 'Tarfas dam', ar se, 'sluag siabra ic losgudh in tigi form ⁊ ic orleach mo muindtiri fon dorus'. 'Ni f[h]uil olc duidsi de sin', ar an ingen, 'acht chena ro tarfas'.

An tan immoro ro badar ar an comradh sin, do chualadar breasm[h]aidhm ica loscudh ⁊ gair na slog siabra ⁊ ndraigechta imon tech.[95]

93 See above, pp. 27–9.

94 See O'Rahilly, *Early Irish History and Mythology*, pp. 121–3; G. Murphy, *The Ossianic Lore and Romantic Tales of Mediaeval Ireland* (Dublin, 1955), p. 185. Murphy considers it 'almost certain that the original bruidhean was an otherworld dwelling equivalent to the Greek Hades'. On the later *bruidhean* tales, see G. Murphy, *Duanaire Finn* III, pp. xxiii–xxxiii, and J. F. Nagy, 'Shamanic Aspects of the *Bruidhean* Tale', *History of Religions* 20 (1981), 302–22.

95 *Aided Muirchertaig Meic Erca*, ed. Nic Dhonnchadha, pp. 26–7: 'Now while he was in that sleep Sín arose and arranged the spears and javelins of the hosts in readiness in the doors and then turned all their points towards the house. She forms by magic

This tale has many overtly Christian elements.[96] The enchantress has seduced the king from 'the teachings of the clerics', and the hosts that surround and fire the house are not his human enemies but demons. It is a small step from a hostel-burning by demons to the burning of a sinner in an infernal hostel. And there are indications that the otherworldly hostels of Irish saga were indeed appropriated by Celtic Christian authors as settings for infernal torments. St John D. Seymour thought that the infernal *hospitium* called *Phristinus* in the *Visio Tnugdali* was modelled on the Irish houses of hospitality.[97] More recently, Robert Easting has argued that the hellish house of torment run by Gulinus in Peter of Cornwall's version of the *Purgatorium S. Patricii* 'is certainly reminiscent of many well appointed otherworld palaces in Celtic legend', and that 'The hospitality of Gulinus ... seems to be a Christianized and therefore demonized version of the traditional hospitality of the sidhe folk.'[98]

Although it seems likely that Ireland was the original milieu of the 'demonized version' of the Iron House motif in 'The Devil's Account', we do not have to assume that an allusion to the secular theme would have been appreciated only by an Irish audience. We have already seen that the Iron House motif appears in a Welsh tale, and Joseph Harris has

many crowds and multitudes around the fortress. She herself goes in and scatters fire in every direction throughout the house and the sidewalls, and then she enters the bed. It was then that the king awoke from his sleep. "What is it?" asked the damsel. "A host of demons has appeared to me, burning the house upon me and slaughtering my people at the door." "Thou hast no hurt from that", said the damsel; "it only seemed so". Now when they were thus in converse, they heard the crash of the burning house, and the shout of the host of demons and wizardry around it' (trans. W. Stokes, in Cross and Slover, *Ancient Irish Tales*, p. 529).

96 See McCone, *Pagan Past and Christian Present*, pp. 146–8.

97 'Studies in the Vision of Tundal', p. 104. Spilling, however, disagrees (*Die Visio Tnugdali*, p. 121, n. 352). As Seymour points out, the Irish versions refer to it as *tech osda*, 'house of hospitality'.

98 'Peter of Cornwall's Account of St. Patrick's Purgatory', *AB* 97 (1979), 397–416, at 407. An Early Modern Irish text personifies Hell as 'the proprietor of the loud-thundering, rough-warlike, woeful, shout-filled establishment; and he has never refused hospitality to old or young, one or many, and he has not spent any night without offering hospitality; however, he has not suffered anyone of those who have visited his house or his threshold or his dwelling (to go) from him, by permission, by force or by stealth' ('An Early Modern Irish "Harrowing of Hell"', trans. W. Gillies, *Celtica* 13 (1980), 32–55, at 49).

argued that it also influenced the description of a *brenna* in an Old Icelandic tale.[99] The motif may therefore have gained sufficient dissemination for an Anglo-Saxon homilist to expect his audience to recognize it. The precise ways in which the Iron House motif was transmitted can only be guessed at. There were certainly sufficient contacts between the Celtic, Anglo-Saxon and Norse cultures for oral transmission of literary motifs to have taken place,[100] although Patrick Sims-Williams thinks the Irish elements in *Branwen* are probably due to a Hiberno-Latin source.[101] An audience familiar with such a terrifying paradigm of violent death might well shudder to learn that a soul which had been in hell for a single night would sleep through it!

THE DEVIL'S ACCOUNT OF HEAVEN

The devil's account of heaven employs the same rhetorical structure as his account of hell:

Swa ðæt dioful cwæð to ðam ancran: 'Þeah þær sy eal smætegylden mor æt sunnan upgange on neorxnawange, ⁊ s[e] oferhlif[ige] ealle iorðan, ⁊ se man mote sittan swa dyre swa cynebearn ofer ðam gyldenan more, ⁊ hæbbe Salemanes wlite ⁊ wisdom, ⁊ him sie eal middangeard on geweald geseald, mid ðam gestreonum þe geond ealne middan[geard] syndon, ⁊ him sy ælce niht niwe bryd to bedde gelæd ⁊ sio hæbbe [Iu]none wlite, Saturnes dohtor, ⁊ ælc stan sy gylden, ⁊ ealle þa streamas hunige flowen, ⁊ him þonne ne sie ofer eorðan nænig wiðerbreca, ⁊ þeah þe [him] syn ealle sundercræftas ⁊ wuldorsangas in gesamnode, ⁊ þeah þe hiene ealle frefran, ⁊ him sien ealle swetnessa togelædde mid þam fægerestan gestreonum, ⁊ him þonne sy singal sumor butan ælcre onwendednes[se], ⁊ he mote alybban [butan] sare, ⁊ þonne gif he wære ær ane niht on heofona rices wuldre, þonne for[lete] he þæt he ær on þyssum wuldre gelyfede, þe ic ær bisæde, ofer þæt heofena rice þe he ær on wæs þa ane niht, ⁊ he eft ne mote to heofena rices wuldre.[102]

[99] 'Folktale and Thattr: the Case of Rognvald and Raud', in *Folklore and Medieval Studies*, ed. C. Lindahl and E. Brady, Folklore Forum 13 (1980), 158–96, at 173–5.

[100] Harris concludes from features shared by Norse and Celtic descriptions of house-burnings that 'some community of (oral) literary tradition seems certain' (*ibid.*, p. 196, n. 48). [101] 'Some Functions of Origin Stories', p. 124, n. 34.

[102] *The Vercelli Homilies*, ed. Scragg, p. 180, line 184 – p. 182, line 200: 'Thus spoke the devil to the anchorite: "Even if there were a mountain of pure gold at the rising of the sun in paradise, and it towered over all the earth, and a man were able to sit as splendid as a royal child on top of that golden mountain, and he had the beauty and

As I have already pointed out, the rhetorical motif of the 'single night' in hell occurs in several Latin and Irish tales, where it is applied to purgatory or hell and contrasted with hypothetical torments that the soul which had experienced the single night would prefer to suffer. In the devil's corresponding account of heaven, a single night in heaven is contrasted with hypothetical *pleasures* (dominion over the entire world, wealth and sensual delights) which the soul would gladly forgo to return there.[103] The motif is similarly applied to heaven in the tenth-century Tripartite Life of St Patrick. King Echu mac Cremthainn, whom Patrick had raised from the dead and baptized after a day and a night, related the pains of hell and the joys of heaven, declaring of the latter that, 'Cía dobertha dam-sa rígi inna huili cuarta, 7 cía arberainn bith o ilbliadnaib, adrímfinn ar nempní i condiulcc in maithiusa tarfas dam.'[104] A kind of hybrid formulation, in which a soul states that it would forgo the hypothetical pleasure of world dominion if it could

wisdom of Solomon, and all the world were given into his power, along with the treasures which exist throughout the world, and a new bride were brought to his bed each night and she had the beauty of Juno, Saturn's daughter, and every stone were golden, and all the streams flowed with honey, and there were no enemy for him upon the earth, and even if all special powers and glorious songs were united in him, and even if they should all comfort him and all pleasantness were proffered him together with the fairest treasures, and then there were perpetual summer for him without any change, and he might live forever without pain, yet if he had spent a single night in the glory of the kingdom of heaven, he would give up what he had experienced in this glory which I described earlier, in favour of the kingdom of heaven in which he had spent a single night, even if he could not return again to the glory of the kingdom of heaven."'

103 The Vercelli text is corrupt here: 'for[lete]' is Scragg's emendation; Szarmach emends to 'forgeate'. M and L agree that the soul would be too sorrowful (for having left heaven) to enjoy such pleasures.

104 *Bethu Phátraic*, ed. K. Mulchrone (Dublin, 1939) I, 110: 'Though all the kingdoms of the world were given to me, and though I should live for many years, I would count it as nothing in comparison to the goodness which has appeared to me.' On the date, see K. Jackson, 'The Date of the Tripartite Life of St. Patrick', *ZCP* 41 (1986), 5–45. In the Latin version of this story in Colgan's *Vita Tertia* the king says, 'Si michi totius orbis regnum daretur, pro nichilo ducens uelut inanem fumum contempnerem in comparatione aeternorum gaudiorum quae uidi. Sed rogo, ut ad illam laeticiam quam uidi quantocius reuertar' (*Four Latin Lives of St. Patrick*, ed. L. Bieler, SLH 8 (Dublin, 1971), 163–4). Cf. *Betha Colmáin maic Lúacháin*, ed. K. Meyer, TLS 17 (Dublin, 1911), 71: 'If this whole world were mine with its kingship this day, / I should barter it for beholding the Kingdom I see.'

escape from hell for a single night, occurs in a poem from the seventeenth-century compilation *Duanaire Finn*. Fionn expresses his gratitude to God for releasing him from hell after sixty years:

Día madh liomsa an bioth bán
eidir crann is cloich is chlár
uaim a n-onóir mo Dhé dhuinn
ar teacht áonoidhche a hifrionn[105]

In these Irish texts, of course, the hypothetical pleasure is not so elaborately compounded as it is in 'The Devil's Account', but both are variations of the same basic rhetorical formula: a soul which has experienced a single night in heaven (or which could escape a single night from hell) would forgo (or despise) dominion over the whole world.[106] The formula may have developed as an elaboration of Ps. LXXXIII.11 ('quia melior est dies una in atriis tuis super milia'), such as the following from Augustine's *De libero arbitrio*:

Tanta est autem pulchritudo iustitiae, tanta iocunditas lucis aeternae, hoc est incommutabilis ueritatis atque sapientiae, ut, etiam si non liceret amplius in ea manere quam unius diei mora, propter hoc solum innumerabiles anni huius uitae pleni deliciis et circumfluentia temporalium bonorum recte meritoque contemnerentur.[107]

The negative descriptions of hell in Vercelli IX also employ variations of the formula, with the substitution of a hypothetical torment for the hypothetical pleasure: one soul which had been in hell a single night would sleep through the fire and din of the iron 'house'; another would

[105] *Duanaire Finn*, ed. Murphy II, 172 (st. 18). Murphy translates: 'If I owned the fair world with its trees and stones and plains, [I would give it all] away in honour of my noble God, for letting me leave Hell for one night.' Murphy (*Duanaire Finn* III, cxvii) dates this poem '*c.* 1400 – *c.* 1500'.

[106] For a secular variation of the formula in an Irish tale dating from the tenth century, see below, p. 211, and for another Old English homily that employs this rhetoric, see below, pp. 232–3.

[107] Ed. G. M. Green, CSEL 74 (Vienna, 1956), 153–4: 'So great is the beauty of justice, so great the joy of eternal light, of the unchangeable Truth and Wisdom, that even though a man were not allowed to remain in its light for longer than a day, yet in comparison with this he would rightly and properly despise a life of innumerable years spent in the delight of temporal goods' (*On Free Choice of the Will*, trans. A. S. Benjamin and L. H. Hackstaff (Indianapolis, IN, 1964), p. 148). Augustine then cites Ps. LXXXIII.11 ('For better is one day in thy courts above thousands').

rather endure the hanging torment for seven thousand years than return to hell.[108] The poem in the story of Cairpre Crom asserts that a soul which could escape from hell would sleep through a night of similar torment.

In the devil's account of heaven, the hypothetical pleasure that St Augustine called simply 'a life of innumerable years spent in the delight of temporal goods' is elaborately and imaginatively compounded with imagery drawn from stock descriptions of the earthly paradise and happy Otherworld. The pampered princeling's paradise includes familiar characteristics of the *locus amoenus*, including the earthly paradise in Christian tradition: eternal life without pain; perpetual summer; streams flowing with honey.[109] The mountain of paradise can be paralleled in apocryphal and visionary sources,[110] and finds its way into Irish tradition, which speaks of a mount 'Partech' or 'Pariath' upon which Adam first saw the sun and uttered his first words.[111] According to the 'Reference Bible', the paradise of delights where Adam lived was 'omnibus montibus alcior uicinus caelo'.[112] The specifically Christian

[108] Cf. the modern Irish 'Poem of the Tor', in *Religious Songs of Connacht*, ed. Hyde I, 272–3, where the same basic pattern is applied to purgatorial torment on a rock in the ocean in preference to torment in hell, much as in the hanging-sinner passage in Vercelli IX. In response to Mary's intercession, Christ allows a soul to remit its punishment through confinement at the Tor, a desolate rock off the Irish coast, with the words, 'surely one thousand years at the Tor were better for you / Than one single hour in foul hell'.

[109] For the stock motifs of perpetual summer and streams flowing with honey, see Murdoch, *The Irish Adam and Eve Story* II, 57–8.

[110] In Ezechiel XXVIII.13–14 the king of Tyre (understood in patristic tradition as Lucifer before his fall), full of wisdom and beauty, is set upon the 'mountain of God', surrounded by the pleasures of paradise, gems and gold. See also Patch, *The Other World*, p. 159, who cites a passage describing a gold mountain in paradise in Godfrey of Viterbo's *Pantheon*.

[111] *Lebor Gabála Érenn*, ed. Macalister I, 177; Seymour, 'The Book of Adam and Eve in Ireland', *PRIA* 36C (1922), 121–33, at 133; *Duan in choícat cest*, ed. Meyer, 'Mitteilungen', p. 235. For a brief discussion, see Carey, 'The Irish Vision of the Chinese', p. 76.

[112] This passage is ed. R. Grimm, *Paradisus Coelestis Paradisus Terrestris* (Munich, 1977), p. 85: 'close to heaven, higher than every mountain'. Stancliffe ('Early "Irish" Biblical Exegesis', p. 369) quotes this passage and the following description of the feasting of the saints in Paradise, and raises the possibility of a connection with Irish mythology, but ultimately decides in favour of a 'non-Irish' apocryphal

element is evident too in the endowment of the princeling with the beauty and wisdom of Solomon. On the other hand, as with the devil's account of hell, the description as a whole is not closely paralleled in Christian descriptions of the earthly paradise or visions of heaven,[113] and one would hardly look to these traditions for the 'new bride' brought to the princeling's bed every night. The earthly paradise of Christian legend is indeed a place of physical pleasure and repose for the glorified elect, but they are not thus entertained. The implied positive valuation of sexual pleasure – though it still cannot compare with the joys of heaven – is surprising, even granting that the speaker is a demon. Here again, I believe, the author of 'The Devil's Account' has effected a conjunction of imagery from both Christian and Celtic Otherworlds.

Tomás Ó Cathasaigh has spoken of 'the duplex character of the Irish Otherworld: it is now benevolent, now malevolent'.[114] If the devil's account of hell is based in part upon a narrative paradigm from Celtic mythology, in which the Iron House represents the Otherworld in its malevolent aspect, it would not be surprising to find elements of the corresponding paradigm of the Celtic Otherworld in its benevolent aspect in the devil's account of heaven. Variously named *tír na n-óg* ('the land of the young'), *tír na mbéo* ('the land of the living') or *tír tairngiri* ('the land of promise'),[115] the benevolent Otherworld in Irish tradition

source. Citing Patch, *The Other World*, p. 47, Stancliffe points out that the mountain paradise is not a native feature of Celtic mythology.

113 The apotheoses of Lothair in the Vision of Charles the Fat, and of Cormac in the *Visio Tnugdali* (ed. Wagner, pp. 43–4) are vaguely similar. For the background of this visionary motif, see T. Silverstein, 'The Throne of the Emperor Henry in Dante's Paradise and the Mediaeval Conception of Christian Kingship', *Harvard Theological Review* 32 (1939), 115–29, at 124–5.

114 *The Heroic Biography of Cormac Mac Airt* (Dublin, 1977), p. 38.

115 For these terms, see Dumville, '*Echtrae* and *Immram*', pp. 81–2. The terms *tír na mbéo* and *tír tairngiri*, identical to the biblical *terra uiuentium* and *terra repromissionis*, are probably not native, although Dumville thinks the former is pre-Christian. An Anglo-Latin poem, Æthelwulf's *De Abbatibus*, ed. A. Campbell (Oxford, 1967), p. 47, line 577, uses the term *castra beorum* for heaven, which the editor believes to be a Latinized form of Irish *tír na mbéo*. Sims-Williams, 'The Evidence for Vernacular Irish Literary Influence', p. 248, cautions that the allusion is too brief to draw any firm conclusions about the nature of Æthelwulf's source for the Irish phrase. See also Meyer, *Learning in Ireland in the Fifth Century*, p. 22, n. 6, and Herren, 'Some New Light on the Life of Virgilius Maro Grammaticus', p. 52, n. 142, who states

is typically a paradise of sensual pleasures in which women and sexuality figure prominently. The hero who visits the Land or Island of Women, as it is called in other tales, is there entertained by a fairy mistress.[116] In several tales the inhabitants of the Otherworld are explicitly excluded from participation in the guilt of Adam, so that sex is literally sinless.[117]

I do not wish to insist on an identification of the devil's sensual paradise and the fairy Otherworld of Irish myth. The gold mountain upon which the princeling sits is no *síd*,[118] and his brides are not fairy mistresses. Yet the description does owe something, I believe, to native Irish conceptions of the Otherworld as a paradise of material and sexual delights. As Mac Cana has pointed out, 'sexual and alimentary licence' regularly characterizes the Otherworld in the Irish *echtrai*, one of the major native genres of voyage literature.[119] In *Echtra Laeghaire meic Crimthainn* ('The Adventure of Laeghaire mac Crimhthainn'), Laeghaire journeys to an otherworldly *síd*, where he and his men are entertained by women and lavished with music, food and drink. Urging him to return, Crimhthann offers Laeghaire 'the kingship of the Three Connaughts, their gold and their silver, their horses and their bridles, and their fair women at your pleasure'; but Laeghaire responds in a poem describing the greater sensual pleasures of the Otherworld, and asserting in a secular variation of the rhetorical motif of the 'single night' in heaven that he would not exchange a single night in the *síd* for all Crimhthann's kingdoms.[120]

that Æthelwulf's term is related to a fanciful etymology of *beatus* found in the Old Irish Treatise on the Psalter.

116 For references to women as residents of the Celtic Otherworld, see T. P. Cross, *Motif-Index*, no. F112.

117 See above, p. 27 and n. 108.

118 The *síd* or fairy mound is one of the most common locations of the Otherworld in Irish tradition, but its denizens live *inside* the *síd*, which is not noted for great height.

119 'The Sinless Otherworld', p. 110. On the genre, see Dumville, '*Echtrae* and *Immram*'.

120 'The Adventure of Laeghaire mac Crimhthainn', ed. K. Jackson, *Speculum* 17 (1942), 377–89, at 386 ('oín adaig d' aidchib sīde / nī thibér ar dó ríge'). Jackson dates the verse sections of the text to 'the second quarter or middle of the tenth century' (p. 378). Cf. Loeg's description of the Otherworld (Mag Mell) in a poem from *Serglige Con Culainn* ('The Wasting Sickness of Cú Chulainn'): 'Were all Ireland mine along with the kingdoms of bright Brega, I would give it (no weak resolve) to dwell in the homestead to which I came' (trans. G. Murphy, *Early Irish Lyrics: Eighth to Twelfth Century* (Oxford, 1956), p. 111). Murphy (p. 223) dates the poem to the late eleventh century.

Similar in rhetorical structure to 'The Devil's Account' is *Siaburcharpat Con Culaind* ('The Phantom Chariot of Cú Chulainn').[121] Cú Chulainn, raised from the dead by St Patrick, describes to the pagan King Loegaire, in elaborate and grotesque detail, his battles against serpents and monsters in the malevolent Otherworlds of Lochlainn and Dun Scáith, the latter a city with seven walls, and an iron palisade on each wall, on which were nine heads, and an iron door on each wall.[122] He then dramatically dismisses these otherworldly hardships with what J. F. Nagy has called 'an evangelical "punch line"',[123] but which may now be defined more specifically as a variation of the motif of the single night in hell:

> An ro chesusa d'imned
> a Loegairi
> for muir 7 tír.
> bá ansa damsa óenadaig
> la demon co n-ír.[124]

[121] Thurneysen, *Die irische Helden- und Königsage*, p. 567, states that the text is not older than the tenth century. G. Murphy dated it to the eleventh (review of R. Christiansen, *The Vikings and the Viking Wars in Irish and Gaelic Tradition* (Oslo, 1931), in *Béaloideas* 2 (1931), 96–9, at 97). McCone, *Pagan Past and Christian Present*, p. 200, says that the language 'is compatible with a roughly ninth- or tenth-century date'.

[122] 'Uii múir imón cathraig sin / ... sonnach íarn for cach múr / forsin bátár nóe cend. / Dorse iarn for cach slis' (*Siaburcharpat Con Culaind*, in *Lebor na Huidre*, ed. Best and Bergin, p. 282, lines 9382, 9384–6). On Lochlainn (literally Norway) as the Otherworld in Irish literature, see P. Mac Cana, 'The Influence of the Vikings on Celtic Literature', in *Proceedings of the [First] International Congress of Celtic Studies*, ed. B. Ó Cuív (Dublin, 1962), pp. 78–118, at 80–7 and 94–7.

[123] 'Close Encounters', p. 132.

[124] *Siaburcharpat Con Culaind*, in *Lebor na Huidre*, ed. Best and Bergin, p. 284, lines 9438–42: 'What I suffered of trouble, / O Loegaire, by sea and land: – / Yet more severe was a single night, / When the demon was wrathful' (trans. J. O'B. Crowe, as adapted by E. Hull, in Cross and Slover, *Ancient Irish Tales*, pp. 353–4). This episode has been discussed by J. Szövérffy, 'Síaburcharpat Conculainn, the Cadoc-Legend, and the Finding of the Táin', *BBCS* 17 (1957), 69–77, who relates it to the cycle of Irish stories influenced by the legend of Macarius (on which see above, n. 9). These include a story told by Tírechán, in which Patrick resuscitates a giant, who expresses gratitude for having been raised 'one hour from many pains' (*una hora a doloribus multis*): *The Patrician Texts in the Book of Armagh*, ed. L. Bieler, SLH 10 (Dublin, 1979), 154. See also Flower, *The Irish Tradition*, pp. 8–9.

After Loegaire has been convinced to believe in God through his descriptions of the pains of hell, Cú Chulainn ends by contrasting the hypothetical pleasure of perpetual life with 'a single reward' in heaven:

Cid latsu bithbetho
talman cona lí.
is ferr óenfocraic i nnim
la Crist mac Dé bí.[125]

Nagy argues that *Siaburcharpat Con Culaind* and related Irish tales preserve a native, 'pre-literate narrative tradition' in which a heroic figure relates a journey to the Otherworld to a 'sacerdotal figure'.[126] This narrative pattern was subsequently appropriated to Christian propaganda in such a way that

> the otherworlds which form the dramatic background of the pre-Christian heroic and mythological traditions are... related to the Christian cosmogonic scheme of things, even if only as foils to the Christian heaven and hell. Cú Chulainn's terrifying supernatural worlds are, as the hero himself points out, nothing compared to the gruesome realm of hell. In the many Fenian *laídi* which are basically poetic dialogues between the culturally conservative Oisín and advocate of Christianity Patrick, the recounted virtues of nature or of the pagan supernatural realms familiar to the old hero are matched or even bested by the qualities of the heavenly realms espoused by the saint.[127]

In 'The Devil's Account of the Next World', the native Otherworld element is introduced within a framework constructed largely of imagery from Christian tradition. The account of the next world is given not by a mythological hero raised from the dead by a saint, but by a devil captured by a hermit, a situation modelled on hagiographic tradition. But the hypothetical torment which the devil dismisses as inconsequential in comparison to hell embodies the secular paradigm of the malevolent Otherworld 'Iron House', just as his hypothetical

[125] *Siaburcharpat Con Culaind*, in *Lebor na Huidre*, ed. Best and Bergin, p. 286, lines 9528–31: 'Though thine were a perpetual life / Of earth, with its beauty, / Better is a single reward in heaven / With Christ, Son of the living God' (trans. Crowe and Hull, in Cross and Slover, *Ancient Irish Tales*, p. 354).

[126] 'Close Encounters', p. 136.

[127] *Ibid.*, p. 135. McCone, *Pagan Past and Christian Present*, pp. 199–202, accepts the existence of the 'close encounters' narrative pattern but doubts that it stems from oral tradition. See also J. E. Rekdal, 'Interaction of Pagan and Christian Traditions in Mediaeval Irish Narratives', *Collegium Medievale* 3 (1990), 5–17, esp. 10–13.

paradise embodies the corresponding paradigm of the benevolent Otherworld. The rhetorical force of 'The Devil's Account of the Next World' lies in the devil's negative revelation that, for all their hyperbolical embellishment, the best and worst of both imaginary Otherworlds are still inadequate to express the realities of a single night in heaven or hell.

5

The literary milieu of Vercelli IX and the Irish tradition in Old English literature

In its indebtedness to Irish sources and literary models, Vercelli IX is by no means unique or isolated. Several of the Old English texts which I shall discuss in this chapter also have an enumerative structure or employ numerical rhetoric, and many incorporate eschatological and cosmological motifs paralleled in Irish sources. A few share specific stylistic and thematic features with Vercelli IX and may be regarded as products of an Irish-influenced literary milieu. The stylistic affinities between Vercelli IX and the *Prose Solomon and Saturn Pater Noster Dialogue*, in particular, are sufficiently striking to attribute these two texts to a common workshop.

Three prominent eschatological themes in anonymous Old English homilies are based on apocryphal traditions transmitted by the Irish: the Three Utterances of the Soul, the Seven Heavens apocryphon and the 'Niall' version of the Sunday Letter. The Three Utterances exemplum, which tells of the exclamations of a good and a bad soul to the angels or demons who lead them to heaven or hell at the moment of death, was adapted independently by three Anglo-Saxon homilists. Versions of this exemplum survive in an Old English Rogationtide homily in Oxford, Bodleian Library, Hatton 114 (Worcester, s. xi²), 102v–105v;[1] in a sermon *Be heofonwarum ⁊ be helwarum* in London, BL, Cotton Faustina A. ix (s. xii¹), 21v–23v, and Cambridge, Corpus Christi College 302 (s. xi/xii), pp. 71–3;[2] and in a Lenten homily in Oxford, Bodleian Library,

[1] *Two Apocrypha*, ed. Willard, pp. 38–54 (partial; Willard's Text H); *Rogationtide Homilies*, ed. Bazire and Cross, pp. 121–3. See Ker, *Catalogue*, no. 331, item 53; Scragg, 'The Corpus of Vernacular Homilies', pp. 253–5.

[2] *Two Apocrypha*, ed. Willard, pp. 38–56 (partial, from the Cotton manuscript; Willard's Text C). Willard also printed the introductory section of the homily

Junius 85/86 (s. xi^{med}; provenance St Augustine's, Canterbury?), 25r–40r.[3] In 1935, Rudolf Willard published a study of this exemplum, with a detailed comparison between the three Old English versions, an Irish version and a single Latin text in an eleventh-century manuscript, Paris, BN, lat. 2628.[4] Two years later Willard published a second Latin text from Oxford, University College 61 (s. xiv).[5] Other copies of the Latin sermon have subsequently come to light. In 1966, Réginald Grégoire edited a version from the Homiliary of Toledo in London, BL, Add. 30853 (s. xi^{ex}), and identified five additional manuscripts.[6] In 1979, R. E. McNally, unaware of Willard's study, published another text from two ninth-century manuscripts, one of the homilies *In nomine Dei summi* that McNally regarded as Hiberno-Latin.[7]

McNally's identification of the Three Utterances sermon as Hiberno-Latin independently confirmed Willard's view that the theme 'reflects, in its early history at least, the Celtic culture of the British Isles'.[8]

(p. 68), as well as another part (pp. 24–5) in connection with the Seven Heavens apocryphon. See Ker, *Catalogue*, no. 153, item 4 and no. 56, item 10; Scragg, 'The Corpus of Vernacular Homilies', pp. 245–7.

3 *Two Apocrypha*, pp. 39–57 (partial; Willard's Text J); *Nuove omelie anglosassoni*, ed. Fadda, pp. 8–21. See Ker, *Catalogue*, no. 336, item 6; Scragg, 'The Corpus of Vernacular Homilies', pp. 235–6. In addition to these homilies, Napier XLVI contains echoes of the Three Utterances combined with material from a version of the *Visio S. Pauli* (see Willard, *Two Apocrypha*, pp. 74–6).

4 *Ibid.*, pp. 31–149. The Paris text was first published by L. Dudley, *The Egyptian Elements in the Legend of the Body and Soul* (Baltimore, MD, 1911), pp. 164–5.

5 'The Latin Texts'.

6 *Les Homéliaires du Moyen Age*, Rerum ecclesiasticarum documenta, Series maior: Fontes 6 (Rome, 1966), 224–5. For the additional manuscripts identified by Grégoire, see p. 177. See also Grégoire's *Homéliaires liturgiques médiévaux* (Spoleto, 1980), pp. 310–11. P. Courcelle printed variants from another text in Orléans, BM, 149 (126), pp. 155–8: 'Fragments non identifiés de Fleury-sur-Loire (III)', *Revue des études Augustiniennes* 2 (1956), 447–55, at 451–2.

7 'Seven Hiberno-Latin Sermons', pp. 134–6 (McNally's Document I). In collaboration with Professor Mary F. Wack (of Stanford University) I have identified over twenty additional manuscripts, in preparation for a new edition and study of the Latin sermon and the Old English versions.

8 Willard, 'The Latin Texts', p. 160; see also *Two Apocrypha*, p. 145. Willard believed, on linguistic grounds which Professor Wack and I do not consider conclusive, that the sermon was translated from a Greek apocryphon (see 'The Latin Texts', pp. 158–61). It seems clear, however, that the ultimate origins of the legend are to be sought in Eastern apocrypha, whether Coptic, Syriac or Greek.

Among the additional manuscripts unknown to Willard or to McNally, many of the earliest show Insular palaeographical symptoms, or are transmitted in manuscripts which contain other Hiberno-Latin texts. These include St Gallen, Stiftsbibliothek, 908 (North Italy or Switzerland, s. viii/ix), which contains a Hiberno-Latin Genesis commentary[9] and other apocryphal material common in Irish tradition,[10] and two of the compilations which I described in ch. 2, the Karlsruhe florilegium and the *Florilegium Frisingense*.[11] These manuscripts confirm that the Irish and Anglo-Saxon missions played an important role in the early transmission of the sermon on the Continent.

Of the three Old English versions of the sermon, the Rogationtide homily and the sermon *Be heofonwarum ⁊ be helwarum* are closest to the previously edited versions of the Latin sermon, though both show significant divergences and are clearly not translated directly from any known Latin text.[12] The Lenten homily in Junius 85/86, however, has a drastically abbreviated variant version of the exemplum, omitting the initial struggle between the devils and angels that occurs in all other versions, as well as the escort and chant of the devils who lead the damned soul away to hell, and incorporating unique variants within the series of utterances of both damned and just souls. A Latin text of this abbreviated recension survives in an early-ninth-century manuscript, Munich, Bayerische Staatsbibliothek, Clm. 28135 (Freising, s. ix^{in}).[13] This manuscript contains other material related to Irish tradition, including a much-expanded version of another of the homilies *In nomine Dei summi*,[14] extracts corresponding to the *Liber de numeris*, including the sequence *de uia iustorum et uia peccatorum* (11v–13r, immediately preceding the abbreviated version of the Three Utterances)[15] and some half-dozen

[9] *BCLL*, no. 1260; Wright, 'Hiberno-Latin', no. *8.

[10] For details, see Wright, 'Apocryphal Lore'.

[11] See above, pp. 56 and 64–6.

[12] See, in addition to Willard, Bazire and Cross's comparisons of the homily in Hatton 114 with the published Latin versions (*Rogationtide Homilies*, pp. 116–19).

[13] For a detailed study of this Latin text and its relationship to the Old English version in Junius 85/86, see Wack and Wright, 'A New Latin Source'.

[14] At 51v–54r, corresponding to McNally's Document IV ('Seven Hiberno-Latin Sermons', p. 140). According to Bischoff (*Schreibschulen*, p. 93), this part of the manuscript (fols. 51–80) is a nearly contemporary addition to the original codex.

[15] See McNally, *Der irische Liber de numeris*, pp. 41–2. McNally considered the passage in Clm. 28135 to be an extract from the *Liber de numeris*.

enumerations,[16] along with the well-known Irish sequence of the twelve abuses (15r). Clm. 28135 also includes a version of the pseudo-Augustinian Doomsday sermon which at an early period was often paired with the Three Utterances sermon.[17] Although no scholar has specifically identified the Doomsday sermon as Hiberno-Latin, its frequent manuscript association with the Three Utterances suggests at least that it was a popular item in Insular circles. As J. E. Cross has shown, the Lenten homily in Junius 85/86 which includes the Three Utterances exemplum also incorporates a translation of part of the Doomsday sermon,[18] further confirming their close association and Insular circulation.

The Seven Heavens apocryphon, which in its original form described the journey and purgation of souls, assigning names to each heaven as well as to the door of each, survives in variant forms in a Latin epitome among the *Apocrypha Priscillianistica* in the Karlsruhe florilegium, in an Old English sermon and in three Irish versions (within *Fís Adamnán* and Recension III of *Tenga Bithnua*, and separately in the Liber Flauus Fergusiorum).[19] As Jane Stevenson points out, 'The Latin homily itself cannot be the direct source of the vernacular versions',[20] but it is obviously related closely to their immediate source or sources. The apocryphon was probably not of Irish origin, although its presence among the *Apocrypha Priscillianistica* and its dissemination in Irish and Old English vernacular versions suggests that its circulation in the West was concentrated in the British Isles and in Insular centres on the Continent. That the conception of the seven heavens was well known in Irish centres is indicated by lists of the heavens in Hiberno-Latin sources such as the *Liber de numeris* and the Reference Bible, and in Irish

16 For these parallels, see McNally's index, *ibid.*, p. 206.

17 At 63v–65r, corresponding to pseudo-Augustine, *Sermo App.* 251 (PL 39, 2210): 'O fratres karissimi, quam timendus est' (see Machielsen, *Clavis*, no. 1036). For manuscripts in which the Doomsday and Three Utterances sermons occur side by side, see Wright, 'Apocryphal Lore', pp. 136–7.

18 'A Doomsday Passage'. The Old English version is in *Nuove omelie anglosassoni*, ed. Fadda, pp. 27–9, lines 262–303.

19 For references, see McNamara, *The Apocrypha in the Irish Church*, pp. 141–3 (no. 108); Wright, 'Apocrypha Priscillianistica'.

20 'Ascent through the Heavens', p. 34.

vernacular sources such as the *Félire Oengusso*.[21] *Saltair na Rann* has a unique name for one of the heavens.[22] An Anglo-Saxon manuscript, London, BL, Royal 8. C. III (Canterbury, St Augustine's, s. x^{ex}), 62v, contains a brief Latin text on the seven heavens, apparently taken from a version of the Reference Bible.[23] The Old English sermon, which combines the Seven Heavens with a selection from the Apocalypse of Thomas, appears among the texts added by a mid-eleventh-century hand in the margins of Cambridge, Corpus Christi College 41 (s. xi^{1}; provenance Exeter). These include certain other pieces with Irish connections,[24] including parts of a Latin hymn to St Patrick for use as a charm,[25] and two other Old English texts with possible affiliations to Irish traditions, Vercelli Homily IV and *Solomon and Saturn I*.[26] Stevenson cautions that 'these texts cannot be taken as a unified group, so the dependence of the "seven heavens" text on an Irish model cannot be proved';[27] but she concludes that 'the facts that there is only one Old English version, and that this is embedded in a manuscript context of material partly derived from Ireland, suggest that the apocryphon was known in Ireland first'.[28]

Although it is true, as Stevenson states, that the Old English translation is unique, one other Old English homily must have drawn upon some version of the Seven Heavens apocryphon. The homily *Be heofonwarum 7 be helwarum*, as Willard showed, includes a description of hell closely related to the descriptions in the Latin and Old English versions of the apocryphon: hell has twelve fiery iron walls and twelve

[21] See McNally, *Der irische Liber de Numeris*, p. 122; Cross, 'Identification', pp. 78–9 and 90.

[22] *The Irish Adam and Eve Story from Saltair na Rann*, ed. Greene and Kelly I, 108, lines 2205–6.

[23] See Reynolds, 'Unity and Diversity', p. 126 and n. 172; Wright, 'Hiberno-Latin', p. 91.

[24] Grant, *Cambridge, Corpus Christi College 41*, pp. 1–26, discusses items in the manuscript connected with Irish traditions; see also *idem*, *Three Homilies*, pp. 6 and 51.

[25] See P. Grosjean, 'Notes d'hagiographie celtique: 54. Un quatrain irlandais dans un manuscrit anglo-saxon', *AB* 81 (1963), 269–71. C. Hohler, in a review of R. Grant, *Cambridge, Corpus Christi College 41* in *MÆ* 49 (1980), 275–8, at 275, suggests that the compiler of these texts may have been from the Glastonbury area.

[26] See below, pp. 233–48 and 260–5.

[27] 'Ascent through the Heavens', p. 22.

[28] *Ibid.*, p. 34.

dragons; each dragon in turn swallows and expels the sinful souls until they are led to Satan.[29] The homily also includes another detail concerning hell, not printed or discussed by Willard, but which probably also derives from the Gnostic sources of the Seven Heavens apocryphon: the fire of hell, according to the homilist, is nine times hotter than the fire of Judgement.[30] None of the surviving versions of the Seven Heavens apocryphon includes this detail, but the Gnostic apocryphon *Pistis Sophia* states that 'the fire of Amenti is nine times hotter than the earthly fire; the fire in the great Chaos is nine times hotter than in Amenti; the fire in the judgments of the rulers who are in the way of the midst is nine times hotter than that in the great Chaos; and, finally, the fire in the dragon of outer darkness is seventy times hotter than the fire of the rulers'.[31] A similar conception of incremental fires, with a change in number, occurs in the Irish text *Airdena inna Cóic Lá nDéc ria mBráth* ('The Fifteen Tokens of Doomsday'):

Oir ceithri teinnti fil ann 7 secht tes gach teinedh dibh naroili, amal isbert aroile ecnaidhi .i. teine talman 7 teine gealain 7 teine bratha 7 teine ifrind.

> Secht tes teinedh talman tais
> a[n] teine ghealain gealbrais,
> secht tes teinedh bratha brais
> a[n] teine ifrinn amhnais.[32]

29 This portion of the homily was printed separately by Willard, *Two Apocrypha*, pp. 24–5, with a discussion of its relation to the other versions of the Seven Heavens apocryphon at pp. 25–8.

30 'An Edition of Previously Unpublished Anglo-Saxon Homilies', ed. Callison, p. 246, lines 63–4: 'þær bið ungemet cyles and hætan .ix. siðan hatre þonne domes dæges fyr'. The conception survived tenaciously in the vernacular. Owst, *Preaching in Medieval England*, p. 337, n. 2, quotes from a description of hell in a Middle English sermon, which says that 'som shall brenne in the grett flameth of fyre, the wiche is ix times hotter than is anny fyre in this worlde'.

31 Cited from Seymour, 'Notes on Apocrypha in Ireland', p. 115.

32 'The Fifteen Tokens of Doomsday', ed. Stokes, p. 314: 'For there are four fires there, and seven (times greater is) the heat of each of them than (that of) another: as said a certain sage, namely, fire of earth, fire of lightning, fire of Doom, and fire of Hell: "Seven (times greater than) the heat of the fire of the soft earth (is) the fire of bright-quick lightning. Seven (times greater than) the heat of the fire of ready Doom (is) the fire of cruel Hell"' (trans. Stokes, p. 315). The Irish text occurs in a fifteenth-century manuscript, London, BL, Add. 30512 (see Flower, *Catalogue of Irish Manuscripts* II, 501–2). On the close relationship of this version of the legend to *Saltair na Rann* and *Tenga Bithnua*, see Heist, *The Fifteen Signs*, pp. 73–93 and

The sermon *Be heofonwarum 7 be helwarum*, which begins with an adaptation of the Three Utterances transferred in context to the Last Judgement, and then continues with a description of hell based partly on a version of the Seven Heavens apocryphon, thus conflates two apocryphal themes most likely transmitted through Irish tradition. It also includes variations of two of the prominent eschatological motifs in Vercelli IX: a description of Satan as the monster of hell (with a hundred heads, a hundred tongues in each head and terrible fingers with a hundred claws on each finger) and a version of the Men with Tongues of Iron.[33]

The two Old English 'Niall' sermons, Napier XLIII and XLIV, which transmit a recension of the Sunday Letter, are explicitly linked with Ireland.[34] The ultimate origins of the Letter of Christ on the observance of Sunday are obscure. It appears first in the sixth century, and by the eighth was popular enough in Frankish territories to elicit condemnation in 745 by a synod in Rome (at the behest of St Boniface) and again in 789 by Charlemagne's *Admonitio generalis*.[35] There are six versions of the Sunday Letter in Old English, representing three separate recensions transmitted to England by different channels. One of these was certainly by way of Ireland, for Napier XLIII and XLIV name an Irish deacon Niall as their source and authority. As we learn from a Latin letter written *c.* 835 by Ecgred, bishop of Lindisfarne, an account of Niall's death, resurrection and subsequent life-long fast was being spread in the early ninth century by an Anglo-Saxon named Pehtred, whose book also contained 'mendacious ravings concerning the Old and New Testaments', among them a version of the Sunday Letter.[36] The common exemplar of the two Old English Niall sermons,

98–105. A Norse homily cited by D. Johnson, 'The Five Horrors of Hell: an Insular Homiletic Motif' (forthcoming in *ES*) states that the fire of hell is seven times hotter than the hottest fire in this world (*Gamal Norsk Homiliebok*, ed. G. Indrebø (Oslo, 1931), p. 33).

33 For these passages see above, pp. 149 and 159.

34 For the following, see the fundamental study by Whitelock, 'Bishop Ecgred, Pehtred and Niall', and the entry on the 'Sunday Letter' by C. Lees in *Sources of Anglo-Saxon Literary Culture*, ed. Biggs *et al.*, pp. 38–40. Napier Homilies XLIII and XLIV are in *Wulfstan*, ed. Napier, pp. 205–26.

35 See Whitelock, 'Bishop Ecgred, Pehtred and Niall', pp. 50–1.

36 Bishop Ecgred's letter is ed. Whitelock, *ibid.*, pp. 48–9, and trans. *idem*, *English Historical Documents c. 500–1042*, English Historical Documents I, 2nd ed. (London, 1979), 875–6 (no. 214).

according to Dorothy Whitelock, must have been based on Pehtred's book; Pehtred himself, Whitelock states, 'probably obtained his text in or from Ireland'.[37] The two Old English sermons, as Whitelock shows, agree in certain respects with an Irish version of the Sunday Letter, *Epistil Ísu* ('Letter of Jesus'), part of the composite tract *Cáin Domnaig* ('Law of Sunday') dating probably from the first half of the eighth century.[38] These common features, which include an allusion to the seventh heaven, a reference to the Sunday respite of souls and a 'Sunday list' or *dignatio diei dominici*,[39] show 'that the same Latin text was used by Pehtred and the Irish translator'.[40] The Latin version most closely related to their common source is that in Munich, Bayerische Staatsbibliothek, Clm. 9550, but an extract of a Sunday Letter in the *Catechesis Celtica*, immediately following a version of the Sunday list, is closer still for the section it preserves.[41] The Sunday lists in the Niall sermons and the *Epistil Ísu* are also related, and each shares certain unusual items with the Hiberno-Latin Sunday lists edited by McNally.[42]

If the author of the archetype of the two Old English 'Niall' sermons had access to Pehtred's book, he must also have had access to a version of Vercelli IX, for both versions incorporate passages from the homily, although each retains different passages – with a single brief but significant exception. Napier XLIV retains a passage from the opening of Vercelli IX, minimally revised to include injunctions to observe Sunday, while Napier XLIII retains instead a reference to the story of the devil and the anchorite, along with a version of the Men with Tongues of Iron.[43] According to Scragg, 'We can be sure that a copy of Vercelli IX (in the version in L rather than that in A) lies behind both Napier XLIII and Napier XLIV',[44] although Scragg also suggests that

[37] 'Bishop Ecgred, Pehtred and Niall', p. 58. Whitelock (p. 50) suggests Mayo as 'a possible habitat for Pehtred'.

[38] For discussion and references, see McNamara, *The Apocrypha in the Irish Church*, pp. 60–3 (no. 52).

[39] For the references to the seventh heaven, see *Wulfstan*, ed. Napier, p. 207, line 2; p. 213, line 13; and p. 217, line 16; for the respite of the souls, *ibid.*, p. 211, line 23; p. 219, line 32 – p. 220, line 1. For the 'Sunday lists', see Lees, 'The "Sunday Letter" and "Sunday Lists"'.

[40] 'Bishop Ecgred, Pehtred and Niall', p. 60.

[41] *Ibid.*, pp. 59–60.

[42] *Ibid.*, pp. 62–4; Lees, 'The "Sunday Letter" and the "Sunday Lists"', pp. 146–9.

[43] The correspondences are noted by Scragg, 'The Corpus of Vernacular Homilies', p. 250, nn. 2, 4 and 5.

[44] *Ibid.*, p. 250.

the extracts from Vercelli IX were 'incorporated separately into the two surviving versions' of the Niall sermon.[45] Both versions, however, retain or omit different material which must have been in their common archetype;[46] more importantly, both versions *do* retain a distinctive clause from another portion of Vercelli IX, also adapted to conform to the new context. In a passage describing the horrors of 'hellehus', Vercelli IX has the sentence, 'Se nama is to geþenceanne ælcum men butan hwæs heorte sie mid diofles stræle þurhwrecen.'[47] Both Niall sermons adapt this sentence to condemn those who might doubt the veracity of the oaths of Pope 'Florentius' and Bishop Peter about the heavenly origins of the Sunday Letter: 'hwylc man is þonne æfre, butan his heorte sy eall mid deofles strælum awrecen, þæt he wene, þæt se halga papa and se biscop dorston swerjan mænne að þurh swa miclan mægenþrymme?'[48] The archetype of the Niall sermons, therefore, probably contained all the passages from Vercelli IX found in the two surviving versions, which includes material from the introduction and the preparatory motif section as well as the allusion to the story of the devil and the anchorite and the Men with Tongues of Iron. As Scragg suggests, Napier XLIV may have omitted the passage referring to the devil and the anchorite because another version of 'The Devil's Account' immediately follows the sermon in the manuscript, Cotton Tiberius A. iii [M].[49] The Niall homilist's text of Vercelli IX would have been an earlier version in the line represented by L since, as Scragg pointed out, there is also parallel phrasing between a passage in the two

45 'Anonymous Old English Homilies', in *Sources of Anglo-Saxon Literary Culture*, ed. Biggs *et al.*, p. 126.

46 See Whitelock, 'Bishop Ecgred, Pehtred and Niall', p. 51.

47 *The Vercelli Homilies*, ed. Scragg, p. 170, lines 117–18: 'The notoriety (of hell) should be remembered by every man whose heart is not pierced with the devil's arrow.'

48 Napier XLIII, in *Wulfstan*, ed. Napier, p. 214, lines 12–15: 'What man is there ever, then, unless his heart were wholly pierced by the arrows of the devil, that he would believe that the holy pope and the bishop dared to swear a false oath by such a great power?' The reading in Napier XLIV, *ibid.*, p. 225, lines 3–6, is closely similar: 'men þa leofestan, hwilc man is þonne efre, butan his heorte se eal mid deofles strealum awrecan, þæt he wæne, þæt se halga papa and se biscup dorstan swerigan menne aþ þus micel megen?'

49 'The Corpus of Vernacular Homilies', pp. 248–9. The version in M is ed. Robinson, 'The Devil's Account of the Next World'.

Niall sermons and a sentence added to the version of Vercelli IX in L.[50] On the other hand, L does *not* retain the phrase used by both Napier XLIII and XLIV. The author of their archetype must therefore have had access to a lost version of Vercelli IX, textually in the line represented in L, but which also retained the phrase that now survives only in the Vercelli Book text [A].

That Vercelli IX and material from Pehtred's book circulated in a common milieu is not surprising. We know from Bishop Ecgred's letter that Pehtred's book contained at least one apocryphal legend explicitly connected with Ireland, and the letter makes it clear that Pehtred's book was a larger compilation of apocryphal material, including eschatology and demonology.[51] We know too that Niall claimed to have been dead for five (or seven) weeks, and subsequently related many marvels concerning his visions of the next world.[52] It is tempting to speculate that some of the apocryphal materials in Vercelli IX had also been transmitted to Anglo-Saxon England through Pehtred and his book. Although Vercelli IX contains none of the heretical views which Bishop Ecgred found objectionable, its contents, like those of the Niall sermon, derive ultimately from Irish tradition, and its eschatological and cosmological focus is consistent with the kind of material Pehtred's book must have contained. While the style and matter of Vercelli IX were clearly congenial to the author of the Niall sermon and to several other anonymous homilists, a more sophisticated and discriminating churchman such as Bishop Ecgred might have found it only slightly less objectionable than the heretical views he singled out for condemnation.

The Old English Three Utterances, Seven Heavens and Niall sermons, like Vercelli IX, testify to the continuing influence of Irish texts and traditions in later Anglo-Saxon England, especially in the realm of apocryphal eschatology and cosmology. Eschatological motifs in Old English literature that appear to derive from Irish sources

[50] 'The Corpus of Vernacular Homilies', p. 230 and n. 8.

[51] R. Priebsch, 'The Chief Sources of Some Anglo-Saxon Homilies', *Otia Merseiana* 1 (1899), 129–47, at 142, argues that Pehtred's book must have been in Old English rather than Latin.

[52] The information concerning Niall in the homilies is confirmed by entries in Irish annals, which variously report that Niall mac Ialláin suffered from paralysis or sickness for twenty-four, thirty-three or thirty-four years (or went thirty years without food and drink), and 'was disturbed by frequent visions, as well false as true' (cited by Whitelock, 'Bishop Ecgred, Pehtred and Niall', p. 49).

include the common stock which Vercelli IX shares with several other Old English homilies, as well as the motif of the three companies at Judgement. Another example is a dramatic Judgement dialogue in an Old English Rogationtide homily (Bazire and Cross no. 3), in which Christ demands a 'pledge' from man, who responds that he has no pledge to offer but his soul. A close Latin parallel occurs in the Karlsruhe florilegium:

Þonne cwyð se eca Cyning to anre gehwyclum, 'Men þa leofestan, sege me hwæt geþohtest þu oððe hwæt gecwæde þu oððe hwæt gedydest þu on þinum life. Syle wed be þysum eallum þe ic for ðe dyde and for ðe þrowude.' Þonne andswarað se man urum Drihtne and cwyð, 'Næbbe ic ænig wedd to syllenne butan mine sawle.'[53]

Oportit enim nos timere uerbum domini quod locutum fuerit in die iudicii ad omnes homines; tunc dicit homini: quid fecisti? quid ambolasti? quid cogitasti? quid uidisti? quid dixisti? da mihi hodie aream. Tunc respondit homo: domine non habeo aream tibi nisi animam meam.[54]

The five questions which Christ asks in the Latin[55] have been reduced

[53] *Rogationtide Homilies*, ed. Bazire and Cross, p. 51, lines 91–6: 'Then the eternal King will say to each one, "Beloved men, tell me what you have thought or what you have said or what you have done in your life. Give a pledge for all these things which I did and suffered for you." Then the man will answer our Lord and say, "I have no pledge to give except my soul."' For further details and discussion, see Wright, 'The Pledge of the Soul'.

[54] 'Fragments retrouvés', ed. De Bruyne, p. 326 (De Bruyne notes, 'Lisez deux fois *arram*' for manuscript *aream*): 'For we ought to fear the word of the Lord which shall be spoken on the day of Judgement to all men. Then he says to man: "What have you done? What have you traversed? What have you thought? What have you seen? What have you said? Give to me today a pledge." Then man answers, "Lord, I have no pledge for you except for my soul."'

[55] Compare the Middle Irish treatise *Dá Brón Flatha Nime* ('The Two Sorrows of the Kingdom of Heaven'), where a similar sequence of questions occurs in connection with the motif of the three companies of heaven, earth and hell: 'Cách ar úair ón dothuisfénaid an athchomairc an atchonnarcatár a súile 7 in atrubratár am béoil 7 a tenga 7 án dorónsat a láma 7 án imándechatár a cossa, Crist mac Dé 7 aingil nime 7 fir thalman 7 fir iffrind ic coistecht fris dóib uile co rólais in tasfénad-sin do dénum' ('Les deux chagrins', ed. Dottin, p. 380). 'Each in turn when requested will reveal what his eyes saw, what his mouth and tongue said, what was done by his hands, and

to three and slightly re-arranged, probably to conform to the 'thought, word and deed' triad, but the homilist clearly had some version of this Latin text before him. It also occurs, with minor variations, in Clm. 19410, pp. 34–5 (where the questions are 'Quid fecisti, quid cogitasti, quid uidisti?'), and in a later English manuscript, Salisbury, Cathedral Library, 9 (Salisbury, s. xi^{ex}), 78r–v.[56] The theme appears elsewhere in Old English in reduced form in an Old English homily for Holy Saturday,[57] and also in the epilogue of Cynewulf's *Elene*, which echoes the formulation of the Rogationtide homily in linking the term *wed* (equivalent to Latin *arra*) with the 'thought, word and deed' triad:

Sceall æghwylc ðær
reordberendra riht gehyran
dæda gehwylcra þurh þæs deman muð,
ond worda swa same wed gesyllan,
eallra unsnyttro ær gesprecenra,
þristra geþonca.[58]

Other Old English homilies draw selectively from Irish sources for specific enumerative or apocryphal motifs, or for exegesis of particular

what was traversed by his feet [cf. 'quid ambolasti?' in the Latin]. Christ, son of God, along with the angels of heaven, and the inhabitants of earth and of hell, will be listening to all until the revelations are completed' (trans. Herbert and McNamara, *Irish Biblical Apocrypha*, p. 20).

56 I am grateful to J. E. Cross for drawing my attention to these additional manuscripts. On Clm. 19410, see above. The Salisbury manuscript is listed by Gneuss, 'A Preliminary List', p. 44 (no. 699). For the crucial term *aream*, Clm. 19410 reads *arram*, which is presumably the correct reading. Salisbury 9 has *aureum* corrected from *arreum*. Has Latin *arr(h)a* ('pledge') been confused with Hiberno-Latin *arreum* ('commutation for penance')? On the latter term (derived from Irish *arrae*), see D. A. Binchy, 'The Old-Irish Table of Penitential Commutations', *Ériu* 19 (1962), 47–72, at 50–6.

57 See Wright, 'The Pledge of the Soul', p. 24, for this passage, and for similar passages in other Old English homilies, none of which, however, uses the distinctive term *wed*. To these should perhaps be added a passage from a Wulfstan homily (*The Homilies of Wulfstan*, ed. D. Bethurum (Oxford, 1957), p. 121, lines 65–9; cf. p. 286 for parallels in Napier XXV and XL), cited by B. Raw, *Anglo-Saxon Crucifixion Iconography and the Art of the Monastic Revival*, Cambridge Studies in Anglo-Saxon England 1 (Cambridge, 1990), 39 (cf. p. 65).

58 *The Vercelli Book*, ed. Krapp, p. 101, lines 1281b–86a: 'Each of those bearing speech must hear judgement from the mouth of the Judge for every deed, and give a pledge for words as well, all folly spoken earlier, presumptuous thoughts.'

biblical passages. Blickling Homily III draws on Hiberno-Latin exegesis for the first part of its exposition of the Temptation of Christ,[59] while another homily on the Temptation, Belfour X, refers to the pinnacle of the temple 'þær þære larþeawselt [*sic*] wæs' ('where the teachers' seat was'), translating the phrase *sedes doctorum*, an Irish symptom found in virtually every Hiberno-Latin commentary on the passage.[60] Another

[59] See Wright, 'Blickling Homily III'. In this article I tentatively suggested that the typological connection between David's five stones and the five books of the Pentateuch may have been an originally Irish interpretation, since it occurs in some five Hiberno-Latin commentaries, and since editors of two of these had not been able to cite a patristic source. In a recent paper, 'The Battle between Christ and Satan in the Tiberius Psalter', *Journal of the Warburg and Courtauld Institutes* 52 (1988), 14–33, K. M. Openshaw shows that the connection can be traced to Augustine, *Enarrationes in Psalmos*, and occurs also in Cassiodorus, Isidore and Hrabanus Maurus. These exegetes, however, interpret the single stone which David selected as showing the unity of the Law, and do not make the more literal-minded equation with the book of Deuteronomy, from which book alone Christ refuted the devil. The Hiberno-Latin commentaries all make this connection (as does the Irish homily in the Leabhar Breac, in *The Passions and the Homilies*, ed. Atkinson, p. 178), which is also implied in the Blickling homilist's comment that although David took five stones from his bag, 'þeah-hweþere mid anum he þone gigant ofwearp; swa Crist oferswiþde þæt deofol mid þisse cyþnesse' (*The Blickling Homilies*, ed. R. Morris, p. 31, lines 18–19). In my earlier article I noted parallels in a sermon by Haymo of Auxerre (PL, 118, 198–9) and in Paschasius Radbertus's commentary on Matthew (now ed. B. Paulus, CCCM, 56, 258; the editor cites only the Irish pseudo-Alcuin commentary for this particular detail). The only other non-Irish exegete I have been able to find who makes this connection is Bede, in his commentary on I Samuel (ed. D. Hurst, CCSL 119, 160). Bede occasionally made use of Hiberno-Latin commentaries for minor details (see above, p. 43, n. 176), and this interpretation may be another case of his indebtedness to Irish exegesis.

[60] *Twelfth-Century Homilies in MS. Bodley 343*, ed. A. O. Belfour, EETS os 137 (London, 1909), 100, lines 21–2. See Kelly, 'Hiberno-Latin Exegesis and Exegetes', p. 58. To the five Hiberno-Latin commentaries cited by Kelly may be added the 'Man' glosses in London, BL, Harley 1802 (Armagh, A. D. 1138), 14r (*BCLL*, no. 350); the *Catechesis Celtica*, Vatican City, Biblioteca Apostolica, Reg. lat. 49, 2r; and the Leabhar Breac homily on the Temptation, in *The Passions and the Homilies*, ed. Atkinson, p. 175 (Irish text) and p. 427 (Latin version). Three continental exegetes also transmit the motif. In the *Expositio libri comitis* of Smaragdus, the source is identified by a marginal notation as the Hiberno-Latin exegete Frigulus (see F. Rädle, *Studien zu Smaragd von Saint-Mihiel*, Medium Aevum 29 (Munich, 1975), 151 and 206). The other two continental exegetes, Haymo of Auxerre and Paschasius Radbertus (see previous note), are known to have drawn heavily on Hiberno-Latin sources (for Haymo, see B. Bischoff, 'Muridac doctissimus plebis,

Rogationtide homily (Vercelli XIX) expands a narrative of the Creation and Fall with a series of apocryphal motifs which appear to have been transmitted through Irish sources, including the creation of Eve from a rib from Adam's left side and the identification of the forbidden fruit as a fig.[61] Finally, a sermon for Easter Sunday draws on Irish traditions for a variety of motifs, including a reference to the seventh heaven of the Trinity, lists of the seven joys of heaven and of miraculous events that occurred on Sundays and of calamitous events on Fridays, and an allusion to the three companies at Judgement.[62]

If Irish texts and traditions contributed significantly to the Old English homiletic tradition prior to Ælfric and Wulfstan, these two Anglo-Saxon homilists turned instead almost exclusively to patristic and continental sources. Apart from the vision of the Irish saint Fursa, which he translated, and the Hiberno-Latin treatise *De duodecim abusiuis saeculi*, which he used on more than one occasion[63] (under the impression that it was an authentic work of St Cyprian), Ælfric seems to have avoided Hiberno-Latin works, and his homilies are virtually free from Irish influence. It is telling that in a rare instance when he does cite from a pseudonymous biblical commentary that modern scholarship has identified as Hiberno-Latin, he is clearly suspicious of its authenticity (Bede had derided a typically Irish interpretation apparently from the same commentary).[64] Ælfric's complaints about the *micel gedwyld* ('great foolishness') which he had encountered in vernacular writings, essentially a reaction against the credulous use of apocryphal texts such as the *Visio S. Pauli*,[65] is in part a reaction against the Irish tradition,

ein irischer Grammatiker des IX. Jahrhunderts', in his *Mittelalterliche Studien* II, 51–6; for Paschasius, see Bischoff, 'Turning-Points', pp. 92–3).

61 See Bazire and Cross, *Rogationtide Homilies*, pp. 7–12; Cross, 'Identification', pp. 79–80; *idem*, *Cambridge Pembroke College MS 25*, p. 99. Most of this information is included in the St Gallen Commentary on the Creation and Fall and in the 'Reference Bible' (see Wright, 'Hiberno-Latin', p. 91).

62 See Lees, 'Theme and Echo'.

63 See above, p. 75, n. 131.

64 See J. E. Cross, 'More Sources for Two of Ælfric's *Catholic Homilies*', *Anglia* 86 (1968), 59–78, at 77–8. The commentary is pseudo-Hilary, *Expositio in VII epistolas catholicas* (*BCLL*, no. 346; Wright, 'Hiberno-Latin', no. 35); for Bede's disparaging allusion, see above, p. 43.

65 See Godden, 'Ælfric and the Vernacular Prose Tradition'; but see also the qualifications of Clayton, *The Cult of the Virgin Mary*, pp. 260–5, who argues that the contrast between Ælfric and the anonymous works has been overemphasized: 'the

which drew freely from the *Visio* and other apocrypha and which was an important conduit – though by no means the only one – for the transmission of apocryphal literature to England. There is no positive evidence that Ælfric specifically associated such objectionable notions with the Irish, but his avoidance of Hiberno-Latin texts in favour of patristic and continental sources suggests that his experience had led him to mistrust the former partly because of their free use of apocrypha.

Once an apocryphal or eschatological motif had entered the vernacular tradition, it could be transmitted and adapted without further direct reliance on Irish sources. Such appears to be the case with the popular motif of the three companies at Judgement, for example, and perhaps also with the Men with Tongues of Iron, since the Old English reflexes of this theme are more fully developed and also more consistent in their formulation than are the Irish. The degree of 'Irish influence' in these homilies thus ranges from direct and thorough-going indebtedness to Irish sources, as in Vercelli IX, to isolated use of motifs which may originally have been transmitted to Anglo-Saxon England through Hiberno-Latin sources but which were then fully assimilated (or 'naturalized', as Kathleen Hughes put it)[66] into the Old English homiletic tradition. In homilies such as *Be heofonwarum ⁊ be helwarum* and the Lenten homily in Junius 85/86, however, the Irish element is sufficiently strong to assume more immediate contact with Hiberno-Latin sources. There is, in addition, a small core of Old English texts which, on stylistic and other evidence, can be associated with Vercelli IX as part of a distinctive literary milieu influenced by Irish learned traditions and literary models.

A Rogationtide homily edited by Joyce Bazire and J. E. Cross (no. 4)[67] draws on apocryphal sources for a description of hell, including a lengthy enumeration of nine separate compartments of hell and the

two cannot be divided simply on an apocryphal/anti-apocryphal basis and a concentration on this distorts the issue' (p. 265). Tristram, *Sex aetates mundi*, pp. 121–2, accepts the notion of 'eine vorreformische Theologie, die im Gegensatz zu Ælfric und Wulfstan auch apokryphe Stoffe und widersprüchliche Lehren (z.B. von den letzten Dingen) tolerierte'. Tristram cautions that not all anonymous sermons are heterodox, but I believe that it is misleading to speak of a 'heterodox tradition' in Old English homilies, or for that matter of a 'heterodox' Irish learned tradition, simply because of the use of apocryphal materials (see above, pp. 38–9).

[66] 'Some Aspects of Irish Influence', p. 61. [67] *Rogationtide Homilies*, pp. 62–4.

punishments suffered by different classes of sinners in each. The editors describe the passage as 'a loose reminiscence' of the *Visio S. Pauli*, but once again the source must have been a variant version of the apocryphon which has not survived.[68] The homily, like Vercelli IX, focuses relentlessly on the pains and the measurements of hell, expressed in a form similar to the numerical *gradatio* (there are nine compartments or 'houses' in hell and each is a mile deep and another wide).[69] It also uses an enumeration to structure a central portion of the text (the punishments of each of the nine compartments are described in turn), employs a brief variation of the 'joys of heaven' motif,[70] and betrays a taste for inexpressibility topoi and hyperbole. The homily includes a variation of the Men with Tongues of Iron, applied not to the pains of hell but to the joys of heaven – specifically the 'seven' heavens.[71] To underscore the pains of hell, the homilist uses another hyperbole:

nis nan man on bocum swa cræftig þæt mage asecgan hwæt innan þam nigo husum sy godes oððe winsumes, swa micel swa an fugel mæg mid his læstan fiðere windes aswingan.[72]

A similar image occurs in two other Old English Rogationtide homilies, applied to both the joys of heaven and the torments of hell. Bazire and Cross Homily 5, which enumerates the three things by which we can maintain God's decree (good thought, word and deed) as well as the three spiritual births,[73] also compares the amount of unpleasantness in heaven and of pleasantness in hell to the song of a little bird, accompanied by an allusion to the 'likenesses' which a certain wise man spoke of concerning heaven and hell:

... næfre nære on heofona rices wuldre swa micel unwynsumes, on ænigum laðe oððe on hungre oððe on þurste oððe on cyle oððe on hætan oððe on adle

[68] See their list of comparisons between the homily and the *Visio*, *ibid.*, p. 58.

[69] *Ibid.*, p. 63, lines 42–3.

[70] *Ibid.*, p. 64, lines 92–3.

[71] For the passage, see above, p. 150.

[72] *Ibid.*, p. 63, lines 43–5: 'There is no man so learned in books that can tell what there may be of good or pleasure within those nine compartments, as much as a bird may beat the wind with his smallest feather' (following Bazire and Cross, p. 65). Or should we read *læstan fiðeres winde* (i.e., the amount of good in hell is so small a bird could 'beat it away with the wind of his smallest feather')?

[73] For these enumerations, see above, pp. 79–80.

oððe on ænigum laðe gewinne, þæt wære swa mycel swa anes lytles fugeles sweg; swylce he cwæð, se ylca witega, þæt nære næfre on hellewyte swa mycel wynsumes swa anes fugeles sweg.[74]

A closely parallel passage occurs in Bazire and Cross Homily 8:

Leofan men, se witega cwæð be heofona rice and be hellewite þæt næfre nære gemet on heofona rices wuldre swa mycel unwynsumnes, on ænigum laðe oððe on hungre oððe on þurste oððe on cele oððe on hæte oððe on ece oððe on adle oððe on ænigum laðe gewinne, þæt wære swa mycel swa anes lytles fugeles sweg; swylce he cwæð, se ylca witega, þæt næfre nære on hellewitum swa mycel wynsumnes swa anes lytles fugles sweg.[75]

The image of a bird is used within inexpressibility topoi in Irish texts as well, as Hildegard Tristram has noted.[76] In the examples she cites, however, the breadth of hell or of heaven is dramatized by stating that the swiftest bird could not traverse it in a thousuand years, as in the second recension of *Tenga Bithnua*:

Adubradar ecnaidi na nEbraidi: 'Indis duind in tuaruscbail ro fuirmistair Dia do phianaib na pecthach'. Frecrais in Tenga Bithnua: 'Ce ro indsind, ni fhetfaind re mbrath mar do gab do med & do domni glenna ifrind. Ce ro comluided in t-en bud luaithi & bad thresi luamain isin bith, robod edoig a rochtain re mile bliadan tar in ngleann sin.[77]

[74] *Ibid.*, p. 71, lines 45–9. See the translation of the parallel passage in the following note. On the theme of 'likenesses' of heaven and hell, see above, pp. 95–102.

[75] *Ibid.*, p. 113, lines 125–31: 'Beloved men, the wise man said concerning the kingdom of heaven and hell-torment that in the glory of the kingdom of heaven would never be found so much unpleasantness, in any pain or in hunger or in thirst or in cold or in heat or in pain or in sickness or in any hateful strife (?), that would be as great as a little bird's cry; and likewise the same wise man said that in hell-torments there would never be as much pleasure as a little bird's cry.'

[76] 'Die *leohtfæt*-metapher in den altenglischen anonymen Bittagspredigten', *NM* 75 (1974), 229–49, at 239; *Vier altenglische Predigten*, pp. 315–16; 'Der "homo octipartitus"', p. 137.

[77] 'The Second Recension of the *Evernew Tongue*', ed. Nic Énrí and MacNiocaill, p. 44: 'The sages of the Hebrews said: "Tell us the tidings of what God has prepared for the torments of sinners." The Evernew Tongue answered: "Though I were to tell, I could not [tell] before doom how great and how deep the valley of hell is. Though the swiftest and strongest-flying bird in the world were to travel it, it would hardly pass over that valley in a thousand years"' (trans. Nic Énrí and MacNiocaill, p. 45). In another manuscript of this recension the image is used in combination with the multiplicity-of-tongues inexpressibility motif (see above, p. 155, n. 174).

In *Scéla Laí Brátha*, virtually the same image is used to describe the great breadth of heaven: 'Is diasneti im[murgu] farsinge 7 lethet na flatha nemda. ar in t-én as luathiu lúamain for bith ni tháirsed dó tóichell ríchid o tossuch domain coa dered.'[78] These Irish examples do not closely parallel the Old English in formulation, therefore, but one Irish text, *Betha Maignenn* ('Life of St Maignenn'), does contrast earthly and heavenly joys by referring to the small *voice* of a bird: 'uair in tén as luga ocus as seirbe glór isin cathair nemda is áibhni é ocus is binne iná maitheas na talman uili'.[79]

The Old English and Irish variations on the bird topos may reflect use of common or similar sources, but are not sufficiently similar to suggest a closer relationship. But elaborate inexpressibility topoi in eschatological contexts are clearly recurrent stylistic features of Vercelli IX and the texts I would associate with its milieu, as they are in Irish literature. Bazire and Cross Homily 4 shares another inexpressibility topos with Vercelli IX:

Swa micel mirhþe is on heofonum, gif þu most ane niht þærinne gewunian, þeah þu ahtest ealles middaneardes gewald, eal þu hit woldest on anum dæge forlæton wið þan þe þu neafre ma of þære eardungstowe eft ne come.[80]

The hypothetical 'single night' in heaven, for which one would give up the hypothetical pleasure of dominion over all the world ('þeah þu ahtest ealles middaneardes gewald'), recalls the rhetorical formula in Vercelli IX and in Irish tradition, according to which a soul would

[78] *Lebor na Huidre*, ed. Best and Bergin, p. 81, lines 2477–9: 'But indescribable are the amplitude and width of the heavenly kingdom. For the bird that is swiftest of flight upon earth, for him the journey of the kingdom would not end (though he flew) from the world's beginning until the end thereof' (trans. Stokes, 'Tidings of Doomsday', p. 257). A closely parallel passage occurs in 'The Fifteen Tokens of Doomsday', ed. Stokes, p. 322.

[79] *Silva Gadelica*, ed. O'Grady I, 37: 'for the bird which in the heavenly city has the least, and that the most discordant voice, is more delightful and sweeter than the whole earth's good things' (trans. O'Grady II, 35, with slight modification). On this Life, see Plummer, *Miscellanea Hagiographica Hibernica*, p. 192 (no. 48), and Kenney, *The Sources*, no. 256, who describes it as 'Late and very fabulous'. The bird turns up in inexpressibility topoi in different formulations in other literatures; see R. Köhler, 'Ein Bild der Ewigkeit', *Kleinere Schriften*, 3 vols. (Weimar, 1898–1900) III, 37–47.

[80] *Rogationtide Homilies*, ed. Bazire and Cross, p. 64, lines 95–7: 'So much happiness is in heaven, (that) if you could dwell therein for one night, even if you had power over all the earth, you would give it all up in a day provided that you never came out of that dwelling-place again.'

forgo any earthly glory and pleasure, 'even if all the world were given into his power' ('7 him sie eal middangeard on geweald geseald').[81]

Bazire and Cross Homily 4 thus shares a series of motifs and stylistic features with Vercelli IX. Also closely related to Vercelli IX in rhetorical structure is the *Prose Solomon and Saturn Pater Noster Dialogue*. It is remarkable that there are no fewer than four Old English texts in which Solomon and Saturn figure as interlocutors in a question-and-answer setting: the two *Solomon and Saturn* debate poems, the *Prose Solomon and Saturn* and the *Prose Solomon and Saturn Pater Noster Dialogue*. To adapt a remark by T. A. Shippey in a different context, one *Solomon and Saturn* debate might be a quirk, but four suggest a taste. Apart from its unique choice of interlocutors, the *Prose Solomon and Saturn*, which belongs to the widespread genre of the *Joca monachorum*, is only tangentially related to the other three.[82] The remaining works, however, comprising the two poetic dialogues and the prose *Pater Noster Dialogue*, clearly belong to a common tradition, although their precise interrelationship remains unclear. Menner pointed to certain differences in content and style between the two poetic dialogues which he considered sufficient to rule out the possibility of common authorship. Dobbie thought the second poetic dialogue an imitation of the first, using material derived from Germanic gnomic tradition.[83] Daniel Donoghue, however, has recently argued for common authorship on the basis of 'mutual peculiarities' in the use of the verbal auxiliary. Donoghue would account for the differences noted by Menner by assuming 'that the same poet worked from two different sources and was influenced differently by each'.[84] The possibility of common authorship of the two poetic dialogues remains an open question, but the differences between them are significant enough to treat them as two quite distinct poems, as indeed the capitalized 'Hwæt' and *gefrægn*-formula in the first line of the second poem clearly demand. The two poems, moreover, are separated in the chief manuscript, Cambridge, Corpus Christi College 422, pp. 1–26 (s. x^{med}), by the fragmentary prose *Pater Noster Dialogue*.[85]

81 *The Vercelli Homilies*, ed. Scragg, p. 180, line 188. See above, pp. 206–9.

82 *The Prose Solomon and Saturn*, ed. Cross and Hill, pp. 25–34. For the use of Hiberno-Latin sources in this dialogue and in the related *Adrian and Ritheus*, see *ibid.*, pp. 9–10.

83 *The Anglo-Saxon Minor Poems*, ed. Dobbie, p. lix.

84 *Style in Old English Poetry: the Test of the Auxiliary* (New Haven, CT, 1987), p. 105.

85 On the manuscript, see Ker, *Catalogue*, no. 70A.

The connections between this prose fragment and the first of the poetic dialogues, *Solomon and Saturn I*, on the other hand, are numerous and striking. Although Menner justly remarked that the rhetorical expression of the prose dialogue is even more extravagant than that of the poetic dialogue,[86] most readers would probably agree that the difference is one of degree rather than kind. The poem does not employ the numerical *gradatio* which, as we shall see, nearly overwhelms the prose fragment and which links it stylistically with 'The Devil's Account'. But both *Solomon and Saturn I* and the *Pater Noster Dialogue* indulge in fantastic personifications of the Paternoster (referred to in both texts with the Latin loanwords *lina*, *cantic* and *organ*) and both dramatize in elaborate and grotesque fashion the combat between the hypostatized Paternoster and the devil: in the poem, the personified letters of the Paternoster attack the devil in succession; in the prose, the Paternoster undergoes a series of transformations countering the transformations of the devil. The poem, moreover, also refers to the shape-shifting of devils (*bleoum bregdað*, line 150a) and specifies that the Paternoster can counteract them, so that the enumeration of the shapes (*bleos*) of the devil and Paternoster and the description of their transformation combat in the prose fragment can be considered an elaboration of an idea expressed in the poem. Finally, the evidence of the manuscript, in which the prose dialogue immediately follows *Solomon and Saturn I* without any indication of a break or new division, suggests that the two texts were at least perceived, if not actually composed, as a unified work.[87] The first poem and the prose dialogue, in fact, may well be translations of two parts of the same Latin source, and, if so, are probably by the same author. His reasons for turning from verse to prose can only be guessed at, but he might well have despaired of versifying the extended and repetitive numerical rhetoric of the second part of his source.[88]

[86] *Poetical Dialogues*, p. 9.

[87] See K. O'B. O'Keeffe, *Visible Song: Transitional Literacy in Old English Verse*, Cambridge Studies in Anglo-Saxon England 4 (Cambridge, 1990), 68, who notes that 'With the exception of the increase of lines (from twenty-three to twenty-four) on pages 7 to 12, there is no distinction between the presentation of prose and verse in this part of the manuscript.'

[88] Menner considers this possibility and decides against it, though he concedes that 'It is, of course, curious that there should be two separate Solomon and Saturn dialogues on the Pater Noster' (*Poetical Dialogues*, p. 9, n. 5).

Certain features of style and content link these *Solomon and Saturn* texts, especially the prose *Pater Noster Dialogue*, with Vercelli IX and 'The Devil's Account'. That the names of Solomon and Saturn also appear in close association in 'The Devil's Account' is unlikely to be a coincidence, as Kemble perceived.[89] In the devil's account of heaven, the princeling lavished with material and sensual pleasures is endowed with 'Solomon's beauty and wisdom', and the new bride conducted to his bed each night has 'the beauty of Juno, Saturn's daughter'.[90] Stylistic parallels confirm that the homily and the *Solomon and Saturn* texts belong to a common literary milieu. The extravagant rhetorical style characteristic of both poems, particularly the hyperbole and use of numbers in grotesque descriptive contexts, suggests a common tradition. The most extensive stylistic parallels with the homily occur, as we shall see, in the prose *Pater Noster Dialogue*, but the single closest parallel occurs in Saturn's book riddle in *Solomon and Saturn II*, which employs a variation of the numerical *gradatio* in a form reminiscent of the Men with Tongues of Iron theme:

> Ac hwæt is se dumba se ðe on sumre dene resteð?
> Swyðe snyttrað, hafað seofon tungan,
> hafað tungena gehwylc twentig orda,
> hafað orda gewhylc engles snyttro, ...[91]

Although the peculiar contents of both *Solomon and Saturn* poems have proved very difficult to parallel, there are good indications that

[89] *The Dialogue of Solomon and Saturnus*, pp. 84–6. The version of 'The Devil's Account' printed by Kemble is that in Cotton Tiberius A. iii [M], ed. Robinson, 'The Devil's Account of the Next World'. This version actually names Samson rather than Solomon, but Kemble rightly assumed a scribal error, and the other versions of the exemplum confirm that the original name was Solomon. Kemble's association of 'The Devil's Account' with the *Solomon and Saturn* group has led to a misunderstanding by some later scholars, who have attributed passages from 'The Devil's Account' in Napier XXX to *Solomon and Saturn*; see Robinson, 'The Devil's Account of the Next World', pp. 362–3, n. 7. 'The Devil's Account' is, of course, an entirely distinct text (or group of texts). Kemble, however, was surely right in supposing some kind of literary connection.

[90] See *The Vercelli Homilies*, ed. Scragg, p. 180, lines 187–8 and 190–1.

[91] *Poetical Dialogues*, ed. Menner, p. 92, lines 221–4 (I omit macrons marking long vowels): 'But what is the mute thing which rests in a vale? It is exceedingly wise, it has seven tongues, each tongue has twenty tips, each tip has the wisdom of an angel'. Tristram, 'Stock Descriptions', p. 108, n. 27, notes the similarity with the Men with Tongues of Iron.

Irish sources have contributed to the strange amalgam of arcane lore. The author of the most detailed edition and study, R. J. Menner, suggested tentatively that 'the dialogues of Solomon and Saturn have come to Old English through Celtic sources'.[92] Menner pointed out that the closest parallels to the hypostasis of the Paternoster occur in Irish prayers and litanies, 'where the *lorica* becomes a kind of all-inclusive protector, and a prayer may come to be spoken of in extravagant terms applicable only to a person'.[93] He also noted[94] that the Leabhar Breac homily on the Paternoster describes the prayer as a weapon against the devil: 'Hic est malleus ferreus, quo contritus est diabolus, sicut dicitur, "malleo ferreo conteram soliditatem tuam."'[95] Martin McNamara has recently traced this comment back to a Hiberno-Latin tradition represented by the *Catechesis Celtica*, in the last of three short expositions of the Paternoster.[96] In the *Catechesis*, this image is followed by a further comparison of the seven petitions of the Paternoster to seven spears, through which seven vices are pierced. In another exposition in the *Catechesis*, partially paralleled in the Reference

[92] *Poetical Dialogues*, p. 43. Although the general form of both poems as debates between Solomon and a representative of pagan wisdom has many antecedents in Hebraic and Christian traditions – a lost *Contradictio Salomonis* condemned in the Gelasian decree has been suggested as a possible source – Solomon's usual antagonist in the later medieval versions is Marculf, a Germanic name apparently corresponding to the Hebrew Marchol, a god represented as Solomon's opponent in some of the most ancient versions of the legend. A relic of this, apparently the original, name for Solomon's opponent occurs in *Solomon and Saturn II*, which mentions *Marculfes eard* (180b) as one of the heathen lands Saturn had visited. The substitution of Saturn for Marculf is a feature unique to the Old English texts, but there is one early Latin source which equates the god Morcholon with Saturn: the *Cosmographia* of 'Aethicus Ister'. On the possible identification of Aethicus Ister with the Irishman Virgil, bishop of Salzburg, see above, p. 26, n. 104; and on the possibility that the *Cosmographia* was drawn on by the poet of *Solomon and Saturn II*, see O'Keeffe, 'The Geographic List', pp. 135–40.

[93] *Poetical Dialogues*, p. 42; cf. p. 111.

[94] *Ibid.*, p. 112.

[95] *The Passions and the Homilies*, ed. Atkinson, pp. 505–6 (for the Irish version, see p. 264, with an English translation at p. 501): 'The Paternoster is the iron hammer by which the power of the devil is broken, as saith Job in the person of the Lord: – "I will break thy power, O devil", saith the Lord, "with an iron hammer", viz: with the Paternoster.'

[96] Vatican, Biblioteca Apostolica, Reg. lat. 49, 11r, cited by McNamara, 'The Irish Affiliations', p. 326: 'Hic est mallus de quo contritus est diabulus, sicut est malleo ferreo ut concutiam soliditatem tuam.'

Bible, the Vienna Commentary on Matthew and the Cracow homily collection, verses of the Paternoster are ranged against statements of the devil in what might be termed a verbal transformation combat:

Diabolus enim dixit: Nescio Deum! Nos humiliter dicere iubemur: *Paternoster qui es in celis*. Diabolus dixit: *Ero similis altissimo*. Nos dicimus: *Adueniat regnum tuum*. Diabolus dixit: *Super astra Dei solium meum exultabo*. Nos dicimus: *Fiat uoluntas tua sicut in celo et in terra*.[97]

The *Catechesis Celtica* and the Vienna commentary, in addition, both refer to the Paternoster with its seven petitions as a branching tree, a tradition which may lie behind the description of the Paternoster as 'palm-twigged' in *Solomon and Saturn I*, although both Hiberno-Latin commentaries associate the Paternoster not with the palm but rather with the flourishing tree of the parable of the mustard seed (Matth. XIII.31–2).[98] The representation of a protecting prayer from Scripture

[97] Vatican City, Biblioteca Apostolica, Reg. lat. 49, 9v: 'For the devil said: "I do not know God!" We are bidden to say humbly: "Our Father who art in heaven" [Matth. VI.9]. The devil said: "I will be like the most High" [Is. XIV.14]. We say: "Thy kingdom come" [Matth. VI.10]. The devil said: "I will exalt my throne above the stars of God" [Is. XIV.13]. We say: "Thy will be done on earth, as it is in heaven" [Matth. VI.10].' Compare the parallel passages from the Vienna Commentary (*BCLL*, no. 772 (i); Wright, 'Hiberno-Latin', no. 24) and Cracow homily collection (*BCLL*, no. 802; Wright, 'Hiberno-Latin', no. 45) printed by T. L. Amos, 'The *Catechesis Cracoviensis* and Hiberno-Latin Exegesis on the *Pater Noster*', *Proceedings of the Irish Biblical Association* 13 (1990), 77–107, at 90–1. A closely similar exposition, with a longer series of antitheses, occurs in the Reference Bible (*BCLL*, no. 762; Wright, 'Hiberno-Latin', no. 1), in Paris, BN, lat. 11561, 152v.

[98] Vatican City, Biblioteca Apostolica, Reg. lat. 49, 10r; Vienna, Nationalbibliothek, 940, 89r. The Vienna commentary, which is much fuller here, specifically contrasts the Paternoster with the incantations of pagan sages: '*granum sinapis* est octo uersiculi orationis dominicae, qui incarnationibus [*read* incantationibus] uatum seculi et magorum et poetarum et philosophorum minores erant. *Homo* tunc, id est humilis [*corr. from* humiles] populus christianus octo hos uersiculos [*corr. from* uersiculus] in agrum bonae naturae; et *in magnam arborem* [Lc. XIII.19] creuere [*read* creuerent], id in fortissimum genus orationis et *maius omnibus holeribus*, id incantationibus quas diximus. *Ut uolucres ueniant*, id est mentes infidelium [*read* fidelium]; *et habitant in ramis eius*, id est in duobus quadraginta ramis de vii uersiculis crescentibus' ('*a grain of mustard seed* is the eight verses of the Lord's prayer, which are smaller than the incantations of the seers of the world and of the magicians and poets and philosophers [cf. *Catechesis Celtica*: '*omnibus holeribus*, loquiis [et] locutionibus philosophorum']. Then *a man*, that is the humble Christian people

as a branching tree is found elsewhere in Irish tradition. A Middle Irish poem describes a vision of St Augustine, who escapes from eight wolves in a forest by climbing a great tree with twenty-two branches. From the leaves of this tree Augustine shakes down drops that fall on the heads of the wolves and destroy them. The tree is Psalm CXVIII, the *Beati*; its branches are the twenty-two divisions of the psalm; the drops are the individual verses which destroy the eight deadly sins.[99]

Menner was not familiar with another, more elaborate example of the hypostasis of the Paternoster as a protecting charm in Irish. The Middle Irish *Geinemain Molling ocus a Bethae* ('Birth and Life of St Moling') includes a prayer in which individual words and phrases of the Paternoster are invoked consecutively against demons, death and other evils, much as *Solomon and Saturn I* personifies the successive letters as weapons against the devil. Since Stokes's edition of this poem is very rare, I shall cite the Irish text in full:

Paternoster ardom-thá frisna huile eccrotá,
rop lemsa mo pater noster rop leosomh a míthorter (*sic*).
Qui es in celis, Dé bī dom snādhadh ar urbhaidhí,
ar demnaib co n-ilar cor snāidsium sanctificetur.
Nomen tuum lim do grés is adueniat mo bithbés,
regnum tuum lim for fect panem nostrum rē n-imtecht.
Cotidianum cach dia et da nobis ō Dia
na rom-farcba dia héis guidem dimit[t]e nobis.
Debita nostra co rós maráen is sicut et nōs
dimittimus lim ar scīs debitoribus nostrīs.
Ar mo cennsiu dēcar bás atchim ne nos inducās
cona ragbat demhnu m'ell atcim in temptacionem.
Sed libera nos a [malo] rom-saera beos mo cara

(sowing) these eight verses in the field of good nature; and they grew *into a large tree*, that is into a very strong kind of prayer and *greater than any herb*, that is the incantations which we mentioned. *So that the birds come*, that is the minds of the faithful; *and they dwell in its branches*, that is in the twenty-four branches growing from the seven verses'). The same exegesis, in similar wording, occurs earlier in the commentary (50v).

[99] B. Ó Cuív, 'Three Middle Irish Poems', *Éigse* 16 (1975), 1–17, at 2–5. The poem is apparently modelled on an episode from Jonas of Bobbio's *Vita S. Columbani* I.8, ed. B. Krusch, MGH, SS rer. Merov. 4 (Hannover and Leipzig, 1902), 61–152, at 74, in which Columbanus, wandering in the woods, is surrounded by twelve wolves, but protects himself by repeating the words *Deus in adiutorium* (Ps. LXIX.2). As Sims-Williams points out, Cassian had recommended this psalm verse as an *inpenetrabilis lurica* (*Religion and Literature*, pp. 277–8).

trāth bas cinnti lim mo scél corop mebhair lem amēn.
Ar t'atach, a Dē nime ar t'itge 'sar t'airnaige
co ris degbethaid glan glē tria ernaighe na patre.
Fir domuin cīa beith da lín cia do[g]net uile mīgnīmh,
ros-aincet tria glere glan a credo, ocus a pater.
Impid he Maire for a Mac for a deacht, for a daenact,
cor'ermaide dam go glē secht n-ernaile na patre.
Fir domuin ce be da lín cia dognet uile mīgnīmh,
nos-ragat uile for nemh da ndernat guide a pater.
Ní mar chumsigedh fri hedh nī mar soilsiged maten,
nī mar baistedh ra hedh ris nach memor a pater.
Pater noster.[100]

In Irish tradition certain hymns, canticles and psalms are frequently accompanied in manuscripts by statements confirming their efficacy as protective charms against physical and spiritual dangers for those who chant them.[101] Here the Paternoster is invoked as just such a charm, as in the statement introducing the personification of the letters of the Paternoster in *Solomon and Saturn I*, which asserts that 'he who will

[100] *The Birth and Life of St. Moling*, ed. W. Stokes (privately ptd, London, 1907), p. 52: '*Pater noster* is for me against all horrid (?) things! / with me be my paternoster: with them be their ... ? / *Qui es in caelis*, O living God, to protect me from bale: / from demons with many sins (?) may *sanctificetur* protect me! / *Nomen tuum* be with me always, and *adueniat* be my lasting use, / *regnum tuum* be with me on an expedition, and *panem nostrum* before a journey. / *Quotidianum* every day and *da nobis* from God, / that He may not leave me behind Him let us pray *dimitte nobis*. / *Debita nostra* so that I shall reach, together with *sicut et nos* / *dimittimus* with me for weariness, *debitoribus nostris*. / To meet me death is seen: I beseech *ne nos inducas*, / that demons may not take advantage of me I beseech *in temptationem*. / *Sed libera nos a malo*, may my Friend still save me. / When my tale is determined, may I remember *amen*. / For beseeching thee, O God of heaven, for entreating Thee and for praying Thee / may I attain a pure-bright good life through praying the *pater*. / The world's men, whatever their number, though they all do misdeed, / their *credo* and their paternoster protect them thro' pure abundance. / Mary's intercession with her Son by his Godhead, by his Manhood, / so that the seven parts of the paternoster may be clearly attained by me. / The world's men, whatever their number, though they all do misdeed, / they will all go to heaven if they pray their paternosters. Not as ... not as morning would shine, / not as ... (is it) with him who remembers not his paternoster' (trans. Stokes, p. 53). Stokes omitted the poems in his earlier, more accessible editions of this text (for which see Kenney, *The Sources*, no. 249).

[101] See Godel, 'Irish Prayer in the Early Middle Ages', pp. 74–5 and 95–7. Cf. *Aided Muirchertaig Meic Erca*, ed. Nic Dhonnchadha, p. 34, lines 967–70, and a poem on prayer for the dead in 'A Miscellany of Irish Verse', ed. Carney, pp. 243–4.

eagerly and carefully sing God's saying and who will always cherish it without sins may put to flight the hostile spirit, the fighting enemy' (lines A84–7). The Paternoster, of course, was widely regarded as a protective charm in Christian tradition,[102] and Valerie Flint has noted that 'Ælfric singles out the Creed and Paternoster as protective prayers.'[103] In Ireland, chanting the Paternoster was a prominent part of devotional exercises during the eighth- and ninth-century anchorite movement associated with the Céli Dé. Documents associated with Mael Rúain of Tallaght refer to cross-vigils of thirty *paters* and regimens consisting of the Paternoster with other psalms and prayers, including a ceremony called the 'Shrine of Piety', which combined the Paternoster with the verse *Deus in adiutorium* (Ps. LXIX.2).[104] Mael Rúain's devotion to the Paternoster was said to have been inspired by a pious Irish nun:

niconeirged cen pater do cantain. Niconsesed cen pater dochetul. Antan atraiged som iarum do gabail na gabail nogebed pater statim iar neirgi ⁊ is iarum tindscanad a gabail. O roscithet iarum ind gabail hísin nósuided ⁊ nogebed pater statim iarsuidiu ⁊ iarum toinscanad ingabail di cétul ina suidiu. Is de tra do forgillsom ind pater hi forciund cacha gabali. Is bés laissim dogres pater do chetul nach tan atraig ⁊ pater nach dand suides.[105]

Another text associated with the Céli Dé, the Old Irish 'Table of Commutations', goes further, claiming that repeating 365 Paternosters

[102] See Menner's survey of the magical use of the Paternoster, *Poetical Dialogues*, pp. 39–42.

[103] *The Rise of Magic in Early Medieval Europe* (Princeton, 1991), p. 313, citing Ælfric's *De auguriis*, in *Ælfric's Lives of Saints*, ed. W. W. Skeat, EETS os 76, 82, 94 and 114 (London, 1881; repr. in 2 vols., 1966) I, 364–82, at 370.

[104] 'The Teaching of Mael Ruain', in *The Rule of Tallaght*, ed. E. J. Gwynn, pp. 6 and 68. The Paternoster is linked with this verse also in the Old Irish 'Table of Commutations' (see below, n. 106).

[105] '*The Monastery of Tallaght*', ed. E. Gwynn and W. J. Purton, *PRIA* 29C (1911), 115–79, at 140. Gwynn translates: 'She would not rise without singing a *pater*. She would not sit down without chanting a *pater*. When she rose to recite the divisions [of the psalms] she used to recite a *pater* immediately after rising, and then she would begin the division. Then when that division was finished she would sit down and she would recite a *pater* immediately after sitting down, and then she would begin to recite the [next] division sitting down. It is by her example that he appoints [?] the *pater* at the end of each division. It is his constant usage to sing a *pater* whenever he rises, and a *pater* whenever he sits down.' The same story (except that it is a 'holy person' rather than specifically a nun) is told in 'The Teaching of Mael Ruain', in *The Rule of Tallaght*, ed. Gwynn, p. 58.

has the power to rescue a soul from hell.[106] The Old English poet attributes the same power to the Paternoster:

He mæg þa sawle of synnihte
gefetian under foldan, næfre hi se feond to ðæs niðer
feterum gefæstnað; þeah he hi mid fiftigum
clausum beclemme, he þane cræft briceð
and þa orþancas ealle tosliteð.[107]

In addition to the general parallels in Irish tradition for the hypostasis of the Paternoster as a weapon against demons and for certain specific motifs and expressions, Menner cited the frequently bombastic style of the poetic dialogues as another possible indication of Irish influence. Referring to the description of the Paternoster, Menner remarked that the 'extravagance of expression is reminiscent of Irish religious literature, and, indeed, the whole tone of this section of the poem savors of Hisperic Latin'.[108] He singled out the poet's statement that the devil casts from his sling 'iron apples – all are grown from the heads of the waves of scorn' (25–9), an expression which he thought 'smacks of the Irish Latin of Aldhelm's school'.[109] Menner rightly noted that 'There is nothing unusual in the use of *æppel* in the general sense of ball',[110] but

[106] Trans. D. A. Binchy in *The Irish Penitentials*, ed. L. Bieler, SLH 5 (Dublin, 1963), 278. For the association of this text with the Céli Dé, see *ibid.*, pp. 49–50. As Godel ('Irish Prayer in the Early Middle Ages. II', p. 74) notes, the Paternoster is here a substitute for Psalm CXVIII, the *Beati*, the text most frequently assigned the power of rescuing souls from hell in Irish tradition.

[107] *Poetical Dialogues*, ed. Menner, p. 84, lines 68–72: 'It can rescue the soul from perpetual night under the earth, though the fiend fastens it never so far down with fetters; though he clasp it with fifty bonds, the Paternoster will break that power and loosen all those devious devices.' The metaphor of prayer breaking the bonds of the dead recalls Bede's story of Imma (*HE* IV.22), which recommends the power of masses to release souls from punishment *in alia uita*. However, as Ælfric makes clear (in a sermon on the Lord's Prayer, and elsewhere) masses do not avail the soul condemned to hell through deadly sin (see Grundy, *Books and Grace*, pp. 233–5). *Solomon and Saturn* and the Old Irish 'Table of Commutations' make no such qualification.

[108] *Poetical Dialogues*, pp. 42–3.

[109] *Ibid.*, p. 109. Aldhelm's Latin style, however, is now thought to have been based primarily on continental models (see below, n. 197).

[110] See P. A. Thompson, '*Æpplede Gold*: an Investigation of its Semantic Field', *MS* 48 (1986), 315–33, at 318 and 327. The attestations are few, however, and one other occurs in the prose *Pater Noster Dialogue*, which says that the Paternoster can crush all creation in his right hand *on anes weaxæples onlicnesse* (*Poetical Dialogues*,

the expression 'iron apples' for missiles is striking and unparalleled in Old English. In Irish, however, the word *uball* is commonly used for missiles and projectiles, and in the LL *Táin* Cú Chulainn casts an 'iron apple' from his *deil chliss*, evidently a kind of sling.[111]

Menner also drew attention to the style of a passage enumerating the virtues of the Paternoster:

He bið sefan snytero and sawle hunig
and modes meolc, mærþa gesælgost.
...
Hungor he gehideð, helle gestrudeð,
wylm toworpeð, wuldor getymbreð.
He is modigra middangeardes
staðole, he is strengra þone ealle stana gripe.
Lamana he is læce, leoht winciendra,
swilce he his deafra duru, deadra tunge,
scildigra scild, Scippendes seld,
flodes feriend, folces neriend,
yþa yrfeweard, earma fixa,
wyrma wlenco, wildeora holt,
westenes weard, weorðmynta geard.[112]

'The tone of the English passage', Menner remarked, 'reminds one, in its extravagant use of figure, of the Old Irish prayers ... and in its general inclusiveness, of the famous *loricae* of St. Patrick and Gildas'.[113] The precise terms applied to the Paternoster in this sequence are difficult to

ed. Menner, p. 170). On this term see also P. Lendinara, 'Tecnicismi nel *Salomone e Saturno* in prosa (ms. CCCC 422)', *Quaderni di filologia germanica* 2 (1981), 97–124, at 110–11.

111 For the reference see *DIL*, s.v. *uball* II (e), with the compound *uballmell*, and s.v. 2 *deil* I (b). For a detailed consideration of the *deil chliss*, see now W. Sayers, 'Warrior Initiation and Some Short Celtic Spears in the Irish and Learned Latin Traditions', *Studies in Medieval and Renaissance History* ns 11 (1989), 89–108.

112 *Poetical Dialogues*, ed. Menner, p. 84, lines 66–7, 73–83: 'He is wisdom of the heart and honey of the soul, milk of the mind, most blessed of glories ... He destroys hunger, plunders hell, turns aside a conflagration, builds up glory. He is bolder than the foundation of earth, he is stronger than the grip of all stones. He is the physician of the lame, light of the blinking, also he is the door of the deaf, the tongue of the dead [ms. B; of the dumb, ms. A], the shield of the guilty, the hall of the Creator, bearer of the flood, saviour of the people, hereditary guardian of the waves, of poor fishes, glory [stream, ms. A] of serpents, forest of wild animals, guardian of the desert, court of honours.'

113 *Ibid.*, p. 111.

parallel,[114] but some appear to be based on Christian litanies, while others are reminiscent of Celtic and Indo-European panegyric tradition.[115] The Paternoster is praised as *wyrma wlenco* ('pride of serpents or dragons'), like a hero in Welsh and Irish praise poetry, who is often acclaimed as a dragon or snake for fierceness in one reflex of what Patrick Sims-Williams has called 'the Celtic figurative tradition in which men and wild beasts were often compared'.[116]

The litanic style of the passage in *Solomon and Saturn I*, 'énumératif' in the sense that Wilmart applied the term to Irish liturgical style, is also similar to the sequences of short parallel *cola* frequently encountered in Irish and Hiberno-Latin texts.[117] The same technique is found in

114 With *yþa yrfeweard* ('hereditary guardian of waves', line 81a) cf. the similar phrase applied to Columba in the *Amra Coluim Cille*, in *The Irish Liber Hymnorum*, ed. and trans. Bernard and Atkinson I, 177 and II, 73: 'Cét cell custói tond' ('Hundred churches' guardian of waves'; but Best and Bergin, *Lebor na Huidre*, p. 34, V. Hull, *ZCP* 28 (1961), p. 248 and *DIL* read *custoid*). With the epithet 'honey of the soul' compare the Latin passage in praise of the Paternoster in Sedulius Scottus's Commentary on Matthew (*Sedulius Scottus Kommentar*, ed. Löfstedt, p. 206: 'Fauus est mellis et est odor suauitatis coram Altissimo, si pura conscientia atque sollerti intensione decantetur' ('It is a honeycomb and it is an odour of sweetness before the most High, if it is sung with a pure conscience and careful attention'). With the phrases 'bolder than the foundation of earth, stronger than the grip of all stones' (lines 75–6), cf. St Patrick's *Lorica*, 'tairismige t[h]alman / cobsaide ailech' ('stability of earth, firmness of rock'; *Thesaurus Palaeohibernicus*, ed. and trans. Stokes and Strachan II, 356), and for the style, cf. the Irish infancy gospel: 'Fairer than earth ... / More wonderful than heaven / Brighter than sun / Clearer than streams / Sweeter than honey / Greater than the universe / Higher than heaven's hosts / Comelier than angels / Nobler than the world / Wider than the universe His speech / Better than the world / More precious than creatures' (trans. E. Hogan, in James, *Latin Infancy Gospels*, p. 110).

115 See the survey of panegyric traditions by Sims-Williams, 'Gildas and Vernacular Poetry', pp. 169–92, with the references cited at 173, n. 30, especially E. Campanile, 'Aspetti della cultura indoeuropea arcaica: I. La raffigurazione del re e dell'eroe', *Studi e saggi linguistici* 14 (1974), 185–227.

116 'Gildas and Vernacular Poetry', p. 190.

117 See above, p. 32 and n. 128. Meyer, *Learning in Ireland in the Fifth Century*, pp. 13–20, argued that the techniques of antithesis and parallelism in Irish vernacular rhetoric were based upon the late Antique *rhetoricus sermo*, brought to Ireland in the fifth century by Gaulish rhetors who fled the barbarian invasions on the Continent. Meyer's theory (based solely on a note in a twelfth-century Leiden manuscript) of an exodus of Gaulish rhetors to Ireland and of their influence on the development of Irish rhetoric was accepted and developed by Chadwick, 'Intellectual Contacts',

vernacular 'rhetorics' or *roscada*, some of which, as Liam Breatnach has shown, are translations of Hiberno-Latin passages from the *Collectio Canonum Hibernensis*.[118] In a broader sense, then, the 'enumerative style' as cultivated by the Irish and their Anglo-Saxon followers includes a predilection for litanic runs of parallel or antithetical *cola*, particularly in liturgical and paraliturgical texts but also in other genres. An Anglo-Latin letter of Alchfrith the anchorite, for example, was printed by Wilhelm Levison, who noted its 'vivid style', including 'the liking of the author for parallelisms of contrasted ideas, by which his admonitions are emphasized'.[119] Kathleen Hughes has pointed out that 'more than half of this letter comes word for word from the Third Sermon of Columbanus ... and Alchfrith's style here is, in fact, that of an earlier and greater Irish exegetist of the ascetic school'.[120] An example of an extended sequence of antitheses in Old English which was taken from a Hiberno-Latin source occurs in the body-and-soul homily in Junius 85/86, which contrasts the teachings of God and of the devil with a list closely paralleled in one of the homilies *In nomine Dei summi*:

God Ælmihtig us lærað wæccan and gebedu, diofol us lærað slæw and slæcnesse.	Docet Deus uigilias. Docet diabulus somnolentiam.
God Ælmihtig us lærаþ fæstan, diofol us lærað oferfylle and untidætas.	Docet Deus ieiunium. Docet diabulus saturitatem.
God Ælmihtig us lærað rummodnesse, diofol us lærað gitsunga.	Docet Deus largitatem. Docet diabulus auaritiam.

pp. 237–50, but has not been supported by more recent scholarship. See E. James, 'Ireland and Western Gaul', p. 370.

118 'Canon Law and Secular Law in Early Ireland: the Significance of *Bretha Nemed*', *Peritia* 3 (1984), 439–59. Compare the Irish and Latin versions of a sequence in the Tripartite Life of St Patrick, cited by Meyer, *Learning in Ireland in the Fifth Century*, p. 28, n. 51.

119 *England and the Continent*, p. 300.

120 'Some Aspects of Irish Influence', p. 59. The attribution of the *Instructiones* to Columbanus, however, is uncertain (cf. *BCLL*, no. 1251). It should also be noted that one extended sequence of parallelisms describing the Christian's fight against the devil is based on Caesarius of Arles, as Levison pointed out (p. 299, n. 4). The same passage from Caesarius was adapted by the author of Vercelli Homily XIX: see P. Szarmach, 'Caesarius of Arles and the Vercelli Homilies', *Traditio* 26 (1970), 315–23, at 319. On the Irish style of the prayers attributed to Alchfrith, see Clayton, *The Cult of the Virgin Mary*, pp. 101–4.

God Ælmihtig us lærað clænnesse,	Docet Deus castitatem.
diofol us læraþ derne geligro.	Docet diabulus fornicationem.
God Ælmihtig us lærað liþnesse and gefeohtsumnesse,	Docet Deus lenitatem.
diofol us lærað yrre and unrotnesse.	Docet diabulus iracundiam.
	Docet Deus patientiam.
	Docet diabulus inpatientiam.
God Ælmihtig us lærað eadmodnesse,	Docet Deus humilitatem.
diofol us lærað ofermetto.	Docet diabulus superbiam.
God Ælmihtig us lærað sibbe and winsumnesse,	Docet Deus pacem.
diofol us lærað unsibbe and wrohte.[121]	Docet diabulus indisceptionem.
	Docet Deus dilectionem proximi.
	Docet diabulus occisionem.

The poet of *Solomon and Saturn I*, as Menner noted, had a 'predilection for parallelism and enumeration'.[122] With the list of the virtues of the Paternoster one may compare the following enumerations of the virtues of chastity from the Hiberno-Latin treatise *De duodecim abusiuis saeculi* and of the virtues of Christ from an Irish version of an Infancy gospel:

[121] *Nuove omelie anglosassoni*, ed. Fadda, p. 169–71, lines 72–83: 'Almighty God teaches us vigils and prayers, the devil teaches us sloth and sluggishness. Almighty God teaches us fasting, the devil teaches us gluttony and untimely eatings. Almighty God teaches us generosity, the devil teaches us avarice. Almighty God teaches us purity, the devil teaches us fornication. Almighty God teaches us gentleness and joyfulness, the devil teaches us anger and sadness. Almighty God teaches us humility, the devil teaches us pride. Almighty God teaches us peace and happiness, the devil teaches us hostility and wrong.' The Latin parallel is in 'Seven Hiberno-Latin Sermons', ed. McNally, p. 141. For further details, see Wright, '*Docet Deus, Docet Diabolus*'. As I pointed out in that article (p. 452, n. 10), the passage from Junius 85/86 was borrowed and adapted by the author of Assmann XIV. For possible echoes of the phrasing of Assmann XIV in the Middle English *Worcester Fragments*, see Heningham, 'Old English Precursors', p. 300.

[122] *Poetical Dialogues*, p. 7.

Pudicitia ornamentum nobilium est, exaltatio humilium, nobilitas ignobilium, pulchritudo uilium, prosperitas laborantium, solamen maerentium, augmentum omnis pulchritudinis, decus religionis, defensio criminum, multiplicatio meritorum, creatoris omnium Dei amicitia.[123]

Is he nert Dé 7 lám Dé,
Is e dess Dé 7 cena Dé,
Is e tacmong na ndúl 7 faircseoir in betha,
Is e bás 7 crith 7 atach na ndúl,
Is e brithem 7 liaig 7 comarci na ndúl, ...

Is e didiu brithem 7 sássad nan aingel, 7 betha múnntire nime 7 luirec imdegla na bethad suthaine cin crich cin forcend, 7 cathbarr coróni na cat(h)rach nemda.[124]

123 *Pseudo-Cyprianus de xii abusivis saeculi*, ed. Hellmann, pp. 42–3: 'Chastity is the distinction of the noble, the exaltation of the humble, the nobility of the ignoble, the beauty of the base, the prosperity of labourers, the comfort of the mournful, the increase of all beauty, the glory of religion, the defence of offences, the multiplication of merits, the friendship of God the Creator of all things.' For similar sequences in praise of particular virtues, compare Sedulius's *Collectaneum Miscellaneum* XIII.xx.23 (ed. Simpson, p. 91) and XXV.vii.9 (p. 164, cf. *Hib.* XXV.18). The first part of a sequence in praise of virginity (XIII.vii.2–3, p. 69; with item 3 cf. *Hib.* XLV.1) is paralleled in Aldhelm's prose *De uirginitate* (*Aldhelmi Opera*, ed. Ehwald, p. 255). The common source, which has not previously been identified, is the *Passio S. Thomae apostoli*, ed. K. Zelzer, *Die alten lateinischen Thomasakten* (Berlin, 1977), p. 10, lines 4–6. Good examples of this kind of extended sequence in a patristic source are found in Ambrose, *De Helia et ieiunio*, ed. C. Schenkl, CSEL 32.2 (Vienna, 1897), 413 and 423–4.

124 *The Irish Nennius*, ed. Hogan, pp. 68–9. Hogan translates: 'He is the strength of God and the hand of God; He is the right hand of God and the wisdom of God, He is the comprehension of creatures, the beholder of the (whole) world, He is the death and terror and refuge of creatures; He is the judge and physician and protection of creatures ... He is also the judge and the nourishment of angels, and the life of the family of heaven, and the breastplate of protection of eternal life, without end, without limit, and the helmet of the crown of the heavenly city.' For 'refuge of creatures' (*atach na ndúl*), *DIL* s.v. *attach* II (c) translates 'he whom the elements beseech'. Tristram, *Sex aetates mundi*, p. 335, illustrates the rhythmic prose style of Irish texts with a similar passage from an Old Irish homily ('An Old-Irish Homily', ed. Strachan, p. 3; I cite from Strachan's translation, p. 8): 'He is King of Kings and Lord of lords, Creator of heaven and earth, Maker of the angels, Teacher of the prophets, Master of the apostles, Giver of the Law, Judge of the men of the world. He is higher than the heavens, lower than the earth, wider than the seas.' The formula of the final sentence is particularly widespread in Irish and Hiberno-Latin

With a second but briefer litanic enumeration of the virtues of the Paternoster in the poem, employing homoioteleuton in a sequence of third-person singular verbs, one may compare a sequence from a passage on the Paternoster found in slightly variant forms in two Hiberno-Latin sources, Sedulius Scottus's Commentary on Matthew and the *Catechesis Celtica*, and paralleled in a vernacular Irish fragment 'In Praise of Hymnody':

Ðæt gepalmtigude heofonas ontyneð, Metod gemiltsað, adwæsceð deofles fyr, onæleð.	Pater noster halie geblissað, morðor gefilleð Dryhtnes	Haec [sc. Oratio Dominica] tumorem superbiae comprimit, iracundiae quoque atque inuidiae furorem refrenat, inpetus carnis atque libidinem extingit, a terrenis mentem auocat, desiderium regni caelestis incendit.[125]

texts, often extended into a longer sequence. Cf. Columbanus (?), *Instructio* VIII, in *Sancti Columbani Opera*, ed. Walker, p. 64, lines 21–3 and p. 94, lines 12–13; R. E. McNally, '"Christus" in the Hiberno-Latin "De ortu et obitu patriarcharum"', p. 179; *Der irische Liber de numeris*, ed. McNally, p. 146; Sedulius Scottus, *Collectaneum Miscellaneum* XVI.24, ed. Simpson, p. 135; *Corpus Iuris Hibernici*, ed. D. A. Binchy, 6 vols. (Dublin, 1978) VI, 2069, lines 24–9 (see the list of Latin citations in D. Ó Corráin, L. Breatnach and A. Breen, 'The Laws of the Irish', *Peritia* 3 (1984), 382–438, at 436); *Florilegium Frisingense*, in *Florilegia*, ed. Lehner, p. 34 (no. 414). Lehner (p. xxix) points out that the ultimate source of the formula is Gregory's *Moralia*: 'coelo excelsior, inferno profundior, terra longior, mari latior' (PL 75, 928). The Hiberno-Latin passages illustrate well the Irish tendency to extract, imitate and extend litanic sequences from patristic sources. An example in Old English occurs in Vercelli V (*Die Vercelli Homilien*, ed. Förster, p. 130, lines 220–3): 'for-þan-þe his miht is ufor þonne heofon ⁊ bradre þonne eorðe ⁊ deopre þonne sæ ⁊ leohtre þonne heofones tungel'. The context of the sequence in the Old English homily, where it is immediately preceded by a 'thought, word and deed' list, and followed by a variation of the 'joys of heaven' theme, suggests that the sequence was derived from an Irish source. For other parallels with Hiberno-Latin sources in Vercelli V, see above, pp. 80–1.

125 *Sedulius Scottus Kommentar*, ed. Löfstedt, p. 206, lines 25–8: 'This (prayer) reduces the swelling of pride, restrains also the furor of anger and envy, destroys the assault of the flesh and lust, directs the mind away from earthly things, kindles desire for the kingdom of heaven.' The passage is attributed by Sedulius to a 'sanctus Iustinus' (Dolbeau, CCCM 67, Supplementum, p. 15, points out that Sedulius in his *Collectaneum* also attributes to 'Iustinus' a passage on the Last Judgement). The portion quoted is closely paralleled in the *Catechesis Celtica*, in Vatican, Biblioteca Apostolica, Reg. lat. 49, 11v, where it is likewise applied to the Paternoster, but

gib e dogebud as a ... imnaidi
corup duan molta intoga ic Dia
dogein, oir scrisaig si na huile
pecud ocus glanaig si ... ibrigi na
colla ocus bathaig si toil in cuirp
d'a aindeoin ocus minig si in
truamdacht ocus ... si gach uile
dasacht ocus brisig si in ferg ocus
luathaigig si na haingil ithfirnd
ocus deluigid si na diabuil ocus
scrisaig si dorchodus na hindtind
ocus methaigid si in naimdacht
ocus comedaig si in tslainte ocus
crichnaidig si na deg-oiprigi ocus
lasaig si tene spirudalta isin croidi
.i. grad Dé ri grad daine ocus
do(ni) si sithchain etir in corp
ocus in t-anum.[126]

For sheer rhetorical extravagance the *Solomon and Saturn* poems must both yield to the prose *Pater Noster Dialogue*. The stylistic similarities between this fragmentary prose text and Vercelli IX, especially 'The Devil's Account', are so impressive that it is tempting to attribute them to a common author. The surviving portion of the dialogue falls into

certain phrases recur in a similar list elsewhere in the *Catechesis* (16r) applied to the virtue of patience. For the style, compare *Pseudo-Cyprianus de xii abusivis saeculi*, ed. Hellmann, pp. 40–1; Sedulius Scottus, *Collectaneum Miscellaneum* XIII.xxxii.1–3, ed. Simpson (pp. 110–11; cf. *Hib.* XII.3); XIII.xxxv.15 (p. 121; cf. *Hib.* XIII.2); XIII.xx.20 (p. 90); also *Hib.* XXXVIII.13b and the sequences *de sobrietate* and *de ebrietate* discussed above, pp. 65–6. A sequence in praise of Scripture, consisting of twenty-five phrases in the same form, occurs in Salisbury, Cathedral Library, 9, 78v, among material from the *Apocrypha Priscillianistica* (see above, n. 56).

126 *The Irish Liber Hymnorum*, ed. Bernard and Atkinson I, 193: 'Whoever should recite the hymnody, would be making a song of praise dear to God, for it wipes out all sins, and cleanses the powers of the body and subdues involuntarily the lusts of the flesh; it lessens melancholy, and (banishes) all madness; it breaks down anger, it expels hell's angels, and gets rid of the devils; it dispels the darkness of the understanding, and increases holiness; it preserves the health, and completes good works, and it lights up a spiritual fire in the heart, i.e. the love of God (in place of) the love of man, and it (promotes) peace between the body and the soul' (trans. Bernard and Atkinson II, 89). Note that the Latin and Irish, like the Old English, state that prayer 'kindles' spiritual desire.

two sections. It opens with an elaborate transformation combat between the Paternoster and the devil, scheduled to go thirty rounds, although the devil fails to answer the bell after the Paternoster's twenty-ninth and ultimate transformation 'on Dryhtnes onlicnesse'.[127] In the second section of the dialogue, Saturn asks a series of questions about the nature and appearance of the Paternoster, to which Solomon replies with the most fantastic descriptive passages in all of Old English literature.[128] The rhetorical structure of this text is remarkably close to that of Vercelli IX. As the homily begins with a series of enumerations 'concerning the likeness of death' ('be deaðes onlicnesse', line 25), including an enumeration of five 'likenesses' of hell, so too the *Pater Noster Dialogue* begins with an enumeration of the thirty 'likenesses' (*onlicnessa*) of the Paternoster and the devil. Even more striking are the stylistic parallels between the homily and Solomon's descriptions of the Paternoster in the second part of the dialogue. The two most distinctive rhetorical patterns of Vercelli IX, the elaborate adynata built upon sequences of *þeah* clauses and the reduplicating numerical *gradatio*, combined in the motif of the Men with Tongues of Iron, also characterize the prose *Pater Noster Dialogue*. In scarcely more than two pages in Menner's edition, there are some half-dozen elaborate examples of this rhetorical scheme, almost all based on the number twelve. Here is a sampling:

And his eagan sindon xii ðusendum siða beorhtran ðonne ealles middengeardes eorðe, ðeah ðe hio sie mid ðære beorhtestan lilian blostmum ofbræded, and æghwylc blostman leaf hæbbe xii sunnan, and æghwylc blostma hæbbe xii

[127] See T. D. Hill, 'The Devil's Forms and the Pater Noster's Powers: "The Prose Solomon and Saturn *Pater Noster* Dialogue" and the Motif of the Transformation Combat', *SP* 85 (1988), 164–76.

[128] The extravagant hyperboles used to describe the Paternoster's physical appearance and properties are sometimes reminiscent of descriptions of fantastic properties of heroes in Irish and Welsh literature. Compare, for example, the description of the Paternoster's gold and silver hair, a single lock of which would shelter the entire world from a downpour of all the waters of heaven and earth (*Poetical Dialogues*, ed. Menner, p. 169), with the description of Fergus's beard in the LL *Táin*, lines 2713–14: 'It would protect fifty warriors on a day of storm and rain if they were under the deep shelter of the warrior's beard' (*Táin Bó Cúailnge Recension I*, trans. O'Rahilly, p. 199).

monan, and æghwylc mona sie sinderlice xii ðusendum siða beorhtra ðonne he ieo wæs ær Abeles slege.[129]

Ond his geðoht he is spryngdra and swyftra ðonne xii ðusendu haligra gæsta, ðeah ðe anra gehwylc gæst hæbbe synderlice xii feðerhoman and anra gehwylc feðerhoma hæbbe xii windas and anra gehwylc wind twelf sigefæstnissa synderlice.[130]

Even the number twelve as the basis of the reduplicating series is paralleled in 'The Devil's Account', which states that Samson had twelve locks, with the strength of twelve men in each lock (where the Bible (Judges XVI.13) states that Samson had seven locks). The elaborate adynata of the dialogue, moreover, are very similar in tone to those in 'The Devil's Account'. With the hypothetical cosmic conflagration posited in the 'Iron House' passage in 'The Devil's Account', for example, compare the following from the *Pater Noster Dialogue*, where a similar conflagration is posited in combination with an inexpressibility topos reminiscent of the Men with Tongues of Iron:

[129] *Poetical Dialogues*, ed. Menner, p. 169: 'And his eyes are twelve thousand times brighter than the earth of all this world, even if it were covered with the blossoms of the brightest lilies, and each blossom's petal had twelve suns, and each blossom had twelve moons, and each moon individually were twelve thousand times brighter than it had been prior to Abel's murder.' The image of the primal brightness of the moon is a variation on a motif, based ultimately on Is. XXX.26 and common in Irish and Anglo-Saxon sources, that prior to the fall of Adam the sun was seven times brighter, and the moon was bright as the sun. The Hiberno-Latin *Liber de ordine creaturarum* was probably the source for the image in *Cáin Domnaig* (see Whitelock, 'Bishop Ecgred, Pehtred and Niall', p. 64) and in Belfour Homily XI and the *Old English Martyrology* (see J. E. Cross, '*De ordine creaturarum liber* in Old English Prose'; *idem*, 'The Influence of Irish Texts and Traditions', pp. 185–6). Cf. the description of the brightness of Christ's face in *Tenga Bithnua*: 'Such are the effulgence and splendour and light of His face that when the nine ranks of heaven shine forth, and every one of those angels is seven times more radiant than the sun, and the souls of the saints shine with the same likeness, and when the sun is brighter seven times than now, the effulgence of the face of the great King Who has made every element will shine beyond them all, so that the light of the Lord surpasseth angels and stars of heaven, and the souls of the saints, even as the light of the sun and his radiance surpass the other stars' ('The Evernew Tongue', trans. Stokes, p. 143). This passage is part of a long series of similar hyperboles.

[130] *Poetical Dialogues*, ed. Menner, p. 170: 'And his thought is more vigorous and swifter than twelve thousand holy spirits, even if each spirit individually had twelve wings and each wing had twelve winds and each wind individually had twelve victories.'

His heorte is xii ðusendum siða beorhtre ðonne ealle ðas seofon heofonas ðe us syndon ofergesette, ðeah ðe hie sien ealle mid ði domescan fyre onæled, and ðeah ðe eall ðeos eorðe him neoðan togegnes byrne, and heo hæbbe fyrene tungan and gyldene hracan and leohtne muð inneweardne, and ðeah ðe eall middangeard sie fram Adames frymðe edniowe gewurden and anra gehwelc hæbbe ða xii snyttro Habrahames and Isaces and Iacobes, and anra gehwylc mote lifigan ðreo hund wintra, ne magon hie ðære tungan gerecnesse ne hire mægnes swiðmodnisse aspyrian.[131]

Despite these stylistic similarities, the *Pater Noster Dialogue* is probably not, after all, by the same author, to judge simply from the difference in phrasing of the catchwords in the reduplicating formula (*þara æghwylc* in the homily versus *anra gehwylc* in the dialogue); but it is surely by a devotee of the same fantastic rhetorical tradition. Menner thought that the style of the *Pater Noster Dialogue* 'savor[s] strongly of Hebrew methods of description', and cited an example of the Men with Tongues of Iron theme from Napier XLIII as evidence that 'this technique found its way into the West'.[132] As I suggested in ch. 3, Rabbinic tradition may well have been an ultimate source, transmitted to the West by way of Christian apocrypha such as the *Visio S. Pauli* and the Seven Heavens, both of which circulated in the British Isles. But the two interpolated motifs from the *Visio S. Pauli* which incorporate the pattern both derive from the relatively late Latin redactions,[133] and the Latin version of the Seven Heavens apocryphon, which also uses the pattern, seems to have been transmitted through Irish channels. The

[131] *Ibid.*, p. 169: '[The Paternoster's] heart is twelve thousand times brighter than the seven heavens that are set over us, even if they were all kindled with the fire of Doomsday, and even if all this earth should burn up from beneath them and it had a fiery tongue and a golden throat and bright inner mouth, and even if the whole world from Adam's creation were renewed, and each man had twelve (times the) wisdom of Abraham and Isaac and Jacob, and each were allowed to live three hundred years, they could not discover the explanation of that tongue, nor the greatness of its might.'

[132] *Ibid.*, p. 8, n. 2. G. Cilluffo, 'Il dialogo in prosa Salomone e Saturno del ms. CCCC 422', *Annali Istituto Universitario Orientale, Napoli, Filologia germanica* 23 (1980), 121–46, at 133, compares a passage from II Baruch XXIX.5 (see above, p. 167, n. 210).

[133] Silverstein attributes the Men with Tongues of Iron and Dragon Parthemon interpolations to the archetypal Redaction α, which he dates to the tenth century (*Visio Sancti Pauli*, p. 60).

possibility of an Irish background for this rhetorical tradition must also be considered. The most concentrated use of the numerical *gradatio* in Irish is in the late-eleventh-century Leabhar Breac redaction of *Aislinge Meic Con Glinne*, which shows how easily the technique could degenerate into scholastic mannerism, and which also implies that it was sufficiently well established to be travestied. But the numerical *gradatio* occurs in Irish vernacular literature dating back as far as the eighth century (*Táin Bó Fraích*), and was probably a mnemonic technique of oral rhetoric. In Old English, on the other hand, the use of the numerical *gradatio* is an isolated phenomenon, without (so far as I am aware) stylistic precedent in native literary tradition, or indeed in Germanic tradition generally. Apart from Vercelli IX, the homily *Be heofonwarum ⁊ be helwarum*, the *Pater Noster Dialogue* and *Solomon and Saturn II*, it occurs in variations of the Men with Tongues of Iron and descriptions of the multi-headed Monster of Hell.[134] For these reasons it seems likely that the technique was transmitted to these Anglo-Saxon writers through Irish sources or Irish versions of apocryphal texts such as the Seven Heavens, and that its sudden and concentrated, but also isolated, appearance in these Old English texts is either a mannered and decadent imitation of an Irish rhetorical technique or a translation of Irish or Hiberno-Latin models. Such a hypothesis would be consistent with the evidence for Irish influence in the contents of Vercelli IX and 'The Devil's Account'.

There is more direct evidence for Irish influence in the *Pater Noster Dialogue*, moreover, in a previously overlooked Hibernicism in the vocabulary. The second sample of the dialogue quoted above, describing the exceeding vigour and swiftness of the Paternoster's thought, includes a piece of Hisperic diction which itself reflects the semantic influence of Old Irish. The twelve winds on the twelve wings of the twelve thousand spirits[135] are said each to have twelve 'victories'

[134] The only other example I can find occurs in Napier LVI, where it refers to the frequency of repeating the Paternoster! See *Wulfstan*, ed. Napier, p. 290, lines 17–19: 'and þu ahst to fyllene þine seofen tidsangas under dæg and niht, þæt is, to ælcan tidsange seofan pr̄ nr̄'.

[135] On the connection between the angels and the wind see the references in 'The Three "Victories" of the Wind', p. 21, n. 39, and add the following item from the Durham Ritual, in *Rituale Ecclesiae Dunelmensis*, ed. Lindelöf, p. 192: 'Dic mihi unde flauescat uentus. id est de seraphin inde dicitur seraphin uentorum', glossed in Old English as 'sæge me hvona geblawað wind þ[æt] is of seraphin of ðon is acvoeden seraphin windana'.

(*sigefæstnissa*). But why does the wind have 'victories'? This is a peculiar usage, even for a text in which peculiarity is the rule. But the phrase 'victories of the wind' has a very specific background traceable to an Irish-Latin learned tradition. Two texts considered Hiberno-Latin by most scholars enumerate three 'victories' or 'triumphs' of the wind. According to the section *De uento* in the A-text of the *Hisperica Famina*, the wind has three *trophea*:

> Trina mormoreus pastricat trophea not[h]us:
> quod spumaticum rapuit tol<l>o diluuium,
> pollentemque tonuit rapere dodrantem,
> ac corporeas perculit tactu effigies;
> nec sibilans intueri queat procella.
> Altusque poli rector
> mormorantibus degesti de pennis euri
> gibrosum reamine censebit lochum.[136]

A parallel for the faminator's list of the three 'triumphs' of the wind occurs in the *Collectanea Bedae*:

> Dic mihi tres uictorias uenti. Prima uictoria inflat, et non uidetur: secunda sanctificauit mundum post diluuium: tertia non comburetur in die iudicii.[137]

Both texts list three 'victories' of the wind, using the synonymous terms *trophea* and *uictoriae*, and both lists agree in essentials, though differing slightly in detail and sequence. The *Hisperica Famina* and the *Collectanea* clearly preserve two versions of the same learned tradition, combining scriptural testimony concerning the wind with elements from wind riddles, which commonly enumerate the marvellous properties and paradoxes associated with this natural force.

No doubt because the diction of the *Hisperica Famina* is consistently strained, no one ever seems to have asked why the wind should have

[136] *The Hisperica Famina I*, ed. Herren, p. 102, lines 489–96: 'The roaring wind has collected three triumphs: because it bore away the foamy deluge in a huge flood, was able to carry off the powerful tidal wave, and overthrew bodily forms with its effect. Nor can it be seen, even though it whistles. And the Ruler of the Universe on high out of the whirring wings of the aforesaid wind shall accuse the human throng of guilt' (trans. Herren, p. 103).

[137] PL 94, 542D: 'Tell me the three victories of the wind. The first victory that it blows, and is not seen; the second, that it sanctified the world after the Flood; the third, that it will not be burned on the Day of Judgement.' The list is here paired with an enumeration of three 'victories' of fire.

'triumphs'. The 'triumphs' of the wind are either its special or unique properties, as reflected in the riddle tradition (it can be heard, but not seen; it can pass through fire and not be burned), or, in the Christianized form of the riddle tradition in the *Hisperica Famina* and the *Collectanea*, the unique roles it is assigned in sacred history (it made the waters of the Flood subside; God will come to Judgement on its 'wings'). The sense required in the context of this riddle is reflected in an Old Icelandic version, which uses the term *afl* ('power', cognate with OE *afol*, *abal*).[138] The Latin words *uictoria* and *tropaeum* are clearly being used in a consistent but apparently unidiomatic sense. This usage, however, can be explained as reflecting the semantic influence of the Irish word *búaid*, for which the *Dictionary of the Irish Language* gives the following senses: '(a) *victory*, *triumph*'; '(b) *special quality* or *attribute*, *gift*, *virtue* ... *pre-eminence*, *excellence*; *prerogative*'.[139] Lists of *búada* – special qualities, virtues or prerogatives – are a recurrent feature of Irish literature. This '*búaid* tradition' has been discussed by Roland Smith, who draws attention to enumerations of *búada* in a variety of Irish texts,[140] including the *búada* of Cú Chulainn, variously numbered three, six, fifteen or twenty-five.[141] A ninth-century poem enumerates five *búada* of Cerball mac Muirecáin.[142] In a poem in *Lebor na Cert* the term *buadha* has technical force, denoting the prerogatives or 'lucky things' (Myles Dillon's rendering) of a king, which are enumerated at several points; another poem lists the *búada* ('prescriptions') of the kings of Ireland, as opposed to *urgarta* or *gessa* ('prohibitions' or 'taboos').[143] An example

[138] 'The Old Icelandic *Joca Monachorum*', ed. Marchand, p. 112: '"Seg mier fra þrimur auflum vinzins." "Fyrst er hann blæss, þad er eigi sem annar seigir, annat at hann hreinse af blæstri allan heimen, þridia att hann mun eigi blása á dooms deigi"' ('"Tell me of the three powers of the wind." "First, that it blows, it is not as others say; second, that it cleanses with its blast all the world; third, that it will not blow on Doomsday"'). Marchand notes the parallel in the *Collectanea*.

[139] See also J. Loth, 'Etymologies celtiques', *Société de Linguistique de Paris*, *Mémoires* 7 (1892), 157–60. A third sense is '(c) good, advantage, profit, benefit'.

[140] 'The Six Gifts'.

[141] For references, see Smith, *ibid.*, pp. 99–102. For other examples (all triads), cf. *Mesca Ulad*, ed. Watson, p. 11, lines 249–51; *Togail Bruidne Da Derga*, ed. Knott, p. 13, lines 439–40; and T. O'Donoghue, 'Advice to a Prince', *Ériu* 9 (1917), 43–54, at 46 (stanza 11).

[142] Cited by Smith, 'The Six Gifts', p. 100, n. 9.

[143] *Lebor na Cert: the Book of Rights*, ed. M. Dillon, ITS 46 (Dublin, 1962), 140–3; at another point in the text (pp. 118–19) *búaid* refers to 'supremacy' in various

from a Christian context is the Leabhar Breac homily on St Michael, which enumerates the archangel's five *búada*, including the roles he will play at the Last Judgement.[144] *The Triads of Ireland*[145] include several enumerations of *búada*, including the three *búada* of a householder (73) and of a gathering (88 and 175), but also of a thing (182, the three *búada* of dress) or of an act (177, the three *búada* of speech). A prayer attributed to Mael Ísu Ua Brolacháin beseeches God to endow the poet with four *búadha* ('qualities', in the specific sense 'virtues').[146] The motif in the *Hisperica Famina* and *Collectanea*, then, probably reflects a vernacular Irish triad that enumerated the *búada* of the wind and drew on popular riddle tradition, but was tricked up in Latin dress with scriptural allusions, glossary words and a learned reference to *phisici*.

In the *Pater Noster Dialogue* the twelve 'victories' of the wind are not specified, but the expression can hardly be dissociated from this Hisperic usage, and its occurrence here provides strong grounds for assuming that the prose *Pater Noster Dialogue* has drawn on Hiberno-Latin sources, or is based on an Irish or Hiberno-Latin original. An Irish background is also suggested by certain other Irish 'symptoms', including a reference to the seven heavens and the naming of the archangels Uriel and Rumiel and of the devil Sathiel.[147]

qualities, a rendering which nicely captures the underlying connection between the two chief senses of the word. For the second poem, see Dillon, 'The Taboos of the Kings of Ireland', *PRIA* 54C (1951), 1–36 (cf. p. 4).

144 *The Passions and the Homilies*, ed. and trans. Atkinson, pp. 216 and 453.

145 *The Triads of Ireland*, ed. Meyer. The following references are to the numbers of the triads in Meyer's edition.

146 The poem is ed. K. Meyer, *Archiv für celtische Lexikographie* 3 (1907), 230–1; the first stanza is trans. D. Ó Laoghaire, 'Irish Spirituality', in *Irland und Europa*, ed. Ní Chatháin and Richter, pp. 73–82, at 74.

147 On invocation of the archangels in Irish and Anglo-Saxon sources, see E. Kitzinger, 'The Coffin-Reliquary', in *The Relics of Saint Cuthbert*, ed. C. F. Battiscombe (Oxford, 1956), pp. 202–304, at 274–7, who points out that 'the name Rumiel has its parallels in Irish texts or texts under Irish influence'; M. R. James, 'Names of Angels'; and Sims-Williams, *Religion and Literature*, p. 286 (with further references at n. 57), who notes that the name Rumiel appears in one non-Insular liturgical source. The name Sathiel is presumably related to Satanael, on which see Wright, 'Apocryphal Lore', p. 138. An Irish gloss in the Southampton Psalter (*BCLL*, no. 509; Wright, 'Hiberno-Latin', no. 13) identifies the *draco* of Ps. LXXIII.14 as *sathel* (*Thesaurus Palaeohibernicus*, ed. Stokes and Strachan I, 5; the editors refer to the *Pater Noster Dialogue*, from Kemble's edition). In the Durham Ritual (*Rituale Ecclesiae Dunelmensis*, ed. Lindelöf, p. 198) occurs the gloss 'Raguel id est fortis id est satahel.'

Like Vercelli IX, then, these three Old English *Solomon and Saturn* texts show significant signs of influence from Irish sources, and their relationship to the homily, suggested by a similar collocation of the names of Solomon and Saturn, is confirmed by stylistic evidence. Most closely related to Vercelli IX is the prose *Pater Noster Dialogue*, which employs the same mannered numerical *gradatio* that characterizes 'The Devil's Account'. The *Pater Noster Dialogue* is itself closely related to *Solomon and Saturn I* in its treatment of the Paternoster. *Solomon and Saturn II*, as Menner perceived, differs in significant ways from the other poem; but it is essentially similar in genre and style, and it has one striking stylistic parallel with Vercelli IX, again a variation of the reduplicating numerical *gradatio*, in a formulation similar to that of the Men with Tongues of Iron.

A few other Old English texts may also be related to this Irish-influenced milieu, but the evidence is slighter and the following suggestions must be regarded as tentative. The Old English *Soul and Body* poem, surviving in two versions,[148] has certain affinities with the *Solomon and Saturn* poems. The occasionally mannered style and grotesque descriptive passages of *Soul and Body* are only superficially similar to the *Solomon and Saturn* poems. The soul's lurid description of the havoc wreaked by Gifer the worm and his fellows on the helpless body, for example, vaguely resembles the description of the savaging of the devil by the letters of the Paternoster in *Solomon and Saturn I*. One line in *Soul and Body*, however, *feldgongende feoh butan snyttro*,[149] is closely paralleled in *Solomon and Saturn I*, *feldgongende feoh butan gewitte* (B23; cf. 154, *feldgongende feoh*). One cannot grant too much significance to such verbal parallels in a formulaic poetic tradition; but it is hard to imagine that a phrase of such restricted application as 'field-roaming beast without sense' ever had wide currency. A more complex and compelling parallel between *Soul and Body* and *Solomon and Saturn II* involves a

148 *The Old English Soul and Body*, ed. Moffat; also in *The Vercelli Book*, ed. Krapp, pp. 54–9 (*Soul and Body I*), and *The Exeter Book*, ed. Krapp and Dobbie, pp. 174–8 (*Soul and Body II*).

149 *The Old English Soul and Body*, ed. Moffat, p. 56, line 80 (citations are to the Exeter Book text, unless otherwise noted). Three lines later occurs the phrase *wyrmcynna þæt wyrreste*, which is paralleled in the separate version of 'The Devil's Account' in M and in one of Ælfric's Lives of Saints (see Scragg, '"The Devil's Account of the Next World" Revisited', p. 109).

numerical hyperbole which occurs in similar rhetorical contexts. In *Soul and Body*, the soul expresses how greatly it wished to be released with the hyperbolic remark that 'it seemed to me very often that it would be thirty thousand winters to your deathday':

þ(æ)t me þuhte ful oft
þæt wære þritig þusend wintra
to þinum deaðdæge.[150]

In *Solomon and Saturn II*, the bird *Vasa Mortis* yearns so greatly for release from captivity that 'it seems to him that it would be thrice thirty thousand winters before he might hear the din of Doomsday' ('ðynceð him ðæt sie ðria ðritig ðusend wintra ær he domdæges dynn gehyre', lines 263–4). The preference for such multiples of three for hyperbolic intervals of time occurs elsewhere in *Soul and Body* (the soul returns to its body every seven days for 'three hundred years', unless Doomsday intervenes) and in *Solomon and Saturn II* (Saturn uses the number 'thrice thirteen thousand' to express how many times *yldo* devours the years of all living creatures). In the prose *Pater Noster Dialogue* multiples of thirty occur in various contexts, in occasional relief from the general mania for the number twelve; one adynaton states that all the men of the world could not describe the greatness of the Paternoster, even if each one could live for three hundred years.[151]

The few specific indications of Irish influence in *Soul and Body* involve particularly vivid eschatological conceptions and expressions. Thomas D. Hill has noted two analogues from Irish penitential sources, including the 'Table of Commutations', for the peculiar notion that punishment at Doomsday will be meted out according to each individual joint of the body (lines 90–3a).[152] Again, the soul's comparison of the body to the 'black raven' (51b) may reflect the influence of Irish soul-

150 *The Old English Soul and Body*, ed. and trans. Moffat, p. 52, lines 35b–37a.

151 Quoted above, p. 251. In Irish literature the most favoured and distinctive number in hyperbolic expressions is 'thrice fifty', but multiples of thirty, including three hundred and thirty thousand, are often used (as in the Irish poem on death cited above, p. 94, n. 199). Puhvel, *Beowulf and Celtic Tradition*, p. 3, n. 11, citing C. W. von Sydow, notes the popularity of the number thirty in Irish literature in connection with *Beowulf*, where thirty is also used as a conventional round number.

152 T. D. Hill, 'Punishment According to the Joints of the Body in the Old English *Soul and Body*', *NQ* 213 (1968), 409–10; *idem*, 'Punishment According to the Joints of the Body, Again', *NQ* 214 (1969), 246.

and-body literature, such as the Three Utterances sermon, which frequently employs the same comparison, although it is usually the wicked *soul* that is thus described.[153] That the soul must return to its body every seven days has generally been regarded as a fusion of two separate traditions emanating from the *Visio S. Pauli*, the visit of the soul to the body and the Sunday respite.[154] The notion of a weekly Sunday return of the soul to its body occurs in an enumerative theme found in a manuscript with Celtic connections, Cambridge, Corpus Christi College 279 (Tours region, s. ix^2; provenance Worcester), pp. 186–7:

Quatuor modis anima uniuscuiusque uisitat post mortem: locum a quo [...] corpore, et locum sepulturae, et locum ubi in corpore uenerat, et locum baptismi. Dominico omni die sepulchrum uisitat sciens quod in dominico die resurget; tedium erga illum quia in eodem caro iterum adsummet illud. Locum baptismi ubi naturam humanam deposuit et spiritalem regenerationem suscipit.[155]

Of the four places the soul visits, it returns to the grave 'every Sunday' (*Dominico omni die*), where it feels (and presumably expresses) loathing (*tedium*) towards the body. The enumeration of the four places visited by the soul circulated in Ireland, for it appears in the vernacular in 'Adomnán's Second Vision':

Ar tecait a n-anmanda sein beos co a n-adnaicthib. Ar is e sin in cetramud inad

[153] See Wack and Wright, 'A New Latin Source', p. 191.

[154] See Healey, *The Old English Vision*, p. 46.

[155] 'The soul of each person visits in four ways after death: it visits the place from which [it exited?] the body, and the place of burial, and the place where it came into the body, and the place of baptism. Every Sunday it visits the grave, knowing that it will rise on a Sunday; there is loathing as regards that place, because in that very same place the flesh shall take that unto itself (?). (And it visits) the place of baptism where it put off human nature and received spiritual regeneration.' On the manuscript, see R. Sharpe, 'Gildas as a Father of the Church', in *Gildas: New Approaches*, ed. Lapidge and Dumville, pp. 193–205. As Sharpe notes, this part of the manuscript (pp. 162–87, which he calls C^2) is a collection of penitential excerpts mostly deriving from the *Collectio Canonum Hibernensis* (see his table of correspondences, pp. 202–5; see also Reynolds, 'Unity and Diversity', p. 105). A fragment of this theme occurs in a marginal note in the Leabhar Breac, in *The Irish Liber Hymnorum*, ed. Bernard and Atkinson I, 61: 'anima uniuscuiusque testat post mortem locum ... erat sic sepulturae et ... uenerat in mundum et locum babtismi'.

torramus in animm iar scarad fria a corp .i. loc a gene 7 loc a báis, loc a baisti 7 loc a hadnaicthi 'na húir mainche dílis. Tic didiu in Coimdiu co .ix. ngradu nime in cech domnach do thabairt bennachtan forsin ndoman 7 forsna heclasib noemu 7 for cech n-oen bís hi sobés inntib.[156]

The body-and-soul theme was richly developed in Ireland, as in England. The Leabhar Breac contains a body-and-soul debate in Irish, with some citation of its lost Latin source.[157] The related theme of the going-out of souls is dramatized in the Hiberno-Latin Three Utterances sermon and in other Irish sources. This is not to suggest that all body-and-soul literature in Old English is dependent on Irish models; body-and-soul themes were transmitted from east to west through various channels, and there are important differences between the surviving Irish and Old English body-and-soul texts. The Leabhar Breac body-and-soul homily, for example, like most Irish examples of the theme, differs significantly in form from the Old English poem in recording a reply of the body. But in the case of the related theme of the going-out of souls in the Three Utterances, for example, the Old English versions were based upon Hiberno-Latin models and, as I have noted, another Old English body-and-soul homily in Junius 85/86 borrowed from a Hiberno-Latin source a passage contrasting the teachings of God and of the devil as a transition between the speeches of the good and bad souls. Irish influence on *Soul and Body* would be consistent with these

[156] 'Adamnán's Second Vision', ed. W. Stokes, *RC* 12 (1891), 420–43, at 425: 'For their souls still come to their burial-places. For that is the fourth place which the soul visits after parting from the body, to wit, the place of its birth, the place of its death, the place of its baptism, and the place of its burial in its own conventual (?) mould. Every Sunday, too, the Lord comes with the nine ranks of heaven to give a blessing to the world, and to the holy churches, and to every one therein who leads a holy life' (trans. Stokes, p. 426). The text is dated '*c*. 1100' by Lapidge and Sharpe, *BCLL*, no. 351. The tetrad looks like a Christian expansion of a popular Irish triad, the 'three sods' of birth, death and burial, on which see Carney, 'Old Ireland and Her Poetry', in *Old Ireland*, ed. McNally, pp. 147–72, at 151–4; M. Carney, '*Fót báis Banaþúfa*', *Arv: Journal of Scandinavian Folklore* 13 (1957), 173–9; A. Holtsmark, 'Fód Báis – Banaþúfa – Heillaþúfa', *Lochlann: a Review of Celtic Studies* 2 (1962), 122–7.

[157] *The Passions and the Homilies*, ed. and trans. Atkinson, pp. 266–73 and 507–14. See H. Gaidoz, 'Le débat du corps et de l'âme en Irlande', *RC* 10 (1889), 463–70; McNamara, *The Apocrypha in the Irish Church*, pp. 109–13 (nos. 91E–F); Seymour, 'The Bringing Forth of the Soul in Irish Literature'.

indications of Irish influence on specific developments of the body-and-soul theme in Anglo-Saxon England.

Another Old English body-and-soul text, Vercelli Homily IV, probably did draw on Irish sources and, like *Soul and Body*, it has verbal and contextual parallels with *Solomon and Saturn II* close enough to suggest use of some common sources, if not a more direct literary relationship. A common source or closely similar sources must have been used by both Vercelli IV and *Solomon and Saturn II* for descriptions of the guardian angel and contending demon:

Solomon and Saturn II:
Ðonne hine ymbegangað *gastas twegen*:
oðer bið golde glædra, oðer bið grundum sweartra;
oðer cymeð . . . .
. . . . *ofer ðære stylenan helle*;
oðer him læreð ðæt he lufan healde
Metodes miltse and his mæga ræd;
oðer hine tyhteð and on tæso læreð,
yweð him and yppeð earmra manna misgemynda ...[158]

Vercelli IV:
Ælce dæge [we] hæbbað *twegen hyrdas*: *oðer cymð* ufan of heofonum, þe us sceall gode bysene on-stellan 7 us gode þeawas tæcan, 7 hæfð him on handa þa scyldas, þe ic ær nemde, 7 þæt sweord, 7 wyle us forstandan æt þam awyrgdan diofle, þe *of þære stylenan helle* cymð mid his scearpum strælum us mid to scotianne.[159]

Menner pointed to a passage in the Shepherd of Hermas as a possible ultimate source for the conception of the two contending spirits, but did not pursue the question further or address the problem of transmission to Anglo-Saxon England.[160] A long version of the *Visio S. Pauli* was

[158] *Poetical Dialogues*, ed. Menner, p. 103, lines 477–88: 'Then two spirits accompany him: one is brighter than gold, the other is blacker than the abyss; one comes ... beyond steel-hard hell; one instructs him that he keep with love the mercy of the Lord and the counsel of his kinsmen; the other seduces him and urges him to ruin, shows and reveals to him the evil thoughts of wretched men'.

[159] *Die Vercelli-Homilien*, ed. Förster, p. 106, lines 371–6: 'Each day we have two guardians: one comes from above from heaven, who is to set a good example for us and teach us good virtues, and he has in his hand the shields which I mentioned earlier and the sword, and he wishes to defend us against the accursed devil, who comes from steel-hard hell with his sharp arrows for shooting us with.'

[160] Menner, *Poetical Dialogues*, p. 143. See now Sims-Williams, *Religion and Literature*, p. 268. For some additional evidence, see my entry on the Shepherd of Hermas in

another source, which supplied the detail that the angels report the deeds of men to God each day at sunrise and sunset, as reported in both *Solomon and Saturn II* and Napier XLVI (and possibly reflected in the phrase 'Ælce dæge' in the abbreviated report in Vercelli IV).[161] Since the Napier homily identifies Gregory as its authority, we may surmise that a Latin pseudo-Gregorian homily which drew on both the Hermas-tradition and a long version of the *Visio S. Pauli* lies behind the passages in *Solomon and Saturn II* and Vercelli IV. Menner thought the distinctive phrase *stylenan helle*, which occurs in both texts in precisely the same context, sufficient to suggest 'a relation between the poem and the homily, both perhaps going back to the same source'.[162]

Vercelli IV also has affinities with both *Solomon and Saturn II* and *Soul and Body*. As Moffat has pointed out, one line in the latter poem, 'ond ic wæs gæst on þe from gode sended', is paralleled in Vercelli IV, 'Ic wæs gast fram Gode on þe sended.'[163] The similar numerical hyperboles that link the two poems also find looser parallels in Vercelli IV, in which the damned soul tells the body that it so eagerly yearned for the body's death that it seemed to the soul that they were together forever: 'ac á me þuhte, þæt wyt wæron to lange æt-gædere'.[164] Later, addressing Death, the soul says that the body lived so long, that it seemed Death had forgotten him: 'swa me þuhte, þæt he moste á lybban 7 næfre deaðes byrgean ... for-neah he moste lifian oð domesdæg'.[165] Although in the homily the soul exaggerates its perception of their time together with the words 'forever' or 'until Doomsday', instead of using a large conventional number as in *Soul and Body* ('it seemed to me ... thirty thousand winters to your deathday'), the hyperbole is generally similar, and it occurs in a similar context, so that one must again reckon with the possibility of a common source or common tradition.

Sources of Anglo-Saxon Literary Culture, ed. Biggs *et al.*, pp. 63–5. I hope to discuss in greater detail elsewhere the sources for these and other passages concerning the two contending spirits in Old English literature, including *Guthlac A* and Napier Homily XLVI.

161 *Apocrypha Anecdota*, ed. James, p. 13, lines 19–34; cf. *Regula Magistri*, ed. A. de Vogüé, *La Règle du Maître*, 3 vols. (Paris, 1964) II, 188.

162 *Poetical Dialogues*, p. 143.

163 *The Old English Soul and Body*, ed. Moffat, p. 52, line 46; *Die Vercelli-Homilien*, ed. Förster, pp. 92–3, lines 225–6: 'I was a soul sent into you from God'.

164 *Ibid.*, p. 94, line 238.

165 *Ibid.*, pp. 95–6, lines 259–60.

A variant text of Vercelli IV occurs in Cambridge, Corpus Christi College 41, among the marginal entries which include a fragment of *Solomon and Saturn I*. Stylistically, Vercelli IV, like *Solomon and Saturn I*, is marked by a litanic style. The homily begins with a lengthy series of antitheses in the form 'Her... ac þær...', with eighteen contrasting pairs, and a similar pattern dominates a later portion of the homily as well. Commenting on another passage in which the soul defines its relation to the body in a sequence of twenty-five parallel terms, Max Förster remarked that 'Eine solche Häufung von Parallelbegriffen ... ist typisch für die liturgische Sprache der Iren. Sollte die lateinische Vorlage unserer Homilie von einem Iren herrühren?'[166] An Irish source probably is indicated by the style, although the Irish *Vorlage* would itself have been a compilation with sources of its own.[167] Another rhetorical sequence, enumerating the virtues of God in similar form, may be

[166] *Ibid.*, p. 99, n. 158.

[167] A homily of Ephrem the Syrian, for example, may have provided the ultimate model for the opening series of antitheses. Cf. the passage from Ephrem's *De Patientia*, trans. T. S. Pattie, 'Ephraem the Syrian and the Latin Manuscripts of "De Patientia"', *British Library Journal* 13 (1987), 1–24, at 19, lines 141–55. On the same stylistic grounds one may suspect a Hiberno-Latin liturgical source for another Old English homily in Cambridge, Corpus Christi College 41, *In laudem Sancti Michaelis* (*Three Homilies*, ed. Grant, pp. 56–64), which employs an extended litanic sequence of twenty-five short paragraphs enumerating Michael's roles in salvation history, each beginning 'Đis is se halga heahengel Sanctus Michael ... ' Grant, who drew attention to Irish influence in other marginalia in CCCC 41, suspected Irish influence on this homily on the basis of its apocryphal content and stylistic extravagance. There is a similar though briefer sequence in praise of Michael in Irish, with a sequence of eleven sentences each beginning 'Is é Michel', in the Liber Flauus Fergusiorum, where it is copied twice (Dublin, Royal Irish Academy 23. O. 48, pt II, 1va, margin, and 34vb). Unfortunately, both copies are barely legible, but the sequence includes references to Michael's Old Testament roles as guide of Abraham, Isaac and Jacob, and protector of the Israelites during the plagues of Egypt and during their forty-year sojourn in the desert, as well as to his roles at the Resurrection and Judgement, corresponding generally to the Old English homily, sections 5–8 and 26. See also *The Poems of Blathmac*, ed. Carney, p. 88. It is likely that both the Irish and the Old English Michael texts depend on a common (Hiberno-Latin?) source, which developed phrases in praise of Michael such as those found in the pseudo-Gregorian *Liber responsalis siue Antiphonarius* (PL 78, 725–850, at 805–6; see J. E. Cross, 'An Unpublished Story of Michael the Archangel and its Connections', in *Magister Regis: Studies in Honor of Robert Earl Kaske*, ed. A. Groos (New York, 1986), pp. 23–35, at 26).

compared to the enumerations of the virtues of the Paternoster in *Solomon and Saturn I*:

Vercelli IV:	*Solomon and Saturn I*:
Þu eart hiht heofendra	He bið sefan snytero
7 þu eart eallre worulde Hælend.	and sawle hunig
7 þu eart geswencendra manna	and modes meolc …
rest;	Lamana he is læce,
7 þu eart blindra manna leoht	leoht winciendra,
7 dumra gesprec	swilce he his deafra duru,
7 deafra gehyrnes	deadra tunge,
7 hreofra clænsung	scildigra scild,
7 healtra gang.	Scippendes seld,
7 eallre biternesse þu eart se	flodes feriend,
sweta swæc.	folces neriend,
7 ealle ge-unrette magon on þe	yþa yrfeweard,
geblissian.	earma fixa,
7 þu eart ealra worca wyrhta	wyrma wlenco,
7 ealra wæstma fruma 7 eallra	wildeora holt,
þystra onlihting.	westenes weard,
Ðu eart se æðela wylle.[168]	weorðmynta geard.[169]

As Patrick Sims-Williams has pointed out, 'the enumeration of the attributes of God or Christ is common in Christian literature', particularly in Gallican liturgy and Insular private prayers.[170] The sequence of epithets with nominative singular nouns and dependent genitive plurals occurs, for example, in Anglo-Saxon prayer books.[171]

168 *Die Vercelli-Homilien*, ed. Förster, p. 89, lines 195–202: 'You are the hope of the mournful and you are the Saviour of all the world. And you are the rest of toiling men; and you are the light of blind men and the speech of the mute and the hearing of the deaf and the cleansing of the leprous and the steps of the lame. And you are the sweet odour of all bitterness. And all unhappy men can rejoice in you. And you are the builder of all works and the origin of all abundance and the illumination of all darkness. You are the noble fountain.'

169 *Poetical Dialogues*, ed. Menner, lines B66–7 and 77–83; trans. above, n. 112.

170 *Religion and Literature*, p. 317.

171 See the examples quoted by Sims-Williams, *ibid.*, pp. 313–16. Cf. also an abecedarian litany ed. N. K. Rasmussen, 'An Early "Ordo Missae" with a "Litania Abecedaria" Addressed to Christ', *Ephemerides Liturgicae* 98 (1984), 198–211, at 200; for Irish symptoms in this *Ordo*, see pp. 209–11.

The sequence in Vercelli IV is specifically modelled on prayers and collects beginning 'Tu es ... ', a formula characteristically extended in Irish books so that 'a long row of titles can follow each other without any recognizable connection of thought'.[172] Sims-Williams notes two examples of such prayers from the Book of Cerne, one of which is thought to be Irish.[173]

In addition to its affinities with Irish liturgical style, there are points of contact between Vercelli IV and other Old English homilies based on Irish eschatological traditions. In the homilist's description of the going-out of the good soul, the angel's blessing of the soul after it has been brought before God, translating Psalm LXIV.5–6, closely echoes the Three Utterances sermon, in which the angels chant the same psalm verses to the blessed soul when it is brought out of the body:

Vercelli IV:	Junius 85/86:	Munich, Clm. 28135:
þonne onfoð þa	Ond þanne syngað	Et sancti angeli
englas þære sawle ⁊	þa halgan ænglas	cantabunt canticum
hire to cweðað:	swiðe gastlingne [*sic*]	spiritalem ... dicentes
'Eadigu eart þu,	sang ... ond hie	ad animam, 'Beatus
sawl; forðan þu	cweðað to ðære	quem elegisti domine
name on þe góde	sawle: 'Beatus quem	et adsumpsisti,
eardunge in þinum	elegisti; replebimur.'	inhabitauit in
huse. ⁊ ic geseah	Hie cweðað: 'Eadig	tabernaculis tuis.
gearwian þin hus on	eart þu sawl, ðu	Replebimur in bonis
ðam halgan heofona-	name gode eardunge	domus tuae; sanctum
rices wuldre. ⁊ we þe	in þinum huse. One	est templum tuum,
lædað to ðam-þe þu	we nu gefyllað mid	mirabile in
ær lufodest.'[174]		aequitate.'[176]

[172] M. Curran, *The Antiphonary of Bangor and the Early Irish Monastic Liturgy* (Dublin, 1984), p. 104; cited by Sims-Williams, *Religion and Literature*, p. 317.

[173] *Ibid.* See *The Book of Cerne*, ed. Kuypers, pp. 95–6, and Hughes, 'Some Aspects of Irish Influence', p. 56.

[174] *Die Vercelli-Homilien*, ed. Förster, p. 84, lines 134–8: 'Then the angels will receive the soul and say to it: "Blessed are you, soul, because you took up for yourself a good dwelling in your house. And I have seen your house prepared in the glory of the holy kingdom of heaven. And we shall lead you to what you formerly desired.'

gode ðin hus, ðin
templ his halig ond
wundorlicre
ðrymnesse.'[175]

At the Last Judgement, the three companies of men, angels and devils are present:

Eala, men þa leofestan, hu us is to ondrædanne, þæt we stælan sculon on domesdæge beforan ealles middangeardes deman 7 beforan eallum mennicum cynne; 7 eall helle-mægen þis gestal ge-hyrað. 7 eal engla werod 7 heah-engla beoð þy [ge]mete beforan Gode.[177]

Finally, a connection with the Seven Heavens tradition in Vercelli IV is Christ's reception of the good soul 'in þone heofon þære halgan þrynesse', a term applied to the seventh heaven in Irish lists, in the Old English version of the Seven Heavens apocryphon, and in the Easter homily edited by Lees, which has a variety of Irish symptoms.[178]

Irish influences in Old English Christian literature could have been transmitted in various ways and at different times and places, so that if the presence of Irish symptoms or the use of Irish sources broadly distinguishes the Old English texts I have discussed, these characteristics alone do not necessarily constitute them as a self-conscious 'school' or historically related literary milieu. Yet Vercelli IX was certainly among the sources of the archetype of the Niall sermons, and stylistic evidence strongly suggests that Vercelli IX and the prose *Pater*

[175] *Two Apocrypha*, ed. Willard, p. 55: 'And then the holy angels will sing a very spiritual song ... and they will say to the soul, "Beatus quem elegisti; replebimur." They say: "Blessed are you, soul, you took up a good dwelling in your house. And we shall now fill your house with goodness, your temple is holy and in marvelous glory.' This parallel was pointed out by Willard, 'The Address of the Soul to the Body', p. 980, n. 77.

[176] Ed. Wack and Wright, 'A New Latin Source', p. 190: 'And the holy angels will sing a spiritual song ... saying to the soul, "Blessed is he whom thou hast chosen and taken to thee: he will dwell in thy courts. We shall be filled with the good things of thy house; holy is thy temple, wonderful in justice."'

[177] *Die Vercelli-Homilien*, ed. Förster, pp. 82–3, lines 107–11: 'Alas, dearest men, how we ought to fear that we must confess on Doomsday before the Judge of all earth and before all mankind; and all the troop of hell will hear this confession. And all the company of angels and archangels will be in that fitting manner before God.' On the theme of the three companies, see above, pp. 85–8.

[178] Above, p. 228.

Noster Dialogue should be attributed to a common workshop. If so, is it possible to be more precise about their historical setting?

Paul Szarmach, in summarizing the conclusions of D. G. Scragg's unpublished dissertation, lists Vercelli IX as 'demonstrably Anglian; probably tenth-century Mercian rather than ninth-century Anglian through an early West Saxon transcription'.[179] Scragg has stated more recently that the homilies VI–X (his group B2a) 'have clear evidence of Anglian origin', and has suggested that 'the exemplar of group B2a was a collection of Anglian homilies assembled in the south-east' in the third quarter of the tenth century.[180] Franz Wenisch, who supports an Anglian origin for Vercelli IX on lexical grounds,[181] also posits an Anglian origin for the *Prose Solomon and Saturn Pater Noster Dialogue*,[182] *Solomon and Saturn I* and *II*, and *Soul and Body I* and *II*.[183] The *Pater Noster Dialogue* and *Solomon and Saturn I* both date probably from the late ninth or early tenth century; both share the late Latin loanword *cantic*, and Menner thinks that Poem I was probably composed later than Poem II.[184] The dialect of Bazire and Cross Homily 4 has not been analysed, but Wenisch considers Vercelli IV to be a copy of a Mercian original, dating at the latest to the first half of the tenth century;[185] and he also classifies as probably Anglian the three Old English versions of the Three Utterances sermon,[186] as well as the Niall versions of the Sunday letter sermon (Napier XLIII and XLIV).[187] The dates of these homilies are uncertain, but Janet M. Bately has recently suggested that many supposedly 'early' Mercian prose texts are likely to be early tenth

179 Szarmach, *Vercelli Homilies*, p. xxii, summarizing Scragg, 'The Language of the Vercelli Homilies' (unpubl. DPhil dissertation, Manchester Univ., 1970).

180 'The Compilation of the *Vercelli Book*', *ASE* 2 (1973), 189–207, at 201.

181 *Spezifisch anglisches Wortgut*, pp. 196–7 and 327.

182 *Ibid.*, pp. 163 (and n. 461), 220, 294 and 327.

183 *Ibid.*, p. 328.

184 See Menner, *Poetical Dialogues*, pp. 13–17. Menner tentatively posits 'an Early West Saxon copy of the late ninth century, or at least very early tenth century' for the poems (p. 17), based on an Anglian original of the ninth century, possibly from Western Mercia.

185 Wenisch, *Spezifisch anglisches Wortgut*, pp. 74 and 327. Vercelli XIX (= Bazire and Cross no. 1), whose Irish symptoms I have noted above, p. 228, is considered late West Saxon by Scragg; Wenisch classifies it as probably Anglian (*ibid.*, pp. 210, n. 823, and 327).

186 *Ibid.*, pp. 197–8 and 327.

187 *Ibid.*, pp. 117, 197, 299 and n. 155, and 327.

century rather than late ninth or earlier,[188] and Mary Clayton has reminded us that 'we have no unambiguous proof that the anonymous works do belong to the pre-reform period, rather than to a date closer to the dates of the compilations of the manuscripts in which they are found'.[189]

Vercelli IX, the *Pater Noster Dialogue* and *Solomon and Saturn I*, therefore, as well as Vercelli IV and the Three Utterances and Niall homilies, can all reasonably (though still conjecturally) be placed in Mercia, between the last quarter of the ninth century and the first three-quarters of the tenth. This is still a large expanse of time and space, and further delimitation will require progress in linguistic and stylistic analysis as well as in source studies. The use of Irish sources and models would have been possible at any time during this period. We know that the scholars at King Alfred's court included Irishmen, and that Alfred received three Irishmen who arrived in England on a pilgrimage for the love of God. The same entry in the *Anglo-Saxon Chronicle* which records this event also notes the death of *Swifneh* (Suibne mac Maele Umai, anchorite of Clonmacnois), 'the greatest teacher among the Irish'.[190] Alfred also drew heavily on Mercian scholars in his efforts to advance English learning. In the tenth century there is abundant evidence of continuing contacts with the Irish, particularly during the reign of Athelstan (924–39). The Irish manuscript known as the Mac Durnan

188 'Old English Prose before and during the Reign of Alfred', *ASE* 17 (1988), 93–138, at 114. Bately takes up the dating of the two Niall homilies on the basis of their use of the terms *Sceotlande* and *Scotta ealonde* for Ireland (a usage shared by the St Chad homily), concluding that the terminology indicates 'either that in the dialect of their authors the use of *Scotland* for *Hibernia* persisted longer than in that of the author(s) of the annals for the last years of Edward the Elder, 912–20, or that these works were composed before the second quarter of the tenth century' (p. 118). Whitelock, 'Bishop Ecgred, Pehtred and Niall', p. 51, believed the definition of Sunday in these homilies indicated a date after 962, but Bately thinks the archetype of the Niall material could possibly be late ninth century (see p. 114, n. 126).

189 *The Cult of the Virgin Mary*, p. 263.

190 *Two of the Saxon Chronicles Parallel*, ed. C. Plummer, 2 vols. (Oxford, 1982) I, 82 (s.a. 891); trans. Keynes and Lapidge, *Alfred the Great*, pp. 113–14. Chadwick, 'The Celtic Background of Early Anglo-Saxon England', p. 347, points out that the spelling of the name indicates an oral source, which, of course, might have been the three Irish pilgrims themselves, as Keynes and Lapidge suggest (*Alfred the Great*, p. 283, n. 14). For Alfred's grants to churches in Ireland, see Asser's Life, *ibid.*, p. 107, and cf. pp. 91 and 101 for other references to contacts with Ireland.

Gospels (London, Lambeth Palace Library, 1370; Armagh, s. ix^2), given by Athelstan to Canterbury, contains an inscription linking the book with Mael Brigte mac Tornáin (d. 927), described in an Irish annal as 'head of the piety of all Ireland and of the greater part of Europe'.[191] Simon Keynes has suggested that although the manuscript could have been brought to England during the reign of Alfred, 'if the juxtaposition of Mael Brigte and Athelstan in the inscription implies a direct link between them it is perhaps more likely that the manuscript was given to Athelstan by Mael Brigte himself... or that it was given to Athelstan in Mael Brigte's memory after his death'.[192] There is also evidence for the presence of a Benedict *Euernensicus* ('the Irishman') in Athelstan's court, in the form of a colophon in a Breton gospel book owned by Athelstan (London, BL, Cotton Otho B. ix; s. ix/x; provenance Chester-le-Street, Durham).[193] Further evidence of contacts with Irish ecclesiastics comes from a later manuscript, Oxford, Corpus Christi College 122 (Bangor, s. xii^{med}), an Irish gospel book containing a description of the *Alea euangelii* ('gospel dice'), an elaborate board game based on the Eusebian Canons.[194] An inscription states that the

[191] See S. Keynes, 'King Athelstan's Books', pp. 153–9; the annal is quoted at p. 154. The inscription was added to the manuscript 'apparently in the second quarter of the tenth century' (p. 153). On the Mac Durnan Gospels see also Kenney, *The Sources*, no. 475; *BCLL*, no. 528; McNamara, *Early Irish Latin Gospels*, pp. 102–11.

[192] 'King Athelstan's Books', p. 154. See also P. McGurk, 'The Gospel Book in Celtic Lands before AD 850: Contents and Arrangement', in *Irland und die Christenheit*, ed. Ní Chatháin and Richter, pp. 165–89, at 165, with a list of other Irish gospel books in tenth-century England at 165, n. 2.

[193] 'King Athelstan's Books', pp. 172–3. Keynes suggests that the Irish Benedict may be identical with a bishop of that name who attested a charter of Athelstan in 931. The manuscript is not included in *BCLL*; for its Breton origin, see Keynes, p. 170, n. 134. A Psalter doubtfully associated with Athelstan, BL Cotton Galba A. xviii, contains a metrical calendar composed after *c.* 902, 'either by an Englishman who had frequent recourse to Irish sources, or, as was suggested by Bishop, and still seems the more likely, by an Irishman working in English court circles' (P. McGurk, 'The Metrical Calendar of Hampson', *AB* 104 (1986), 79–89, at 89, referring to E. Bishop, *Liturgica Historica*, pp. 253–6); see also M. Lapidge, 'A Tenth-Century Metrical Calendar from Ramsey', *RB* 94 (1984), 326–69, at 347–8. The author of the calendar made use of the *Félire Oengusso* (for references, see Bullough, 'The Educational Tradition', p. 463 and n. 19). On the questionable association of the manuscript with Athelstan, see Keynes, 'King Athelstan's Books', pp. 193–6.

[194] *BCLL*, no. 307; see Robinson, *The Times of St Dunstan*, pp. 69–71 and 171–81;

game was brought away from the court of Athelstan by Bishop Dub Innse of Bangor (d. 953): 'Incipit Alea Euangelii, quam Dubinsi episcopus Bennchorensis detulit a rege Anglorum, id est a domu Adalstani regis Anglorum, depicta a quodam Francone et a Romano sapiente, id est Israel.'[195]

It is tempting, therefore, to place the Irish-influenced literary milieu of Vercelli IX in Mercia during the reign of King Athelstan.[196] Certain charters of King Athelstan show a marked taste for rhetorical extravagance, exemplifying what Michael Lapidge has termed 'the hermeneutic style' in tenth-century England.[197] As Lapidge shows, this Latin style is based on continental sources and not, as previously believed, on Irish models such as the *Hisperica Famina*, although there is an Hisperic element in the charters, which D. A. Bullough would trace to Celtic (Breton or Welsh) influence.[198] There are no specific similarities, in any case (so far as I am aware), between the Latin hermeneutic style and the extravagant style of 'The Devil's Account' and the *Pater Noster Dialogue*, and indeed what is by definition a Latin style would hardly be translatable in the vernacular;[199] but although different origins must be sought for each style, they reflect similar rhetorical predilections. Moreover, if the inscription associating the *Alea euangelii* with Athelstan's court is accurate ('one of those games of numbers which made Irish scholars popular at the court of Athelstan',

F. J. Byrne, *A Thousand Years of Irish Script: an Exhibition of Irish Manuscripts in Oxford Libraries* (Oxford, 1979), p. 17.

195 Ed. Robinson, *The Times of St Dunstan*, p. 173: '*Alea Euangelii*, which Dubinsi bishop of Bangor brought away from the king of the English, that is, from the house of Adelstan king of the English; depicted by a certain Frank and a Roman sage, that is, Israel' (trans. Robinson, p. 70).

196 The obit of Athelstan is recorded in the Annals of Clonmacnois and in the Annals of Ulster, which calls him 'pillar and dignity of the western world' (see McNamara, *Early Irish Latin Gospels*, p. 103).

197 'The Hermeneutic Style'. M. Winterbottom, 'Aldhelm's Prose Style and its Origins', *ASE* 6 (1977), 39–76, has exploded the theory that Aldhelm's prose style was based on the *Hisperica Famina*. On stylistic similarities between a group of 'alliterative' charters and the inscription in the Mac Durnan Gospels, see Keynes, 'King Athelstan's Books', pp. 156–9.

198 'The Educational Tradition in England', pp. 466–76.

199 The macaronic poem *Aldhelm* (in *The Anglo-Saxon Minor Poems*, ed. Dobbie, pp. 97–8) is a rare attempt to do just that; see Lapidge, 'The Hermeneutic Style', p. 83.

as Denis Bethell has remarked),[200] it suggests a fascination with the kind of Irish-inspired numerical rhetoric we find in both Vercelli IX and the *Pater Noster Dialogue*.[201]

Even if some of these Old English texts date from as late as the Benedictine reform, there would be no difficulty in positing an Irish background for them. Dunstan himself, according to the *Vita S. Dunstani* by the anonymous B., 'applied himself attentively' (*diligenter excoluit*) to the books of the Irish *peregrini* at Glastonbury – one of the few entirely credible stories regarding the Irish presence at Glastonbury.[202] In the late tenth century, Hiberno-Latin texts such as the tract *De duodecim abusiuis saeculi* and the *Expositio in VII epistolas catholicas* of pseudo-Hilary were known to Ælfric.[203] Extensive and well-documented English contacts with Wales and Brittany during the entire century also provided avenues for transmission of Hiberno-Latin texts,[204] and contacts with

[200] 'English Monks and Irish Reform', p. 117. Bethell does not specifically mention the *Alea euangelii*, but I assume he had this example in mind.

[201] Tristram, *Sex aetates mundi*, pp. 152–3 and 336, speculates on the possible influence of the Irish rhetorical style in early Old English homilies (with reference to Napier XLIX), and of transmission through Mercia.

[202] See M. Lapidge, 'The Cult of St Indract at Glastonbury', in *Ireland in Early Mediaeval Europe*, ed. Whitelock *et al.*, pp. 179–212, at 182. For a possibly Hiberno-Latin text in St Dunstan's Classbook, see above, p. 92. See also J. P. Carley and A. Dooley, 'An Early Irish Fragment of Isidore of Seville's *Etymologiae*', in *The Archaeology and History of Glastonbury Abbey: Essays in Honour of the Ninetieth Birthday of C. A. Ralegh Radford*, ed. L. Abrams and J. P. Carley (Woodbridge, 1991), pp. 135–61, for a fragment of an Irish manuscript of *c.* 680–700 which was in Glastonbury by the twelfth century. Carley and Dooley speculate that the fragment might be 'a survivor from the Irish collection, one of the very books used by Dunstan himself as a student' (p. 152).

[203] See above, p. 228.

[204] For Hiberno-Latin exegetical themes in Welsh manuscripts, see Lapidge, 'Latin Learning in Dark Age Wales'. Hiberno-Latin texts survive in Breton compilations, including the *Catechesis Celtica* (*BCLL*, no. 974) and *Dies Dominica* (*BCLL*, nos. 903 and 905). London, BL, Royal 5. E. XIII, a ninth-century Breton manuscript that was at Worcester in the tenth century, contains the *Collectio Canonum Hibernensis*, as well as a piece corresponding to the *Apocrypha Priscillianistica* (*BCLL*, no. 1252) and a Latin fragment of the Book of Enoch. Frantzen, *The Literature of Penance*, p. 130, states that 'We may safely assume that this manuscript entered England amid the "furore in Bretonism" so marked in the history of the period.' See also C. Brett, 'A Breton Pilgrim in England in the Reign of King Athelstan', in *France and the British Isles in the Middle Ages and Renaissance: Essays by Members of Girton College, Cambridge,*

Ireland itself continued through the end of the Anglo-Saxon period.[205]

This study of the Irish tradition in Old English literature is intended to be suggestive rather than comprehensive. As I have pointed out in the Introduction, our knowledge of Irish Christian literary traditions in the early Middle Ages is limited by the relative paucity and inaccessibility of early sources. Moreover, the distinctiveness of themes and stylistic features characteristic of Irish Christian literature cannot always be confidently assessed until all the texts in Bischoff's corpus of Hiberno-Latin and Irish-influenced biblical commentaries have been critically edited with identification of their sources. Until fairly recently, Old and Middle Irish religious texts have been studied chiefly for their linguistic interest, so that even when editions and translations are available, they have rarely been accompanied by adequate source analysis, or comparison with Hiberno-Latin writings. As the essential work of editing and source-study proceeds, it should become easier to sort out the distinctively Irish element from the Christian-Latin tradition upon which Irish Christian literature is ultimately based. But I believe that sufficient progress has been made to justify the preliminary assessment I have offered in the present book. I hope that it will encourage and facilitate future research on Irish and Anglo-Saxon literary relations in the early Middle Ages.

in Memory of Ruth Morgan, ed. G. Jondorf and D. Dumville (Woodbridge, 1991), pp. 43–70. For contacts during the reign of King Edmund (939–46), see D. Dumville, *The Historia Brittonum*, III: *The 'Vatican' Recension* (Cambridge, 1985), pp. 18–22. Dumville's forthcoming O'Donnell Lectures, *England and the Celtic World in the Ninth and Tenth Centuries*, will apparently deal comprehensively with Anglo-Celtic cultural links during this period.

205 For other Irish–English contacts in the tenth and eleventh centuries, see Bethell, 'English Monks and Irish Reform'.

Appendix

Vercelli Homily IX and 'The Devil's Account of the Next World'

In addition to the text in the Vercelli Book, Vercelli, Biblioteca Capitolare, CXVII (s. x^2), 61r–65r [A],[1] the homily occurs also in Oxford, Bodleian Library, Bodley 340 (+ 342) (?Canterbury, s. xi^{in}; provenance Rochester), 35v–40v [E], in an abbreviated version which, however, partly makes good a lacuna in the Vercelli Book text.[2] Extensive passages from a lost, 'markedly different (and probably earlier) version' of Vercelli IX were used in another sermon in Oxford, Bodleian Library, Hatton 115, fols. 140–7 (s. xi^2; provenance Worcester) [L].[3] Briefer extracts from the line represented by L are incorporated

[1] First ed. M. Förster, 'Die Vercelli-Codex CXVII nebst Abdruck einiger altenglischer Homilien der Handschrift', in *Festschrift für Lorenz Morsbach*, ed. F. Holthausen and H. Spies, Studien zur englischen Philologie 50 (Halle, 1913), 20–179, at 100–16; also in *The Vercelli Homilies*, ed. Szarmach, pp. 3–7. On the variant versions of Vercelli IX, see Scragg's edition, pp. 151–7, and his 'Anonymous Old English Homilies', pp. 126–7. On the manuscript, see *idem*, 'The Compilation of the Vercelli Book' and 'The Corpus of Vernacular Homilies', pp. 229–30 (I adopt Scragg's manuscript sigla). For a facsimile of the manuscript, see C. Sisam, *The Vercelli Book* (*Vercelli Biblioteca Capitolare cxvii*), EEMF 19 (Copenhagen, 1976).

[2] Förster, Szarmach and Scragg all use E to supply part of the lacuna. Scragg records all the variants from E in his apparatus. On the probable contents of the lacuna, presumably a single leaf, see Scragg, 'Napier's "Wulfstan" Homily XXX', pp. 201–2, where he suggests that E does not contain all that was in the lacuna of A. See also Szarmach, 'The Vercelli Homilies: Style and Structure', p. 242. In E the sermon is rubricated 'Dominica .II. post Theophania et quando uolueris'.

[3] Quotation from Scragg, 'Homilies and Homiliaries', p. 126. See also *idem*, 'The Corpus of Vernacular Homilies', p. 247, for details of the correspondences. L is also ed. Scragg, along with A on facing pages; it was first ed. Fadda, *Nuove omelie anglosassoni*, pp. 186–211. Folios 140–7 were originally a separate booklet, written in an earlier hand; see P. R. Robinson, 'Self-Contained Units in Composite Manuscripts of the Anglo-Saxon Period', *ASE* 7 (1978), 231–8 at 235–8; C. Franzen, *The Tremulous Hand of Worcester: a Study of Old English in the Thirteenth Century* (Oxford, 1991), p. 40.

in the two versions of the 'Niall' Sunday Letter sermon, Napier XLIII [N] and XLIV [*M*],[4] while Napier XXX [O] borrows passages from the A line as represented by the Vercelli Book version.[5] The exemplum, 'The Devil's Account of the Next World', was one of the most popular vernacular religious tales in the tenth and eleventh centuries. In addition to the versions found in A and E (both defective) and in L, it occurs separately in London, BL, Cotton Tiberius A. iii, fols. 2–173 (s. xi^{med}; provenance Christ Church, Canterbury), 87r–88v [M],[6] and in a précis headed 'De inclusis' in Cambridge, Corpus Christi College 303 (Rochester, s. xii^{1}), p. 202 [H].[7] Finally, the badly damaged manuscript London, BL, Cotton Otho B. x, pt A (s. xi^{1}) [f^{g}] once had a sermon that used the exemplum.[8]

For the convenience of the reader I provide the following text and literal translation of the entire homily and exemplum.[9] The text is that of Scragg's edition of AE, supplemented by L for one passage where AE lack a section of

4 In *Wulfstan*, ed. Napier, pp. 205–15 and 215–26; Scragg prints the relevant passages in his apparatus. See also *idem*, 'The Corpus of Vernacular Homilies', pp. 230 and 250. In his edition Scragg designates Napier XLIV as *M* to distinguish it from a separate version of 'The Devil's Account' in the same manuscript [M]. In 'Anonymous Old English Homilies', p. 126, Scragg states that two different extracts were 'incorporated separately into the two surviving versions', but there is a third brief extract from Vercelli IX used by both versions in precisely the same position and context. The archetype, therefore, probably contained all the extracts from Vercelli IX found in the two surviving redactions. See above, pp. 222–4.

5 In *Wulfstan*, ed. Napier, pp. 143–52. Scragg prints the relevant passages in his apparatus, and uses one passage from O to supply a lacuna in A. See also *idem*, 'Napier's "Wulfstan" Homily XXX'.

6 Scragg prints the relevant passages from M in his apparatus. The complete sermon is ed. Robinson, 'The Devil's Account of the Next World'; it was first ed. Kemble, *The Dialogue of Solomon and Saturnus*, pp. 84–6. Scragg, '"The Devil's Account of the Next World" Revisited', *American Notes and Queries* 24 (1986), 107–10, shows that the version in M is a late compilation based on a version of Vercelli IX. According to Scragg, the location of the anchorite in the Thebaid is an innovation of the compiler of this version. I have therefore abandoned 'Theban Anchorite legend' as a designation for the tale, in favour of Robinson's title, 'The Devil's Account of the Next World'. But I will refer to all versions of the exemplum (not just the separate version in M) as 'The Devil's Account'.

7 Ed. Scragg, in his apparatus; earlier ed. Fadda, *Nuove omelie anglosassoni*, pp.187–8. See Scragg, 'The Corpus of Vernacular Homilies', pp. 243–4.

8 *Ibid.*, p. 263. Humphrey Wanley had described the contents of Otho B. x before it was damaged in the Cotton Library fire.

9 A translation of Szarmach's text by P. Quattrin has recently appeared in *The Vercelli Book Homilies: Translations from the Anglo-Saxon*, ed. L. E. Nicholson (Lanham, MD, 1991), pp. 65–71.

'The Devil's Account'.[10] In the notes I translate some of the most significant variant readings and additions in the different versions.[11]

[10] Scragg supplies the gap in AE with the text of O because the extracts from Vercelli IX in O are textually closer to A. I use L because, as Scragg notes, LM seem to represent better the original version of this passage in several significant respects, including the description of Samson, the identification of the bellows as blacksmiths' (see Scragg, *The Vercelli Homilies*, pp. 156–7 and 157, n. 1) and the reference to iron *walls*.

[11] For the purposes of this translation I accept Scragg's emendations throughout, and translate Scragg's texts for all variant readings mentioned in the notes.

TEXT

[1–15] Men ða leofestan, manað us ⁊ myngaþ þeos halige boc þæt we sien gemyndige ymb ure sawle þearfe, ⁊ eac swa ures þæs nehstan dæges ⁊ þære tosceadednesse ure sawle þonne hio of ðam lichoman lædde bion. ⁊ læten we us singallice bion on gemyndum ⁊ on geþancum þæs egesfullican dæges tocyme, on ðam we sculon Gode riht agifan for ealles ures lifes dædum þe we sið oððe ær gefremedon fram fruman ures lifes [oð] ende; for ðan þe we nu magon behydan ⁊ behelian ura dæda, ac hie bioð þonne opena ⁊ unwrigena. For þan we habbað micle nydþearfe, þa hwile þe we her syndon on þys lænan life ⁊ on þyssum gewitendlicum, þæt we þonne on þære toweardan woruld[e] mægen ⁊ moton becuman to life þæs heofoncundan rices ⁊ to þam wu[l]dre þære ecean eadignesse, þær we moton siððan orsorglice lybban ⁊ rixian butan ælcre onwendednesse mid him, emne swa ure dryhten hælende Crist, ⁊ mid eallum his halgum, gif we hit gearnian willað mid urum godum dædum.

[16–31] Nis þonne næniges mannes gemet þæt he mæge asecgan þara goda ⁊ þara yðnessa þe God hafað geearwod eallum þam þe hine lufiað ⁊ his b[eb]odu healdan willað ⁊ gelæstan. Gif þæt þonne bið þæt we willað wyrcean his willan ⁊ on his lufe þurhwunian, þonne magon we ægðer ge us heofonrice geearnian ge ðonne eac þæt we magon gesæliglice befleon þa stowe ⁊ þa dimman tintregan þær helle dioflu on syndon, mid eallum hyra weagesiðum, ⁊ mid þam sawlum þe hyra larum hlystað ⁊ be hyra larum lybbað ⁊ to Gode gecyrran nellað þurh soðe andetnesse mæssepreosta ⁊ þurh soðe bote. Swa se halega lareow cwæð: 'Wa, la, ðam mannum þe sculon mid dioflum habban geardungstowa, for ðam þær is sar butan frofre, ⁊ þær is yrmð butan are, ⁊ þær is weana ma þonne hi ænig man wite to asecganne.' Swa hit on ðam sealme by ðam awriten standeð; he cwæð, se sealmscop, þurh dryhtnes gife: 'Hwylc man is [on deaðe] þætte he sie dryhtnes gemyndig, oððe hwylc is ðætte hyne on helle andette?' ⁊ se sealmscop us sang þis be deaðes onlicnesse ⁊ be helle gryre.

[32–40] Þonne syndon þry deaðas liornode on bocum: þæt is þonne se æresta deað her on worulde þæt se man mid manegum synnum oferhealden bið; þonne is se æftera deaþ þæra sawle gescead ⁊ lichoman; þonne is se þridda deað þæt þa sawla sculon eardigan on helle, þær nis nænig man þætte mæge his scippend herigan for ðam sare þe him onsitet. Emne swa ða þry deaðas syndon fyrenfulra, swa þænne syndon þreo lif be ðam soðfæstum: an lif is þæt he bið

TRANSLATION

[1–15] Most beloved men, this holy book exhorts and admonishes us that we be mindful of our soul's need and also of our last day and the separation of our souls when they[12] will be led out from the body. And let us continually be mindful and thoughtful of the approach of that terrible day, on which we must render account to God for the deeds of all our life which we have committed late or early from the beginning of our life until the end; because now we can hide and conceal our deeds, but then they will be open and revealed. Therefore we have great need, as long as we are here in this fleeting life and in these transitory times, that thereafter in the future world we may be permitted to attain to the life of the heavenly kingdom and the glory of eternal blessedness, where we may thenceforth live without care and reign without any change with him, even as our Lord Saviour Christ, and with all his saints, if we are willing to earn it with our good deeds.

[16–31] It is not within any man's capacity to express the good and pleasant things which God has prepared for all those who love him and are willing to keep and fulfil his commands. If it will be, then, that we are willing to do his will and persevere in his love, then we can both earn the kingdom of heaven and also happily escape that place and those dark tortures wherein are the devils of hell, with all their companions in misery, and with the souls which obey their teaching and live by their instruction and which are not willing to turn to God through true confession of masspriests and through true repentance. As the holy teacher said: 'Woe, alas, to those men who must have dwelling-places with devils, because in that place is sorrow without comfort, and there is misery without grace, and there is greater evil than any man knows how to express it.' Just as it stands written in the psalm concerning this matter; the psalmist said through the Lord's grace: 'Which man is there in death that may be mindful of God, or which that may praise him in hell?'[13] And the psalmist sang us this concerning the likeness of death and the terror of hell.

[32–40] Then there are three deaths learned from books. The first death here in the world is that a man is overcome with many sins; the second death is the separation of the soul and body; the third death is that the souls must dwell in hell, where there is no man who can praise his Creator on account of the suffering that oppresses him. Just as there are three deaths of the sinful, so then there are three lives with regard to the righteous: one life is that in the flesh;

[12] I translate the plural *ura sawla* from E, and follow Scragg's suggestion (*ibid.*, note to line 3) to read *hi* for *hio*.

[13] Ps. VI.6: 'quoniam non est in morte qui memor sit tui / in inferno autem quis confitebitur tibi'.

on flæsce; þonne is oðer lif ðæt [he] bið on god[um] w[eorc]e; ⁊ þridde lif is on þære toweardan worulde mid eallum halgum.

[41–58] ⁊ se deað is þænne for þan to ondrædanne for ðan hine ne mæg nænig man forflion. ⁊ se deað is nyðerlic [⁊ uplic]. ⁊ he is for þan nyðerlic, se deað, þeah se man gewite in ða neowlestan scrafa ⁊ on þa deoppestan dene þe on middangearde sy, þonne sceal he þeahhwæðere sweltan. And se deað is for þam uplic, þeah se man astige ofer þone yfemystan dæl þæs hyhstan holtes, swa þeahhwæðere hiene se deað geseceð. And se deað is swiðe manigfealdlic ⁊ egeslic. ⁊ he is for þan mænigfealdlic, þeah se man eardige in middum burgum ⁊ on midre his mægðe ⁊ betweox hundteontegum þusenda manna, þonne sceal he hwæðere sweltan. ⁊ se deað is for þan egeslic þæt nænig man swa feor ne gewiteð ut on westen, swa þeah he ne mæg þone deað forflion. Se deað is gionlic, for þan þe cild [s]wel[t]að ⁊ unmagan, ⁊ se deað is freolic ⁊ [ð]eo[w]lic, for þan cyningas sweltaþ ⁊ eac þeowe men, ⁊ se deað is [d]islic ⁊ snotorlic, for þan þe ge[dwol]an sweltaþ ⁊ uðwitan. For ðan se deað is unrotlic ⁊ bliðelic, for þan synfulle sweltaþ ⁊ eac halige. Þy byð wel wyrð þæt se deað sy unrotlic fyrenfullum mannum. For þan is [se] deað to ondrædanne, for þan he ne myrneð geongum [ne ealdum].

[59–67] For ðan we sculon ure sawle georne tilian ⁊ he geornlice Gode gegearwian. Ne mæg þonne eall manna cyn mid hyra wordum ariman þa god þe God hafað soðfæstum sawlum geearwod togeanes for hyra gastlicum worcum. ⁊ se deað is for þan to [on]drædenne for þan ealle þa ged[w]æledan sawla h[e t]odæleð. ⁊ þonne bið eallum [un]cuð þæt sio sawl gedeð beforan hire, ⁊ þonne hwæðere bið beforan hyre gemeted swa god swa yfel swa he[o] ær geearnod hæfde. Is us eac þonne to behealdanne þæt we nu onwarigan þone tocyme, þæt hira ne sy to feala.

the second life is that in good work;[14] and the third life is in the future world with all the saints.

[41–58] And death is then to be feared, because no man may escape it. And death is low and high. And death is low for this reason, even if a man should go into the deepest caves and into the deepest valley on earth, yet none the less he must die. And death is high for this reason, even if a man should climb above the topmost part of the highest forest, nonetheless death will seek him out. And death is exceedingly multiple and terrible.[15] And it is multiple for this reason, even if he should dwell in the middle of a fortress and in the midst of his kindred and among a hundred thousand men,[16] yet none the less he must die. And death is for this reason terrible, that no matter how far any man might go out into the desert, still he cannot escape death. Death is youthful, because children and orphans die. And death is freeborn and servile, because kings die and so do slaves, and death is foolish and wise, because madmen and wise men die. Death is sad and happy for this reason, because sinners and saints die. For it is entirely fitting that death should be sad to sinful men.[17] Therefore death is to be feared, because it cares neither for the young nor the old.

[59–67] We must therefore zealously tend to our souls and eagerly prepare them for God. All the race of men with their words could not reckon the good that God has prepared for righteous souls in return for their holy deeds. And death is therefore to be feared because it separates all the perverted souls. And then it will be unknown to all what the soul will offer before itself, and yet none the less just as good or as evil as it had previously merited will be encountered before it. Consequently, we ought also to take care that we now prepare for the (second) coming, that there should not be too many of them.[18]

[14] Scragg's emendation of A's *godes wuldre* accords better with the Latin analogue for the motif in the *Collectanea Bedae*; see above, p. 93.

[15] Scragg suggests that the word *egeslic* has replaced an original *synderlic*, 'singular', which would supply the expected opposition with *manigfealdlic*, 'multiple'.

[16] L adds: 'with weapon's edges, and even if he were locked in an iron casket a hundred thousand fathoms under the earth, none the less he must die' (*The Vercelli Homilies*, ed. Scragg, p. 163, lines 44–6).

[17] L here has a fuller but partly corrupt reading: 'It is well fitting that it should be sad to the sinful because they never come after it or are met before (?) on account of the extent [Scragg's suggestion for *gemetnesse*] of the eternal torments where they must always remain without end. And death is happy to holy men because of the separation from earthly riches, which had been alien to their spirit, and because of the vision of their Lord' (*ibid.*, p. 165, lines 50–5).

[18] Scragg's paraphrase of this whole passage (*ibid.*, p. 186, note to lines 65–7) does much to clarify the sense, but I take the phrase *beforan hyre gemeted* to refer to the weighing of the soul's good and evil deeds. The meaning of the last two sentences,

[68–83] Þonne is þæt ærest[e] gedal wið eallum his freondum, for ðam him nænig æfter ne we[n]deð þæt him ænig to cyme. Æghwylcre sawle bið onsundrum toscyred, 7 sio bið swylce hyre se lichoma ær geworhte. Þonne hreoweð hyre swiðe þa yfelan dæda, 7 þonne hie hit awendan ne magon þonne nellað hie ... 7 ðonne is þæt þridde gedal wið eallum eorðw[el]um, for þan he næfre eft to eorðw[el]um ne gehwyrfeð. Ne bið funden beforan him ne huru æfter boren [nan god], buton he ær his gast mid godum weorcum gefrætewod hæfde, þa hwile þe he wære mid mannum. Ðonne bið þæt feorðe gedal þæt hine man gedæle wið þyssum eor[ð]licum þrymme 7 plegan 7 blisse, 7 him for þyssa nænegum ne bið gleng witod. Þonne bið hit swa egeslic for þære biternesse þe on him bið gecyðed, for þan he betyneð þa eagan fram gesyhðe 7 þa earan fram gehyrnesse 7 þa weloras fram spræce 7 þa fet fram gange 7 þa handa fram weorce 7 þa næsðyrelu fram stence. Ðonne æfter þon betyneð he ða scyldegan on helle. Wa ðam þæt bið þæt he þonne sceal bion betyned on helle!

[84–113] Þonne is leornod on bocum þæt on þysse worulde syn fif onlicnessa be helle gryre. Sio æreste onlicnes is nemned wræc, for ðan se wræc bið miceles cwelmes ælcum þara þe he to cymeð, for ðan hine sona ne lysteð metes ne drynces, ne him ne bið læten gold ne seolfor, ne ðær ne bið ænig wuldor mid him þæt he fore wynsumige, þeah him syndon ealle wuldordreamas to gelædde. Þonne is þære æfteran helle onlicnes genemned oferyldo, for þan him amolsniað þa eagan for ðære oferyldo ða þe wæron gleawe on gesyhðe, 7 þa earan adimmiað ða ðe ær meahton gehyran fægere sangas, and sio tunge aw[l]is[p]að þe ær hæfde gerade spræce, 7 þa [fet] aslapað þe ær wæron ful swifte [7 hræde] to [gange], 7 þa handa aþindað þe ær hæfdon ful hwate fingras, 7 þæt feax af[ealle]ð þe ær wæs on fullere wæstme, 7 þa teð ageolewiað þa þe [ær] wæron

[68–83] The first separation then is from all his friends, because no one goes in pursuit of him in order that any may reach him.[19] Each soul is individually segregated, and it will be in such condition as the body had formerly earned for it. Then it will regret greatly those evil deeds, and when they cannot change it they will not wish ... [20] Then the third separation is from all the earth's riches, because he will never return to the earth's riches again.[21] No good will be found before him nor indeed will any be carried after him, unless he had previously adorned his spirit with good works while he was among men. The fourth separation is that he is separated from this earthly glory and sport and bliss, and certainly there will be no splendour for him in place of any of these. Then it will be so terrible on account of the bitterness which will be manifest in him, because death will close the eyes from seeing and the ears from hearing and the lips from speaking and the feet from walking and the hands from working and the nostrils from smelling. Then after that he will close up the guilty one in hell. Woe to the one who must then be closed up in hell!

[84–113] It is learned from books that there are five likenesses of hell-torment in this world. The first likeness is called pain, because pain is a great torment to each of those it afflicts, because at once food and drink do not please him, nor do gold and silver remain for him, nor is there any glory with him that he might rejoice in, even if all glorious pleasures were brought before him. The second likeness of hell is called old age, because the eyes weaken from old age, which had been keen in sight; and the ears grow dull,[22] which had been able to hear fair songs; and the tongue lisps, which once had skilful speech; and the feet are paralysed, which had been very quick and swift to walk;[23] and the hands swell up, which once had very nimble fingers; and the hair falls out, which had been in fuller growth; and the teeth yellow, which had been white

as I now understand them, is that although no one can know what good or evil deeds the soul will present at Judgement, they will be judged exactly as the soul had earned in this life. Therefore we should take care that there not be too many evil deeds to tip the scale against us (cf. lines 74–6).

19 I adopt Scragg's suggested translation (*ibid.*, p. 186, note to lines 68–83) for this sentence and the beginning of the next. E (as translated by Szarmach, *Vercelli Homilies*, p. 8) reads: 'for no man is so much afraid (as when he is afraid that) he will not come to them (i.e., his friends)'.

20 Here A is defective, and there is no closely corresponding sentence in E or L.

21 Scragg emends AE *eorðwarum* 'earth-dwellers' on the basis of L, which is also defective for the four 'separations', listing only a first, of the body and soul, and a third, from all the earth's riches (*eorþweolum*).

22 L reads 'grow deaf'.

23 In this clause A refers to the ears for a second time; Scragg emends on the basis of L.

hwite on hywe, 7 þæt oroð afulað þe wæs ær swete on stence. Đonne is þære þriddan helle onlicnes her on worulde deað genemned, for þan þonne se man sceal sweltan, þonne swyrceð him fram þæs huses hrof ðe he inne bið; þonne nis nænig strengo þæt hine arære, for ðan he ne bið gelustfullod metes, ne he ne gymeð þysses eorðlican rices torhtnessa. Đonne is ðære feorðan helle onlicnes byrgen nemned, for þan þæs huses hrof bið [gehnæg]ed þe him onufan ðam breostum siteð, 7 him mon þonne deð his gestreona þone wi[r]sestan dæl, þæt is þæt hine [mon siw]eð on anum [hræg]le. Hafað him þonne syððan þry gebeddan, þæt is þonne greot 7 molde 7 wyrmas. Þonne is þære fiftan helle onlicnes tintrega genemned, for ðan þænne nis nænig man þæt mæge mid his wordum asecgan hu mycel þære fiftan helle sar is. 7 þeah .vii. men sien, 7 þara hæbbe[12] æghwylc twa 7 hundsiofontig gereorda, swa feala swa ealles þysses middangeardes gereorda syndon, and þonne sy þara seofon manna æghwylc to alife gesceapen, 7 hyra hæbbe æghwylc siofon [heafdu, 7 þara heafdu ælc hæbbe siofon] tungan, 7 þara tungena ælc hæbbe isene stemne, 7 þonne hwæðre ne magon þa ealle ariman helle witu.

[114–30] 7 emne swa mycel swa fram heofenes hrofe is to þysse eorðan, þonne is leornod on halgum bocum þæt sio hel sie swylc twa deop, 7 nis na ðe unwidre. Þæt hus is mid swiðe ongristlice f[yre] afylled, 7 helle hus hafað forc[i]las micle. Se nama is to geþenceanne ælcum men butan hwæs heorte sie mid diofles stræle þurhwrecen. For þy nis nan man þæt he þ[an]on aweg hine astyrian mæge, for ðam is mycel þearf æghwylcum men to onwariganne, þam þe ænig andgit hæbbe oðð[e] wisdomes ænigne dæl, þæt he þis symle hæbbe on gemyndum þære egesfullan stowe. For ðan gif hwylc man bið on helle ane niht, þonne bið him leofre, gif he þanon mot, þæt he hangie siofon þusend wintra on þam lengestan treowe ufeweardum þe ofer sæ standeð on þam hyhstan sæclife, [7 syn þa fet gebundene to ðam hehstan telgan 7 þæt heafod hangige

* Here and in similar lists of hypotheticals I translate the present subjunctives *hæbbe* and *sy* as 'had' and 'were'.

in colour; and the breath stinks, which once had smelled fresh. The third likeness of hell here in the world is called death, because when a man must die, the roof of the building in which he lies grows dark before him;[24] then there is no power that can raise him, for he has not delighted in food, nor does he care for the splendours of this earthly realm. The fourth likeness of hell is called the grave, for the roof of the house that sits upon his breast is bent down, and the meanest portion of his treasures is taken from him, that is someone sews it up in a bag. Thereafter he has three bedfellows, that is earth, dust and worms. The fifth likeness of hell is called torment, because there is no man who can express with his words how great the pain of the fifth (likeness of) hell is. And even if there were seven men, and each of them had seventy-two languages, as many languages as there are in this world, and then if each of those men were created with eternal life, and each one of them had seven [heads, and each of the heads had seven][25] tongues, and each of the tongues had an iron voice, yet none the less they could not enumerate all the pains of hell.[26]

[114–30] And just as far as from the roof of heaven to this earth, then it is learned in holy books that hell is twice[27] as deep and no less wide. That house is filled with exceedingly terrible fire, and the house of hell has intense cold.[28] The notoriety (of hell) should be remembered by every man whose heart is not pierced with the devil's arrow.[29] For there is no man who can bestir himself from there, and therefore there is great need for every man who has any understanding or any portion of wisdom to beware that he always bear this in mind concerning that terrible place.[30] For if any man were in hell for a single night, thereafter it would be more agreeable to him, if he could escape from there, that he should hang for seven thousand years atop the tallest tree that stands on the highest seacliff,[31] [and that his feet should be bound to the highest

24 I adopt Scragg's translation of this clause.

25 Scragg supplies the reference to the seven heads, omitted in A by homeoteleuton.

26 For variations of the motif of the Men with Tongues of Iron, see above, pp. 145–56. In Napier XLIII (N) the corresponding passage is attributed to the captive devil.

27 L omits 'twice'.

28 Scragg emends AE *forclas* ('pitchforks' ?) to *forcilas* (= *færcilas*).

29 I adopt Scragg's translation for this sentence.

30 In M the passages corresponding (with considerable variation) to A.122–50 are attributed to the devil, in response to the anchorite's demand to reveal the terror of hell and fairness of heaven. The opening paragraph of M reads: 'It happened once on a certain occasion that an anchorite seized a demon through the power of God, and he was an anchorite in the Thebaid, having become a man of very holy life through the power of God. Then the anchorite began to press the devil to tell him all the terrors of hell-torment and also the fairness of the kingdom of heaven.'

31 The lacuna in A begins here; the bracketed passage is supplied from E.

ofdunrihte ⁊ þa fet uprihte, ⁊ him sige þæt blod ut þurh þone muð, ⁊ hine þonne gesece ælc þæra yfela þe æfre on helle sy, ⁊ hine ælc yð gesece mid þam hehstan þe seo sæ forðbringð, ⁊ þeah hine ælc tor gesece þe on eallum clyfum syndon, þonne wile he eall þis luflice þrowian wið ðan þe he næfre eft helle ne gesece.

[131–43] Wa bið þam mannum þe beoð geteohhode to ðære stowe, for ðan þær is wop butan frofre ⁊ hreow butan reste, ⁊ þær bið þeowdom buton freodome, ⁊ þær bið unrotnys buton gefean, ⁊ þær bið biternys buton swetnysse, ⁊ þær bið hungor ⁊ þurst, ⁊ þær bið granung ⁊ geomrung ⁊ micel wroht. ⁊ hi wepað heora synna swiðe biterlicum tearum, ⁊ on heom sylfum beoð ealle heora synna gesene, þa ðe hi ær geworhton, ⁊ ne mæg nan oðres gehelpan. Ac hi þonne onginnað singan swiðe sorhfulne sang ⁊ swiðe wependre stemne: 'Nu we magon sceawian ealle ure synna beforan ealre þysse mænigo, þeah we heo ealle ær geworhton.' Ne bið þær gesibbes lufu to oðrum, ⁊ nis þær nænig man þæt þær sy his scyppendes gemyndig for ðam sare þe him onsiteð. ⁊ þær beoð þa sawle forgytene ealra þæra þe hi ær on eorðan gemetton.

[144–50] Sægeð hit eac on bocum þæt sum deofles gast sæde anum ancran ealle helle ger[yne] ⁊ þara sawla tintrega. ⁊ he wæs cweðende þæt eall þes middaneard nære þe mare dryges landes ofer þone micclan garsegc þe man ænne prican aprycce on anum brede, ⁊ nis þes middaneard swilce se seofoða dæl ofer þone micclan garsecg, se mid micclum ormætnyssum ealle þas eorðan utan ymbligeð. ⁊ lytel dæl is under heofonum dryges landes þæt hit ne sy mid garsecge oferurnen.

[L.140–51] Þa cwæþ þæt deoful to þæm ancran: 'Þeah mon þone garsecg mid isernum weallum utan betyne, ⁊ hine þonne fyres afylle up oþ heofnes hrof,

branch, and his head should hang upside down and his feet upright, and the blood flow out[32] through the mouth, and every evil that ever existed in hell should afflict him, and every wave with the highest the sea produces, and even if every rock from all cliffs should beset him, yet will he endure all this provided that he should never again visit hell.[33]

[131–43] Woe to those men who will be assigned to that place, because there is weeping without comfort and grief without rest, and there is servitude without freedom, and there is sadness without joy, and there is bitterness without sweetness, and there is hunger and thirst, and there is groaning and lamentation and great misery. And they weep with very bitter tears for their sins, and upon themselves will be seen all their sins which they had committed, and no one will be able to help another. But then they will begin to sing a very sorrowful song and with a very mournful voice: 'Now we can perceive all our sins before all this multitude, though we had committed them all at an earlier time.' There will be no familial love for another there, and there is no man who can be mindful of his Creator there on account of the grief that oppresses him.[34] And there the souls will be forgotten by all those they had met on earth.

[144–50] It also says in books that a certain devilish spirit told an anchorite all the mystery of hell and the torments of souls. And he was saying that all this earth would be no more of dry land beside the great Ocean than a point pricked on a tablet,[35] and this earth is not but as the seventh part over the great Ocean which with great immensity encircles all this earth on the outside. And there is little portion of dry land under heaven that it is not covered over with the Ocean.[36]

[L.140–51] Then the devil said to the anchorite: 'Even if the Ocean were closed up from without with iron walls, and then filled with fire up to the roof

[32] L adds: 'in six directions'.

[33] L reads: 'then he will gladly endure all this, even if he should have to be (there) six thousand years and also the thousand on which Doomsday takes place, provided that he never again visit hell'.

[34] Here L interpolates a long passage (*The Vercelli Homilies*, ed. Scragg, p. 173, line 106 – p. 175, line 133) from Vercelli II; see Scragg, 'The Corpus of Vernacular Homilies', p. 247.

[35] M and L read 'wax-tablet', as does a gloss in Napier XXX.

[36] M and L differ considerably from A for this paragraph. M reads: 'This earth that the water does not flow upon would be, with all its growth ... and yet that earth (itself) would by no means be greater in its extent than is that vast hell. And the great ocean which lies around the outside of this earth is tremendously large, such that all this earth is no bigger in comparison to it than a point which is pricked on a wax-tablet' (first part of the sentence as translated by Robinson, 'The Devil's Account of the Next World', p. 369).

7 hine þonne utan besette mid smiþbylium 7 heora æghwylc oðrum ætrine, 7 sy to ælcum þara man togeset and ælc þara manna hæbbe Samsones strenge (7 se Samson ealle F[i]llestina þeode gererde 7 heora duguþe afylde, 7 he hæfde twelf loccas 7 on ælcum locce he hæfde twelf manna mægen) 7 man þonne sette iserne þele ofer þæs fyres hrof 7 þæt sy eall mid mannum afylled 7 heora æghwylc hæbbe hamor on honda, 7 hit þonne aginne eal samod brastlian 7 þa bylias blawan 7 þæt fyr dynian 7 þa hamoras beatan, hweþere for eallum þyssum gedyne ne mæg seo sawl awacian seo þe wæs ær ane niht on helle.'

[164–82] Wa bið þam sawlum þe on helle beon sceolon, for ðan þe þæt helle hus is mid swiðe laðlicum gastum afylled! Ac utan we, men ða leofestan, nu we syndon gegaderode on ðysne drihtenlican dæg, þæt we þæs for Godes lufan on geornysse syn, þæt we] beflion þa helle wita, for þan hit is ðærinne swiðe sarlic to wuniganne. Ac utan geearwian us nu ða mid inneweardum gebedum 7 mid gæstedome, þæt we ne weorðan aslidene innon þa fyrenfullan þystro þæt synfullum sawlum is geearwod on helle togeanes. Ac utan þydan us to þam uplican rice, for ðan þær is þæt wuldor, þæt nænig man ne mæg mid his wordum asecgan ða wynsumnesse þæs heofoncundan lifes. Ðær bið lif butan deaþe 7 god butan ende 7 yld butan sare 7 dæg butan nihte, and þær bið gefea butan unrotnesse 7 rice butan awendednesse. 7 ne þearf man næfre ne sunnan ne monan ne æniges eorðlices liohtes, for ðan þær is se ælmihtiga dryhten scinendra 7 liohtra þonne ealle oðre lioht. 7 þær æfre aspringað ða wuldorlican dreamas 7 þa þrymlican sangas ðam ðe on hyra midlene wiorðan [mot]. Þær bið se sweta stenc 7 sio syngalu lufu 7 sio wiensumnes butan ælcere unwynsumnesse. Ne þær ne bið hunger ne ðurst ne cyle ne bryne ne nænig unwynsumnes gemeted.

[183–205] Þonne swa ðæt dioful sæde þam ancran be helle geryne, swa he him ær sæde be heofena rices wuldre. Swa ðæt dioful cwæð to ðam ancran: 'Þeah þær sy eal smætegylden mor æt sunnan upgange on neorxnawange, 7 s[e]

of heaven, and then surrounded by smith's bellows so that each touched the other, and a man were placed at each bellows and each of those men had the strength of Samson (and that Samson stirred up all the people of the Philistines and felled their troops, and he had twelve locks and in each lock he had the strength of twelve men)[37] and an iron plate were then placed over the roof of the fire and it were all filled with men and each had a hammer in his hand, and then all together began to crash it, and blow the bellows and cause the fire to roar[38] and beat the hammers, none the less despite all this commotion the soul that was earlier in hell for a single night could not wake up.'[39]

[164–82] Woe to those souls who must be in hell, because the house of hell is filled with exceedingly hateful spirits! But let us, most beloved men, now that we are gathered on this day of the Lord, be zealous for God's love so that we] may escape the torments of hell, for it is exceedingly painful to dwell therein. But let us prepare ourselves now with earnest prayers and with spirituality, so that we will not fall within the fiery darkness that is prepared for sinful souls in hell. But let us submit ourselves to the celestial kingdom, because there is such glory that no man can express with his words the joy of the heavenly life. There will be life without death and good without end and old age[40] without pain and day without night, and there will be joy without sadness and kingdom without change. And one never has need of sun or moon or other earthly light, because there the almighty Lord is more resplendent and brighter than all other light. And there continually spring forth glorious joys and majestic songs for those who are allowed to be in their midst. There will be the sweet odour and unceasing love and joy without any unpleasantness. Neither hunger nor thirst nor cold nor burning nor any unpleasantness will be encountered there.

[183–205] Then just as the devil told the anchorite about the mystery of hell, so he had earlier told him about the glory of the kingdom of heaven. Thus spoke the devil to the anchorite: 'Even if there were a mountain of pure gold[41]

[37] O (Napier XXX) reads more simply: 'he who was the strongest of all earth-dwellers who have lived before or after'.

[38] M omits 'and blow the bellows and cause the fire to roar'.

[39] A marginal note in L adds: 'it would be so oppressed and troubled'. O (Napier XXX) and H agree with L that the soul would not wake up despite all the noise and fire. N reads: 'he would never wake up despite all this, so weary he would be because of that single night's space'. O reads: 'despite all this misery the weary soul would not arise because of the pain which it had suffered in hell for a single night'. The reading of M differs: 'none the less despite all this din the soul that was earlier in hell for a single night could not rest within from those terrors it had earlier seen sufficiently that he could ever forget that misery for half an hour' (as translated by Robinson, 'The Devil's Account of the Next World', p. 370).

[40] L reads 'health'; see above, p. 105.

[41] M adds: 'all set with gems'.

oferhlif[ige] ealle iorðan, 7 se man mote sittan swa dyre swa cynebearn ofer ðam gyldenan more, 7 hæbbe Salemanes wlite 7 wisdom, 7 him sie eal middangeard on geweald geseald, mid ðam gestreonum þe geond ealne middan[geard] syndon, 7 him sy ælce niht niwe bryd to bedde gelæd 7 sio hæbbe [Iu]none wlite, Saturnes dohtor, 7 ælc stan sy gylden, 7 ealle þa streamas hunige flowen, 7 him þonne ne sie ofer eorðan nænig wiðerbreca, 7 þeah þe [him] syn ealle sundercræftas 7 wuldorsangas in gesamnode, 7 þeah þe hiene ealle frefran, 7 him sien ealle swetnessa to gelædde mid þam fægerestan gestreonum, 7 him þonne sy singal sumor butan ælcre onwendednes[se], 7 he mote alybban [butan] sare, 7 þonne gif he wære [æ]r ane niht on heofona rices wuldre, þonne for[lete] he þæt he ær on þyssum wuldre gelyfede, þe ic ær bisæde, ofer þæt heofena rice þe he ær on wæs þa ane niht, 7 he eft ne mote to heofena rices wuldre. 7 him þær ne bið nanes gefean to lytel, for þan he mot þær alybban [on wlite] 7 on wu[l]dre 7 on wiorðunge butan ælcre onwendednesse mid þara nigon endebyrdnessa engla 7 heahengla [þe] þær wæron Gode gecweme. Þær bið eallum halgum alif sceapen betweox englum 7 heahenglum 7 heahfæderum 7 witegum 7 apostolum 7 mid martyrum.'

[206–13] 7 þencen we togeanes his tocyme, þæt is se egesfullica dæg, þæt us þonne ne ðurfe scamigan þonne he us nealæcð þæt he us gesion wille. For þan þæt bið mycel scamu þæt man his sylfes scamige on þam myclan gemote. [Hw]æt, we nu gehyrdon secgan þæt we ure synna geswican sculon 7 þa betan dæges 7 nihtes. 7 þurh þa ylcan þing we magon þe eað gedon þæt eorðcundlice men magon gewiorðan hiofonwlitige, gif hie willað eaðmodlice Gode þeowigan 7 hyran, 7 þær bið gelic hiofena rices wlite.

at the rising of the sun in paradise, and it towered over all the earth, and a man were able to sit as splendid as a royal child on top of that golden mountain,[42] and he had the beauty and wisdom of Solomon,[43] and all the world were given into his power, along with the treasures which exist throughout the world, and a new bride were brought to his bed each night and she had the beauty of Juno, Saturn's daughter, and every stone were golden, and all the streams flowed with honey, and there were no enemy for him upon the earth, and even if all special powers and glorious songs were united in him, and even if they should all comfort him and all pleasantness were proffered him together with the fairest treasures, and then there were perpetual summer for him without any change, and he might live forever without pain, yet if he had spent a single night in the glory of the kingdom of heaven, he would give up what he had experienced in this glory which I described earlier, in favour of the kingdom of heaven in which he had spent a single night, even if he could not return again to the glory of the kingdom of heaven.[44] And there will not be too little of any joy for him there, because he may live there forever in beauty and in glory and in honour without any change with the nine orders of angels and archangels which were pleasing to God there. There eternal life is ordained for each of the saints among the angels and archangels and patriarchs and prophets and apostles and martyrs.'

[206–13] And let us give thought to his coming, that is that dreadful day, so that we need not be ashamed when he approaches in order to see us. Because that will be a great shame that one must be ashamed of oneself in that great assembly. Lo, we have now heard that we must cease our sins and pray day and night. And by the same means we may the more easily bring it about that earthly men can become radiant as heaven, if they are willing to humbly serve and obey God, and there it will be like the splendour of the kingdom of heaven.[45]

[42] L and M both add a phrase to the effect that this royal child (*cynebearn*) would be in the prime of life; M also adds: 'and he might sit there always until the end of his life'.

[43] M has 'Samson', an error noticed by Kemble and corrected by Robinson.

[44] L reads: 'he would not wish to remain in all this glory if he had been a single night in heaven'. M reads: 'And yet nevertheless, for sorrow he will not wish (?) that he should dwell in all this splendour if he formerly were a single night in heaven and could go back there again and see there the countenance of the king of heaven and the delights which are in heaven' (first part of the sentence as translated by Robinson, 'The Devil's Account of the Next World', pp. 370–1).

[45] Scragg suggests, 'Presumably what is meant is that as men improve their behaviour, the likeness of heaven's beauty will appear in them, an explanation of the preceding *hiofonwlitige*' (*The Vercelli Homilies*, p. 189).

[214–21] Eala mycel is on bocum leornod 7 hit is soðlice eal gesewen; sagað hit þæt on helle sy an hund. Ne meahte hit þæt dioful þam ancran eall asecgan hu mycel þær[e] s[aw]le witu bioð þe to him bioð gescyrede. He hafað hundteontig heafda, 7 he hafað on ælcum heafde hund eagena, 7 ælc þara egena is fyre hat, 7 he hafað .c. handa, 7 on ælcre handa hundteontig fingra, 7 on ælcum fingre .c. nægla, 7 hyra is ælc on nædran wisan ascyrped. Eala, min dryhten, laðlic is hit for ðy on helle to bionne. Wa ðam sawlum þe ðær bion sculon!

[222–8] Hwæt, we nu gehyrdon secgan hwylc hit is on helle to bionne. For ðan we sculon geswican urra synna 7 Gode eaðmode bion mid ælmessum 7 mid godum weorcum. 7 secen we ure cyrcean mid clænesse 7 mid hlutran mode, 7 bidden we eaðmodlice bene þæt we ne wiorðan geteodde on þa helle witu. Gif we þænne swa don wyllað swa us dryhten beden hafað, þonne moton we mid him 7 mid his þam halegan gæste wunigean in ealra worulda woruld, amen.

[214–21] Oh, much is learned from books and it is all truly known; it says that in hell there is a hound.[46] The devil could not tell fully to the anchorite how great are the soul's torments that are assigned to them. He has a hundred heads, and he has a hundred eyes in each head, and each of the eyes is hot as fire, and he has a hundred hands, and on each hand a hundred fingers, and on each finger a hundred nails, and each of the nails is sharpened in serpent fashion. Alas, my Lord, hateful it is therefore to be in hell. Woe to those souls who will have to be there!

[222–8] Lo, we have now heard what it is like to be in hell! Therefore we must cease our sins and be humble towards God with almsgiving and good works. And let us attend our church with purity and with clean spirit, and let us humbly ask in prayer that we not be assigned to the torments of hell. If we then will do as the Lord has bidden us, we can dwell with him and with his Holy Spirit forever and ever, amen.

[46] An erasure after *hund* in E suggests that the original reading may have been an enumeration (a hundred of something, presumably torments; see above, pp. 156–7).

Bibliography

Allen, M. J. B. and D. G. Calder, trans., *Sources and Analogues of Old English Poetry: the Major Latin Texts in Translation* (Cambridge and Totowa, NJ, 1976)

Assmann, B., ed., *Angelsächsische Homilien und Heiligenleben*, Bibliothek der angelsächsischen Prosa 3 (1889; repr. with a supplementary introduction by P. Clemoes, Darmstadt, 1964)

Atkinson, R., ed. and trans., *The Passions and the Homilies from Leabhar Breac*, TLS 2 (Dublin, 1887)

Baesecke, G., *Der Vocabularius Sti. Galli in der angelsächsischen Mission* (Halle, 1933)

Banks, M. M., ed., *An Alphabet of Tales*, 2 vols., EETS os 126–7 (London, 1904–5)

Batiouchkof, T. D., 'Le débat de l'âme et du corps', *Romania* 20 (1891), 1–55 and 513–78

Bauerreiss, R., 'Das frühmittelalterliche Bistum Neuberg im Staffelsee', *Studien und Mitteilungen zur Geschichte des Benediktiner-ordens und seiner Zweige* 60 (1946), 375–438

Bazire, J., and J. E. Cross, ed., *Eleven Old English Rogationtide Homilies*, 2nd ed., King's College London Medieval Studies 4 (London, 1990)

Becker, E. J., *A Contribution to the Comparative Study of the Medieval Visions of Heaven and Hell, with Special Reference to the Middle English Versions* (Baltimore, MD, 1895)

Bensley, R. L., ed., *The Fourth Book of Ezra*, with an Introduction by M. R. James, Texts and Studies 3.2 (Cambridge, 1895)

Benson, L. D., gen. ed., *The Riverside Chaucer*, 3rd ed. (Boston, 1987)

Bernard, J. H., and R. Atkinson, ed. and trans., *The Irish Liber Hymnorum*, 2 vols., HBS 13–14 (London, 1898)

Best, R. I. and O. Bergin, ed., *Lebor na Huidre: Book of the Dun Cow* (Dublin, 1929)

Bethell, D., 'English Monks and Irish Reform in the Eleventh and Twelfth Centuries', in *Historical Studies VIII*, ed. T. D. Williams (Dublin, 1971), pp. 111–35

Bieler, L., 'Ireland's Contribution to the Culture of Northumbria', in *Famulus Christi*, ed. Bonner, pp. 210–28

Bieler, L., ed., *The Irish Penitentials*, SLH 5 (Dublin, 1963)

Biggs, F. M., *The Sources of Christ III: a Revision of Cook's Notes*, Old English Newsletter Subsidia 12 (Binghamton, NY, 1986)

Biggs, F. M., T. D. Hill, and P. E. Szarmach., ed., *Sources of Anglo-Saxon Literary Culture: a Trial Version* (Binghamton, NY, 1990)

Bischoff, B., *Die südostdeutschen Schreibschulen und Bibliotheken in der Karolingerzeit*, I: *Die Bayrischen Diözesen* (Wiesbaden, 1960)

Mittelalterliche Studien: Ausgewählte Aufsätze zur Schriftkunde und Literaturgeschichte, 3 vols. (Stuttgart, 1966–81)

'Paläographische Fragen deutscher Denkmäler der Karolingerzeit', in his *Mittelalterliche Studien* III, 73–111

'Turning-Points in the History of Latin Exegesis in the Early Irish Church: A. D. 650-800', in *Biblical Studies: the Medieval Irish Contribution*, ed. M. McNamara (Dublin, 1976), pp. 74–160 (trans. of 'Wendepunkte in der Geschichte der lateinischen Exegese im Frühmittelalter', in *Mittelalterliche Studien* I, 205–73)

'Lorsch im Spiegel seiner Handschriften', in *Die Reichsabtei Lorsch: Festschrift zum Gedenken an ihre Stiftung 764*, 2 vols. (Darmstadt, 1977) II, 7–128

Bishop, E., *Liturgica Historica: Papers on the Liturgy and Religious Life of the Western Church* (Oxford, 1918)

Blumenthal, U.-R., ed., *Carolingian Essays: Andrew W. Mellon Lectures in Early Christian Studies* (Washington, DC, 1983)

Boethius: De consolatione Philosophiae, 2nd ed., CCSL 94 (Turnhout, 1984)

Bonner, G., ed., *Famulus Christi: Essays in Commemoration of the Thirteenth Centenary of the Birth of the Venerable Bede* (London, 1976)

Bonner, G., D. Rollason and C. Stancliffe, ed., *St Cuthbert, His Cult and His Community to AD 1200* (Woodbridge, 1989)

Boswell, C. S., *An Irish Precursor of Dante* (London, 1908)

Bradshaw, B., 'The Wild and Woolly West: Early Irish Christianity and Latin Orthodoxy', in *The Churches, Ireland and the Irish*, ed. W. J. Sheils and D. Wood (London, 1989), pp. 1–23

Brandes, H., ed., *Visio S. Pauli: ein Beitrag zur Visionslitteratur mit einem deutschen und zwei lateinischen Texten* (Halle, 1885)

Brown, C., '*Beowulf* and the *Blickling Homilies* and Some Textual Notes', *PMLA* 53 (1938), 905–16

Bullough, D. A., 'The Educational Tradition in England from Alfred to Ælfric: Teaching *Utriusque Linguae*', in *La Scuola nell'occidente latino dell'alto medioevo*, Settimane di studio del Centro Italiano di studi sull'alto medioevo 19 (Spoleto, 1972), 453–94

Cagin, P., *L'Euchologie latine étudiée dans la tradition de ses formules et de ses formulaires*, I: *'Te Deum' ou 'Illatio'*?, Scriptorium Solesmense 1.1 (Solesmes, 1906)

Calder, D. G., P. K. Ford and D. F. Melia, trans., *Sources and Analogues of Old English Poetry, II: the Major Germanic and Celtic Texts in Translation* (Cambridge and Totowa, NJ, 1983)

Callison, T. C., ed., 'An Edition of Previously Unpublished Anglo-Saxon Homilies in MSS. CCCC 302 and Cotton Faustina A. IX' (unpubl. PhD dissertation, Univ. of Wisconsin, 1973)

Campbell, J., 'The Debt of the Early English Church to Ireland', in *Irland und die Christenheit*, ed. Ní Chatháin and Richter, pp. 332–46

Carey, J., 'Cosmology in *Saltair na Rann*', *Celtica* 17 (1985), 33–52

'The Heavenly City in *Saltair na Rann*', *Celtica* 18 (1986), 87–104

'The Irish Vision of the Chinese', *Ériu* 38 (1987), 73–9

'Ireland and the Antipodes: the Heterodoxy of Virgil of Salzburg', *Speculum* 64 (1989), 1–10

'*Visio Sancti Pauli* and the *Saltair*'s Hell', *Éigse* 23 (1989), 39–44

Carney, J., 'A Miscellany of Irish Verse', *Éigse* 1 (1940), 239–48

Studies in Irish Literature and History (Dublin, 1955)

'The Dating of Early Irish Verse Texts, 500–1100', *Éigse* 19 (1983), 177–216

Carney, J., ed. and trans., *The Poems of Blathmac Son of Cú Brettan, together with the Irish Gospel of Thomas and a Poem on the Virgin Mary*, ITS 47 (Dublin, 1964)

Chadwick, N. K., 'The Celtic Background of Early Anglo-Saxon England', in *Celt and Saxon*, ed. Chadwick, pp. 323–52

The Age of the Saints in the Early Celtic Church (London, 1961)

Chadwick, N. K., ed., *Celt and Saxon: Studies in the Early British Border* (Cambridge, 1963)

Charlesworth, J. H., ed., *Old Testament Pseudepigrapha*, 2 vols. (New York, 1983–5)

Clayton, M., *The Cult of the Virgin Mary in Anglo-Saxon England*, Cambridge Studies in Anglo-Saxon England 2 (Cambridge, 1990)

Clemoes, P. and K. Hughes, ed., *England before the Conquest: Studies in Primary Sources presented to Dorothy Whitelock* (Cambridge, 1971)

Coccia, E., 'La cultura irlandese precarolina: miracolo o mito?', *Studi Medievali* 3rd ser. 8 (1967), 257–420

Colgrave, B. and R. A. B. Mynors, ed. and trans., *Bede's Ecclesiastical History of the English People* (Oxford, 1969)

Collins, R. L., 'Blickling Homily XVI and the Dating of *Beowulf*', in *Medieval Studies Conference Aachen 1983*, ed. W.-D. Bald and H. Weinstock (Frankfurt, 1984), pp. 61–9

Contreni, J. J., 'Carolingian Biblical Studies', in *Carolingian Essays*, ed. Blumenthal, pp. 71–98

Coulton, G. G., *Five Centuries of Religion*, I: *St Bernard, His Predecessors and Successors, 1000–1200 A.D.* (Cambridge, 1923)

Courcelle, P., 'Histoire du cliché virgilien des cent bouches', *Revue des études latines* 33 (1955), 231–40

Cross, J. E., 'The Literate Anglo-Saxon – on Sources and Disseminations', *PBA* 58 (1972), 67–100

'*De ordine creaturarum liber* in Old English Prose', *Anglia* 90 (1972), 132–40

'Portents and Events at Christ's Birth: Comments on Vercelli V and VI and the Old English Martyrology', *ASE* 2 (1973), 209–20

'The Influence of Irish Texts and Traditions on the *Old English Martyrology*', *PRIA* 81C (1981), 173–92

'A Doomsday Passage in an Old English Sermon for Lent', *Anglia* 100 (1982), 103–8

'Towards the Identification of Old English Literary Ideas – Old Workings and New Seams', in *Sources of Anglo-Saxon Culture*, ed. Szarmach, pp. 77–101

'The Insular Connections of a Sermon for Holy Innocents', in *Medieval Literature and Antiquities*, ed. M. Stokes and T. L. Burton (Cambridge, 1987), pp. 57–70

Cambridge Pembroke College MS 25: a Carolingian Sermonary Used by Anglo-Saxon Preachers, King's College London Medieval Studies 1 (London, 1987)

Cross, J. E. and T. D. Hill, ed. and trans., *The Prose Solomon and Saturn and Adrian and Ritheus*, McMaster Old English Studies and Texts 1 (Toronto, 1982)

Cross, T. P., *Motif-Index of Early Irish Literature*, Indiana University Publications, Folklore Series 7 (Bloomington, IN, 1952)

Cross, T. P. and C. Slover, trans., *Ancient Irish Tales* (1936; repr. with revised bibliography by D. W. Dunn, Totowa, NJ, 1969)

Daly, L. W. and W. Suchier, ed., *Altercatio Hadriani Augusti et Epicteti Philosophi*, Illinois Studies in Language and Literature 24.1–2 (Urbana, 1939)

David, P., ed., 'Un recueil de conférences monastiques irlandaises du VIIIe siècle', *RB* 49 (1937), 62–89

De Bruyne, D., ed., 'Fragments retrouvés d'apocryphes priscillianistes', *RB* 24 (1907), 318–35

Dekkers, E. and A. Gaar, ed., *Clavis Patrum Latinorum*, 2nd ed. (Steenbrugge, 1961)

Dinzelbacher, P., 'Die Messersäule', *Bayerisches Jahrbuch für Volkskunde* 1980–1, 41–54

Dobbie, E. V. K., ed., *The Anglo-Saxon Minor Poems*, ASPR 6 (New York, 1942)

Dolbeau, F., 'Du nouveau sur un sermonnaire de Cambridge', *Scriptorium* 42 (1988), 255–7

Donahue, C., 'Beowulf, Ireland and the Natural Good', *Traditio* 7 (1949–51), 263–77

Dopsch, H. and R. Juffinger, ed., *Virgil von Salzburg: Missionar und Gelehrter* (Salzburg, 1985)

Dottin, G., *Manuel d'irlandais moyen*, 2 vols. (Paris, 1913)

Dottin, G., ed., 'Les deux chagrins du royaume du ciel', *RC* 21 (1900), 349–87

Dumville, D., 'Biblical Apocrypha and the Early Irish: a Preliminary Investigation', *PRIA* 73C (1973), 299–338

'*Echtrae* and *Immram*: Some Problems of Definition', *Ériu* 27 (1976), 73–94

'Towards an Interpretation of *Fís Adamnán*', *SC* 12/13 (1977–8), 62–77

'"Beowulf" and the Celtic World: the Uses of Evidence', *Traditio* 37 (1981), 109–60

Dunleavy, G. W., *Colum's Other Island: the Irish at Lindisfarne* (Madison, WI, 1960)

Dwyer, M. E., ed., 'An Unstudied Redaction of the *Visio Pauli*', *Manuscripta* 32 (1988), 121–38

Earl, J. W., 'Literary Problems in Early Medieval Hagiography' (unpubl. PhD dissertation, Cornell Univ., 1971)

Ehwald, R., ed., *Aldhelmi Opera*, MGH, Auct. antiq. 15 (Berlin, 1919)

Fadda, A. M. L., ed., *Nuove omelie anglosassoni della rinascenza benedettina*, Filologia germanica, Testi e Studi 1 (Florence, 1977)

Flower, R., *Catalogue of Irish Manuscripts in the British Museum*, II (London, 1926)

The Irish Tradition (Oxford, 1947)

Ford, P. K., ed., *Celtic Folklore and Christianity: Studies in Memory of William W. Heist* (Santa Barbara, CA, 1983)

Ford, P. K., and K. Borst, ed., *Connections between Old English and Medieval Celtic Literature*, Old English Colloquium Series 2 (Berkeley, CA, 1982)

Förster, M., ed., *Die Vercelli-Homilien*, I: *I. – VIII Homilie*, Bibliothek der angelsächsischen Prosa 12 (Hamburg, 1932)

'A New Version of the Apocalypse of Thomas in Old English', *Anglia* 73 (1955), 6–36

Frantzen, A. J., *The Literature of Penance in Anglo-Saxon England* (New Brunswick, NJ, 1983)

Frede, H. J., *Kirchenschriftsteller: Verzeichnis und Sigel*, Vetus Latina 1.1 (Freiburg, 1981), with supplements: *Aktualisierungsheft 1984* (Freiburg, 1984) and *Aktualisierungsheft 1988* (Freiburg, 1988)

Freytag, H., *Kommentar zur frühmittelhochdeutschen Summa Theologiae*, Medium Aevum 19 (Munich, 1970)

Gamber, K., ed., *Niceta von Remesiana Instructio ad competentes: frühchristliche Katechesen aus Dacien*, Textus patristici et liturgici, fasc. 1 (Regensburg, 1964)

Gantz, J., trans., *Early Irish Myths and Sagas* (New York, 1981)

Gatch, M. McC., 'Two Uses of Apocrypha in Old English Homilies', *Church History* 33 (1964), 379–91

Gneuss, H., 'A Preliminary List of Manuscripts Written or Owned in England up to 1100', *ASE* 9 (1981), 1–60

Godden, M. R., 'Ælfric and the Vernacular Prose Tradition', in *The Old English Homily and its Backgrounds*, ed. Szarmach and Huppé, pp. 99–117

'An Old English Penitential Motif', *ASE* 2 (1973), 221–39

Godel, W., 'Irish Prayer in the Early Middle Ages', *Milltown Studies* 4 (1979), 60–99; 5 (1980), 72–114 (trans. of 'Irisches Beten im frühen Mittelalter', *Zeitschrift für katholische Theologie* 85 (1963), 261–321 and 389–439)

Gougaud, L., 'La croyance au répit périodique des damnés dans les légendes irlandaises', *Annales de Bretagne* 1927 (*Mélanges offerts à J. Loth*), pp. 63–72

Christianity in Celtic Lands, trans. M. Joynt (London, 1932)

Grant, R. J. S., *Cambridge, Corpus Christi College 41: the Loricas and the Missal*, Costerus ns 17 (Amsterdam, 1979)

Grant, R. J. S., ed. and trans., *Three Homilies from Cambridge, Corpus Christi College 41* (Ottawa, 1982)

Greene, D., ed., *Fingal Rónáin and Other Stories*, MMIS 16 (1955)

Greene, D. and F. Kelly, ed. and trans., *The Irish Adam and Eve Story from Saltair na Rann*, I: *Text and Translation* (Dublin, 1976)

Greene, D., and F. O'Connor, ed. and trans., *A Golden Treasury of Irish Poetry, A.D. 600–1200* (London, 1967)

Greene, R., trans., *Boethius: The Consolation of Philosophy* (Indianapolis, IN, 1962)

Grosjean, P., 'A propos du manuscrit 49 de la Reine Christine', *AB* 54 (1936), 113–36

Grundy, L., *Books and Grace: Ælfric's Theology*, King's College London Medieval Studies 6 (London, 1991)

Gwynn, A., ed. and trans., *The Writings of Bishop Patrick 1074–1084*, SLH 1 (Dublin, 1955)

Gwynn, E. J., ed. and trans., *The Metrical Dindshenchas*, 5 vols., TLS 8–12 (Dublin, 1906–35)

The Rule of Tallaght, Hermathena 44, 2nd suppl. (Dublin, 1927)

Haddan, A. W. and W. Stubbs, ed., *Councils and Ecclesiastical Documents Relating to Great Britain and Ireland*, 3 vols. (Oxford, 1869–71)

Hall, T. N., 'Apocryphal Lore and the Life of Christ in Old English Literature' (unpubl. PhD dissertation, Univ. of Illinois, 1990)

Hamel, A. G. van, ed., *Immrama*, MMIS 10 (Dublin, 1941)

Hamman, A., ed., *Patrologiae cursus completus, Series Latina: Supplementum*, 5 vols. (Paris, 1958–74)

Hayes, R. J., *Manuscript Sources for the History of Irish Civilization*, XI: *List of Manuscripts* (Boston, 1965); with a *First Supplement* (Boston, 1979)

Healy, A. diP., ed., *The Old English Vision of St. Paul*, Speculum Anniversary Monographs 2 (Cambridge, MA, 1978)

Heist, W. W., *The Fifteen Signs before Doomsday* (East Lansing, MI, 1952)

Hellmann, S., ed., *Pseudo-Cyprianus de xii abusivis saeculi*, TU 1.1 (Leipzig, 1909)

Heningham, E. K., 'Old English Precursors of *The Worcester Fragments*', *PMLA* 55 (1940), 291–307

Hennecke, E. and W. Schneemelcher, ed., *New Testament Apocrypha*, trans. and ed. R. McL. Wilson, 2 vols. (Philadelphia, PA, 1964)

Henry, P. L., *The Early English and Celtic Lyric* (London, 1966)

Herbert, M. and M. McNamara, ed., *Irish Biblical Apocrypha: Selected Texts in Translation* (Edinburgh, 1989)

Herren, M. W., 'Some New Light on the Life of Virgilius Maro Grammaticus', *PRIA* 79C (1979), 27–71

Herren, M. W., ed. and trans., *The Hisperica Famina*, I: *The A-Text* (Toronto, 1974)

The Hisperica Famina, II: *Related Poems* (Toronto, 1989)

Hill, T. D., 'Literary History and Old English Poetry: the Case of *Christ I, II*, and *III*', in *Sources of Anglo-Saxon Culture*, ed. Szarmach, pp. 3–22

Himmelfarb, M., *Tours of Hell: an Apocalyptic Form in Jewish and Christian Literature* (Philadelphia, PA, 1983)

Hogan, E., ed. and trans., *The Irish Nennius from L. na Huidre and Homilies and Legends from L. Brecc*, TLS 6 (Dublin, 1895)

Holder, A., *Die Reichenauer Handschriften*, I: *Die Pergamenthandschriften* (1906; repr. with bibliographical addenda, Wiesbaden, 1970)

Horstmann, C., *Yorkshire Writers*, 2 vols. (London, 1895)

Hughes, K., 'The Distribution of Irish Scriptoria and Centres of Learning from 730 to 1111', in *Studies in the Early British Church*, ed. N. K. Chadwick (Cambridge, 1958), pp. 243–72

'Irish Monks and Learning', in *Los monjes y los estudios* (Poblet, 1963), pp. 61–86

'Some Aspects of Irish Influence on Early English Private Prayer', *SC* 5 (1970), 48–61

'Evidence for Contacts between the Churches of the Irish and English from the Synod of Whitby to the Viking Age', in *England before the Conquest*, ed. Clemoes and Hughes, pp. 49–67

Early Christian Ireland: Introduction to the Sources (Ithaca, NY, 1972)

Hull, V., ed. and trans., 'Apgitir Chrábaid: the Alphabet of Piety', *Celtica* 8 (1968), 44–89

Hyde, D., *The Religious Songs of Connacht*, 2 vols. (London, 1906)

Jackson, K. H., ed., *Aislinge Meic Con Glinne* (Dublin, 1990)

James, E., 'Ireland and Western Gaul in the Merovingian Period', in *Ireland in Early Mediaeval Europe*, ed. Whitelock *et al.*, pp. 362–86

James, M. R., 'Names of Angels in Anglo-Saxon and Other Documents', *JTS* 11 (1909–10), 569–71

'Irish Apocrypha', *JTS* 20 (1918–19), 9–16

James, M. R., ed., *Apocrypha Anecdota [First Series]: a Collection of Thirteen Apocryphal Books and Fragments*, Texts and Studies 2.3 (Cambridge, 1893)

Latin Infancy Gospels (Cambridge, 1927)

James, M. R., trans., *The Apocryphal New Testament* (Oxford, 1924; repr. with corrections, 1953)

Kelly, J. F., 'Irish Influence in England after the Synod of Whitby: Some New Literary Evidence', *Éire – Ireland* 10 (1975), 35–47

'Hiberno-Latin Exegesis and Exegetes', *Annuale Mediaevale* 22 (1981), 46–60

'A Catalogue of Early Medieval Hiberno-Latin Biblical Commentaries', *Traditio* 44 (1988), 537–71; 45 (1989–90), 393–434

Kemble, J. M., *The Dialogue of Solomon and Saturnus*, Ælfric Society 8, 13 and 15 (London, 1848)

Kenney, J. F., *The Sources for the Early History of Ireland*, I: *Ecclesiastical* (1929; repr. with addenda by L. Bieler, New York, 1966)

Ker, N. R., *Catalogue of Manuscripts containing Anglo-Saxon* (Oxford, 1957)

Keynes, S., 'King Athelstan's Books', in *Learning and Literature in Anglo-Saxon England*, ed. Lapidge and Gneuss, pp. 143–201

Keynes, S. and M. Lapidge, trans., *Alfred the Great: Asser's Life of King Alfred and Other Contemporary Sources* (Harmondsworth, 1983)

Klaeber, F., ed., *Beowulf and the Fight at Finnsburg*, 3rd ed. with 1st and 2nd supplements (Boston, 1950)

Knott, E., ed., *Togail Bruidne Da Derga*, MMIS 8 (Dublin, 1936)

Krapp, G. P., ed., *The Junius Manuscript*, ASPR 1 (New York, 1931)

The Vercelli Book, ASPR 2 (New York, 1932)

The Paris Psalter and the Meters of Boethius, ASPR 5 (New York, 1932)

Krapp, G. P. and E. V. K. Dobbie, ed., *The Exeter Book*, ASPR 3 (New York, 1936)

Kuypers, A. B., ed., *The Prayer Book of Aedeluald the Bishop, commonly called The Book of Cerne* (Cambridge, 1902)

Lapidge, M., 'The Hermeneutic Style in Tenth-Century Anglo-Latin Literature', *ASE* 4 (1975), 67–111

'Latin Learning in Dark Age Wales: Some Prolegomena', in *Proceedings of the Seventh International Congress of Celtic Studies*, ed. D. E. Evans, J. G. Griffith and E. M. Jope (Oxford, 1986), pp. 91–107

Lapidge, M. and D. Dumville, ed., *Gildas: New Approaches* (Woodbridge, 1984)

Lapidge, M. and H. Gneuss, ed., *Learning and Literature in Anglo-Saxon England: Studies presented to Peter Clemoes* (Cambridge, 1985)

Lapidge, M. and M. W. Herren, trans., *Aldhelm: the Prose Works* (Cambridge and Totowa, NJ, 1979)

Lapidge, M. and R. Sharpe, *Bibliography of Celtic-Latin Literature 400–1200* (Dublin, 1985)

Leabhar Breac: the Speckled Book [lithographic reproduction of J. O'Longan's transcript] (Dublin, 1872–6)

Lees, C., 'The "Sunday Letter" and the "Sunday Lists"', *ASE* 14 (1985), 129–51

'Theme and Echo in an Anonymous Old English Sermon for Easter Sunday', *Traditio* 42 (1986), 115–42

Lehner, A., ed., *Florilegia: Florilegium Frisingense (Clm 6433); Testimonia Divinae Scripturae*, CCSL 108D (Turnhout, 1987)

Lehner, A., and W. Berschin, ed., *Lateinische Kultur im VIII. Jahrhundert: Traube Gedenkschrift* (St Ottilien, 1989)

Levison, W., *England and the Continent in the Eighth Century* (Oxford, 1946)

Lindelöf, U., ed., *Rituale Ecclesiae Dunelmensis: the Durham Collectar*, Surtees Society 140 (London, 1927)

Little, A. G., ed., *Liber Exemplorum ad Usum Praedicantium* (Aberdeen, 1908)

Löfstedt, B., ed., *Sedulius Scottus Kommentar zum Evangelium nach Matthäus 1,1–11,1*, Aus der Geschichte der lateinischen Bibel 14 (Freiburg, 1989)

Lowe, E. A., *Codices Latini Antiquiores*, 11 vols. and supplement (Oxford, 1934–71; 2nd ed. of vol. II, 1972)

Löwe, H., ed., *Die Iren und Europa im früheren Mittelalter*, 2 vols. (Stuttgart, 1982)

Loyn, H. R., 'The Conversion of the English to Christianity: Some Comments on the Celtic Contribution', in *Welsh Society and Nationhood: Historical*

Essays presented to Glanmor Williams, ed. R. R. Davies, R. A. Griffiths, I. G. Jones and K. O. Morgan (Cardiff, 1984), pp. 5–18

Macalister, R. A. S., ed. and trans., *Lebor Gabála Érenn*, 5 vols., ITS 34, 35, 39, 41 and 44 (Dublin, 1938–56)

Mac Cana, P., *Branwen Daughter of Llŷr: a Study in the Irish Affinities and of the Compilation of the Second Branch of the Mabinogi* (Cardiff, 1958)

'The Sinless Otherworld of *Immram Brain*', *Ériu* 27 (1976), 95–115

Machielsen, J., *Clavis Patristica Pseudepigraphorum Medii Aevi, 1A – B: Opera Homiletica*, CCSL (Turnhout, 1990)

Malone, K., 'Grendel and His Abode', in *Studia Philologica et Litteraria in Honorem L. Spitzer*, ed. A. G. Hatcher (Bern, 1958), pp. 297–308

Marchand, J. W., 'The Old Norwegian Christmas Homily and the Question of Irish Influence', *Arv: Journal of Scandinavian Folklore* 31 (1975), 23–34

Marchand, J. W., ed. and trans., 'The Old Icelandic *Joca Monachorum*', *Mediaeval Scandinavia* 9 (1976), 99–126

Mayr-Harting, H., *The Coming of Christianity to Anglo-Saxon England*, 3rd ed. (University Park, PA, 1991)

McCone, K., *Pagan Past and Christian Present in Early Irish Literature*, Maynooth Monographs 3 (Maynooth, 1990)

McNally, R. E., *Der irische Liber de numeris: eine Quellenanalyse des pseudo-isidorischen Liber de numeris*, Inaugural-Dissertation (Munich, 1957)

'Isidorian Pseudepigrapha in the Early Middle Ages', in *Isidoriana: Estudios sobre San Isidoro de Sevilla en el XIV centenario de su nacimiento*, ed. M. Díaz y Díaz (León, 1961), pp. 305–16

'"Christus" in the Pseudo-Isidorian "Liber de ortu et obitu patriarcharum"', *Traditio* 21 (1965), 167–83

'Old Ireland, Her Scribes and Scholars', in *Old Ireland*, ed. McNally, pp. 120–46

'The Imagination and Early Irish Biblical Exegesis', *Annuale Mediaevale* 10 (1969), 5–27

'"In Nomine Dei Summi": Seven Hiberno-Latin Sermons', *Traditio* 35 (1979), 121–43

McNally, R. E., ed., *Old Ireland* (New York, 1965)

Scriptores Hiberniae Minores I, CCSL 108B (Turnhout, 1973)

McNamara, M., 'A Plea for Hiberno-Latin Biblical Studies', *Irish Theological Quarterly* 39 (1972), 337–53

The Apocrypha in the Irish Church (Dublin, 1975)

'The Irish Affiliations of the *Catechesis Celtica*', *Celtica* 21 (1990), 291–334

Studies on Texts of Early Irish Latin Gospels (A.D. 600–1200), Instrumenta Patristica 20 (Steenbrugge, 1990)

McNamara, M., ed., *Biblical Studies: the Medieval Irish Contribution* (Dublin, 1976)

Menner, R. J., ed., *The Poetical Dialogues of Solomon and Saturn* (New York, 1941)

Meyer, K., 'Stories and Songs from Irish MSS, 1. The Vision of Laisrén', *Otia Merseiana* 1 (1899), 113–19

'Mitteilungen aus irischen Handschriften', *ZCP* 4 (1903), 234–40

Learning in Ireland in the Fifth Century and the Transmission of Letters (Dublin, 1913)

Meyer, K., ed. and trans., *Aislinge Meic Conglinne: the Vision of MacConglinne* (London, 1892)

The Triads of Ireland, TLS 13 (Dublin, 1906)

Migne, J.-P., ed., *Patrologiae cursus completus, Series Latina*, 221 vols. (Paris, 1844–64)

Moffat, D., ed., *The Old English Soul and Body* (Woodbridge, 1990)

Morris, R., ed. and trans., *Old English Homilies and Homiletic Treatises of the Twelfth and Thirteenth Centuries*, EETS os 34 (London, 1868)

An Old English Miscellany, EETS os 49 (London, 1872)

Old English Homilies of the Twelfth Century, EETS os 53 (London, 1873)

The Blickling Homilies of the Tenth Century, EETS os 58, 63, and 73 (1874–8; repr. as one vol., 1967)

Murdoch, B., *The Irish Adam and Eve Story from Saltair na Rann*, II: *Commentary* (Dublin, 1976)

Murphy, G., ed. and trans., *Duanaire Finn: the Book of the Lays of Finn*, II – III, ITS 28 and 43 (Dublin, 1933 and 1953)

Nagy, J. F., 'Close Encounters of the Traditional Kind in Medieval Irish Literature', in *Celtic Folklore and Christianity*, ed. Ford, pp. 129–49

Napier, A. S., ed., *Wulfstan: Sammlung der ihm zugeschriebenen Homilien nebst Untersuchungen über ihre Echtheit* (1883; repr. with a supplement by K. Ostheeren, Dublin, 1967)

Nic Dhonnchadha, L., ed., *Aided Muirchertaig Meic Erca*, MMIS 19 (Dublin, 1964)

Nic Énri, U. and G. MacNiocaill, ed. and trans., 'The Second Recension of the Evernew Tongue', *Celtica* 9 (1971), 1–59

Ní Chatháin, P. and M. Richter, ed., *Irland und Europa: die Kirche im Frühmittelalter* (Stuttgart, 1984)

Irland und die Christenheit: Bibelstudien und Mission (Stuttgart, 1987)

Nyberg, T., ed., *History and Heroic Tale: a Symposium* (Odense, 1985)

Ó Corráin, D. *et al.*, ed., *Sages, Saints and Storytellers: Celtic Studies in Honour of James Carney* (Maynooth, 1989)

Ó Cróinín, D., review of McNamara, *The Apocrypha in the Irish Church*, in *Éigse* 16 (1976), 348–56

'Rath Melsigi, Willibrord, and the Earliest Echternach Manuscripts', *Peritia* 3 (1984), 17–49

'"New Heresy for Old": Pelagianism in Ireland and the Papal Letter of 640', *Speculum* 60 (1985), 505–16

O'Dwyer, P., *Céli Dé: Spiritual Reform in Ireland 750–900*, 2nd ed. (Dublin, 1981)

O'Grady, S. H., ed. and trans., *Silva Gadelica*, 2 vols. (London, 1892)

O'Keeffe, K. O'B., 'The Geographic List of *Solomon and Saturn II*', *ASE* 20 (1991), 123–41

Ó Laoghaire, D., 'Irish Elements in the *Catechesis Celtica*', in *Irland und die Christenheit*, ed. Ní Chatháin and Richter, pp. 146–64

O'Meara, J. J., trans., *The Voyage of Saint Brendan: Journey to the Promised Land* (Dublin, 1978)

Ó Néill, P. P. [P. P. O'Neill], 'The Old English Introductions to the Prose Psalms of the Paris Psalter: Sources, Structure, and Composition', *SP* 78 (1981), 20–38

'The Date and Authorship of *Apgitir Chrábaid*: Some Internal Evidence', in *Irland und die Christenheit*, ed. Ní Chatháin and Richter, pp. 203–15

O'Rahilly, T. F., *Early Irish History and Mythology* (Dublin, 1946)

Os, B. van, *Religious Visions: the Development of the Eschatological Elements in Mediaeval English Religious Literature* (Amsterdam, 1932)

Owen, D. D. R., 'The *Vision of St Paul*: the French and Provençal Versions and their Sources', *Romance Philology* 12 (1958), 33–51

Owst, G. R., *Preaching in Medieval England: an Introduction to Sermon Manuscripts of the Period c. 1350–1450* (Cambridge, 1926)

Patch, H. R., *The Other World according to Descriptions in Medieval Literature*, Smith College Studies in Modern Languages ns 1 (Cambridge, MA, 1950)

Picard, J.-M., trans., *The Vision of Tnugdal* (Dublin, 1989)

Plummer, C., *Miscellanea Hagiographica Hibernica*, Subsidia Hagiographica 15 (Brussels, 1925)

Plummer, C., ed., *Vitae Sanctorum Hiberniae*, 2 vols. (Oxford, 1910)

Plummer, C., ed. and trans., *Bethada Náem nÉrenn: Lives of Irish Saints*, 2 vols. (Oxford, 1922)

Pope, J. C., ed., *Homilies of Ælfric: a Supplementary Collection*, 2 vols., EETS os 259 and 260 (London, 1967–8)

Pöschl, V., H. Gärtner and W. Heyke, *Bibliographie zur antiken Bildersprache* (Heidelberg, 1964)

Puhvel, M., *Beowulf and Celtic Tradition* (Waterloo, Ontario, 1979)

Quin, E. G., gen. ed., *Dictionary of the Irish Language based mainly on Old and Middle Irish Materials*, Compact Edition (Dublin, 1983)

Reynolds, R., 'Unity and Diversity in Carolingian Canon Law Collections: the

Case of the *Collectio Hibernensis* and its Derivatives', in *Carolingian Essays*, ed. Blumenthal, pp. 99–135

The Ordinals of Christ from their Origins to the Twelfth Century, Beiträge zur Geschichte und Quellenkunde des Mittelalters 7 (Berlin, 1978)

Robinson, F. C., ed., 'The Devil's Account of the Next World', *NM* 73 (1972), 362–71

Robinson, J. A., *The Times of Saint Dunstan* (Oxford, 1923)

Rosenthal, C. L., *The 'Vitae Patrum' in Old and Middle English Literature* (Philadelphia, 1936)

Sauer, H., 'Die 72 Völker und Sprachen der Welt: ein mittelalterliche Topos in der englischen Literatur', *Anglia* 101 (1982), 29–48

Sayers, W., '*Mani maidi an nem …*': Ringing Changes on a Cosmic Motif', *Ériu* 37 (1986), 99–117

Schwab, U., *Die Sternrune im Wessobrunner Gebet*, Amsterdamer Publikationen zur Sprache und Literatur 1 (Amsterdam, 1973)

Scott, H. von E. and C. C. S. Bland, trans., *The Dialogue on Miracles: Caesarius of Heisterbach*, 2 vols. (London, 1929)

Scragg, D. G., 'The Compilation of the Vercelli Book', *ASE* 2 (1973), 189–207

'Napier's "Wulfstan" Homily XXX: its Sources, its Relationship to the Vercelli Book and its Style', *ASE* 6 (1977), 197–212

'The Corpus of Vernacular Homilies and Prose Saints' Lives before Ælfric', *ASE* 8 (1979), 223–77

'Anonymous Old English Homilies', in *Sources of Anglo-Saxon Literary Culture: a Trial Version*, ed. Biggs *et al.*, pp. 124–30

Scragg, D. G., ed., *The Vercelli Homilies and Related Texts*, EETS os 300 (London, 1992)

Selmer, C., ed., *Navigatio Sancti Brendani Abbatis* (Notre Dame, IN, 1959)

Seymour, St J. D., 'The Bringing Forth of the Soul in Irish Literature', *JTS* 22 (1920–1), 16–20

'The Eschatology of the Early Irish Church', *ZCP* 14 (1923), 179–211

'The Seven Heavens in Irish Literature', *ZCP* 14 (1923), 18–30

'Notes on Apocrypha in Ireland', *PRIA* 37C (1924–7), 107–17

'Studies in the Vision of Tundal', *PRIA* 37C (1924–7), 87–106

'The Vision of Adamnan', *PRIA* 37C (1924–7), 304–12

Irish Visions of the Other-World (London, 1930)

Siegmund, A., *Die Überlieferung der griechischen christlichen Literatur in der lateinischen Kirche bis zum zwölften Jahrhundert* (Munich, 1949)

Silverstein, T., ed., *Visio Sancti Pauli: the History of the Apocalypse in Latin together with Nine Texts*, Studies and Documents 4 (London, 1935)

'Dante and the Legend of the *Mi'rāj*: the Problem of Islamic Influence on the

Christian Literature of the Otherworld', *Journal of Near Eastern Studies* 11 (1952), 89–110 and 187–97

'The Vision of Saint Paul: New Links and Patterns in the Western Tradition', *Archives d'histoire doctrinale et littéraire du moyen âge* 34 (1959), 199–248

Simpson, D., 'The *Proverbia Grecorum*', *Traditio* 43 (1987), 1–22

Simpson, D., ed., *Sedulii Scotti Collectaneum Miscellaneum*, CCCM 67 (Turnhout, 1988); with a *Supplementum*, ed. F. Dolbeau (Turnhout, 1990)

Sims-Williams, P., 'Thought, Word and Deed: an Irish Triad', *Ériu* 29 (1978) 78–111

'The Significance of the Irish Personal Names in *Culwch ac Olwen*', *BBCS* 29 (1980–2), 600–20

'The Evidence for Vernacular Irish Literary Influence in Early Mediaeval Welsh Literature', in *Ireland in Early Mediaeval Europe*, ed. Whitelock *et al.*, pp. 235–57

'Gildas and Vernacular Poetry', in *Gildas: New Approaches*, ed. Lapidge and Dumville, pp. 169–92

'The Visionary Celt: the Construction of an Ethnic Preconception', *CMCS* 11 (Summer 1986), 71–96

Religion and Literature in Western England 600–800, Cambridge Studies in Anglo-Saxon England 3 (Cambridge, 1990)

Sisam, K., *Studies in the History of Old English Literature* (Oxford, 1953)

Smith, R., 'The Six Gifts', *JCS* 1 (1950), 98–104

Smyth, M., 'The Physical World in Seventh-Century Hiberno-Latin Texts', *Peritia* 5 (1986), 201–34

'Isidore of Seville and Early Irish Cosmography', *CMCS* 14 (Winter 1987), 69–102

Spilling, H., *Die Visio Tnugdali: Eigenart und Stellung in der mittelalterlichen Visionsliteratur bis zum Ende des 12. Jahrhunderts*, Münchener Beiträge zur Mediävistik und Renaissance-Forschung 21 (Munich, 1972)

Stahl, W. H., trans., *Macrobius: Commentary on the Dream of Scipio* (New York, 1952)

Stancliffe, C., 'Early "Irish" Biblical Exegesis', *Studia Patristica* 12 (Berlin, 1975), 361–70

'Red, White and Blue Martyrdom', in *Ireland in Early Mediaeval Europe*, ed. Whitelock *et al.*, pp. 21–46

Stegmüller, F., *Repertorium Biblicum Medii Aevi*, 11 vols. (Madrid, 1950 –)

Steinmeyer, E. and E. Sievers, *Die althochdeutschen Glossen*, 5 vols. (Berlin, 1879–1922)

Stevenson, J., 'Ascent through the Heavens, from Egypt to Ireland', *CMCS* 5 (Summer 1983), 21–35

Stokes, W., ed., *The Saltair na Rann*, Anecdota Oxoniensia, Mediaeval and Modern Series 1.2 (Oxford, 1883)

Stokes, W., ed. and trans., 'Tidings of Doomsday: an Early-Middle-Irish Homily', *RC* 4 (1879–80), 245–57

'The Evernew Tongue', *Ériu* 2 (1905), 96–162

Félire Oengusso Céli Dé: the Martyrology of Oengus the Culdee, HBS 29 (London, 1905)

'Three Legends from the Brussels Manuscript 5100–4', *RC* 26 (1905), 360–77

'The Fifteen Tokens of Doomsday', *RC* 28 (1907), 308–26

Stokes, W., and J. Strachan, ed. and trans., *Thesaurus Palaeohibernicus: a Collection of Old-Irish Glosses, Scholia, Prose, and Verse*, 2 vols. and supplement (Cambridge, 1901–10)

Stokes, W., and E. Windisch, ed., *Irische Texte*, 4 vols. (Leipzig, 1884–1909)

Strachan, J., ed. and trans., 'An Old-Irish Homily', *Ériu* 3 (1907), 1–7

Suchier, W., ed., *Das mittellateinische Gespräch Adrian und Epictitus nebst verwandten Texten (Joca Monachorum)* (Tübingen, 1955)

Szarmach, P. E., 'The Vercelli Homilies: Style and Structure', in *The Old English Homily and its Backgrounds*, ed. Szarmach and Huppé, pp. 241–67

Szarmach, P. E., ed., *Vercelli Homilies IX–XXIII*, Toronto Old English Series 5 (Toronto, 1981)

Sources of Anglo-Saxon Culture (Kalamazoo, MI, 1986)

Szarmach, P. E. and B. F. Huppé, ed., *The Old English Homily and its Backgrounds* (Albany, NY, 1978)

Thomson, D. S., ed., *Branwen Uerch Lyr*, Mediaeval and Modern Welsh Series 2 (Dublin, 1961)

Thurneysen, R., *Die irische Helden- und Königsage bis zum siebzehnten Jahrhundert* (Halle, 1921)

Tranter, S. N. and H. L. C. Tristram, ed., *Early Irish Literature – Media and Communication*, Scriptoralia 10 (Tübingen, 1989)

Tristram, H. L. C., 'Der "homo octipartitus" in der irischen und altenglischen Literatur', *ZCP* 34 (1975), 119–53

'Stock Descriptions of Heaven and Hell in Old English Literature', *NM* 75 (1976), 102–13

Sex aetates mundi: die Weltzeitalter bei den Angelsachsen und den Iren, Anglistische Forschungen 165 (Heidelberg, 1985)

Tristram, H. L. C., ed., *Vier altenglische Predigten aus der heterodoxen Tradition* (Freiburg im Breisgau, 1970)

Tubach, F., *Index Exemplorum: a Handbook of Medieval Religious Tales*, FFC 86 (Helsinki, 1969)

Turville-Petre, J., 'Translations of a Lost Penitential Homily', *Traditio* 19 (1963), 51–78

Tveitane, M., 'Irish Apocrypha in Norse Tradition? On the Sources of Some Medieval Homilies', *Arv: Journal of Scandinavian Folklore* 22 (1966), 111–35

Wack, M. F. and C. D. Wright, 'A New Latin Source for the Old English "Three Utterances" Exemplum', *ASE* 20 (1991), 187–202

Wagner, A., ed., *Visio Tnugdali lateinisch und altdeutsch* (Erlangen, 1882)

Walker, G. S. M., ed. and trans., *Sancti Columbani Opera*, SLH 2 (Dublin, 1957)

Walsh, P., ed., *Mil na mBeach* (Dublin, 1911)

Ward, H. L. D., *Catalogue of Romances in the British Museum*, 3 vols. (London, 1883–1910)

Wasserschleben, F. W. H., ed., *Die irische Kanonensammlung*, 2nd ed. (Leipzig, 1885)

Watson, J. C., ed., *Mesca Ulad*, MMIS 13 (Dublin, 1967)

Wenisch, F., *Spezifisch anglisches Wortgut in den nordhumbrischen Interlinearglossierungen des Lukasevangeliums*, Anglistische Forschungen 132 (Heidelberg, 1979)

Whitelock, D., 'Bishop Ecgred, Pehtred and Niall', in *Ireland in Early Mediaeval Europe*, ed. Whitelock *et al.*, pp. 47–68

Whitelock, D. *et al.*, ed., *Ireland in Early Mediaeval Europe: Studies in Memory of Kathleen Hughes* (Cambridge, 1982)

Willard, R., *Two Apocrypha in Old English Homilies*, Beiträge zur englischen Philologie 30 (Leipzig, 1935)

'The Address of the Soul to the Body', *PMLA* 50 (1935), 957–83

'The Latin Texts of The Three Utterances of the Soul', *Speculum* 12 (1937), 147–66

Willis, J., ed., *Macrobius: Commentarii in Somnium Scipionis* (Leipzig, 1970)

Wilmart, A., ed., 'Catéchèses celtiques', in his *Analecta Reginensia*, Studi e Testi 59 (Vatican City, 1933), 29–112

Wilmart, A., E. A. Lowe and H. A. Wilson, *The Bobbio Missal: Notes and Studies*, HBS 61 (London, 1924)

Wright, C. D., 'Irish and Anglo-Saxon Literary Culture: Insular Christian Traditions in Vercelli Homily IX and the Theban Anchorite Legend' (unpubl. PhD dissertation, Cornell Univ., 1984)

'Apocryphal Lore and Insular Tradition in St Gall, Stiftsbibliothek MS 908', in *Irland und die Christenheit*, ed. Ní Chatháin and Richter, pp. 124–45

'*Docet Deus, Docet Diabolus*: a Hiberno-Latin Theme in an Old English Body-and-Soul Homily', *NQ* 232 (1987), 451–3

'Blickling Homily III on the Temptations in the Desert', *Anglia* 106 (1988), 130–7

'The Irish "Enumerative Style" in Old English Homiletic Literature, Especially Vercelli Homily IX', *CMCS* 18 (Winter 1989), 27–74

'Apocrypha Priscillianistica', in *Sources of Anglo-Saxon Literary Culture: a Trial Version*, ed. Biggs *et al.*, pp. 69–70

'Hiberno-Latin and Irish-Influenced Biblical Commentaries, Florilegia, and Homily Collections', in *Sources of Anglo-Saxon Literary Culture: a Trial Version*, ed. Biggs *et al.*, pp. 87–123

'The Pledge of the Soul: a Judgment Theme in Old English Homiletic Literature and Cynewulf's *Elene*', *NM* 91 (1990), 23–30

'Some Evidence for an Irish Origin of Redaction XI of the *Visio Pauli*', *Manuscripta* 34 (1990), 34–44

'The Three "Victories" of the Wind: a Hibernicism in the *Hisperica Famina*, *Collectanea Bedae*, and the Old English Prose *Solomon and Saturn* Pater Noster Dialogue', *Ériu* 41 (1990), 13–25

Index

Material in footnotes is included in the general page reference.